LIFE OF LORD NELSON.

NELSON AS A MIDSHIPMAN

NELSON

THE PUBLIC AND PRIVATE LIFE

OF

Horatio, Viscount Nelson

AS TOLD BY

HIMSELF, HIS COMRADES, AND HIS FRIENDS

Reprinted 1999 from the 1891 edition.
Trident Press International
Copyright 1999

ISBN 1-888777-67-2 Standard Edition.

Printed in Slovenia by
DELO Tiskarna

BY

G. LATHOM BROWNE

*Author of " Wellington," " Narratives of State Trials in the
Nineteenth Century," &c., &c.*

" REMEMBER NELSON "
Captain Hoste's Signal at the battle of Lissa

" GO THOU AND DO LIKEWISE "
Concluding words of Nelson's Autobiography

London
T. FISHER UNWIN
PATERNOSTER SQUARE

MDCCCXCI

𝕮𝖔

HER MOST GRACIOUS MAJESTY

𝕿𝖍𝖊 𝕼𝖚𝖊𝖊𝖓

THIS ATTEMPT TO TELL THE STORY OF THE

PUBLIC AND PRIVATE LIFE OF

HORATIO VISCOUNT NELSON,

DUKE OF BRONTE,

FROM HIS DESPATCHES AND LETTERS,

AND THOSE OF HIS COMRADES AND FRIENDS,

𝖎𝖘 𝕯𝖊𝖉𝖎𝖈𝖆𝖙𝖊𝖉,

BY HER MAJESTY'S SPECIAL GRACIOUS PERMISSION,

BY HER DUTIFUL AND HUMBLE SUBJECT AND

SERVANT,

GEORGE LATHOM BROWNE.

PREFACE.

T the suggestion of my friend, Arthur Duke Coleridge, I have endeavoured to frame a Life of Nelson, as told by himself, his relations, and friends, on the same principle as that of " Wellington," so favourably received by the critics.

In this attempt I have to acknowledge the kind and valuable aid of Earl Nelson and Viscount Bridport, the present Duke of Bronte, and of his son, the Honble. Alexander Hood, under whose superintendence the photographs were taken of the Nelson relics at Cricket St. Thomas, of which illustrations are now given, and who has furnished me with the description of the present estate of Bronte, of which for seventeen years he has been the resident manager. The portraits of Nelson from the Earl's collection as a young post-captain and that of him wearing the Sultan's aigrette have, I believe, never been as yet engraved.

I have also to thank Mrs. Herbert Jones and the proprietors of *The Century Magazine* (New York) for their permission to make use of the letters of Sir Thomas Troubridge, relating to Copenhagen, which Mrs. Jones edited for that serial.[1]

[1] *The Century Illustrated Monthly Magazine*, vol. 37, No. 1 (November, 1888). Century Company, Union Square, New York ; T. Fisher Unwin, Paternoster Square, London.

I have also been permitted by Mr. Alfred Morrison, of Fonthill House, to inspect his interesting collection of letters of and to Lord Nelson.

These letters, which were purchased by Mr. Morrison, in March, 1886, were the property of Mr. Finch Hatton, to whom they had descended from his grandfather, Robert Fulke Greville, brother of Charles Greville, the heir of Sir William Hamilton, to whom Emma Lyons was transferred by him. As might be expected they relate almost entirely to her connection with and desertion by Greville, and have been made of full use by Mr. John Paget in his article in *Blackwood*, in May, 1888, and by Mr. Cordy Jeffreson in his lately published volumes. This portion of Lady Hamilton's life does not come into my present venture.

Of the works already in print forming materials for a life of Lord Nelson, the Biography by Clarke and McArthur and the invaluable collection of Despatches and letters compiled by the late Sir Harris Nicolas occupy the foremost place. In the former work we have the most interesting autobiography of Nelson up to the close of the Battle of the Nile. In the latter, nearly the whole of the contents of the thirty-seven volumes of Despatches and Letters of Nelson now in the Library of Viscount Bridport at Cricket St. Thomas have been laid under contribution by Sir Harris Nicolas.[1]

Another printed volume from which I have quoted is that by the late Honble. Captain Plunkett, giving a history of " The Last Great War," as told in the Letters

---

[1] "Despatches and Letters of Vice-Admiral Sir Horatio Nelson," edited by Sir H. Nicolas, 7 vols., 1844–45. "Life and Services of Lord Nelson," edited by Clarke and Dr. J. McArthur, 3 vols., 1840. Of these papers, a selection illustrating the professional life of Nelson has been made by Professor J. K. Laughton, Professor of Modern History in King's College, London, a valuable text-book for the naval cadet. London, 1886, 1 vol., Longmans.

of the then Captain Jurien de la Gravière, contributed by him to the *Revue de Deux Mondes.* In this able history of the great battles in which Nelson fought with the French and Spanish fleets, we have not only a most noble tribute to our hero, but very valuable information of the state of the French and Spanish navies during that bitter contest which practically closed at Trafalgar.[1]

The Diary of Miss Cornelia Knight, better known to us as the much respected companion of the Princess Charlotte, furnishes many anecdotes of Nelson, with whom she first became acquainted in the year of the battle of the Nile, and accompanied him and the Hamiltons on the journey through Germany on his return after the battle.[2]

Of the published letters of Lady Hamilton I take but little account, so disfigured are they in what would apparently be their most important sentences, by omissions and asterisks, and also rendered more doubtful by the fact that most of them evidently never came through the post, and that not a few bear no date. I have discussed the value of the most important of them as the occasion arose in the narrative.[3]

With Southey's ever popular narrative there is little fault to be found, writing as he did before the truth was known about the Carraciolo incident and the other points which made, according to the evidence of that day, against the character of Nelson. It is, however, to be much regretted that this otherwise charming Life has very lately

---

[1] "The Last Naval War," being translations from the letters of Captain Jurien de la Gravière in the *Revue Des Deux Mondes*, by the Honble. Captain Plunkett, 2 vols., 1848, Longmans. These letters, six in number, entitled *La Derniere Guere Maritime*, appeared in the *Revue* from Nov. 1845 to 1847.

[2] "Autobiography of Miss Cornelia Knight, with Extracts from her Diary," &c., 2 vols., 1861.

[3] "Letters of Lady Hamilton to Lord Nelson," &c., 2 vols., London, 1814.

been republished without so much as a footnote to show
that these accusations have been, now some forty years
back, thoroughly refuted.[1]   With the Lady Hamilton incidents, from the view which I have felt justified in taking
of the relationship between her and Nelson, it has
been unnecessary for me to go into detail.   Mr. Cordy
Jeffreson has dealt so thoroughly with her case and that
of the Queen of Naples that, however much one may in
some points disagree with his conclusions, it would be
mere copying to go more fully into these moot questions.[2]

Among the smaller biographies of Lord Nelson,
published about the time of his death, one of the most
interesting is that of Archibald Duncan, the author of the
" British Trident and the Mariners Chronicle," published
in 1805, from which I have borrowed some characteristic
anecdotes.[3]

To Earl Nelson, in addition to the two portraits before
mentioned, I am indebted for the original copper-plate of
the House at Merton—long since pulled down—originally
published in a " Lady's Memorandum Book," soon after
Nelson's death, and also for the clear and able refutation
of the scandalous stories told of the life of Nelson and
the Hamiltons at Merton, contributed to *The Times* in
1861 by Nelson's grandnephew.

The " Recollections of the Life of Rev. A. J. Scott,
D.D., Lord Nelson's Chaplain," contain most reliable
notices of Nelson's private character ; and the " Nelsonian
Reminiscences " of Lieut. G. S. Parsons, who was present

---

[1] Southey's "Life of Nelson," Morley's Universal Library, 1 vol.,
Routledge, 1886.

[2] "Lord Nelson and Lady Hamilton," by J. Cordy Jeffreson, 2 vols.,
London, 1888.

[3] "Life of Horatio Viscount Nelson," &c., London, James Cundee, Ivy
Lane and J. Nuttal, Liverpool.

at the Battle of St. Vincent and the trial of Carraciolo, furnish facts of value.[1]

Harrison's " Life of Nelson," written under the influence, if not by the direction, of Lady Hamilton, with the object of supporting her claim to a pension, is so filled with exaggerations, evidently dictated by her, as to be too unreliable to admit of any but the most scanty reference.[2]

Dr. Pettigrew's volumes, as Professor Laughton truly says, " are better suited for the ' School of Scandal' than the student of naval history."[3]   With the history of the letter of the King of Spain and the well-known " Fountain of Arethusa " letter I have dealt in their places in the Life.   Having carefully examined the letters from Lady Hamilton in the volumes of the Private Correspondence at Cricket, I feel convinced that Dr. Pettigrew was imposed upon, in the latter case, by a clever imitation of Nelson's handwriting made by the lady herself. Nelson's left-handed writing is so dangerously like that of Lady Hamilton as to give good ground for this suspicion.   With reference to the letter of the King of Spain, I have cited, from Tucker's " Life of Lord St. Vincent," Sir J. Jervis's letter to the Admiralty on his appointment to the command in the Mediterranean, which appears to me to throw further doubts on Lady Hamilton's story.

Besides these leading authorities there are several of a less pretentious character, to which I have referred in the Notes.

ATHENÆUM CLUB,
     Trafalgar Day, 1889.

---

[1] " Life of Dr. Scott," by his son, Saunders and Ottley, London, 1 vol., 1842.   " Nelsonian Reminiscences," Saunders and Ottley, 1843.

[2] " Life of Lord Nelson," by James Harrison, 2 vols., London, 1806.

[3] " Memoirs of the Life of Vice-Admiral Viscount Nelson," by T. J. Pettigrew, London, 2 vols., 1849.

POSTSCRIPT.

Whilst this volume was being printed, I have had the advantage of reading Mr. Clark Russell's " Nelson," published by Messrs. Putnam's Sons, of New York, with its graphic descriptions of Nelson's great battles. To such attractive descriptions I make no claim, content to tell plainly, and I hope clearly, from the writings of Nelson and his colleagues, the share which he bore in each of his battles. It is very satisfactory to me to find, that Mr. Clark Russell takes the view of the Carraciolo incident so ably shown by my old friend, Mr. John Paget, and agrees with Mr. Cordy Jeffreson in giving little credit to the claims advanced by Lady Hamilton to the stealing and transmission of the letter of the King of Spain, and to her romantic story of the letter of the Queen of Naples respecting the victualling of the fleet at Syracuse. As Mr. Clark Russell appears to believe in the so-called letters of Nelson to Lady Hamilton, published in 1814, by Lovewell and Co., London, we must agree to differ as to the relations between Nelson and her, and as to the parentage of the child Horatia, and leave my readers to judge between us. For some other matters I refer to such notes as I have been able to add to the text of my volume, during its passage through the press.

Woodridings, Pinner
August, 1890.

CONTENTS.

CONTENTS.

CHAPTER IV.

AT HOME AND IN THE MEDITERRANEAN.

1787–1795.

CHAPTER V.

NELSON AS A SOLDIER.

1794–5.

CHAPTER VI.

BLOCKADE OF THE GENOESE COAST.

1795.

CHAPTER VII.

1796.

NELSON AS A COMMODORE.

CHAPTER VIII.

1797.

THE BATTLE OF ST VINCENT.

CHAPTER IX.

1797.

SANTA CRUZ—TENERIFFE.

CHAPTER X.

THE BATTLE OF THE NILE.

CHAPTER XI.

AFTER THE NILE.

1798–1800.

CHAPTER XII.

COPENHAGEN.

1801.

CHAPTER XIII.

1801–2.

THE BOULOGNE FLOTILLA.

CHAPTER XIV.

1803–5.

THE CHASE TO THE WEST INDIES.

CHAPTER XV.

1805.

THE LAST COMMAND.

CHAPTER XVI.

1805.

TRAFALGAR.

CHAPTER XVII.

PERSONAL I.: NELSON'S PERSONAL INFLUENCE.

CHAPTER XVIII.

1779 to 1805.

PERSONAL II.: NELSON AND HIS FAMILY.

CHAPTER XIX.

1801 to 1805.

PERSONAL III.: NELSON AT HOME AND ABROAD.

CHAPTER XX.

1805 to 1806.

CONCLUSION.

APPENDICES.

CONTENTS.

LEADING EVENTS.

1758	Sept. 29	Born.
1770	about Dec.	Midshipman of *Raisonable*.
1771	about June	To West Indies in a merchant ship.
1772	to July	Midshipman, *Triumph*.
1773	August	To the North Pole in *Carcass*.
1774–6	Feb. to Aug.	*Triumph*, *Seahorse*, and *Dolphin*.
1777	April 8	Passed examination for Lieutenant.
	April 9	Lieutenant of *Lowestoffe*.
1778	December 8	Commander, *Badger* Brig in West Indies.
1779	June 11	Post-Captain, *Hinchinbrook*.
1780	January	San Juan Expedition.
	August	Invalided home ; at Bath.
1781	August	Appointed to the *Albermarle* 28.
	October	Employed in the North Sea.
1782	April to Nov.	American Station.
1783	Jan. to July	West Indies ; attempt on Turk's Island.
	July 3	Paid off *Albermarle*; on half pay.
	November	Visit to France.
1784	March to May 1787	Captain of the *Boreas* 28, Leeward Isles Station. Engaged in suppressing the illegal traffic in the Leeward Islands.
1787	March 12	Marriage with Mrs. Nisbet.
	July 4	Spithead on half pay, till January, 1793.
1793	January 30	Appointed to *Agamemnon* 64.
	May	To Mediterranean under Lord Hood.
1794	April to May	Siege and capture of Bastia.
	June to August	Siege and capture of Calvi ; loss of his right eye.
1795	March	Action with the *Ca Ira*.
	April 4	Distinguishing Pendant.
	June 1	Colonel of Marines.

1795	July 13	Lord Hotham's second action.
1796	August 11	Broad Pendant with a Captain.
1796	The whole year	Gulf of Genoa and Corsica ; Capture of *La Sabina*, Spanish frigate.
1797	February 14	BATTLE OF ST. VINCENT.
	March 17	KNIGHT OF THE BATH.
	July 3	Bombarding Cadiz ; desperate action with Spanish gunboat.
	July 23 and 24	Attacks on Santa Cruz ; loss of his right arm ; invalided home ; REAR-ADMIRAL OF THE BLUE.
1798	March 29	Hoists his flag on the *Vanguard*.
	April 30	Joins Lord St. Vincent's fleet in the Mediterranean.
	May 2	Appointed to the detached squadron.
	May 20	The storm ; *Vanguard* dismasted.
	June and July	The chase after the French Fleet.
	August 1 and 2	BATTLE OF THE NILE.
	November 22	Surrender of Leghorn.
	December 21	Embarked the Royal Family for Palermo.
1799	Feb. 14–June 21	VICE-ADMIRAL OF THE RED ; off Maritimo and at Palermo.
	June 21	Left Palermo for Naples, and heard on the voyage of the capitulation with the rebels, which he at once annulled.
	June 24–29	At Naples ; took possession of the castles of Uovo and Nuovo ; Carraciolo seized, tried, and executed.
	July 10–13	Arrival of the King of Naples ; refusal to obey Lord Keith's orders.
	July 31	Surrender of Capua and Gaeta to Troubridge.
	August 5	Sailed for Palermo with the King.
	August 13	CREATED DUKE OF BRONTE.
1800	January 14	Joins Lord Keith's Fleet.
	February 18	Capture of *Le Généreux*.
	March	Capture of *Le Guillame Tell*.
	June 10	Sailed from Palermo to Leghorn with the Queen of Naples and family and the Hamiltons.
	July 13	Struck his flag.

1800	June 14	The Queen landed at Leghorn.
	June 17	Nelson with the Hamiltons ; left on their way to England through Germany.
	November 6	Landed at Yarmouth.
	December 20	Took his seat in the House of Lords.
1801	January 1	VICE-ADMIRAL OF THE BLUE; hoists his flag in the *San Josef.*
	January 13	Separation from Lady Nelson.
	February	Shifted flag to the *St. George ;* joined the Baltic Expedition under Sir Hyde Parker.
	March 12	Sailed with the fleet.
	March 29	Shifted flag to the *Elephant.*
	April 2	BATTLE OF COPENHAGEN.
	April 9	Signed Armistice with Denmark.
	May 22	VISCOUNT NELSON ; Commander-in-chief in the Baltic.
	June 19	Resigned the command and sailed for England; at Merton.
	July 24	Commander-in-chief of squadron to resist Boulogne Flotilla.
	August 16	Unsuccessful attack on the Flotilla.
	August 18	New Patent of the Barony of Nelson with special remainders.
	August 27	On leave of absence.
	August 29	Took his seat as Viscount Nelson.
	December	At Merton.
1802	January	Vice-Admiral in command of Channel Fleet.
	April 10	Struck his flag ; Peace of Amiens.
1803	May 15	Commander-in-chief in the Mediterranean.
	July 1	Joined the fleet off Toulon ; commencement of blockade.
1804	April 23	VICE-ADMIRAL OF THE WHITE.
	October	War with Spain.
1805	January 11	Escape of French Fleet and return to Toulon after a short cruise.
	March 30	Final escape of the French Fleet ; Nelson in pursuit.
	June 1	Nelson at Barbadoes.
	June 13	Sailed from Antigua, in pursuit of French Fleet, to England.

1805	June 18	Gibraltar.
	August 13	Home ; struck his flag.
	September 15	His last command ; sailed for Cadiz.
	September 20	Joined fleet off Cadiz.
	October 21	Battle of Trafalgar. Death of Nelson.

DESCRIPTION OF THE ILLUSTRATIONS.

Portrait of Nelson as a Midshipman, exhibited by Dr. Ridge, M.D., in a Loan Collection, and reputed to be by Gainsborough; from a photograph now at South Kensington. Though it is very doubtful whether the original picture is by Gainsborough, there is such a similarity between the lower portion of the face with the portrait of Nelson's niece, who married Lord Bridport, that it may be regarded as likeness. Where the original portrait now is I have been unable to discover, Dr. Ridge having died the year before last, and its whereabouts now is not known to his present representatives ... *Frontispiece*

For the following illustrations I am indebted to the kindness of Earl Nelson of Trafalgar :

Rigaud, R.A. Now at Trafalgar ; purchased by Earl Nelson from the Locker family ... *To face p.* 23.

3.—Portrait of Nelson wearing the "Chellinck"— the diamond ornament given to him by the Sultan, painted by Guzzardi for the King of Naples. Now in the possession of Earl Nelson at Trafalgar .... *To face p.* 203.

4.—Merton House from the original copper-plate published in 1805, published, at Bury St. Edmunds, in Gedge's "Ladies Memorandum Book." This house has long since been pulled down ... ... *To face p.* 267.

5.—Facsimile of a Letter from Nelson's father to the Rev. Bryan Allott, Whitehaven, Cumberland, dated Oct. 16, 1798 ... *To face p.* 450, *Appendix*.

For the following illustrations I am indebted to the kindness of Viscount Bridport, Duke of Bronte. These were photographed for me when staying at Cricket St. Thomas in August last by Mr. Higgins, photographer, of Chard, Somerset :

1.—Facsimile of Lord Nelson's Visiting Card, given to me by Viscount Bridport .... *Tailpiece to p.* xxxi

2.—The last Letter written by Nelson with his right hand on the eve of the final attack on Santa Cruz ... ... *To face p.* 165

3.—The Sicilian Medal struck by the order of the King of Sicily to commemorate his return to Naples in Nelson's flagship. On the obverse is the portrait of the king, with the inscription, FERDINAND IV., D.G. SICILIAR ET HIE REX.

On the reverse is a medallion of Nelson carried by Fame, the *Foudroyant*, his flagship, the royal army advancing headed by a priest carrying the cross, and the rebels in full flight, with Naples and Vesuvius in the background. At the foot is the following inscription : PER MESSO DELLA PROVIDENTIA DELLE LUI VERTUTE DELLA FEDE ET ENERGIA DEL SUO POPOLO DEL VALORE DE SUOI ALLEATI ET PARTICULARE GL' INGLESI GLORIOSTE RESTABILITO IO JUGLIO, 1799 ...   .   *To face p.* 211

4.—A Letter in 1805 showing his left-handed writing
To face p. 285

5.—The bust of Nelson, executed by Flaxman, R.A.
To face p. 298

6.—Trophy of the Medals, Orders, and Relics of Nelson preserved at Cricket St. Thomas arranged by Lord Bridport's third son, the Hon. Alexander Nelson Hood ...   *To face p.* 351

Medals, Orders, and Relics of Admiral Viscount Nelson, Duke of Bronte, in the possession of General Viscount Bridport, Duke of Bronte, K.C.B. :

On the Left.	*In the Centre.*	*On the Right.*
Grand Cross of the Order of St. Ferdinando.	Star of the Turkish Order of the Crescent.	Jewel of the Order of St. Ferdinando.
Trafalgar Medal.	Neapolitan medal of the king's return to Naples.	Turkish Order of the Crescent.
Casket with the Freedom of London.		Obverse of the Nile Medal.

On the Left.	*In the Centre.*	*On the Right.*
	Chronometer worn at Trafalgar.[1]	
Ivory box with his own hair.		Box with the Freedom of Thetford.
Diamond-hilted sword from the King of Naples.	Box with the Freedom of Plymouth.	Gold and enamelled sword, gift of the Captains of the Fleet, presented after the Victory of the Nile.
Jewel of the Order of S. Joachim.	Medal for Battle of St. Vincent.	
	Nile Medal.	
	Combined gold knife and fork.	Grand Cross of the Order of St. Joachim.
	Jewel and Ribbon of the Order of the Bath.	

7.—View of the Castello Maniace, the ducal residence at Bronte. Duplicate of one of the Photographs of Bronte and its neighbourhood, originally taken for Her Majesty ... *To face p.* 390

Plans of the Battles of St. Vincent (*facing p.* 137), the Nile (*facing p.* 179), Copenhagen.

---

[1] On the case is the following inscription :—

THE CHRONOMETER OF
ADMIRAL VISCOUNT NELSON
WHICH HE WORE AT THE BATTLE OF TRAFALGAR
PLACED IN THIS CASE BY HIS NIECE
CHARLOTTE MARY LADY BRIDPORT
TO BE PRESERVED FOR
THE USE OF HIS DESCENDANTS WHO MAY
ENTER THE NAVY.

(*facing p.* 247), Trafalgar (*facing p.* 329), from various authorities.

The Davison Memorial, constructed of the eighty-four guineas found in Nelson's purse at his death.   For this very curious and hitherto unengraved relic of Nelson I am indebted to Mr. J. Griffin, of the Hard, Portsmouth ... *To face p.* 444

FACSIMILE OF NELSON'S VISITING CARD.

ERRATA.

Heading to Chap. vi. " Strict " for " Struck," page 99.
    „   „   „ vii. " First " „   " Fresh "   „   115.

FROM SCHOOLBOY TO CAPTAIN.

CHAPTER I.

FROM SCHOOLBOY TO CAPTAIN.

(1758–1780.)

Nelson at school—Enters the Navy in his twelfth year—A good pilot—
The North Pole Expedition—The White Bear Hunt—Examination
for his Lieutenancy—Appointed to the *Lowestoffe*—The American
Privateer—Commander of the *Badger*, 1778—Post-Captain in the
Hinchinbrook, 1779—The San Juan Expedition, 1780—Invalided
home.

S far as the close of the year, 1799, the
simple Autobiography which Nelson
then sent to Dr. McArthur forms the
most reliable and natural ground of any
Memoir of the Hero of the Nile. I
commence, therefore, with his own
" *Sketch of his life* " from his schooldays until he became qualified for his Lieutenancy.

" I was born Sept. 29, 1758, in the Parsonage-house (Burnham
Thorpe),[1] was sent to the High School at Norwich, and afterwards
removed to North Walsham ; from whence, on the disturbance with
Spain relative to the Falkland Islands, I went to sea with my uncle,
Captain Maurice Suckling, in the *Raisonable* of 64 guns (*æt.* 12).
But the business with Spain being accommodated, I was sent in a West
India ship belonging to the house of Hibbert, Parrier, and Horton,

---

[1] Nelson thus briefly states his parentage : " Horatio Nelson (fourth)
son of the Rev. Edmund Nelson, Rector of Burnham Thorpe, in the
County of Norfolk, and of Catherine his wife, daughter of Dr. Suckling,
Prebendary of Westminster, whose grandmother was a sister of Sir R.
Walpole, Earl of Orford."

with Mr. John Rathbone, who had formerly been in the Navy, in the
Dreadnought with Captain Suckling.   From this voyage I returned to
the *Triumph* at Chatham, in July, 1772, and if I did not improve my
education, I returned a practical seaman, with a horror of the Royal
Navy, and with a saying then constant with the seamen, ' *Aft the most
honour, forward the better man.*'—It was many weeks before I got
reconciled to a Man of War, so deep was the prejudice rooted, and
what pains were taken to instil this erroneous principle in a young
mind.   However, as my ambition was to be a seaman, it was always
held out as a reward, that if I attended well to my navigation, I should
go in the cutter and decked long-boat which was attached to the
Commanding Officer's ship at Chatham.   Thus, by degrees, I became
a good pilot, for vessels of that description from Chatham to the
Tower of London, down the Swin and the North Foreland, and
confident of myself amongst rocks and sands, which has many times
been of great comfort to me.   In this way I was trained, till the
Expedition towards the North Pole was fitted out, when though no
boys were allowed to go in the ships (as of no use), yet nothing could
prevent my making every interest to go with Captain Lutwidge in the
Carcass, and as I fancied I was to fill a man's place, I begged I might
be his cockswain ; which finding my ardent desire for going with him,
Captain Lutwidge complied with, and has continued the strictest
friendship to this moment.   Lord Mulgrave, whom I then first knew,
maintained his kindest friendship and regard to the last moment of
his life.   When the boats were fitting out to quit the two ships blocked
up in the ice, I exerted myself to have the command of a four-oared
cutter raised upon, which was given me, with twelve men (*æt.* 15) ;
and I prided myself in fancying I could navigate her better than any
other boat in the ship.

    "On our arrival in England, being paid off, Oct. 15, I found that a
squadron was fitting out for the East Indies, and nothing less than such
a distant voyage could in the least satisfy my desire of maritime
knowledge.   I was placed in the *Seahorse* of 20 guns, with Captain
Farmer, and watched in the foretop ; from whence in time I was
placed on the quarter-deck ; having in the time I was in this ship,
visited almost every part of the East Indies, from Bengal to Bassorah.
Ill health induced Sir Edward Hughes (Commander-in-chief in the
East Indies), who had always shown me great kindness, to send me to
England in the *Dolphin* of 20 guns, with Captain James Pigot, whose
kindness at that time saved my life.   This ship was paid off at Wool-
wich, on the 24th Sept., 1775.   On the 26th I received (from Sir

James Douglas, who commanded at Portsmouth) an order to act as Lieutenant of the *Worcester* 64, Captain Mack Robinson, who was ordered to Gibraltar with a convoy. In this ship I was at sea with convoys till April 2, 1777, and in very bad weather. But although my age (*æt.* 19) might have been sufficient cause for not entrusting me with the charge of a Watch, yet Captain Robinson used to say, 'he felt as easy when I was on deck, as any Officer in the ship.' "

Of the schoolboy period of Nelson's life, we have the following anecdotes :—

"The Master, Mr. Jones, had some remarkably fine pears, which his scholars had often wished for, but the attempt to gather them was in their opinion so hazardous, that no one would undertake it ; when Horatio, on seeing all his companions so staggered, came forward, and offered to brave the danger. He was accordingly one night lowered down from the dormitory by some sheets tied together, and thus at considerable risk secured the prize ; but the boldness of the deed was all that the young adventurer regarded : for on being hauled up again, he shared the pears among his schoolfellows without reserving any for himself ; and added, 'I only took them because every other boy was afraid.' Five guineas was offered next morning to discover the plunderer ; but young Nelson was too much beloved for any boy to betray him." [1]

It is also related of him, by the same writer, that at an earlier period, when he was quite a child, he strayed from his grandmother's house at Hillborough, after birds' nests with a cow-boy. The dinner-hour arriving without his appearance, the alarm of the family became very great ; for they apprehended that he had been carried off by the gipsies. Search was instantly made in various directions, and at length he was discovered, without his companion, sitting with the utmost composure by the side of a stream which he had been unable to pass. "I wonder, child," exclaimed the old lady on seeing him, "that hunger and fear did not drive you

---

[1] Clarke and McArthur's "Life of Nelson," vol. i. p. 15.

home."—" Fear never came near me, grandmamma,"
replied Horatio.[1]

" When the brothers, William and Horatio, were going to school on
their ponies, William, who did not much like the journey, having
advanced a short distance from his father's gate, and found that a
great deal of snow had fallen, returned with his brother to the
parsonage and informed Mr. Nelson ' that the snow was too deep to
venture.' 'If that be indeed the case,' replied the father, 'you
shall not go : but make another attempt, and I will leave it to your
honour. If the road should be found dangerous, you may return.
Yet, remember, boys ! I leave it to your honour.' They accordingly
proceeded, and though various difficulties presented themselves,
which offered a plausible reason for their return home, Horatio was
proof against them all, exclaiming, ' We have no excuse ! Remember,
brother, it was left to our honour.' " [2]

In 1802, Mr. Levett Hansom, a schoolfellow of
Nelson at North Walsham, in a letter respecting Lord
Nelson being offered the dignity of a Knight Grand
Commander of the Chapteral Order of St. Joachim,
makes the following reminiscence of their schooldays :

" HAMBURGH, *September* 29, 1802.
" MY LORD,—Dean Swift closes, or terminates, a letter to the
great Earl of Peterborough, by telling that nobleman ' that he should
be happy to show one of his Lordship's letters to his parishioners.'
You, my Lord, have not suffered me to languish respecting *that point.*
For these some months past I have had it in mind to show to my
acquaintance and friends a letter from you, and thereby to convince
them I had once the pleasure of being your schoolfellow, and have

---

[1] Clarke and McArthur, vol. i. p. 18. On this incident, which, with
the previous ones, I have taken from Clarke and McArthur, a late
writer remarks : "As to the reply to his grandmother about fear,
Nelson's temperament was not impervious to fear—his daring was full
of consciousness of the danger. He could not but see fear very closely,
and the absolute charm that he experienced in going into the hottest fire
was due to the mastery of mere physical shrinking, and the delight of
subordinating it to his will " (*Edinburgh Review,* vol. clxiv. p. 563).

[2] Clarke and McArthur, vol. i. p. 16.

now the honour of being considered your friend. In truth, my Lord, we never were otherwise, though not intimate.

"Your Lordship, though in the second class when I was in the first, were five years my junior, or four at least, and at that period of life such a difference in point of age, is considerable. I well remember where you sat in the schoolroom. Your station was against the wall, between the parlour door and the chimney : the latter to your right. From 1769 to 1771 we were opposites. Nor do I forget that we were under the lash of Classic Jones, as arrant a Welshman as Rees-ap-Griffith, and as keen a flogger as merciless Bushby, of birch-loving memory. Happy I am, indeed, my Lord, to find, by your very kind letter, that *Hæc Meminisse Juvat!* According to an old sentimental toast, we imprecate the meeting 'an old friend with a new face.' Consequently, how very pleasing it is to find *that* not to be the case respecting an old schoolfellow ! As a philosopher, I observe, my Lord, with great satisfaction, that your honours have not changed you. Reasonable men always behold those things through the proper medium. Titles and peerages may honour Lord Barington, or Lord Carrington, or Lord Lavington, or Lord Boringdon : Lord Nelson confers an honour upon them by his acceptance. 'I regard my old schoolfellow as the saviour and deliverer of Europe in general, and my country in particular : and in my eyes those titles are superior to all honours.' " [1]

"In 1770, when his father was at Bath for his health, on reading in the papers that his Uncle Maurice Suckling was appointed to the *Raisonable* 64, young Nelson, then only twelve years old, asked his elder brother to write to their father and tell him that he should like to go to sea with his uncle. To the letter which his father wrote to Captain Suckling, came this reply. 'What has poor Horatio done, who is so weak, that above all the rest, he should be sent to rough it at sea? But let him come ; and the first time we go into action a cannon-ball may knock off his head and so provide for him.' "

In consequence of the speedy settlement of the dispute with Spain, Nelson's first experience of the navy was

[1] Pettigrew's "Nelson," vol. ii. pp. 262 3.

short-lived ; and, as he tells us in his Autobiography, he
filled up his spare time with a voyage in a West Indian
merchantman, and in perfecting his knowledge of the
pilotage of the Thames, until the North Sea Expedition
was decided on.

In this expedition (which was suggested to the King
in 1773, in consequence of an application from the
Royal Society), under Captain the Hon. Constantine
John Phipps, Nelson sailed as cockswain to Captain
Lutwidge of the *Carcass.* He was then only fifteen,
and of a weak and aguish constitution. The expedition,
consisting of the *Racehorse* and the *Carcass* left the
Nore, June 4, 1773, and made the land off Spitzbergen
on the 28th. Within two days the ice, which had
considerably impeded their progress, became alarming.
Whilst the ships were embayed in the ice-floe the
following adventure is characteristic of Nelson's habitual
daring.

"Among the gentlemen on the quarter-deck of the *Carcass,* who
were not rated midshipmen, there were besides Nelson a daring ship-
mate of his, to whom he had become attached. One night, during the
mid-watch, it was concerted between them that they should steal
together from the ship and endeavour to obtain a bear's skin. The
clearness of the nights in those high latitudes rendered the accomplishment of this object extremely difficult ; they seem, however, to
have taken advantage of the haze of an approaching fog, and thus
to have escaped undetected. Nelson in high spirits led the way over
the frightful chasms in the ice, armed with a rusty musket. It was
not, however, long before the adventurers were missed by those on
board, and as the fog had come on very thick, the anxiety of Captain
Lutwidge and his officers was very great. Between three and four
in the morning the mist somewhat dispersed, and the hunters were
discovered at a considerable distance, attacking a large bear. The
signal was instantly made for their return, but it was in vain that
Nelson's companion urged him to obey it. He was at this time
divided from his shaggy antagonist by a chasm in the ice, which
probably saved his life ; for the musket had flashed in the pan, and

their ammunition was expended. 'Never mind,' exclaimed Horatio, 'do let me get a blow at this devil with the butt-end of my musket, and we shall have him.' His companion, finding that entreaty was in vain, regained the ship. The captain, seeing the young man's danger, ordered a gun to be fired to terrify the enraged animal. This had the desired effect; but Nelson was obliged to return without his bear, somewhat agitated with the apprehension of the consequence of this adventure. Captain Lutwidge, though he could not but admire so daring a disposition, reprimanded him rather sternly for such rashness, and for conduct so unworthy of the situation he occupied; and desired to know what motive he could have for hunting the bear. Being thought by his captain to have acted in a manner unworthy of his situation made a deep impression on the high-minded cockswain; who, pouting his lip, replied, 'Sir, I wished to kill the bear, that I might carry its skin to my father.'" [1]

Whilst suddenly blocked in by the ice, when a little to the north of Spitzbergen, the ship's companies endeavoured to cut a passage to the westward through the floe, which was in some places twelve feet thick, but with so little success that after a whole day's hard work they could not move the ships for more than two hundred yards. It was whilst thus blocked for several days that young Nelson obtained the command of a cutter with twelve men, for the purpose of exploring the channels and breaking the ice. At length on the 7th of July the wind and the current shifted, and the ships were borne into the open sea. Convinced that it was impossible to penetrate further, the expedition entered the harbour of Smeerenberg, and thence sailed for home, where in the month of October, 1773, they were paid off. The next four years of his life at sea are told in his autobiography. A strict attention to his professional duties, added to seven years almost unbroken practice, had rendered Nelson a complete seaman, though he had not attained his nineteenth year.

[1] Clarke and McArthur, vol. i. pp. 21-2.

On the 8th of April, 1777, Nelson went in for examination for his Lieutenancy. The record of his services for six years and three months showed that he had filled every office necessary for his promotion, and the certificate noted that "he had produced journals kept by himself in the ships on which he had served— that he can splice, knot, reef a sail, &c., is qualified as an able seaman and midshipman."

"At his examination, his uncle, Maurice Suckling, who was now Comptroller of the Navy, was present, but concealed his relationship from the examiners. When his nephew had recovered from his confusion, his answers were prompt and satisfactory, and indicated the talents he so eminently possessed. They ended in a manner very honourable to him. His uncle then introduced him as his nephew." [1]

I now continue the extracts from the autobiography :

"On the 8th of April, 1777, I passed my examination as a lieutenant, and received my commission the next day as second lieutenant of the *Lowestoffe* frigate of 32 guns, captain (afterwards Lieutenant-Governor of Greenwich Hospital), William Locker. In this ship I went to Jamaica : but even a frigate was not sufficiently active for my mind, and I got into a schooner tender to the *Lowestoffe* (the *Little Lucy*). In this vessel I made myself a complete pilot for all the passages through the (Keys) Islands, situated on the north side of Hispaniola. Whilst in this frigate an event happened which presaged my character; and as it conveys no dishonour to the officer alluded to, I shall insert it.

"Blowing a gale of wind (between Cape Maize and Cape Nicolo Malo 20th October, 1777), and a very heavy sea, the frigate captured an American letter-of-marque. The first lieutenant was ordered to board her, which he did not do, owing to the very heavy sea. On his return the Captain said, 'Have I no officer in the ship who can board the prize?' On which the master ran to the gangway to get into the boat, when I stopped him, saying, 'It is my turn now; and

---

[1] Clarke and McArthur, vol. i. p. 14.

if I come back, it is yours.' This little incident has often occurred to my mind, and all know it is my disposition that difficulties and dangers do but increase my desire of attempting them." [1]

Whilst Nelson was in command of the tender to the *Lowestoffe* (the *Little Lucy*), they came up with a French frigate and a schooner, which the frigate seemed to be convoying, and Nelson was sent to examine the latter though under the guns of the frigate. Standing a little ahead of the *Lowestoffe*, a volley of musketry was poured into the tender, and she was ordered by Captain Locker to come under the frigate's stern. On this Nelson hoisted out his boat and asked Captain Locker ' if it would not be advisable to bring the tender men on board, as a brush with the frigate seemed inevitable." " At all events," replied Captain Locker, " I am determined to examine the schooner." The French captain then allowed it, and she proved to be a Frenchman.

To continue the autobiography—

" Sir Peter Parker soon after his arrival at Jamaica took me into his own flagship, the *Bristol*, as third lieutenant, from which I rose by succession to be first (September 4, 1778). Nothing particular happened whilst I was in this ship, which was actively employed off Cape François, it being the commencement of the French War."

" On the 8th December, 1778, I was appointed as commander of the *Badger* brig, and was first sent to protect the Mosquito shore and the bay of Honduras from the depredations of the American

---

[1] The following is Lieutenant Bromwich's correction of this incident, Bromwich at the time was a midshipman on board the *Lowestoffe* :—
" The first Lieutenant, afterwards an Admiral, never left the ship. On receiving his order he went below to get his sword, which was mislaid, and could not be found. During his absence Captain Locker came on deck, and anxious lest the boat should founder, used the words stated, when Nelson came forward. So waterlogged was the American ship, that Nelson's boat went in and out again in the scud. When at last he got on board he was long separated from the *Lowestoffe* by the gale " (Clarke and McArthur, vol. i. pp. 28–9).

privateers. Whilst on this service I gained so much the affection of the settlers that they unanimously voted me their thanks, and expressed their regret on my leaving them, entrusting me to describe to Sir Peter Parker and Sir John Dalling (Commander-in-chief in Jamaica) their situation should a war with Spain break out.

" Whilst I commanded this brig, H.M.S. *Glasgow*, Captain Thomas Lloyd, came into Montego Bay, Jamaica, where the *Badger* was lying ; in two hours afterwards she took fire from a cask of rum, and Captain Lloyd will tell you that it was owing to my exertions, joined to his, that her whole crew were rescued from the flames.

" On the 11th of June, 1779—*æt.* 21—I was Post into the *Hinchin-brook* (28 guns)—when being at sea, and Count d'Estaing arriving at Hispaniola with a very large fleet and army from Martinico, an attack on Jamaica was expected. In this critical state I was, both by the Admiral and the General, entrusted with the command of the batteries at Port Royal ; and I need not say, as this place was the key to the whole Naval force, the town of Kingston and Spanish Town, the defence of it was the most important post in the whole island."

" In January, 1780, an expedition being resolved on against San Juan, I was chosen to direct the sea part of it. Major Polson, who commanded, will tell you my exertions. How I quitted my ship, carried troops in boats an hundred miles up a river, which none but Spaniards since the time of the Buccaneers, had ever ascended. It will then be told how I boarded, if I may be allowed to use the expression, an outpost of the enemy, situated on an island in the river ; that I made batteries and afterwards fought them, and was the principal cause of our success. From this scene I was appointed to the *Janus* 44, at Jamaica, and went to Port Royal in the *Victor* sloop."

The object of the San Juan Expedition was to capture the fort of that name on the river which flows from the Lake of Nicaragua into the Atlantic, and to make itself the master of that lake, and of the cities of Granada and Leon, thus cutting off the communication of the Spaniards between their northern and southern possessions in South America. Though the force destined for the enterprize was ample, no one was really acquainted with the nature of the country through which it was to be carried out, nor had a single man in the force ever been up the river, or knew the distance of the fortification from its mouth. How far the enterprise might have succeeded, even if it had been attempted at a suitable season, may be a grave question, but as it was not until the 24th of March that the force reached the mouth of the river, its eventual failure from the heat and deadly climate was inevitable. With the landing of the troops Nelson's duty was to have ended, but with his natural determination not to fail, he embarked two hundred soldiers in the boats of the *Hinchinbrook*, which despite the shallowness of the stream, the sailors dragged against it, and by the 9th of April reached the Spaniards' outpost, where he, to use his own expression, " leaped upon the beach at the head of a few seamen, and boarded the battery." Sixteen miles more had yet to be covered before the fortress of San Juan could be reached. Two days after the capture of the outpost the English reached the fort, and on the 24th of April it surrendered. And now the worst of the danger commenced. The castle was worse than a prison, and contained nothing to assist the sick or to preserve those yet unaffected. The huts that served for hospitals were surrounded with filth ; medicines had been left behind for want of craft enough to transport them, and the river now swollen by the descending torrents rendered it all but impossible to send them. For five months the English persisted in their war against the climate to retain the fortress, and then leaving a few men to hold it until the Spaniards could retake it, abandoned their horrid task. Out of eighteen hundred men sent to different posts, barely three hundred and eighty returned, and of the two hundred of the crew of Nelson's ship, eighty-seven took to their beds in one night, and in the end not more than ten survived.

"Had the expedition," Nelson wrote, "arrived in San Juan's harbour in the month of January, the violent torrents would have subsided, and of course the whole army would not have had occasion to get wet three or four times a day in dragging the boats. They would have arrived at the castle by the middle of February, and had between two or three months of fair season to have established themselves, with all the stores, in the healthy country of Granada and Leon, and then I think a road for carriages might have been made to the Lake Nicaragua.

"The fever which destroyed the Army and Navy attached to the expedition was invariably from twenty to thirty days before it attacked the new-comers, and I cannot give a stronger instance than in the *Hinchinbrook*, with a complement of two hundred men, eighty-seven took to their beds in one night; and of the two hundred, 145 were buried in one night, in mine and Collingwood's time; and I believe very few, not more than ten, survived of that ship's crew : a proof how necessary expedition is in those climates."[1]

To show that Nelson, from his earliest days of service, never forgot to give praise where praise was due, I quote his letter to Captain Polson, who commanded the land force in this unfortunate expedition :

"To Captain Polson, 60th Regiment.
"Port Royal, *June* 2, 1780.

"Dear Polson,—I assure you nothing gave me more pleasure than to hear of your reducing the fort, before the arrival of Kemble (Colonel of the regiment) or any of the folks of the 2nd Division. When I arrived at Jamaica I saw General Dalling several times (Governor of Jamaica), and told him of all your transactions from our first setting out; our troubles on the Mosquito shore, &c., which I thought you would wish, as no letters had arrived. He expressed himself very much pleased with your conduct on every occasion, and was very sorry he was obliged to send down older officers. But when the news arrived of the reduction of the fort, I assure you he expressed the greatest pleasure it happened to you; and the news arriving of the plundering of the Black River by the Governor of Camayagoa, I told him of your sending back the Black River company, and only taking

---

[1] Nelson's remarks in second edition of Dr. Mozeley's "Tropical Diseases," 1803-4.

forty men from the *Tempest* instead of one hundred and fifty ; and advising to send two hundred men to Black River, and that those forty men had run away, so that not one Indian was taken to the westward of the Cape.   He was much pleased with those matters, as it takes off all reflection of taking the inhabitants of the shore to go upon the expedition.

"I am sorry you and so many officers are not well ; but I hope sincerely you are recovered before this.   General Dalling will be with you by the middle of July, you may depend on it.   Pray remember me kindly to the two Despards,[1] Bulkeley Harrison, Mounsey, and all good friends about you ; and believe me, with very great esteem,

"Your ever wellwisher and obedient servant,

"HORATIO NELSON."

The anxiety of the expedition and the effects of the climate had so serious an effect on Nelson, bringing on gout in the chest, that on the 30th of April he was invalided home, " and sailed for England in the *Lion,* the care and attention of whose captain, the Honble. W. Cornwallis, saved his life."   At Bath, under the care of Dr. Woodward, he began to slowly recover, but it was not until August, 1781, that he was again fit for service.   Of Dr. Woodward it is related that when Nelson expressed his surprise at the smallness of his fees, he replied, " Allow me to follow what I consider my professional duty.   Your illness, sir, has been brought on by serving your king and your country, and believe me, I love both too well to be able to receive any more." [2]   Happily, Nelson obeyed his doctor's orders, and earned his verdict of having been the best of patients.

[1] Captain Andrew Despard, and Lieutenant, afterwards Colonel, Edward Marcus Despard of the 79th Regiment—the latter was tried and convicted of treason, February, 1803, at whose trial Nelson testified to his loyalty and bravery.   See " Narratives of State Trials," vol. i. See also reference to his conduct in the protection of Jamaica.

[2] Clarke and McArthur, vol. i. p. 43.   " Ex Relatione Viscountess Nelson."   In May, 1781, he was under the care of Mr. Adair, the eminent surgeon, for the temporary loss of the use of his left arm, and nearly of the left leg and thigh.

It was at this time that the portrait of the young captain, of which I give a copy, was painted by Mr. Rigaud,
R.A.   "As to my portrait," Nelson writes to William
Locker, " it will be nothing in the least like what I am
now, that it is certain ; but you may tell Mr. Rigaud to
add beauty to it, and it will be much mended." [1]   It is
apparently to this period that the following anecdote
relates :—

" I felt impressed with an idea that I should never rise in my profession.   My mind was staggered with a view of the difficulties I had
to surmount, and the little interest I possessed.   I could discover no
means of reaching the object of my ambition.   After a long and
gloomy reverie, in which I almost wished myself overboard, a sudden
glow of patriotism was kindled within me, and presented my king and
country as my patron.   My mind exulted in the idea.   ' Well, then,'
I exclaimed, ' I will be a hero, and confiding in Providence, brave
every danger.'   The spirit of Nelson revived, and from that hour, in
his mind's eye, as he often declared to his friend Captain Hardy, a
radiant orb was suspended, which urged him onward to renown. " [2]

---

[1] To William Locker, Bath, 1781.   This portrait is now the property
of Earl Nelson, by whose permission this engraving is inserted.

[2] Related to Mr. W. R. Spencer in after years during their walks in
the romantic scenery of Downton Castle, Herefordshire, the seat of Mr.
Knight.   (Clarke and McArthur, vol. i. pp. 23-4).

NELSON'S SIGNATURE TO HIS "BOOK OF NAVIGATION," ON HIS
APPOINTMENT AS LIEUTENANT OF THE *LOWESTOFFE*, TRACED
FROM THE BOOK NOW IN THE POSSESSION OF EARL NELSON.

THE VISIT TO FRANCE.

CHAPTER II.

THE VISIT TO FRANCE.

(1781–1784.)

On the American Station—Attempt to recapture Turk's Island—First
interview with Prince William Henry—The Prince's portrait of
Nelson—Return to England on the Peace with France, 1783—
Exertions to obtain for his sailors their pay—A hard case—The
result of the war to Nelson—Visit to France—The Prince de Deux
Ponts — First love — A despairing lover — Appointment to the
Boreas—Leeward Islands Station.

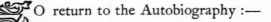 O return to the Autobiography :—

"In August, 1781, I was commissioned for the
Albermarle, and it would almost be supposed to
try my constitution, was kept the whole winter
in the North Sea. In April, 1782, I sailed with
a convoy for Newfoundland and Quebec, under
the orders of Captain Thos. Pringle. From Quebec, during a cruise
off Boston, I was chased by three French ships-of-the-line and the
Iris frigate ; as they all beat me in sailing very much, I had no chance
left but running them amongst the shoals of St. George's Bank. This
alarmed the line-of-battle ships, and they quitted the pursuit, but the
frigate continued, and at sunset was little more than a gun-shot distant,
when, the line-of-battle ships being out of sight, I ordered the main-
top-sail to be laid to the mast ; on this the frigate tacked and stood to
rejoin her consorts."

To the period of his North Sea voyage, the following
indignant denial of harsh conduct to a middy applies :—

"To WILLIAM LOCKER.

"*Feb.* 2, 1781.

"MY DEAR SIR,—The instant I received your letter, the latter part

struck me so very much, that perhaps I write to you sooner than
otherwise I should have done.   I need not say it to you, but what in
the name of God could it be to me whether a midshipman in my ship
had not a farthing or fifty pounds a year ?   Therefore, I must tell you,
as far as I know, his wish to leave the ship.   When he came on board,
I sent him into Mr. Bromwich's mess (third lieutenant) where he was
two or three days.   In that time they spoke to me, that they hoped I
would not take amiss, but they could not think of keeping that young
man (I forget his name) in their mess, as he could not pay his part of
their small expenses.   I am sure that you will not think I should
attempt to force any people who were ·behaving exceedingly well in
the ship (which would have been *tyrannical* in the highest degree)
against their inclination.   Whether the lad, sent to speak to me, or I
sent for him, I do not recollect; but I told him of what the mess had
said.   He seemed very uneasy at what I told him, and said he could
not afford to live in a mess that cost anything; and then said he wished
to leave the ship.   Next day he pressed me much to discharge him,
as he could not live in any of the mid. messes.   Much against my
inclination, I did discharge him.   What he took the idea of £30 a
year from, I know not, but I declare I never opened my lips to him
upon the subject.   To a youngster in the ship whose friends are Norfolk people, who had not made an allowance for their son, I took upon
me to allow £20 a year.

   " I assure you, I hold myself under very great obligations to you,
that you asserted it was an *infamous lie ;* had I in the least suspected
the story he has told, he should have stayed on board, and might have
lived as he pleased.   It was ndeavouring to put him in a comfortable situation that has made any person speak ill of me." [1]

On his return to the Downs from his North Sea cruize
Nelson was all but shipwrecked in a terrible gale. According to his biographers, Nelson, at the moment when the
gale burst on the shipping, was on shore, calling on the
senior officer ; and the *Brilliant*, store-ship, came athwart
hawse of the *Albermarle.* The sequel, if true, was a
striking illustration of Nelson's fearlessness in the discharge of his duty.   It is quoted on their authority : —

   " Captain Nelson immediately ran to the beach, and with his

   [1] Clarke and McArthur, vol. i. p. 52.

wonted contempt of danger, when any duty called for his exertions, employed every method he could devise to return on board, fearing lest the *Albermarle* might drive on the Goodwin Sands, but the dreadful surf and the increasing gale made even the skilful mariners of Deal regard the attempt as utterly impracticable.   At length some of the most intrepid offered to make the trial for fifteen guineas ; this produced a competition, and Nelson, to the astonishment of all beholders, was long seen struggling with a raging sea-surf, in which the boat was continually immersed.   After much difficulty he got on board his ship." [1]

This romantic incident, so characteristic of Nelson, may be true, but it is not even alluded to in the letter which he wrote to his brother William immediately after the occurrence.   In this he details his hopes with great particularity :—

"All done in five minutes.   What a change ! " he writes; " but we ought to be thankful we did not founder.   We have been employed since in getting jury-masts, yards, and boat-sprits, and stopping holes in our sides.   What is to become of us now I know not.   We must go into dock, and I fear be paid off, she has received so much damage. But, however, we must take the rough with the smooth ; these are the blessings of a sea life." [2]

Of his voyage to Quebec and his escape from the too powerful squadron of the French, he gives the following brief account in his letter to his good friend William Locker :—

"To William Locker.
"Isle of Bec, River St. Lawrence,
"*Oct.* 19, 1782.

"In the end our cruise has been an unsuccessful one ; we have taken, seen, and destroyed more enemies than is seldom done in the same space of time, but not one has arrived in port.   But, however, I do not repine at our loss ; we have in other things been very fortunate,

---

[1] Clarke and McArthur, vol. i. p. 48.
[2] To the Rev. W. Nelson, Jan. 28, 1782.

for on the 14th of August we fell in with, in Boston Bay, four sail-of-the-line and the *Iris*, French man-of-war, part of M. Vaudreuil's squadron, who gave us a pretty dance for between nine and ten hours. But we beat all except the frigate, though we brought to for her, after we were out of sight of the line-of-battle ships, she tacked and stood from us."

The following extract from the Autobiography briefly relates to three interesting incidents in Nelson's Life—the commencement of that friendship with the young Prince William Henry, the future William IV., which became most intimate and lasted during the whole of Nelson's life ; his trip to and residence in France, whither he went for the sake of acquiring greater facilities in the use of the French tongue ; and the attempt to recover Turk's Island from the French.

" In October," writes Nelson in his autobiography, " I sailed from Quebec with a convoy to New York, where I joined the Fleet under the command of Lord Hood ; and in November I sailed with him to the West Indies, where I remained till the Peace ; when I came to England being directed in my way to attend on H.R.H. the Duke of Clarence on his visit to the Havannah ; and was paid off at Portsmouth on July 3rd, 1783. In the autumn I went to France, and remained there all the spring of the year 1784 ; when I was appointed to the *Boreas* frigate, of 28 guns, and ordered to Leeward Island Station."

" Off Cape Tiberoon,
" *Feb.* 25, 1783.

" My situation in Lord Hood's Fleet must be in the highest degree most flattering to a young man. He treats me as if I was his son, and will, I am convinced, give me anything I can ask of him : nor is my situation with Prince William Henry less flattering. Lord Hood was so kind as to tell him (indeed I cannot make use of expressions strong enough to describe what I felt) that if he wished to ask questions relative to Naval Tactics, I could give him as much information as any officer in the fleet. He (the Prince) will be, I am certain, an ornament to our service. He is a *seaman*, which you could hardly suppose. Every other qualification you may expect from him. But he will be a *disciplinarian*, and a strong one : he says he is determined

NELSON AS A CAPTAIN (ÆTAT 22), BY RIGAUD, R.A.

every person shall serve his time before they are provided for, as he is obliged to serve himself. With the best temper, and great good sense, he cannot fail to be pleasing to every one." [1]

Referring to this interview with Nelson—

" I was then," said the Prince, " a midshipman on board the *Barfleur*, lying in the Narrows off Staten Island, and had the watch on deck, when Captain Nelson came in his barge alongside, who appeared to be the merest boy of a captain I ever beheld : and his dress was worthy of attention. He had on a full-laced uniform ; his lank unpowdered hair tied in a stiff Hessian tail of extraordinary length ; the old-fashioned flaps of his waistcoat added to the general quaintness of his figure and produced an appearance of particularity which attracted my attention. I had never seen anything like it before, nor could I imagine who he was, nor what he came about. My doubts were, however, removed when Lord Hood introduced me to him. There was something irresistibly pleasing in his address and conversation ; and an enthusiasm, when speaking on professional subjects, showing me he was no common being." [2]

Attempt on Turk's Island :—

" As it would be a very little loss in my getting to the Eastward," wrote Nelson, " making the Turk's Island, I determined to look what situation the French were in, and if possible to retake it. The *Tartar* who joined company a few hours afterwards, I ordered to put herself under my command, which with the *Resistance* (44) and *La Coquette*, a French man-of-war, prize to the *Resistance*, made a tolerable outward show. On Friday evening the *Albermarle*, *Resistance*, and *Drake* (14) anchored at the island. The *Tartar*, Captain Fairfax, I imagine, could not keep his anchorage on the bank. I can have no doubt but Captain Fairfax has good reasons why he did not join me again. This reduced our small force one *third* (the *Coquette*, a larger ship, kept off and on the whole time of our stay). I sent Captain Dixon on shore with a flag of truce to demand the surrender of the islands. With much confidence of his

---

[1] To William Locker.
[2] Minutes of a conversation with the Duke of Clarence at Bushey Park (Clarke and McArthur, vol. i. p. 53).

superior situation, the commander of the French troops sent an answer that he should defend himself.

" On Saturday morning, at daylight, 167 seamen and marines were landed from the ships under the command of Captain C. Dixon, who very much obliged me by offering to command them. At eleven o'clock Captain Dixon thought a division of the enemy's force might be made by sending the brigs off the town, to give him an opportunity of pushing on to the enemy's works. I ordered the *Drake*, under the command of Lieutenant Hinton, and (the ?) *Admiral Barrington*, Lieutenant Cunningham, who joined at this instant, to go off the town and batter it. Upon their getting within shot, I was very much surprised to see a battery of three guns open upon them, but notwithstanding this unexpected attack, they were both brought to an anchor opposite the battery in a masterly manner ; and the steady constant fire they kept up for upwards of an hour does great honour to the gentlemen who commanded them, and to their officers and men. The master of the *Drake* is wounded, and the boatswain and six men on board the *Admiral Barrington*. Captain Dixon at this time observed that the guns were fought by seamen, and that the troops were waiting to receive him with several field pieces ; and that they had a post upon the side of the hill with two pieces of cannon. With such a force, and their strong situation, I did not think anything further could be attempted." [1]

On the signature of the Peace with France, in 1783, Nelson returned home in the *Albermarle*, which was paid off ; but Nelson had still much to do for his sailors.

" My time, ever since I arrived in town, has been taken up in attempting to get the wages paid to my *good fellows*, for various ships they have served in during the war. The disgust of the seamen to the Navy is all owing to the infernal plan of turning them over from ship to ship, so that men cannot be attached to their officers or the officers care twopence about them." [2]

---

[1] To Rear-Admiral Lord Hood, March 9, 1783 (vol. i. p. 73). This attempt to recover Turk's Island is not mentioned in any Life of Nelson. In Schomberg's " Naval Chronology " (vol. i. p. 37) the attempt is noticed, but the *Albermarle* and Nelson are omitted, and it is inferred that the ships of the squadron were under the command of Captain King of the *Resistance*.

[2] To Captain Locker, 3, Salisbury Street, Strand, July 12, 1783.

"To HERCULES ROSS, ESQ., LATE A MERCHANT IN JAMAICA.

"*Aug.* 9, 1783.

"I have closed the war without a fortune; but I trust, and from the attention that has been paid to me, believe, that there is not a speck in my character. True honour, I hope, predominates in my mind above riches."

"To ADMIRAL VISCOUNT KEPPEL, FIRST LORD OF THE ADMIRALTY,

Aug. 20.

"MY LORD,—What now obliges me to address you, is the unfortunate case of a gentleman who was second lieutenant of the *Albermarle* by a commission from Lord Hood, approved by Admiral Pigot (successor to Lord Rodney as commander-in-chief in West Indies), but an unfortunate event, his having been a seaman and an officer, is in a fair way to hinder his getting confirmed as a lieutenant.

"When the *Hector*, Sir J. Hamilton, was ordered home from Jamaica, no Pilot could be got to carry the ship through the Windward passage. This gentleman being ordered a passage home in the *Hector*, and having been for several years on the Jamaica Station, Sir John requested, as appears by his certificate, he would take charge of the ship. Sir John ordered him to be borne as pilot till the ship got through the passage; but by a mistake of the clerks when he was discharged from being pilot, he was not entered upon any of the ship's books for the remainder of the passage, by which loss of time the pilot's time not being allowed in his servitude (and the mistake of not entering him upon any books afterwards), instead of having served his time the 20th March, 1783, five weeks previous to the date of his commission, he had not served his time till the 27th of June, a week before the ship was paid off.

"Depend upon it, my Lord, I should not have interested myself so much about this gentleman did I not know him to be a brave and good officer, having been with me for several years : therefore I beg that as my apology for troubling your Lordship with this letter. He has passed his examination at the Navy Office since the ship was paid off." (Clarke and McArthur, vol. i. p. 81.)

Notwithstanding this clear explanation, the Admiralty said this could not be done, and this really able officer did not get his promotion till 1793. In the autumn of 1783, Nelson and his friend Captain Macnamara visited France, in order to perfect themselves in the language.

In the following letter to William Locker, we have a graphic picture of French life at that period :

"We dined at Canterbury the day we parted from you—slept at Dover, and next morning at seven o'clock put to sea with a fair N.W. wind, and at half-past ten we were safe at breakfast at Monsieur Grandsire's house at Calais. His mother kept it when Hogarth wrote his 'Gate of Calais.' Sterne's 'Sentimental Journey' is the best description I can give of our tour. Mac (Captain Macnamara) advised me to go to St. Omer, as he had experienced the difficulty of attempting to fix in any place where there are no English. After dinner we set off, intended for Montreuil, sixty miles from Calais : they told us we travelled *en poste*, but I am sure we did not get on more than four miles an hour. I was highly diverted with looking what a curious figure the postillions in their jack boots and their rats of horses made together. Their chaises have no springs, and the roads are paved like London streets ; therefore you will naturally suppose we were pretty well shook together by the time we had travelled two posts and a half, which is fifteen miles to Marquise. Here we were shown into an inn—they called it—I should have called it a pigstye : we were shown into a room with two straw beds, and with great difficulty they mustered up clean sheets, and gave us two pigeons for supper upon a dirty tablecloth, and wooden-handled knives.—O *what a transition from happy England!*

"We laughed at the repast, and went to bed with the determination that nothing should ruffle our tempers. Having slept well, we set off at daylight for Boulogne, where we breakfasted ; this place was full of English, I suppose because the wine is so cheap. We went on after breakfast for Montreuil, and passed through the finest corn country that my eye ever beheld, diversified with fine woods, sometimes for two miles together through noble forests. The roads mostly were planted with trees, which made as fine an avenue as to any gentleman's seat. Montreuil is thirty miles from Boulogne, situated upon a small hill, in the middle of a fine plain, which reached as far as the eye could carry you towards the sea, which is about twelve miles from it. We put up at the same house, with the same jolly landlord that recommended La Fleur to Sterne. Here we wished much to have fixed, but neither good lodgings, nor masters could be had here ; for there are no middling class of people : sixty noblemen's families lived in the town, who owned the vast plain round it, and the rest very poor indeed. This is the finest country for game that ever was ; partridges twopence halfpenny a couple, pheasants and woodcocks in proportion, and, in short, every species of poultry. We dined, supped, and lay, and breakfasted the next day, Saturday : then we proceeded on our tour, leaving Montreuil you will suppose with great regret.

"We reached Abbeville at 8 o'clock ; but unluckily for us, two Englishmen, one of whom called himself *Lord Kingsland* (I can hardly suppose it to be him), and a Mr. Bullock, decamped at 3 o'clock in debt to every shopkeeper in the place. These gentlemen kept elegant houses, horses, &c. We found the town in an uproar, and as no master could be had in this place that could speak a word of English, and all masters that could speak English grammatically, attend at the places that are frequented by the English, which are, St. Omer, Lisle, Dunkirk, and Boulogne, to the northward of Paris, and as I had no intention of travelling to the South of France till the spring at any rate, I determined with Mac's advice to steer for St. Omer, where we arrived last Tuesday : and I own I was surprised to find, that instead of a dirty, nasty town, which I had always heard it represented, to find a large city, well paved, good streets, and well lighted.

"We lodge with a pleasant French family and have our dinners from the *traiteur's*. There are two very agreeable young ladies, daughters, who *honour* us with their company pretty often ; one always makes our breakfast, and the other our tea, and play a game at cards in an evening. Therefore I must learn French if it is only for the pleasure of talking to them, for they do not speak a word of English. Here are a great number of English in this place, but we visit only two families : for if I did I should never speak French. Two noble captains are here—Ball and Shephard. You do not know, I believe, either of them ; they wear fine epaulettes,[1] for which I think them great coxcombs ; they have not visited me, and I shall not, be assured, court their acquaintance. You must be heartily tired of this long epistle, if you can read it ; but I have the worst pen in the world, and can't mend it. God bless you and be assured,

"I am your sincere friend

"and affectionate humble servant,

"HORATIO NELSON."[2]

[1] Epaulettes were ordered to be worn in the navy on June 1, 1795. The name shows that they were French, and were worn by French officers 1793. In a letter to the same, November 26th, Nelson says, "You may suppose I hold them very *cheap* for putting on any part of a Frenchman's uniform " (vol. i. p. 89). See *post* what a different opinion Nelson afterwards had of Captain Ball, the future Governor of Malta.

[2] To William Locker, Esq., St. Omer, Nov. 2, 1783 (Clarke and McArthur, vol. i. p. 83).

Again Nelson writes to William Locker of the politeness of his late prisoner the Duke de Deux Ponts :—

"If I am not in England before the winter is over, I shall go to *Paris* in the spring; where I have received a most polite invitation from the officer whom I detained off Porto Caballo.[1]   I did not know his rank at the time, or after, till I came here ; he went by the name of Count de Deux Ponts.   He is a prince of the Empire, a general of the French army, Knight of the Grand Order of St. Louis, and was second in command at the capture of York Town.   His brother is heir apparent to Electorate of Bavaria, and of the Palatinate. The present Elector is eighty years of age, and this gentleman's brother is on his death-bed ; so most probably I shall have the honour of having taken prisoner a man who will be a sovereign prince of Europe, and brings into the field near 100,000 men : his letter is truly expressive of the attention that was paid him when on board my ship" (Nov. 26, 1783.   Clarke and McArthur, vol. i. p. 90).

At St. Omer, Nelson fell violently in love with one of the daughters of a clergyman of the name of Andrews, whom in true lovers' language he described as "Very beautiful—the most accomplished woman my eyes ever beheld !"   So strong was his attachment that when he returned to England he wrote to his Uncle Suckling :

"There is a lady I have seen, of a good family and connections, but with a small fortune—£1,000, I understand.   The whole of my income does not exceed £130 per annum.   Now I must come to the point : will you, if I should marry, allow me yearly £100 until my income is increased to that sum, either by employment or by any other way ?   A very few years I hope would turn something up, if my friends will but exert themselves.   If you will not give me the above sum, will you exert yourself either with Lord North or Mr. Jenkinson, to get me a guard-ship, or some employment in a public office where the attendance of the principal is not necessary, and of which they must have numbers to dispose of ?   In the India Service

---

[1] Captured in a Spanish launch March, 1783, with other French officers on a scientific tour, and immediately released : his brother lived to 1795 and died without issue.

I understand (if it remains under the Directors) their marine force is to be under the command of a captain in the Royal Navy ; that is the station I should like.

" You must excuse the freedom with which this letter is dictated, not to have been plain and explicit in my distress would have been cruel to myself. If nothing can be done for me, I know not what I have to trust to. Life is not worth preserving without happiness, and I care not where I may linger out a miserable existence. I am prepared to hear your refusal, and have fixed my resolution if that should happen ; but in every situation, I shall be a well-wisher to you and your family, and pray they or you may never know the pangs which at this instant tear my heart." [1]

Whether his uncle did or did not console the despairing lover—a matter of doubt—the engagement, however, fell through, and Nelson instead of being shelved on a guard-ship or sent to command the East Indian pilot navy, returned to the scene of his future glory. On January 12, 1784, Nelson returned to London, and on the 18th of March was appointed to the *Boreas* frigate 28 guns, and sent to the Leeward Islands, with Lady Hughes and her family (the wife of the admiral on that station) as passengers. The *Boreas* sailed on the 30th of May, with his brother William as his chaplain. In writing to that brother at this time said Nelson, " You ask me by what interest, did I get a ship ? I answer, having served with credit was my recommendation to Lord Howe, First Lord of the Admiralty. Anything in reason I can ask, I am sure of obtaining, from his justice."

[1] To William Suckling, Jan. 14, 1784.

HIS MARRIAGE WITH MRS. NISBET.

CHAPTER III.

HIS MARRIAGE WITH MRS. NISBET.

(1784–1787.)

On the Leeward Islands Station—Troubles with the American traders—
Determined action of Nelson—Proceedings against him by the
traders—The trial—Remonstrance with his Commander-in-chief—
The frauds of the Americans—Approval of Nelson's conduct by the
King and the Admiralty—Nelson and the brothers Collingwood—
The Spaniards and the Bullion license—Nelson and the French
frigate—His kindness to his midshipmen—Sketch of Nelson in 1785
by a female friend of Mrs. Nisbet—Introduction to Mrs. Nisbet—
Love letters to her—Prince William Henry under Nelson's command
—His character as an officer—Pardon of a sailor sentenced to death
at the request of the Prince—Marriage March 12, 1787—*Boreas* paid
off—Return to Burnham.

HIS Station (the Leeward Island)," continues
Nelson, in his Autobiography, " opened a new
scene to the officers of the British Navy. The
Americans, when colonists, possessed almost
all the trade from America to our West India
Islands ; and on the return of peace, they forgot, on this occasion, that they became foreigners, and, of course, had no right to trade in
the British Colonies. Our governors and Custom-House officers
pretended, that by the Navigation Act they had a right to trade and
all the West Indians wished what was so much to their interest.

" Having given Governors, Custom-House officers, and Americans
notice of what I would do, I seized many of their vessels, which
brought all parties upon me ; and I was persecuted from one island
to another, so that I could not leave my ship. But conscious recti-
tude bore me through it ; and I was supported, when the business
became to be understood, from home ; and I proved (and an Act

of Parliament has since established it), that a captain of a man-of-war
is bound to support all the Maritime Laws, by his Admiralty commission alone, without becoming a Custom-House officer."

The difficulties with the American traders to our
West Indian Islands, to which Nelson so briefly alludes
and which for a time involved him in lawsuits, and
appeared likely, to put him at issue with the Admiralty,
afford such a proof of his determination to do his duty,
despite every opposition, and to meet trickery with firmness, that some extracts from the very full correspondence
caused by them must be given. His position was most
difficult. In addition to the ingenious evasions and
frauds of the American shipowners and captains, and the
wish of the islanders to continue the trade with America,
which had proved so profitable to them, he had to deal
with the weakness of the Commander on the Station and
the indecision—for a time—of the Admiralty. The
result was, as he wrote to William Locker, on January
15, 1785 :—

"that the longer I am on this station the worse I like it. Our
Commander has not that opinion of his own sense that he ought
to have. He is led by the advice of the islanders to admit the
Yankees to a trade ; at least to wink at it. He does not give himself
that weight that I think an English Admiral ought to do. I for one
am determined not to suffer the Yankees to come where my ship is ;
for I am sure, if once the Americans are admitted to any kind of
intercourse with these islands, the views of the Loyalists on settling
Nova Scotia are entirely done away. They will first become carriers,
and next have possession of our islands, are we ever again embroiled
in a French war. The residents of these islands are Americans by
connection and interest, and are inimical to Great Britain. They
are as great rebels as ever were in America, had they the power to
show it.

"After what I have said, you will believe I am not very popular
with the people. They have never visited me, and I have not had
a foot in any house since I have been on the station, and all for doing

my duty by being *true to the interests of Great Britain*. A petition from
the President and Council has gone to the Governor-General and the
Admiral, to request the admission of the Americans. I have given
my answer to the Admiral upon the subject ; how he will take it, I
know not ; but I am determined to suppress the admission of foreigners
all in my power. I have told the Customs that I will complain if
they admit any foreigner to an entry—an American arrives ; sprung
a leak, a mast, and what not, makes a protest, gets admittance, sells
his cargo for ready money, goes to Martinico, buys molasses, and
so round and round. But I hate them all. The Loyalist cannot do
it, consequently they must sell a little dearer." [1]

How he dealt with his weak Commander-in-chief is
shown in the following masterly letter to Sir Richard
Hughes of January, 1785 :—

"To Rear-Admiral Sir Richard Hughes, Bart.
"*Jan.* 11 or 12, 1785.

"Sir,—I received your order of the 29th of December, wherein
you direct me in execution of your first order dated 12th of November
(which is, in fact, strictly requiring us to put the Act of Navigation,
upon which the wealth and safety of Great Britain so much depends,
in force) to observe the following directions, viz., to cause foreigners
to anchor by His Majesty's ship under my command, except in cases
of immediate and urgent distress, until her arrival and situation in all
respects shall be reported to His Majesty's Governor or his Representative at any of the islands where I may fall in with such foreign
ships or vessels ; and that if the Governor or his Representative
should give leave for admitting such vessels, strictly charging me not
to hinder them or interfere in their subsequent proceedings.

"I have ever been, as in duty bound, always ready to co-operate
with His Majesty's Governors or their Representatives in doing what
is for the benefit of Great Britain. No Governor will, I am sure,
do such an illegal act as to countenance the admission of foreigners
into the ports of their islands, nor *dare* any officer of His Majesty's
Customs enter such foreigners without they are in such distress that
necessity obliges them to unlade their cargoes, and then only to sell
such a part of it, as will pay the costs. In distress, no individual shall

---

[1] To William Locker, *Boreas*, Basseterre Roads, Jan. 15, 1785 (Clarke
and McArthur, vol. i. p. 113).

exceed me in acts of generosity; and in judging of their distress, no person can know better than sea-officers, of which I shall inform the Governors, &c., when they acquaint me for what reason they have countenanced the admission of foreigners.

"I beg leave to hope that I may be properly understood, when I venture to say, that at a time when Great Britain is using every endeavour to suppress illicit trade at home, it is not wished that ships upon this station should be singular, by being the only spectators of the illegal trade, which I know is carried on in these islands. The Governors may be imposed upon by false declarations; we, who are on the spot, cannot. General Shirley told me and Captain Colling-wood how much he approved of the methods that we were carrying on for the suppressing the illegal trade with America; that it had ever been his wish, and that he used every means in his power, by proclamation and otherwise, to hinder it; but they came to him with protests, and swore everything (even as the sea-phrase is, 'Through a nine-inch plank') therefore got admittance, as he could not examine the vessels himself; and further, by the *Thynne* packet he had received a letter from Lord Sydney, one of His Majesty's principal Secretaries of State, saying that the Administration were determined that American ships and vessels should not have any intercourse with our West India Islands; and that he had, upon an Address from the Assembly, petitioning that he would relax the King's proclamation for the ex-clusion of Americans, transmitted it to Lord Sydney to be laid before the King. The answer to General Shirley was that His Majesty firmly believed and hoped that all his orders which were received by the Governors would be strictly obeyed.

"Whilst I have the honour to command an English man-of-war, I never shall allow myself to be subservient to the will of any Governor, nor to co-operate with him in doing *illegal acts*. Presidents of Council I feel myself superior to. They shall make proper appli-cation to me, for whatever they may want to come by water.

"If I rightly understand your order of the 29th of December, it is founded upon an opinion of the King's Attorney-General, viz., 'That it is legal for Governors or their Representatives to admit Foreigners into the Ports of their Government, if they think fit.' How the King's Attorney-General conceives he has a right to give an illegal opinion, which I assert the above is, he must answer for. I know the Navigation Laws.

"I am Sir, &c.,

"HORATIO NELSON."[1]

---

[1] Clarke and McArthur, vol. i. p. 114.

Again, on the 30th of March in the same year, he wrote the following exposure of the system of fraud and evasion to Lord Sydney, the Secretary of State. After repeating his attempts to suppress the illegal traffic of the American ships, Nelson adds :

"At times the King's ship is obliged to sail to the neighbouring islands to procure wood, water, and provisions : constantly when I returned, have I been informed from good authority, that the Americans had free egress and regress to our ports. The Custom House does not admit them to an entry, only the Master of the American makes a Protest (what they say and are ready to swear to) that their vessel leaks, has sprung a mast, or some excuse of that sort. Then the Customs grant a Permit to land a part or the whole of their cargo to pay expenses, under which Permits they land innumerable cargoes ; could the number of them be found out, which I fear I cannot, your lordship would be astonished. At this island (St. Christopher's) the Customs have refused to give answers to the King's officers. When I send for information, they have answered me, they do not know any right I have to ask : they are not amenable to a Captain of the Navy for their conduct. Yesterday an American brig came into this port, said by the Master to be in distress. I told him he must not have any communication with the shore till I had ordered a survey upon his vessel. People from the shore in boats had spoke to him, and he told them his distress. Now, my lord, let my heart speak for me. It was dispersed all over the island (for my information came from Sandy-Point, the extremity of it) that in the night I intended to turn him out of port, and he would certainly sink before morning. There only wanted this report to represent me both cruel and unjust ; the account was believed by the great part of the island. This, as the honour of my gracious King and my country were at stake, has made me take the liberty of addressing your lordship; for so far from treating him cruelly, I sent an officer, a carpenter, and some men, to take care of the vessel, which they did by pumping her all night; and this morning I moored her into a safe harbour."

With a few more extracts I leave this subject— American seizures.

In a memorial to the king, detailing his proceedings

in stopping American ships at St. Christopher and Nevis, and the issue of writs against him by the masters for £4000 for assault and imprisonment, Nelson states that he is advised by H.M. Attorney-General of Nevis, "that it is unsafe at present to rely too much on the justice of his cause, and put himself upon the country for trial." Hence he is obliged to keep himself confined to his ship to the injury of his health.[1] He then describes the trial and its issue :—

"To William Locker, Esq.

"*Boreas, March* 5, 1786.

"When the trial came on I was protected by the judge for the day, but the Marshal was desired to arrest (me), and the merchants promised to indemnify him for the act ; but the judge, having declared he would send him to prison if he dared to do it, he desisted. I fortunately attached myself to an honest lawyer ; and, don't let me forget, the President of Nevis offered in court to become my bail for £10,000, if I chose to suffer the arrest. He told them I had only done my duty, and although he suffered more in proportion than any of them, he could not blame me. At last, after a trial of two days, we carried our cause, and the vessels were condemned. I was a close prisoner on board for eight weeks, for had I been taken, I must assuredly have been cast for the whole sum (£4,000). I had nothing left but to send a memorial to the King, and he was good enough to order me to be defended at his expense, and sent orders to Mr. Shirley to afford me every assistance in the execution of my duty, and referring to my letters, &c., as there was in them what concerned him not to have suffered.

"The Treasury, by the last packet, has transmitted thanks to Sir Richard Hughes and the officers under him, for their activity and zeal in protecting the commerce of Great Britain. Had they known what I have told you (and if my friends think I may, without impropriety, tell the story myself, I shall do it when I get home), I don't think they would have bestowed thanks in that quarter and have neglected me. I feel much hurt that, after the loss of health and risk of fortune, another should be thanked for what I did against his orders. I rather deserved to be sent out of the service, or, at least,

---

[1] June 28, 1785 (Clarke and McArthur, vol. i. pp. 136–7).

have had some little notice taken of me. They had thought it
worthy of notice, and have neglected me ; if this is the reward for
a faithful discharge of my duty, I shall be careful and never stand
forward again ; but I have done my duty, and have nothing to accuse
myself of" (Clarke and McArthur, vol. i. p. 158).[1]

During this period Captain Cuthbert Collingwood,
who had succeeded Nelson in the *Hinchinbrook*, and his
brother Wilfrid, Captain of the *Rattler*, co-operated
actively with Nelson into carrying into execution the
provisions of the Navigation Laws, thus violated by the
citizens of the United States, with the connivance of
the West Indian proprietors.

"What an amiable, good man Collingwood is," writes Nelson to
William Locker in March, 1786 ; "he is a valuable member of
society. You accuse me too justly of not writing, but really for the
last year I have been plagued to death. Had it not been for Collingwood, this station would have been the most disagreeable I ever saw.
It was near the hurricane months when I arrived in this country,
consequently nothing could be done until they were over in
November, when the squadron arrived at Barbadoes, and the ships
were to be sent to the different islands with only orders to examine
anchorages, and whether there was wood and water. This did not
appear to me the intent of placing men-of-war on this station in
peaceable times, therefore I asked Collingwood to go with me to the
Admiral, for his sentiments and mine were exactly similar. I there
asked him (Sir R. Hughes) if we were not to attend to the commerce
of our country, and to take care that British trade was kept in those
channels which the Navigation Laws pointed out. He answered,
he had no orders, nor had the Admiralty sent him any Acts of Parliament. I told him it was very odd, as every captain of a man-of-
war was furnished with the Statutes of the Admiralty, in which was

---

[1] Captain Wallis says in his narrative that Governor Shirley, feeling
irritated at Nelson's remonstrances, told him, "that old generals were
not in the habit of taking advice from young gentlemen," to which Nelson
replied, "I have the honour, sir, of being as old as the Prime Minister of
England, and think myself as capable of commanding one of His
Majesty's ships as that Minister is of governing the state." General
Thomas Shirley, Captain-General of Leeward Islands, 1781 ; created
baronet, 1786 ; died at Bath, February, 1800.

the Navigation Act, which was directed to Admirals, Captains, &c., to see to its execution. He said he had never seen the book ; but having produced and read the laws to him, he seemed convinced that men-of-war were sent abroad for some other purpose than to be made a show of. He then gave orders to all the squadron to see the Navigation Act carried into execution." [1]

The rest of the story is told in Nelson's letter to the Admiral.

In this difficult business Wilfred Collingwood was the principal director, as said his brother " he understood it much better than any of them." Unhappily for the service, Wilfred died early. How those who knew his worth grieved for his loss we may judge from Nelson's letter to his brother.

" *Boreas*, NEVIS,

" *May* 3, 1787.

" MY DEAR COLLINGWOOD,—To be the messenger of bad news is my misfortune, but still it is a tribute which friends owe each other. I have lost a friend—you an affectionate brother ; too great a zeal in serving the country hastened his end. The greatest consolation the survivor can receive is a thorough knowledge of a life spent with honour to himself and of service to the country. If the tribute of tears be valuable, my friend had it. The esteem he stood in with His Royal Highness was great. His letter to me on his death is the strongest testimony of it. 'Collingwood, poor fellow, is no more. I have cried for him, and most sincerely do I condole with you on his loss. In him His Majesty has lost a faithful servant, and the service a most excellent officer.' A testimony of regard so honourable is more to be coveted than anything this world could have afforded,

---

[1] " In 1776," writes Lord Collingwood in his autobiographical letter to the editor of a naval publication, January 7, 1806, " I went to Jamaica as Lieutenant of the *Hornet* sloop ; and soon after the *Lowestoffe*, of which Lord Nelson was Lieutenant, came to the same station. We had been long before in habits of great friendship ; and it happened here, that as Admiral Sir P. Parker, the Commander-in-chief, was the friend of both, whenever Lord Nelson got a step in rank, I succeeded him ; first on the *Lowestoffe,* then on the *Badger*, into which ship I was made Commander in 1779, and afterwards on the *Hinchinbrook*, a 28-gun frigate, which made us both post-Captains " (" Correspondence and Memoir of Lord Collingwood," p. 7).

and must be balm to his surviving friends. The *Rattler* had been refitting in an English harbour, and when I arrived there in the middle of April, Wilfred was a little complaining ; but I did not think that at first anything dangerous was to be apprehended. But in a few days I perceived he was in a rapid decline, and Dr. Young told me to send him to sea, as the only chance. He sailed on Tuesday for Grenada, where I was in hopes, could he have reached Mr. Haines, some fortunate circumstance might turn out ; but it pleased God to order it otherwise. On Friday, the 21st of April, at ten at night, he left this life without a groan or a struggle. The ship put into St. Vincents, where he was interred with all military honours ; the regiment, President, and Council attending him to the grave. It is a credit to the people of St. Vincents which I did not think they would have deserved. Adieu, my good friend, and be assured I am, with the truest regard, your affectionate friend,

" HORATIO NELSON." [1]

The effect of this determined course of action on the part of Nelson and Collingwood, which eventually was entirely approved of by the Government, may be judged from the following letter to the Secretary of the Admiralty, of August 27, 1786.

In a letter to P. Stephens, Secretary of the Admiralty, Antigua, August 27, 1786, Nelson advises him, that the Spaniards, under the pretence of bringing bullion, bring live stock to sell to the islanders ; and that on his seizing a ship thus laden, the Collector of Customs sent off Treasury order of 1763, with the words " live stock " written in after " bullion," and declared it had been so ever since he had been in office and approved by the Board of Customs. And then says :

"As the American vessels are now pretty tired of venturing amongst our islands, their vessels, after delivering their cargoes in the French islands, or at the Dutch settlements of Surinam, Demerara, &c., upon the Main, repair to the island of Trinidada, where they obtained from

---

[1] "Correspondence and Memoir of Lord Collingwood," p. 13.

the Governor a qualification to make their vessels Spanish for a given
time.   They, in general, take a Spanish Creole, or two, to give colour
to the fraud; and thus prepared, they, under Spanish colours, visit
our islands, and the Custom Houses, under the cloak of the order of
(the) Treasury, 1763, and the sanction they pretend to have from the
Board of Customs, admit these Americans ; and I have little doubt,
although their decks are loaded with cattle, that in their hold they
bring American produce."

It was during this portion of his service that Nelson
had the following amusing incident with a French
frigate, affording another instance of the determination
of this young captain at the age of twenty-six years.

" After the hurricane months were over, and the *Boreas* at anchor
in Nevis roads, a French frigate passed to leeward, close along shore.
Captain Nelson had information that this frigate was destined on a
survey of our islands, and had on board two general officers and some
engineers for that purpose, which information proved correct.
Captain Nelson immediately determined to attend her, and prevent
their intentions : therefore, he immediately got under weigh and
pursued her.   On the day he found her at anchor in the road of St.
Eustatia, and the *Boreas* was anchored about two cables' length on the
French frigate's quarter.   After a reciprocity of civilities and salutes,
&c., had been passed on all sides, Captain Nelson with his officers
were invited to meet the French officers at dinner next day at the
Dutch Governor's, which was accepted ; and it was at this dinner
that Nelson made known his intentions to the Captain of the French
frigate.   He said that, understanding he intended visiting the English
Islands, he thought it his duty to accompany him in the English frigate,
that attention might be paid to his most Christian Majesty, which he was
sure every Englishman in the islands would be proud of an opportunity
of doing.   This declaration did not appear palatable to the French
Generals, and was politely refused by them as well as by the Captain
of the French frigate, saying that their intention was only to take a
cruise round the islands without stopping at any.   However, Captain
Nelson was determined not to be outdone in *civility*, and strictly
adherred to his purpose.   The Frenchman perceiving the English
commander's drift, in a few days abandoned his project, got under
weigh, and beat up to Martinique.   Nelson availed himself of the
same opportunity, and beat up to Barbadoes, by which he never lost

sight of the French frigate until she got into Martinique, where she came from." [1]

The following description of Nelson's system of teaching his youthful officers is taken from a letter written by Lady Hughes (Nelson's passenger to join her husband in the West Indies), to her nephew, Mr. Matcham, subsequently to the fatal victory of Trafalgar.

"I was too much affected when we met at Bath to say every particular in which he displayed the infinite cleverness and goodness of heart of our beloved hero.   As a woman, I can only judge of those things that I could comprehend, such as his attention to the young gentlemen who had the happiness of being on his quarter-deck.   It may reasonably be supposed that among the number of thirty, there must be timid as well as bold : the timid he never rebuked, but always desired to show them he desired nothing of them that he would not instantly do himself, and I have known him say—'Well, sir, I am going a race to the mast-head, and I beg I may meet you there.'   No denial could be given to such a wish, and the poor fellow instantly began his march.   His lordship never took the least notice with what alacrity it was done, but when he met in the top, instantly began speaking in the most cheerful manner, and saying how much a person was to be pitied that could fancy there was any danger or even disagreeable in the attempt.   In like manner he every day went to the schoolroom and saw them do their nautical business, and at twelve o'clock he was first upon the deck with his quadrant.   No one there could be behindhand in his business when their captain set them so good an example.   One other circumstance I must mention which will close the subject, which was the day we landed at Barbadoes. We were to dine at the Governor's.   Our dear Captain said, 'You must permit me, Lady Hughes, to carry one of my aid-de-camps with me,' and when he presented him to the Governor, he said, 'Your Excellency must excuse me for bringing one of my midshipmen, as I make it a rule to introduce them to all the good company I can ; they

---

[1] Captain Wallis' narrative.   The events put by him in 1795 ; but see letter to Mrs. Nisbet, March 25, 1786, in which he writes, " For the last week a French man-of-war has been here, and going about with them so much in the sun has given violent headaches."

have few to look up to besides myself during the time they are at sea.'
This kindness and attention made the young people adore him; and
even his wishes could they have been known, would have been
instantly complied with. It was your wish, sir, to have the above
particulars; an abler pen might have described them better; but I
hope that my simple narration may, in a faint degree, describe his
lordship's excellent manner of making his young men fancy the
attaining nautical perfection was more a play than a task. Who is
there but must allow these methods to be dictated by great skill, as
well as a great goodness of heart that never caused a fear or disgust to
any one? How sincerely is such a loss lamented! But we have
nothing to say, but, 'The Lord giveth, the Lord taketh away; blessed
be the name of the Lord.'" [1]

On this cruise Nelson was introduced, in May, 1785,
to the widow of Dr. Nisbet, of Nevis—his future wife—
the niece of Mr. Herbert, the Governor of that island,
who had previously received the following description of
her future lover from a female friend :—

"We have at last seen the captain of the *Boreas*, of whom so much
has been said. He came up first before dinner, much heated, and
was very silent, yet seemed, according to the old adage, to think the
more. He declined drinking any wine (at dinner); but after dinner,
when the President, as usual, gave the following toasts, 'The King,'
'The Queen and Royal family,' and 'Lord Hood,' this strange man
regularly filled his glass, and observed that these were always bumper
toasts with him; which having drank, he uniformly passed the bottle,
and relapsed into his former taciturnity. It was impossible, during
this visit, for any of us to make out his real character; there was such
a reserve and sternness in his behaviour, with occasional sallies, though
very transient, of a superior mind. Being placed by him, I endeavoured to rouse his attention by showing him all the civilities in
my power; but I drew out little more than 'yes' and 'no.' If you,
Fanny, had been here, we think you would have made something of
him, for you have been in the habit of attending to these odd sort of
people" (Clarke and McArthur, vol i. p. 57).

---

[1] Letter of Lady Hughes, passenger on the *Boreas* to the West Indies,
1783, to Mr. Matcham, Clifton, June 24, 1808 (Clarke and McArthur,
vol. i. p. 124, note).

His courtship was short, as within a month he wrote to his brother :

"St. Kitts, *June* 28, 1785.

"Postscript *Entre Nous*. Do not be surprised to hear I am a *Benedict*, for if at all, it will be before a month. Do not tell."

His love letters are so characteristic, that space must be found for specimens of these usually somewhat absurd productions.

"*Boreas*, English Harbour, *Sept.* 11, 1785.

"Indeed, my dear Fanny, I had buoyed myself up with hopes that the Admiral's schooner would have given me a line from you ; but the tidings she brought of the release of poor Mrs. Herbert from this world, sufficiently apologise for your not thinking of an absentee. Yet this believe from my heart, that I partake in all the sorrows you experience ; and I comfort myself, that however great your grief at this moment may be, at losing a person so deservedly dear to you, as your good aunt ; yet, when reason takes place, you must rather have pleasure in knowing she is released from those torments she had undergone for months past. Time ever has, and in the present instance I trust may have, a tendency to soften grief into a pleasing remembrance ; and her unspotted character must afford you real comfort. Call religion to your aid ; and it will convince you, that her conduct in this world was such as insures everlasting happiness in that which is to come.

"I have received a letter from Mr. Herbert, in answer to that which I left at Nevis for him. My greatest wish is to be united to you ; and the foundation of all conjugal happiness, real love and esteem, is, I trust, what you believe I possess in the strongest degree towards you. I think Mr. Herbert loves you too well, not to let you marry the man of your choice, although he may not be so rich as some others, provided his character and situation in life render such an union eligible. I declare solemnly, that did I not conceive I had full possession of your heart, no consideration should make me accept your hand. We know that riches do not always insure happiness ; and the world is convinced that I am superior to pecuniary considerations in my public and private life ; as in both instances I might have been rich. But I will have done, leaving all my present feelings to operate in your heart. Only of this truth be convinced, that I am your affectionate,

" Horatio Nelson.

" P.S. Do I ask too much, when I venture to hope for a line? or otherwise I may suppose my letters may be looked upon as troublesome."[1]

" To the Same.

'" *Aug.* 19, 1786.

" As you begin to know something about sailors, have you not often heard, that salt water and absence always wash away love. Now I am such a heretic as not to believe that faith : for, behold, every morning since my arrival, I have had six pails of water at daylight poured over my head, and instead of feeling what the seamen say to be true, I perceive the contrary effect, and if it goes on so contrary you must see me before my fixed time. But patience is a virtue and I must exercise it on this occasion, whatever it costs my feelings.

" I am alone in the commanding officer's house, while my ship is fitting, and from sunset until bedtime I have not a human creature to speak to : you will feel a little for me, I think. I did not use to be overfond of sitting alone. The moment old *Boreas* is habitable in my cabin, I shall fly to it, to avoid mosquitoes and melancholics. Hundreds of the former are now devouring me through all my clothes. You will, however, find I am better ; though when you see me, I shall be like an Egyptian mummy, for the heat is intolerable. But I walk a mile out at night without fatigue, and all day I am housed. A quart of goat's milk is also taken every day, and I enjoy English sleep, always baring mosquitoes, which all Frank's care with my net cannot keep out at present.

" What nonsense I am sending you : but I flatter myself the most trivial article concerning me, you feel interested in. I judge from myself ; and I would rather have what passes in your mind, than all the news you could tell me which did not concern you."

" To the Same.

" *Jan.* 1, 1787.

" What is it to attend on princes? Let me attend on you, and I am satisfied. Some are born for attendants on great men. I rather think it is not my particular province. His Royal Highness often tells me, he believes I am married, for he never saw a lover so easy.

---

[1] Clarke and McArthur.

or say so little of the object he has regard for. When I tell him I certainly am not he says, ' Then he is sure I must have a great esteem for you, and that is not what (vulgarly), I do not like the use of that word, called love.' He is right : my love is founded on esteem, the only foundation that can make the passion last. I need not tell you, what you so well know, that I wish I had a fortune to settle on you ; but I trust I have a good name, and that certain events will bring the other thing about : it is my misfortune, not my fault ; therefore I ought to make you a good husband, and I hope that it will turn out that I shall. You are never absent from my mind in any place or company. I never wished for riches, but to give them to you ; and my small share shall be yours to the extreme. A Happy New Year, and that many of them may attend you, is the most fervent wish of your affectionate,

" H. N." [1]

Towards the end of the year 1786, the young Prince William Henry, now captain of the *Pegasus* frigate, was placed under Nelson's command, and from that period the intercourse between them became close. His judgment of the Prince as a young captain, is shown in the subsequent letters.

" To Mrs. Nisbet.

" Off Antigua, *Dec.* 12, 1786.

" Our young Prince is a gallant man : he is indeed volatile, but always with great good nature. There were two balls during his stay, and some of the old ladies were mortified that H. R. H. would not dance with them ; but he says, he is determined to enjoy the privilege of all other men, that of asking any lady he pleases.

" *Wednesday.* We arrived here this morning at daylight. His Royal Highness dined with me, and of course the Governor. I can tell you a piece of news, which is, that the Prince is fully determined, and has made me promise him, that he shall be at our wedding, and he says he will give you to me. His Royal Highness has not yet been in a private house to visit, and is determined never to do so except in this case."

---

[1] Private Correspondence (vol. i. p. 206).

"To William Locker.
"English Harbour, *Dec.* 29, 1786.

" You will know long before this reaches you, that Prince William is under my command : I shall endeavour to take care he is not a loser by that circumstance. He has his foibles as well as private men, but they are far overbalanced by his virtues. In his professional line, he is superior to near two-thirds, I am sure, of the List ; and in attention to orders and respect to his superior officers, I hardly know his equal : this is what I have found him. Some others, I have heard, will tell another story. The islanders have made vast entertainments for him. But all this you will see in the English papers. The Prince is to remain in these seas until May, when he returns to Nova Scotia." [1]

" To the Same.
" *Feb.* 9, 1787.

" His Royal Highness keeps up strict discipline in his ship, and without paying him any compliment, she is one of the finest-ordered frigates I have seen. He has had more plague with his officers than enough " (Clarke and McArthur, vol. i. p. 215). [2]

In April, 1787, at the intercession of Prince William Henry, Nelson had remitted the sentence of death passed on a seaman of the *Rattler*. To the rebuke which he received from the Admiralty for this act of mercy, Nelson wrote the following manly reply on his return to England :—

" Spithead, *July* 11, 1787.

" A man belonging to the *Rattler* was sentenced to death. As senior officer of five ships, or as an officer detached from the fleet by a

---

[1] Clarke and McArthur, vol. i. p. 205.

[2] The following is the testimony of Captain Hon. W. Cornwallis to the abilities of the Prince. Letter to Nelson, *Phœnix*, Diamond Harbour, *Aug.* 13, 1790 :

" Our Royal Duke is, I hear, almost tired of the shore, but how he will be able to employ himself in time of peace at sea, it is not easy to determine. It would, however, be a pity that any of the zeal and fondness he has so evidently shown for the Service should be suffered to abate, as there is every reason to believe that with his ability he will one-day carry its glory to a greater height than it has yet attained " (vol. i. p. 241, note).

Commander-in-chief, I had not leave to carry a sentence of death into execution. Sir Richard Hughes' flag was struck, and I was only under the orders of their lordships; therefore I felt myself empowered to carry any sentence of death into execution; which would have been the case of the unhappy man belonging to the *Rattler*, had not his Royal Highness interceded for his pardon. Thus I was near, if not of cutting the thread of life, at least of shortening a fellow creature's days. The law might not have supposed me guilty of murder, but my feelings would nearly have been the same. I was always bred up with the idea of obeying my commanding officer most correctly; and what must I feel at finding the Commander-in-chief's directions a mere nullity." [1]

On March 12, 1787, Nelson was married at St. Kitts to Mrs. Nisbet. "To-morrow," writes Lady Nelson to her husband from Bath on March 11, 1797, "is our wedding-day, when it gave me a dear husband and my child the best of fathers." Young Nisbet, the son of her former husband, was the Josiah of the future correspondence, but educated for the Navy and brought forward—perhaps too forward for his future work—by his kind stepfather.

At the close of this year the *Boreas* was paid off, and Nelson with his wife and stepson returned to live at his father's parsonage.

[1] Clarke and McArthur, vol. i. p. 246.

AT HOME AND IN THE MEDITERRANEAN.

CHAPTER IV.

AT HOME AND IN THE MEDITERRANEAN.

(1787–1795.)

Life at Burnham—Qualifications for a sea officer—Advice to Prince William Henry—West Indian frauds—The condition of the labourers in Norfolk—Appointment to the *Agamemnon* 64 on the Mediterranean Station—A bull feast—No prize after all the trouble—Action with French frigates—First engagement in the *Agamemnon*—The Bey of Tunis—Letter from his father—The horrors of the evacuation of Toulon.

F the next six years of his life, Nelson gives but a brief account in his Autobiography :—

"The *Boreas*, being paid off at Sheerness on November the 30th, 1 lived at Burnham Thorpe, county of Norfolk, in the Parsonage House. In 1790, when the affair with Spain, relative to Nootka Sound, had nearly involved us in a war, I made use of every interest to get a ship, ay, even a boat, to serve my country, but in vain ; there was a prejudice at the Admiralty evidently against me, which I can neither guess at, nor in the least account for. . . ." [some words here omitted in the print in Clarke and McArthur's : original MS. has not been found.]

Two very interesting letters, however, are found in the correspondence during the few months that elapsed between his arrival at Spithead, and his retirement to Burnham Thorpe when the *Boreas* was paid off. In the first, Nelson advises the Earl of Cork on the qualifications

necessary, in his view of the service, for a naval officer.
In the second, he speaks with commendable plainness to
his friend the Prince on his hasty conduct in censuring
Lieut. Schomberg, one of the officers of the *Pegasus*, and
on the care which persons in the Prince's position should
take in the selection of their friends, on whose judgment
they were only too ready to rely. From the first of these
letters the following extract is given ; the second letter is
too good not to be quoted in full :—

"To the Earl of Cork.
"Portsmouth, *July* 2, 1787.

"In the first place, my Lord, it is necessary that he (his son,
Courtenay Boyle) should be made complete in his Navigation ; and if
the Peace continues, French is absolutely necessary. Dancing is an
accomplishment that probably a sea officer may require. You will
see almost the necessity of it when employed in foreign countries;
indeed, the honour of the nation is so often entrusted to sea officers,
that there is no accomplishment which will not shine with peculiar
lustre in them." [1]

The case of Lieut. Schomberg, the well-known author
of "The Naval Chronology," was due to equally hasty
temper in the Prince and his lieutenant. The Prince had
given orders that no boat should leave his ship without
his permission, or, if he was absent, without being
reported to him on his return. His lieutenant, either
from ignorance or presuming that such an order could not
apply to an officer in his position, disobeyed, and was
publicly reprimanded by the Prince for his conduct. On
that he applied for a court-martial. From the absence of
sufficient ships on the station, this could not be held at
the time, and he was placed under arrest to await its
being held. At this demand for a court-martial, at a
time when it could not be held, and thus compelling the
chief of the station to confine the officer and deprive the

squadron of his services, Nelson was justly angry : the case lingered for months, and was at last only arranged without the need of trial by the Commodore on the Jamaica Station. Hence the following letter to the Prince :—

"PORTSMOUTH, *July* 27, 1787.

"If to be truly great is to be truly good (as we are taught to believe), it was never stronger verified that in your Royal Highness, in the instance of Mr. Schomberg. You have supported your character, yet at the same time, by an amiable condescension, have saved an officer from appearing before a court-martial, which must ever hurt him. Resentment, I know, your Royal Highness never had, or, I am sure, ever will bear any one : it is a passion incompatible with the character of a man of honour. Schomberg was too hasty in writing his letter; but now you are parted, pardon me, my Prince, when I presume to recommend that Schomberg may stand in your Royal favour, as if he had never sailed with you; and that at some future day you will serve him. There only wants this to place your character in the highest point of view. None of us are without failings : Schomberg's was being rather too hasty; but that, put in competition with his being a good officer, will not, I am bold to say, be taken in the scale against him.

"I wish this matter could have been settled on my station, and I am sure your Royal Highness will join me when I acquaint you that I have been reprimanded for allowing you to proceed to America by way of Jamaica.[1] More able friends than myself your Royal Highness may easily find, and of more consequence in the State ; but one more attached and affectionate is, I am bold to say, not so easily met with. Princes seldom, very seldom, find a disinterested person to communicate their thoughts to. I do not pretend to do otherwise ;

---

[1] At Jamaica, Commodore Gardner arranged this unpleasant affair without a court-martial; but Nelson, on his return to England, was called upon to give his reasons for sending the *Pegasus* and *Rattler* to Jamaica. On July 10, 1787, he did so, and received the following rebuke : "My Lords are not satisfied with the reasons you have given for altering the destination of the *Pegasus*, and for sending the *Rattler* sloop to Jamaica ; and that for having taken upon you to send the latter away from the station to which their Lordships had appointed her, you will be answerable for the consequence, if the Crown should be put to any needless expense upon that account."

but of this truth be assured, by a man who, I trust, never did a dishonourable act, that I am interested only that your Royal Highness should be the greatest and best man this country ever produced. In full confidence of your belief of my sincerity, I take the liberty of saying that, having seen a few more years than yourself, I may, in some respects, know more of mankind. Permit me then to urge a thorough knowledge of those you tell your mind to. Mankind are not always what they seem. Far, very far, be it from me to mean any person whom your Royal Highness thinks proper to honour with your confidence : but again let me impress on your Royal mind what I have before mentioned.

"When I go to town I shall take care to be presented to His Majesty and the Prince of Wales, that I may be in the way of answering any question they may think proper to ask me. Nothing is wanting to make you the darling of the English nation, but truth. Sorry I am to say much to the contrary has been dispersed. Lord Hood and the good Commissioner have made many inquiries about you. Permit me to subscribe myself

"Your Royal Highness's attached and affectionate
"HORATIO NELSON." [1]

During his residence with his father at Burnham Thorpe, Nelson turned his attention to the garden or the farm, digging with his own hands for exercise, but not neglecting the current periodicals of the time, studying charts, and drawing plans. His American enemies followed him home, prosecuting him for seizing their vessels, even threatening to arrest him, and making him resolve, if the Government did not defend him at their own expense, to go abroad, and so get out of the way of his persecutors, and leave an ungrateful country.

The *Boreas,* on being paid off, was made a receiving ship at the Nore for impressed seamen, at which act, according to one of his biographers, Nelson was so irritated that he told the senior officer in the Medway that "he would never set his foot on board a King's ship again, and would go to Lord Howe and resign his

[1] Clarke and McArthur, vol. i. p. 250.

commission," and that it was only from the kind reception
he met with from the First Lord, and his gracious reception by the King, that he was induced to alter his
reputed determination.[1]   This anecdote may be true, but
strange it is, if it is true, that not an allusion to any of
the incidents are to be found in the private correspondence,
and it is certainly inconsistent with his letter of August
12, 1787, in which he wrote, " If we are to have a battle,
I do not want to come on shore.   I begin to think I am
fonder of the sea than ever."[2]   No doubt Nelson had
much reason to be angry with the Admiralty ; he had too
much zeal to suit the Government officials ; but if he
ever did talk as it has been reported, it must have been in
a temporary fit of temper.

There was yet another source of trouble for Nelson in
his reports to the authorities at home on the frauds in
several of the Government departments in the West
Indies.   These were brought to Nelson's notice in the
voluntary statements of Messrs. Wilkinson and Higgins,
employées in one of the departments, and transmitted to
the Home Authorities, but for some time no notice was
taken of them.   In 1785, however, Nelson was asked by
the Commissioners of Sick and Wounded if these charges
were likely to be true, as they had no other reason for
suspecting these officers and were not willing to institute
an inquiry without reasonable cause.   Nelson, in his reply
at the end of April, stated his grounds for believing the
statements of his informants :—

" Messrs. W. and H. made their representations to H.R.H. P. W.
H. and myself of various frauds in several departments of Government
in such a strong manner as, I humbly conceived, fully authorized me to
transmit them to the Minister and First Lord of the Admiralty, that

---

[1] Clarke and McArthur, vol. i.
[2] Despatches, vol. i. p. 252.

they might direct such measures to be taken as to them appeared proper. It is a very delicate task to handle the character of an officer, more especially one who most certainly pays every attention to the sick and wounded seamen placed under his direction, and is in every respect a most humane man to all who fall sick in the fleet. In respect to myself, I feel under particular obligation to Dr. Y. for his care and attention to me during my last station. Messrs. W. and H. have made in other departments such proof of improper conduct, as, I think, certainly entitles them to credit in this case. Every honest man, after such a letter as I wrote you, I should conceive would wish a strict inquiry into his conduct rather than let the matter drop."[1]

It was not, however, until 1789 that the papers were sent to the solicitor of the Navy Board, and at last, we are told by Mr. Rose, that "all the representations of Nelson were attended to, and every step that he recommended was adopted. He thus put the investigation into a proper course, which ended in the detection and punishment of some of the parties whose conduct was complained of." Whether, as is most probable, the friends of the peculators were too powerful, that they succeeded not only in so seriously impeding the inquiry, but in raising a prejudice against Nelson at the Board of Admiralty, which he could not for many years subdue, rests on an unvouched statement of Southey. This much, however, is certain, that the warmest thanks of the Public Boards were offered to Nelson in 1788 for his zeal, and the Duke of Richmond concluded his letter of 2nd of June, 1789, with these words : " With respect to yourself, I can only renew the assurances of my perfect conviction of the zeal for His Majesty's service, which has induced you to stir in this business."[2]

When, in 1792, the Radical clubs arose in England, in imitation of the French Republicans, the Duke of Clarence took a prominent part in supporting the

---

[1] Despatches, vol. i. p. 272.
[2] Note Despatches, vol. i. p. 284.

measures of repression which were introduced by the
Government of that time, and brought down many severe
remarks on his apparent desertion of the political party
of which he had hitherto been a member. Out of this
incident arose the following most able description by
Nelson of the state of the agricultural labourers in his
own county. On the severe remarks that had been made
on the Duke's parliamentary conduct, Nelson, having
written to his old pupil, received this manly explanation
of the Duke's conduct :—

> "I am so fully persuaded of your real regard for me, that no fresh
> mark can be wanting to convince me ; still, however, at the present
> moment, when the public have two opinions, the one good and the
> other disadvantageous of my parliamentary conduct, I feel highly
> obliged to you, as a person qualified to judge, to deliver your senti-
> ments. I am by no means a friend to the present ministry ; but my
> conduct can never militate against the good of my country, and I
> think it is the duty of every citizen to prevent, if possible, that con-
> fusion which might throw our kingdom into the wretched, deplorable
> state of France." [1]

To this letter Nelson wrote the following reply :—

"To the Duke.

"Burnham, *Dec.* 10, 1792.

"Our Lord-Lieutenant has summoned a meeting of the Norfolk justices on Tuesday next, the 11th ; and I have no doubt but they will
resolve to do collectively what none of them choose to do individually
—to take away the licenses from those public-houses who allow of
improper societies meeting at them, and to take up these incendiaries
who go from alehouse to alehouse advising the poor people to pay no
taxes, &c. In this neighbourhood a person of the name of Priestley
(Dr. P.),[2] a clergyman, has held this language to a circle of ten miles
round him ; and a few days past I asked a justice of the peace, ' Why,
as such a man's conduct was known, that he was not taken up.' His
answer was, ' that no justice would render himself unpopular at this

---

[1] Note Despatches, vol. i. p. 292.
[2] The famous Dr. Priestley ; he was a Unitarian minister.

time by being singular, for if the mob rose his life and property was gone ; but that when the justices all agreed to act in an uniform manner this man should certainly be taken hold of, if he went on with such conduct.'

" That the poor labourer should have been seduced by promises and hopes of better times, your Royal Highness will not wonder at, when I assure you that they are really in want of everything to make life comfortable.[1] Part of their wants, perhaps, were unavoidable from the dearness of every article of life, but much has arose from the neglect of the county gentlemen in not making their farmers raise their wages in some small proportion as the prices of necessaries increased. The enclosed paper will give your Royal Highness an idea of their situation. It is most favourable, but I have been careful that no county gentleman should have it in his power to say I had pointed out the wants of the poor greater than they really are. Their wages have been raised within these three weeks, pretty generally, one shilling a week ; had it been done some time past they would not have been discontented, for a want of loyalty is not amongst their faults, and many of their superiors, in many instances, might have imitated their conduct with advantage. The wise precautions of Government have certainly given a vigour to the loyal of the nation, who are undoubtedly by far a majority, and the disaffected join them at present for fear of being suspected ; therefore, I have no doubt for our tranquillity."

In the enclosure, Nelson gave the particulars of the expenses and earnings (under advanced prices) of a labourer with a wife and three children, supposed not to have been unemployed for one whole day in the year. The expenses of clothes, candles, coals, and rent amounted to £8 13s. 10d., the advanced wages including harvest pay and woman's gleaning to £23 1s., leaving for the food of five people, £14 7s. 2d., " Not quite twopence a day for each person ; and to drink nothing but water, for beer our poor labourers never taste, unless they are tempted, which is too often the case, to the alehouse." [2]

---

[1] Nelson wrote originally : " Hunger is a sharp thorn, and they are not only in want of food sufficient, but of clothes and firing."

[2] Note Despatches, vol. i. p. 295.

When our naval preparations in anticipation of the declaration of war by France, in 1793, commenced, Nelson, on the 30th of January of that year, was offered the command of the *Agamemnon* (64), "in the handsomest way, and put under the command of that great man and excellent officer, Lord Hood, appointed to the command in the Mediterranean." From this time Nelson had all the opportunities for which he had so long yearned, to prove the great qualities of his character. As he wrote to his wife from London, Jan. 7, 1793 :—

"*Post Nubila Phœbus* — After clouds comes sunshine. The Admiralty so smile upon me that I am really as much surprised as when they frowned. Lord Chatham yesterday made many apologies for not having given me a ship before this time, and said that if I chose to take a sixty-four to begin with I should be appointed to one as soon as she was ready, and whenever it was in his power I should be removed into a seventy-four. Everything indicates war ;[1] one of our ships looking into Brest has been fired into ; the shot is now at the Admiralty. Will you send my father this news, which I am sure will please him. Love to Josiah, and believe me,

"Your most affectionate,

"H. N."[2]

"Five years of undesired repose," writes the gallant French captain in his noble tribute to Nelson, "had created in him a degree of impatience and a restless desire of employment, which he could hardly restrain. He was then in the prime of life, pointed out by public opinion as one of the first officers of the navy, and so ambitious of glory that the opportunity of acquiring could not be wanting in the field where England and France again stood opposed. His first care was to choose a ship's company. We have already seen that this was no easy matter then ; but by dint of activity, and also from his good name—for English sailors do not volunteer equally with all captains—Nelson, already dreaming of fortune, honours, battles, prize money, collected a crew, the sight of which filled him with joy and

---

[1] War with France declared Feb. 11, 1793—appointed to *Agamemnon* Jan. 30, 1793.   Josiah Nisbet entered the navy in his ship.
[2] Despatches, vol. i. p. 297.

hope. 'I have under my feet,' he wrote to his brother, 'the finest ship of sixty-four guns that England possesses; my officers are all men of merit; my men are brave and healthy; what matters it to what part of the globe they send me.' . Happily, for his future glory, it was to the Mediterranean he was sent." [1]

By the close of June Nelson was in the Mediterranean, off Gibraltar, from whence he sent to his wife his first impression of the fighting value of the Spanish fleet :—

" To Mrs. Nelson.

" *Agamemnon* at Sea, *Sunday, June* 23, 1793.
" The Spaniards are very civil to us. We dined on board the *Concepcion*, of 112 guns, with the Admiral ; and all restraints of going into their arsenals and dockyards were removed. They have four first-rates in commission at Cadiz, and very fine ships, but shockingly manned. If those twenty-one sail-of-the-line which we are to join in the Mediterranean are not better manned they cannot be of much use. I am certain if our six barges' crews, who are picked men, had got on board one of their first rates they would have taken her. The Dons make fine ships—they cannot however make men."

Whilst at Gibraltar Nelson, with some of the officers of the fleet, went to a bull feast, of which he gives the following account to his wife :—

" A bull feast was exhibited, for which the Spaniards are famous, and from the dexterity in attacking and killing these animals the ladies choose their husbands. We English had certainly to regret the want of humanity in the dons and the donnas. The amphitheatre will hold sixteen thousand people, and twelve thousand were present. Ten bulls were selected, and one brought out at a time. Three cavaliers on horseback and footmen with flags were the combatants. We had what is called a fine feast, for five horses were killed, and two men very much hurt : had they been killed it would have been quite complete. We felt for the bulls and horses, and I own it would not have

---

[1] " The Last Naval War," by Captain Jurien de la Gravière, translated by the Hon. Captain Plunkett, R.N., vol. i. p. 44. Nelson's crew was mainly composed of Norfolk sailors.

displeased me to have seen some of the dons tossed by the enraged animal.   How women can even sit out, much less applaud, such sights, is astonishing.   It even turns us sick, and we could hardly go through it : the dead, mangled horses with the entrails torn out, and the bulls covered with blood were too much.   However, we have seen one bull-feast, and agree that nothing shall tempt us to see another. The better sort of people never miss one if within reach of them ; and the lowest will sell his jacket or go without his victuals rather than be absent.

 " P.S.—We arrived here (Gibraltar, June 24) last night, and in a few days' sail shall be up the Mediterranean.   God bless and preserve you.

"H. N."

Further acquaintance with the Spanish Fleet when at sea did not improve Nelson's opinion of his future adversaries :—

"We saw a fleet off Alicant on the close of the 7th, and lay-to mid-channel between that place and Iviça.   At daybreak we formed our line ; soon perceived them to be the Spanish Fleet, 24 sail-of-the-line.   The Dons did not, after several hours' trial, form anything which could be called a line of battle ahead.   However, after answering our private signals, the Spanish Admiral sent down two frigates with answers to Lord Hood's letter by *L'Aigle*, acquainting us that, as the fleet was sickly 1,900 men, he was going to Carthagena. The captain of the frigate said ' *it was no wonder they were sickly, for they had been sixty days at sea.*'   This speech appeared to me ridiculous ; for from the circumstance of having been longer than that time at sea do we attribute our getting healthier.   It has stamped me with the extent of their nautical abilities ; long may they remain in their present state.   It appeared odd to me that no salutes were fired. *Leda* was sent on the 9th to Barcelona, and on yesterday, the 13th, the frigate rejoined the fleet.   Inglefield (acting captain of the fleet) brings nothing new respecting the Toulon Fleet, except that the French are preparing their ships with forges for shot.   This information, I humbly think (if true), would have been as well kept secret ; but as it is known, we must take care to get so close that their red-shot can do no mischief.   The fleet received orders yesterday (July 14) to consider Marseilles and Toulon as invested, and to take all vessels of whatever nation bound into these ports. This has pleased us, and may possibly induce these red-hot gentlemen to come out." [1]

"There seems to be no French ships at sea, at least we have seen nothing like one. We fell in with the Spanish Fleet a week ago returning to port, I believe glad we were arrived, and they mean to leave to us the honour of keeping the French in order. I really expect never to see them again." [2]

In the next letter to his wife, when off Toulon, Nelson records his determination not to leave the *Agamemnon* for a more powerful ship :—

"To Mrs. Nelson.
"Off Toulon, *August* 4, 1793.

"Whether the French intend to come out seems uncertain. They have a force equal to us. Our Jacks would be very happy to see it, and our fleet is in the fullest health. I dare say we should give a good account of them. I hardly think the war can last, for what are we at war about? How I long to have a letter from you. Next to being with you, it is the greatest pleasure I can receive. The being united to such a good woman I look back to as the happiest period of my life, and as I cannot here show my affection to you, I do it to Josiah, who deserves it, as well on his own account as yours, for he is a real good boy and most affectionately loves me.—Lord Hood has sent to offer me a seventy-four, but I have declined it ; as the Admiralty chose to put me into a sixty-four, there I stay. I cannot give up my officers, and Lord Hood approved of my reasons ; so far well." [3]

On the 23rd of August commissioners from Marseilles, expecting to meet others from Toulon on a like mission, came on board Lord Hood's flag-ship with a proposal for peace on the basis of deposing the Republic and replacing monarchical government in France, encouraged by the approach of a Royalist force, and on the 28th Toulon

[1] Letter to the Duke of Clarence, *Agamemnon,* off Cape St. Sebastian 14th July to 3rd of August (Despatches, vol. i. p. 311).

[2] To Mrs. Nelson, Gulf of Lyons, July 15, 1793.

[3] Despatches, vol. i. p. 316.

surrendered to Lord Hood with the fleet that lay in its ports.[1] On this Lord Hood issued a proclamation to the people of the South of France, and sent off the *Agamemnon*, a fast sailer, to Naples with the news. Thus, as he relates in his next letter to his wife, Nelson became for the first time acquainted with the Hamiltons :—

"To Mrs. Nelson.
                                  Naples, *September* 12, 1793.

"My other letter will arrive with this. Our news (fall of Toulon) will be received here with the greatest satisfaction. The King has twice sent for me, and I dine with him to-morrow, after he has paid me a visit, which he is to do on board the *Agamemnon*. We are called by him the saviours of Italy, and of his dominions in particular. I have acted for Lord Hood with a zeal no one could exceed, and am to carry from the King the handsomest letter, in his own handwriting, that possibly could be. This I got through Sir W. Hamilton and the Prime Minister (Sir John Acton), who is an Englishman. Lady Hamilton has been wonderful good and kind to Josiah. She is a young woman of amiable manners, who does honour to the station to which she is raised. I am to carry Lord Hood six thousand troops from hence"[2] (Despatches, vol. i. p. 326).

In a letter from William Hoste to his father we have a

[1] Lord Hood received the ships in trust for Louis XVII. Of the fifty-eight ships in the harbour, in the end, only twenty-two fell into our hands, and of these, on the recapture of Toulon, nine were burnt as they lay, three were taken away by the Sardinians and Spaniards, and four, with six frigates, accompanied the English fleet to the island of Hieres.

[2] The following is Lady Hamilton's exaggerated account of the first interview with the Hamiltons :—"Sir William, after returning home from the first interview with Nelson, told Lady Hamilton that he was about to introduce her to a little man who could not boast of being very handsome, but who would become the greatest man ever England produced. 'I know it from the very few words of conversation I have already had with him. I promise that he will one day astonish the world. I have never entertained an officer at my house, but I am determined to bring him here ; let him be put in the room prepared for Prince Augustus.' Nelson is stated to have been equally impressed with Sir William's merits. 'You are a man after my own heart ; you do business in my own way ; I am now only a captain, but if I live I will be at the top of the tree'" (Harrison, vol. i. p. 108).

graphic account of Nelson's first disappointments of prize
money :—

> "WITH NELSON OFF CAGLIARI, *September* 24, 1793.
> "On Sunday afternoon we saw two ships close in shore, which we
> supposed were French frigates. Accordingly we gave chase. They
> had, however, the good fortune to get under the protection of a fort
> before we could cut them off. We stood in after them, but as it was
> late in the evening and dark, we could not with safety go into harbour,
> though we were almost within gun-shot. The fort fired at us, but
> their balls fell short ; we returned the compliment and reached them.
> In the morning Captain Nelson intended to send in our boats to burn
> them, but they thought proper to save us the trouble by coming out
> of the harbour with five or six vessels in consequence of a message
> Captain Nelson sent them by a neutral vessel, which had its effect.
> They proved to be all Genoese, and therefore we could not make
> prizes of them. They informed us that the French had one man
> killed. The country people were running up the mountains crying
> out 'Mon Dieu,' very much frightened. Six hundred of the militia
> were sent down to oppose our landing. The name of the harbour is
> Cagliari, about twelve leagues to the east of Toulon. We have taken
> a prize valued at £15,000 or £16,000 "[1] (Note Despatches, vol. i. p.
> 329).

Unfortunately for the people of Toulon a Spanish fleet
arrived as ours entered the harbour :—

> "The Spaniards behave so infamously that I sincerely wish not one
> ship or soldier was in Toulon ; they will do nothing but plunder and cut
> the throats of poor wretches who have surrendered to the British."[2]

Nelson soon left Naples. "I was hurried," he writes
to his wife from off Leghorn on the 27th of September,
"by information of a French ship of war and three vessels

---

[1] She was cleared as a neutral, see letter to Mrs. Nelson, Leghorn,
September 27th : "I am sorry to say the vessel I sent in here is cleared,
so all my hopes, which I own were not very sanguine, are gone. Prizes
are not to be met with, except so covered by neutral papers, that you may
send in fifty, and not one turn out good."

[2] To W. Sucking, off Corsica, October 14, 1793, from the *Athenæum*,
vol. i. p. 331.

under her convoy being off. I had nothing left but to get to sea, which I did in two hours ; expedition, however, has not crowned my endeavours with success, for I have seen nothing of them. I am here plagued with a French 40-gun frigate, who was to have sailed the day I arrived, and will take the first dark moment to get out. I am determined to pursue him. I hope to sail tomorrow if this gentleman does not, and shall lie in his route to intercept him if he sails." Nelson then gives the report that the French crew had mutinied, deposed their captain in favour of a lieutenant of marines. "What a state," he adds ; "they are mad enough for anything." This is one of the many instances that Captain Jurien de la Gravière gives of the effect of the revolutionary ideas in rendering the French fleet so easy a victim to the discipline of our navy, and the long practical education of our officers, by placing ignorant fellows in the posts of those of the well-tried sailors of the old Royal Navy of France. As the frigate would not come out, Nelson was ordered to Sardinia, and on the way had his first brush with the enemy.

"At two a.m. saw five sail standing across us to the north-west by the wind. At half-past two they tacked by signal rockets, then about three miles on our weather bow ; at four got within hail of a frigate, but was careful not to fire into her, thinking she might be a Neapolitan or Sardinian frigate with convoy. On receiving no answer and the ship making sail, fired a shot ahead of her, when she set all her sails, and steering two points from the wind, we after with every sail set, keeping her two points on the bow, to prevent her getting before the wind ; the other ships on our weather quarter steering after us. The chase made many signals during daylight, when she hoisted national colours, and began firing stern-chasers, and by yawing, which her great superiority in sailing enabled her to do, gave us many broadsides. We could only at times bring any guns to bear upon her, and then only a few of the foremost ones. At seven, took the ships on our weather quarter to be one of the line, two frigates and an armed brig, but whilst the breeze continued, the chase and ourselves left them fast. At nine o'clock we run into almost a calm, the ships on our quarter bearing N.W. by W., coming fast up with us ; the chase hauled up to join them, being in a shattered condition, and making signals to her consorts, who steered to join her when they brought to, hoisted out their boats and sent to her. The enemy were four frigates, two of them carrying twenty-eight eighteen-pounders on their main decks. The enemy from this time to noon had the option of bringing us to action whenever they pleased ; but we having our maintopmast shot to pieces, mainmast, mizenmast and foreyards baaly wounded, could not haul our wind till noon, repairing our rigging, masts, and yards. Forward we had one man killed and six wounded." [1]

It was about this time whilst preparing for the hazardous siege of Bastia, that Nelson received the following letter from his father, the first that has been preserved :—

"BURNHAM, *July* 12, 1793.

"Every mark of my affection you may justly expect ; and it gives me satisfaction to reflect on the many proofs I have had of your disposition to observe those duties which each relation in life calls for. The approbation of your own mind is far more pleasing than any supposed partiality of mine ; though a reward infinitely short of what moral virtue, which is attendant on religion, shall one day receive. The principal domestic occurrence at this juncture is that of your brother's ordination (Suckling Nelson). Thus far, thank God, our design is accomplished : all proceeds favourably, and there is good hope that he may prove a worthy member of society. Farming goes on well ; and at Christmas I look forward for the auditing my accounts in my own person ; *Agamemnon* and her crew being honourably discharged, and laid up for the winter in safety. O England ! blessed art thou among the Isles, for thy internal prosperity. In peace and plenty may thy counsellors preserve thee. . . . As to myself the material machine keeps pretty nearly the same periodical movement ; the repairs must be by a very nice delicate touch, and my mind is so fortified as to meet all common events with calmness—ever steady to my position, that the good of every man's life preponderates over the evil—God bless you." [2]

---

[1] Memorandum of consultation with his officers that they were not in a condition to risk further action, the frigate apparently ready to sink when the calm came on.—Extract from Log sent to Lord Hood (Despatches, vol. i. p. 334).

[2] Clarke and McArthur, vol. i. p. 183.

On Nov. 15, 1793, Nelson was ordered to put himself under the command of Commodore Linzee, and sent by him on secret orders to look after the French frigates which he had engaged on Oct. 22nd, and to prevent ships going to the port of Genoa, then invested by Lord Hood.   Linzee was " to expostulate with the Bey of Tunis in the strongest and most impressive manner, on the impolicy of his giving countenance and support to so heterogeneous a government as the present one in France, comprised of murderers and assassins, who have recently beheaded their Queen in a manner that would disgrace the most barbarous savages" (Lord Hood's order).   The Bey, who was a very clever man, is said at the conference with Nelson to have disconcerted him by his reply, dryly observing that " nothing could be more heinous than the murder of their sovereign ; and yet, Sir, if your historians tell the truth, your own countrymen once did the same thing." [1]

For Nelson's account of this interview see following letter to William Suckling :—

"MY DEAR SIR,—I am just returned from Tunis, where I have been under Commodore Linzee to negotiate for a French Convoy from the Levant.   You will believe we English seldom get much by negotiation, except the being laughed at, which we have been : and I don't like it.   Had we taken the men of war and convoy, with at least £300,000, how much better we should have negotiated—given the Bey £50,000, he would have been glad to have put up with the insult offered to his dignity.   The French sent him very great presents ; and he bought, through fear of us, several rich cargoes for one-third of their value.   The ships of war so much believed we should have attacked them, that, at first, they hauled their ships almost aground ; but latterly almost insulted us.   Thank God, Lord Hood whom Linzee sent to for orders how to act, after having negotiated, ordered me from under his command, and to command a squadron of frigates off Corsica and the coast of Italy, to protect our trade, and

---

[1] Clarke and McArthur, vol. i. p. 138.

that of our new ally, the Grand Duke of Tuscany, and to prevent any ship or vessel of whatever nation going into the port of Genoa. I consider this command as a very high compliment—there being five older captains in the fleet." [1]

William Hoste to his father, Nov. 27, 1793 :—

"When we got to Tunis we found only the *Duquesne*, 80 guns, and merchantmen ; the four frigates were gone, of which *Agamemnon* had nearly been too sensible, as these were the very frigates we met in our voyage to Cagliari, which if they had acted as they ought to have done, would have prevented our joining the Commodore. On our arrival at Tunis, we expected that the Bey would have given leave to take out the *Duquesne* and the merchantmen, but he would not allow the neutrality of the port to be broken, however superior we were in these seas ; nor would the *Duquesne* give herself to the French king, notwithstanding all our negotiations." [2]

"To Mrs. Nelson,
"*Agamemnon*, Dec. 27, 1793.

"My Dear Fanny,—Everything which domestic wars produce is multiplied at Toulon. Fathers are here without their families, families without their fathers. In short, all is horror. I have the Count de Grasse under my command, in a French frigate (*La Topaze*), his wife and family are at Toulon. Lord Hood put himself at the head of the flying troops, and was the admiration of every one : but the torrent was too strong. Many of our posts were carried without resistance : at others, which the English occupied, every one perished. I cannot write all ; my mind is deeply impressed with grief. Each letter makes the scene more horrible. Lord Hood showed himself the same collected officer which he always was. I have only time to say, God bless you.

"Horatio Nelson." [3]

"To the Same.
"*Jan.* 6, 1794.

"I have promised my people, as soon as we have taken Corsica, that I would ask for a month's rest for them. Except to get provision, I have not been at anchor for pleasure since April 23, but I can assure you I was never in better health, as is Josiah."

---

[1] *Athenæum*, Despatches, vol. i. p. 340.   [2] Ibid., vol. i. p. 337.
[3] Ibid., vol. i. p. 345.

NELSON AS A SOLDIER.

CHAPTER V.

NELSON AS A SOLDIER.

(1794-5.)

The Invasion of Corsica—Sieges of Bastia and Calvi—Omission of his name in the despatches—Loss of an eye at Calvi—Kindness to a prisoner—Pursuit of the French fleet—Admiral Hotham's actions of March, 1795—Capture of the *Ca Ira* and *Le Censeur*—Letters from and to his father and wife.

 T the time when Toulon was evacuated, Nelson," writes his gallant and honourable French biographer, " had gained the esteem and friendship of Lord Hood by the zeal he displayed in the various duties he was charged with. In the space of six months his ships had not been twenty days at anchor, and while the English fleet occupied Toulon, and disputed possession of it with the Republican batteries, Nelson one day at Naples, the next on the Coast of Corsica, had not ceased to keep under weigh. Running from Corsica to Sardinia, or Tunis, or Leghorn, negotiating, fighting, knowing neither fear nor rest, he already showed all the daring and *brusquerie* of his character." [1]

He was now to show this daring on shore in an attempt to conquer Corsica, where Paoli had promised

---

[1] Letters of Captain Jurien de la Gravière, in the *Revue de Deux Mondes* translated by the Honble. Captain Plunkett—" The Last Naval War," vol. i. pp. 60–61.

to make the people rise and invoke the protection of
England, if Lord Hood would first expel the French
garrisons from the northern part of the island. Hence
the determination to reduce the fortified towns of Bastia
and Calvi, which difficult and hazardous enterprises were
entrusted to Nelson with the help of some two thousand
soldiers under Major-General Dundas, now disposable
after the evacuation of Toulon. The disembarkation of
these troops was safely effected in the Bay of San
Fiorenzo; the defences of that town successively carried,
but the capture of Bastia and Calvi practically left to
Nelson and his sailors and marines; San Fiorenzo had
been taken on the 17th of February, 1794, and two days
afterwards we have in the following letter of Nelson's
to Lord Hood, Nelson's first report on Bastia. Within
the walls of this town, he had driven the French on
that day, by a sudden attack on the tower of Miomo,[1]
having previously captured the town of Maginaggio, as
he records in his journal :—

"*February 8th.* At eight o'clock anchored with *Tartar* off the town
of Maginaggio : sent a flag of truce on shore to demand immediate
surrender. Having received a very insolent answer, viz., 'We are
Republicans, that is sufficient. Go to San Fiorenzo, to Bastia or
Calvi—there you will get such an answer as you desire; the troops
which I command are ready to give you a meeting, are true French
soldiers'—I immediately landed, when this famous commander and
his troops ran away, and I had the satisfaction of striking the
National flag with my own hand. We found the town full of
provisions for Bastia, which we destroyed, and ten sail of vessels.
Within a few hours, ten times our numbers could be got together to
oppose us, therefore we could take nothing away."[2]

The following extracts from his journal give the
history of the following days :—

"*February* 19th. Went on shore with sixty troops five miles to

---

[1] Nelson's Journal A.   2. Despatches.   [2] Despatches, vol. i. p. 364.

the north of Bastia. Marched to within two miles and a half off Bastia, where we took the village and tower of Miomo, the French running away. These successes induced the Corsicans in this part of Corsica to declare for us, and they are now acting against the French."

"On the 21st received Lord Hood's letter, announcing fall of Fiorenzo.—23rd. Wishing to reconnoitre Bastia, and to the southward of it close, I passed a battery of six guns, which began on us, the ships proceeding as named, *Agamemnon, Romulus, Tartar.* At the third shot we got the distance so exact, that we very soon drove the French out of the battery, and destroyed it, getting within shot of the town. They began on us with shot and shells, and from the works over the town. I backed our maintopsail, and passed slowly along the town. The cannonading lasting one hour and three-quarters. We did them great damage as we see, and by a Dane who immediately came out, we hear they lost a number of men. We suppose they fired on us with twenty-seven guns and four mortars, besides those on the outworks ; and, although each ship was struck in the hull, yet not a man was killed or wounded. Our troops were just in sight on the hills, having marched overland from Fiorenzo, which is only twelve miles distant. General Dundas sent an express to give him (Lord Hood) an account of it. It must have been a fine sight from the hills.—On the 25th. Getting too near in a calm, they fired on me with shot and shells, some of which burst very near us, so as to shake *Agamemnon.* Our troops are not yet got to work. I can't think what they are at.[1]

" *March* 3rd. Lord Hood made my signal, and acquainted me of the retreat of our troops from the heights, and of their return to St. Fiorenzo. Saw Dundas's letter to Lord Hood, as also Paoli's. What the General could have seen to have made a retreat necessary, I cannot conceive. The enemy's force is one thousand regulars, and one thousand to fifteen hundred irregulars. I wish not to be thought arrogant, or presumptuously sure of my own judgment, but it is my firm opinion that the *Agamemnon* with only the frigates now here lying against the town for a few hours with five hundred troops ready to land, when we had battered down the sea walls, would to a certainty carry the place. I presumed to propose it to Lord Hood, and his lordship agreed with me ; but that he should go to Fiorenzo, and hear what the General had to say, and that it would

---

[1] To his brother William, March 1st, vol. i. p. 363.

not be proper to risk having our ships crippled without the co-operation of the army, which consists of sixteen hundred regulars, and one hundred and eighty artillery men, all in good health, and all as good troops as ever marched. We now know from three Ragusan ships and one Dane, that our cannonade on Sunday the 23rd, threw the town into the greatest consternation : that it almost produced an insurrection ; that La Combe St. Michel, the commissioner from the Convention, was obliged to hide himself, for had he been found and massacred, to a certainty the town would have surrendered to me. But St. Michel having declared he would blow up the citadel with himself, was the only thing which prevented a boat coming off to us with offers. A magazine blew up, and the people believe we fired nothing but hot shot. The French shot were all hot ; that by our cannonade on Tuesday afternoon, the 25th of February, the camp was so much annoyed that the French ran, and in the town they so fully expected that I should land, that St. Michel sent orders for La Flêche to be burnt ; but it falling calm, I could not lay near enough to the town to do good service. . . . My ship's company behaved most amazingly well.   They begin to look upon themselves as invincible, almost invulnerable ; believe they would fight a good battle with any ship of two decks out of France.   Lord Hood offered me *Courageux* 74, but I declined it ; shall stay by *Agamemnon*." [1]

San Fiorenzo having been taken by Lord Hood, February 17th, he proposed to Lieut-General Dundas, commander of the forces there, to march on Bastia, which he refused to do without a reinforcement of two thousand men. On this, Lord Hood wrote the following decided letter to the General :—

"*Victory*, IN MARTELLO BAY, *March* 6, 1794.

"I am honoured with your letter of yesterday's date, in which you are pleased to say, 'after mature deliberation, and a personal in-spection of all circumstances local as well as others, I consider the siege of Bastia, with our present means and force, to be a most visionary and rash attempt, such as no officer could be justified in undertaking.'   In answer to which, I must take the liberty to observe, however visionary and rash an attempt to reduce Bastia may be in your opinion, to me it appears very much the reverse, and to be a perfectly right measure ; and I beg here to repeat my answer to you, upon your saying two days ago, that I should be of a different opinion to what I had expressed, were the responsibility upon my shoulders, 'that nothing would be more gratifying to my feelings than to have the whole responsibility on me'; and I am now ready and willing to undertake the reduction of Bastia at my own risk, with the force and means at present here, being strongly impressed with the necessity for it.'"[1]

"To Lord Hood.

"Off Bastia, *March* 16, 1794.

"I send this overland, and shall thank your lordship to signify your wishes by the bearer of the letter. We are really without firing, wine, beef, pork, flour, and almost without water ; not a rope, canvass, twine, or nail in the ship. The ship is so light she cannot hold her side to the wind ; yet if your lordship thinks or wishes me to remain off Bastia, I can by going to Porto Ferrajo get water and stores, and twenty-four hours at Leghorn will give us provisions, and our refitting which will take some time can be put off a little. . . . My wish is to be present at the attack on Bastia ; and if your lordship intends me to command the seamen who may be landed, I assure you, I shall have the greatest pleasure in doing it, or any other service where you may think I can do most good ; even if my ship goes into port to refit, I am ready to remain. We are certainly in a bad plight at present, not a man has slept dry for many months"[2]

Nelson wrote to his brother William off Bastia, March 20th :—

"Our General, D'Aubant (successor to Dundas), with two thousand as fine troops as ever marched, has thought it improper to attack Bastia, which has eight hundred Frenchmen to defend it, and that as to taking it, that is impossible. As I had examined the ground, perhaps more than the General, Sir J. Erskine St. Clair, Major Koehler, Colonel Moore (Sir John, K.B.), or any other, I ventured to give my opinion very freely to Lord Hood, and that not to attack our enemy I shall consider a national disgrace. An artillery officer of great merit, Lieut. Duncan, I requested his lordship would ask the

---

[1] Clarke and McArthur, note to p. 358 of Despatches.
[2] After the gale of the 14th, which compelled press of sail to clear Cape Corse in thick weather. (Despatches, vol. i. p. 372.)

General to permit him to come to me. He came with Mr. De Butts,
a young engineer. They agreed with me in opinion, the place might be
attacked, probably with success. Lord Hood sent for me to Fiorenzo
to concert measures. The General has refused us a single soldier,
and scarcely any stores. We have only about seven hundred men to
land, troops who embarked to serve as marines, whilst the General
has thirteen hundred troops and artillery to defend St. Fiorenzo. I
am to command the seamen. Our irregulars are surely as good as
the enemy's, and in numbers we far exceed them. I truly feel
sorrow, and hope, and confidence that all will end well." [1]

"*April* 4, 10 a.m. The troops landed for the siege of Bastia at
tower of Miomo, three miles to northward, under Lieutenant-Colonel
Villettes and Captain Horatio Nelson, who had under him Captains
Hunt, Scorocold and Bullen. At noon troops encamped about 2500
yards from the citadel—all night cutting down trees to form *abattis*
and clear the ground to the tower of Torga, whence access to our
camp by no means difficult." [2]

"To Mrs. Nelson.

"*April* 6 to 16, 1794.

"We are in high health and spirits besieging Bastia. The final
event, I feel assured, will be conquest. Lord Hood is at anchor
near the town, and our troops are active. Our batteries opened on
the 11th, and apparently have done great execution. Time, I hope,
indeed have no doubt, will crown our zealous endeavours with success.
We are but few, but of the right sort: our General at St. Fiorenzo
not giving one of the five regiments he has lying idle there.[3] Lord
Hood sent a flag of truce on the 11th, at seven a.m., in one of the
Victory's boats. The officer on his landing was grossly abused, until
the arrival of La Combe St. Michel, the commissioner from the
Convention, when the mob became quiet. Having offered his letters
to St. Michel, our officer was informed by the commissioner, that
he could not receive Lord Hood's summons: 'I have hot shot,' he
exclaimed, 'for your ships, and bayonets for your troops: When
two-thirds of our troops are killed, I will then trust to the generosity
of the English.' On the officer's return with this message, Lord
Hood hoisted a red flag at the main-top-gallant-mast-head of the
Victory; when our batteries opened upon the town, citadel, and

---

[1] Despatches, vol. i. pp. 375–378.
[2] Journal C, vol. i. p. 380.   [3] Despatches, vol. i. p. 381.

redoubt of Camponella, English colours having been hoisted over my tent, and every man giving three cheers." [1]

" To the Same.

"*April 22nd.*

" I have a great reason, my dearest Fanny, to be thankful to that Being who has ever protected me in a most wonderful manner, and on none more than since my landing here. If it is His good pleasure, I shall in nothing more rejoice, than in being once more with you : when we will talk over all these stories, and laugh at them. We are here with a force not equal to our wishes or wants, and with only half that is present in this island. General D'Aubant will not attack our enemy with two thousand as fine troops as ever marched, whilst we are here beating them from post to post with one thousand. . . . It is very hard service for my poor seamen, dragging guns up such heights as are scarcely credible. The loss of the enemy we know has been very great, report states it as much as five hundred killed and wounded, ours not more than twenty. The *Agamemnon* has to number five among them : they are not the men to keep out of the way." [2]

" To Lord Hood.

"*April 24th.*

" Your lordship knows exactly the situation I am in here. With Colonel Villettes I have no reason but to suppose, that I am respected in the highest degree ; nor have I occasion to complain of want of attention to my wishes for the good of the service from any parties; but yet I am considered as not commanding the seamen landed. My wishes may (be) and are complied with ; my orders would probably be disregarded ; therefore, if we move from hence, I would wish your lordship to settle that point. Your lordship will not, I trust, take this request amiss. I have been struggling with it since the first day I landed."

" To the Same.

"*April 25th.*

" I am happy that my ideas of the situation I am in here so perfectly agree with your lordship's. Captain Hunt is a most exceeding good young man, nor is any one more zealous for the service. I don't complain of any one, but an idea has entered into

---

the heads of some who serve under him, that Captain Hunt's command was absolutely distinct from me, and that I had no authority whatever over him, except as a request. It was even doubted whether I had a right to command the officers and seamen landed from the *Agamemnon*—that word 'attached to the batteries' was wrested to a meaning very different from your lordship's thoughts. Your kind intention to Captain Hunt I had the honour of telling your lordship should be furthered by every means in my power, and my regard for him, I assure you, is undiminished. At present no letter can be necessary, but when your lordship may judge it proper, I will thank you for an order to command the seamen without any distinction as to any particular service.

" The conduct of Brigadier-General D'Aubant is so extraordinary, that anything he possesses [even his life] appears not sufficient to atone for such an expression as 'will not entangle himself in any co-operation." [1]

A few days later Nelson wrote to his wife :—

."*May* 1*st* to 4*th*.

" MY DEAR FANNY,—I need not, I am certain, say that all my joy is placed in you, I have none separated from you. I am convinced you feel interested in very (every) action of my life ; and my exultation in victory is twofold, knowing that you partake of it. Only recollect that a brave man dies but once, a coward all his life long. We cannot escape death ; and should it happen in this place, remember that it is the will of Him in whose hands are the issues of life and death. I have no fears about the final issue of the expedition ; it will be victory, Bastia will be ours ; and if so, it must prove an event to which the history of England can hardly boast an equal. Time will show the enemy's force ; if it is small, the Fiorenzo commander ought to be blamed; if it is large, they are highly culpable for allowing a handful of brave men to be on service unsupported. My only fears are, that these soldiers will advance when Bastia is about to surrender, and deprive us of part of our glory. The King, we trust, will draw the line of our deserts." [2]

The condition of the garrison of Bastia was steadily getting worse. From letters that were picked up from a boat, it was known on the 12th May, that the com-

[1] Despatches, vol. i. p. 387-8.   [2] Ibid., vol. i. p. 390.

mander had written that they could not hold out till the end of the month, and before that, on the 19th, from the fear entertained of the excesses the Corsican irregulars would most probably commit if the town was stormed, the town surrendered, and next day the troops from San Fiorenzo made their appearance upon the hills above the city, just in time to witness the capture of some four thousand fighting men by a thousand troops and marines and two hundred seamen.[1]

Early in June his little squadron was off again to sea.

"We are just off to sea after the French fleet," Nelson writes to his wife on the 5th of June, "which we hear is out of Toulon; our squadron is after them, steering for Calvi, where I fear they will get in, in spite of Admiral Hotham's endeavours. Lord Hood only got the account last night at eleven o'clock, and by seven this morning we were under all sail. The *Agamemnon* had two hundred tons of ordnance to get out, and Lord Hood had given me orders to follow him as fast as possible : I was enabled to sail in half an hour after him, and we are alongside the *Victory*. I pray God we may meet this fleet.

"If any accident should happen to me, I am sure my conduct will be such as will entitle you to royal favour : not that I have the least idea but I shall return to you, and full of honour; if not, the Lord's will be done. My name shall never be a disgrace to those who belong to me. The little I have you know I have given to you, except a small annuity. I wish it was more ; but I have never got a farthing dishonestly : it descends from clear hands. Whatever fate awaits me, I pray God to bless you, and preserve you for your son's sake. I think always in the most affectionate manner of my father ; tell him so, and ever believe me, your affectionate husband,

"HORATIO NELSON."

The French fleet succeeded in getting into Gourjean Bay, and as it was found impossible to attack them, Hotham was left to watch them, and the *Agamemnon* sailed

[1] Nelson to his wife: Camp, May 20th, vol. i. p. 397. The total loss of the besiegers was nineteen killed and thirty-seven wounded, of whom more than half were seamen.

for Bastia on the 10th, and arrived on the 12th, to assist at the siege of Calvi.

On the 17th of June, the troops under General Stuart landed near Calvi—fourteen hundred and fifty regulars and seventy volunteers from transports, thirty men from the *Inflexible*, and one hundred from the *Agamemnon*, and orders were sent for a small number of troops from Bastia.

" Our landing-place," wrote Nelson to Lord Hood, " is very bad ; the rocks break in this weather very far from the shore, and the mountain we have to drag the guns up is so long and so steep, that the whole of yesterday we were only able to get one gun up, and then we have at least a mile and a half to drag them. I hope before long we shall be able to land some to the eastward of Cape Revellata. Your lordship knows our want of seamen here, that I am sure I need not mention it. We have more than forty pieces of ordnance to drag over these mountains and my numbers are two hundred, barely sufficient to move a twenty-four pounder." [1]

Again, a few days after, he wrote to his wife :—

CAMP, *July* 5, 1794.

" MY DEAR FANNY,—I long to hear from you, for a post has arrived without a letter. Our batteries opened yesterday, and it is possible you may have heard that a captain of the navy has fallen. To assure you it is not me, I write a few lines, for if such a report should get about, I well know your anxiety of mind. We shall take Calvi in time, and I hope without much loss of men. I am very busy, yet own I am in all my glory : except with you, I would not be anywhere but where I am for the world. I am well aware my poor services will not be noticed. I have no interest : but however services may be received, it is not right in an officer to slacken his zeal for his country." [2]

" At daylight on the 12th, the enemy opened a heavy fire from the town and San Francesco, which in an extraordinary manner seldom missed our battery : and at seven o'clock I was much bruised in my face and eyes by sand from the works struck by shot." [3]

---

[1] To Lord Hood, June 21, 1794.
[2] From Clarke and McArthur, vol. i. p. 180 ; Despatches, vol. i. p. 424.
[3] Journal C, Despatches, vol. i. p. 432.

"To Lord Hood.

"Camp, *July* 12*th.*

"Reports, we know, get about, and as neither time nor many other circumstances may be mentioned, it is best to say of myself, I got a little hurt this morning : not much as you may judge by my writing."[1]

The following letter from his father on hearing of the loss of his eye, though out of date, is naturally here inserted :—

[No date given.   About *Sept.* 27 or 28, 1794.]

"My dear Horatio,—It is well known that the predestinarian doctrine is amongst the creeds of military men.   It may sometimes be useful; yet it must not exclude the confidence Christianity preaches of a particular providence, which directs all events.   It was an unerring power, wise and good, which diminished the force of the blow by which your eye was lost ; and we thank the hand that spared you—spared you for future good, for example, and instruction in many subsequent years.   There is no fear that flattery can come from me ; but I sometimes wipe away the tear of joy, at hearing your character in every point of view so well spoken to.   The letters received from you, give me and your good wife the pleasing intelligence that your health has not suffered from the long fatiguing service you are professionally obliged to go through ; and also that success has generally been the issue of your endeavours to make yourself known to the world as a man of probity and judgment; not only towards the things that are your own, but to those of others also.   Your lot is cast, but the whole disposing thereof is of the Lord : the very hairs of your head are numbered—a most comfortable doctrine.

"Upon the whole, I am as strong as can be looked for : how many do I see and hear of that have either fallen or are much more afflicted by age than myself.   Bless God, my days are lengthened, I hope for some good purpose.   Accept, my dear son, the usual but most hearty expressions of love and friendship from your affectionate father,

"Edmund Nelson."

The " little hurt " caused him the loss of his right eye.   Lord Hood wrote : " I am truly sorry to hear you

[1] From the Hood Papers ; Despatches, vol. i. p. 432.

have received a hurt, and hope you tell the truth in
saying it is not much. I shall send some one round
in the morning to know how you are, and whether you
would have assistance. Ever, my dear Nelson, most
sincerely yours,—HOOD." [1]

"To LORD HOOD.
"CAMP, *July* 13*th.*

"My eye is better, and I hope not entirely to lose the sight. I
shall be able to attend to my duty this evening if a new battery is to
be erected." [2]

Nelson complained of Lord Hood's description of the
taking of Bastia as follows :—

"CAMP, *July* 16*th.*

"You will be surprised when I say I was wounded in the head
by stones from the merlon of our battery. My right eye is cut
entirely down ; but the surgeons flatter me I shall not entirely lose
my sight of that eye. At present I can distinguish light from dark,
but no object : it confined me one day, when, thank God, I was
enabled to attend to my duty. I feel the want of it ; but such is
the chance of war, it was within a hair's breadth of taking off my
head.

"Lord Hood and myself were never better friends, nor—*although
his letter does*—did he wish to put me where I never was—in the
rear. Captain Hunt, who lost his ship, he wanted to push forward,
for another—a young man who never was in a battery, or ever
rendered any service during the siege : if any person ever says he
did, then I submit to the character of a story-teller. Poor Serocold,
who fell here, was determined to publish an advertisement, as he
commanded a battery under my orders. The whole operations of
the siege were carried on through Lord Hood's letters to me. I was
the mover of it—I was the cause of success. Sir Gilbert Elliot
(Governor of Corsica) will be my evidence, if required. I am not
a little vexed, but shall not quarrel. We shall be successful here ;
and a stranger and a *landsman* (General Stuart) will probably do me
that credit which a *friend* and brother officer has not given me." [3]

---

[1] Hood Papers, vol. i. p. 433, note.   [2] Ibid. ; Despatches, vol. i. p. 434.
[3] To Wm. Suckling, Esq., from the *Athenæum* (Despatches, vol. i. p.
438).

Again there was, as before Bastia, jealousy between the General and the young Captain. Soldier officers could not understand the siege tactics of the sailors, and the latter attributed the hesitation of the General to other motives than professional caution.[1] Thanks, however, to Lord Hood's firmness, no other injury than delay resulted, and by the 19th of July the outworks of the town were taken, with a trifling loss on the part of the besiegers. A letter of inquiry to the Commandant of the garrison however only resulted in an answer that the garrison would hold out to the last extremity. The condition of the besiegers was serious. "More troops, more seamen are wanted," wrote Nelson to Lord Hood, "and powder and shot. The army is harassed to death. Every man landed is barefooted. Every gun is dragged and fought by seamen."[2] But the end was very nigh : by the 26th flags of truce were passing, and on the 10th of August Calvi surrendered its garrison of 300 regulars and 247 armed Corsicans, to the perseverance of the assailants. The following letter to the Duke of Clarence gives a graphic account of the last days of Calvi :—

"The *Gazette* will tell your Royal Highness the general outline of this siege, which I believe is novel in form. We landed about four miles to the westward of Calvi on the 19th of June and on the 19th of July, were in full possession of every outpost of the enemy, with trifling loss. The batteries were erected with impunity in situations which the enemy ought to have prevented. Had they kept a moderate look-out our loss of life must have been great : every battery being within reach of grape-shot from its opponent. On the 19th of July, General Stuart sent in to ask if they had any terms to offer : their answer, the motto of the town, '*Civitas Calvi, Semper fidelis.*' We were then only 560 yards from the citadel wall, and they allowed us to erect strong, very strong batteries under a mask—

---

[1] See letter from Lord Hood to Nelson, July 17th, and Nelson's answer of July 18th.

[2] Nelson to Lord Hood, July 20th.

they must, ought to have known what we were after—without firing
a shot or shell.

"On the 28th, in the morning, our batteries, 560 yards from the
citadel walls, were ready to open their force, consisting of twenty-one
cannon, five mortars, and four howitzers. The General sent in to
say that he should not fire on the black flags (hospitals). This note
produced a negotiation, by which the enemy wanted to obtain a
truce of twenty-five days ; and then surrender, if no succour had
arrived, the town, frigates, &c., to Lord Hood and the General ; but
while this was going on, four small vessels got in, which gave them
hope of more effectual relief : for on the 30th they rejected our
offer, and our fire opened with all the effect we could expect. On
the 1st of August, at eleven o'clock, when much of the parapet was
beaten down, and the houses in the citadel were either in ruins or
in flames, the enemy hung out a white flag, and requested a suspension
of hostilities for a few hours to prepare terms. In twenty-four hours
everything was settled—that on the 10th of August we were put in
full possession, and the garrison, and such of the inhabitants as chose,
were to be transported to Toulon, without being prisoners of war,
provided no effectual succours were thrown in by the French. Thus
is likely to end the attack on Corsica, the possession of which will,
I hope, benefit our country. Whilst there are such men as Sir
Gilbert Elliot to point out the advantages, it would be impertinent
in me to attempt it. The loss to the French will be very great ; they
got from it all their deals, that are excellent, for their decks, and
timbers for their topsides, with pitch and tar, which, although of
inferior quality, they employed at Toulon for many uses. We also
get the *Melpomene*, the most beautiful frigate I ever saw, 14 ports,
13 eighteen-pounders. The *Mignonne* with 12 pounders, but not a
very fine ship, at least compared with the other.

"The climate here from July to October, is most unfavourable for
military operations. It is now what we call the dog-days, here it
is called the Lion Sun : no person can endure it ; we have upwards
of one thousand sick out of two thousand, and the others not much
better than so many phantoms. We have lost many men from the
season, very few from the enemy. I am a reed amongst the oaks ;
all the prevailing disorders have attacked me, but I have not strength
enough for them to fasten upon : I bow before the storm, whilst the
sturdy oak is laid low. One plan I pursue, never to employ a
doctor : Nature does all for me, and Providence protects me. Always
happy, if my humble but hearty endeavours can serve my King and
country."

Speaking of his visit to the Turkish troops at Eupatoria, May, 1855, Lord Stratford de Redcliffe gives the following anecdote of Nelson, presumably during the siege of Calvi.

" The troops (Turkish) were drawn out in line along the ramparts of the town, and observing that their persons were considerably exposed to missiles in that position, I was told, in reply to my inquiry, that they were expected neither to duck nor swerve however near the enemy's shot might come. This puts me in mind of what I was told by a veteran admiral many years before. His story was that serving at a battery in Corsica, when the French were defending the island, he saw Lord Nelson come up and plant his telescope towards a redoubt from which the French were firing. His Lordship, being asked what the enemy were about, replied, ' You will hardly believe it, but these fellows duck when the shot passes over their heads.' I knew, said my admiral, what he meant, for heads at our battery had gone down under fire just before. I kept silence, he added, till a fresh volley came, and Nelson had ducked in company with the rest of us. Then I thought my time had come, and I said, ' You see, My Lord, the bravest are not exempt from the common instinct.' " [1]

In the October of this year Lord Hood returned to England, leaving the temporary command of the fleet to Vice-Admiral Hotham. It was to the regret and surprise of every well-wisher of the navy, that, when on the point of resuming his command, Lord Hood was curtly ordered to strike his flag, and never more employed in the service to which he had brought such credit and honour. Well aware of the insufficiency of the force kept on the Mediterranean station, he had repeatedly complained of its neglect by the Admiralty, and at last addressed such strong remonstrances on this neglect, that the offended dignity of " My Lords " could not be appeased by less

[1] "Life of Stratford Canning," by S. Lane-Poole, vol. ii. pp. 403-4. When the old Admiral told this story, he had been so accustomed to speak of *Lord* Nelson, that he forgot that Nelson was only Captain and no " Lord," when in the sieges in Corsica.

than the practical removal of one of the best of admirals from active service.

" The absence of Lord Hood," wrote Nelson, " was a national calamity." For a year, therefore, Hotham held the chief command—a chief by no means after Nelson's idea of what the chief in that inland sea should be—" as good a man," wrote Nelson, " as any in the world, but he has taken things too coolly. We want here an active, enterprising man, and he is neither the one nor the other : As long as the month passes without any loss on our side, he is satisfied."

It was during this period of unsatisfactory idleness that Nelson received the following letter of New Year's Day from his aged invalid father, which he acknowledged in the letter to his wife of the last day of that month.

" BATH, *New Year's Day,* 1795.

" MY DEAR HORATIO,—I have received your letter with those contents, which are expressive of a benevolent and truly Christian heart, and I have endeavoured to distribute your Chris.mas gift in the best manner I could think of, chiefly in a little warm clothing to the widow and orphans, and very old men.[1] Blessed is the man who considereth the poor and needy. He who has been marvellously your shield will still, I hope, and pray, be your protector. Before I see Burnham, I must shake hands with the *Agamemnon's* captain, Horatio Nelson, whose friendship as well as affection, I can rely upon. The prospect that the *Agamemnon* would soon come into an English port, is for the present clouded ; yet at a day not far distant it will again appear. Old ships and wearied men must be repaired. Your good wife, whose attention to me I cannot sufficiently praise, is here. Accept our New Year's Gift, Good Wishes, the poor man's all. God bless you with prosperous events. Farewell from an affectionate father,

" EDMUND NELSON."

---

[1] Nelson had sent £200 to his father for the poor of Burnham.

"To Mrs. Nelson.

"Fiorenzo, *Jan.* 31, 1795.

"It is with inexpressible pleasure that I have received within these two days past your letters, with our father's of January the 1st. I rejoice that my conduct gives you pleasure, and I trust I shall never do anything which will bring a blush on your face or on that of any of my friends. It is very true that I have served faithfully, and ever has it been my fate to be neglected ; but that shall not make me inattentive to my duty. I have pride in doing my duty well, and a self-approbation, which if it is not so lucrative, yet perhaps affords more pleasing sensations. I trust the time will come when I may be rewarded, though really I don't flatter myself that it is near. Lord Hood tells me that my loss of my eye should be represented to the King. Lord Chatham carried my papers to the King; but now he is out, all hopes will be done away. My eye grows worse, and it is almost total darkness, and very painful at times ; but never mind, I can see very well with the other.

"I believe I shall inform Lord Hood, what I never told him yet, that after everything was fixed for the attack on Bastia, I had information given me of the enormous number of troops we had to oppose ; but my honour, Lord Hood's honour, and the honour of my country, must have all been sacrificed, had I mentioned what I knew ; therefore, you will believe what must have been my feelings during the whole siege, when I had often proposals made to me by men, now rewarded, to write to Lord Hood to raise the siege." [1]

Again, too, he complains to his uncle of the neglect of his services at Bastia.

"To William Suckling.

"Fiorenzo, *Feb.* 7, 1795.

"When I recollect that I was the cause of our re-attacking Bastia, after our generals gave it over, from not knowing the force, fancying it two thousand men ; that it was I, who, landing, joined the Corsicans, and with only my ship's party of marines drove the French under the walls of Bastia ; that it was I, who, knowing the force in Bastia to be upwards of four thousand men, as I have now only ventured to tell Lord Hood, landed with twelve hundred men, and kept the secret until within this week past. What I must have felt during the whole siege may be easily conceived. Yet I am scarcely

---

[1] Clarke and McArthur, vol. i. p. 199 ; Despatches, vol. ii. p. 2.

mentioned. I freely forgive, but I cannot forget. This and much more ought to have been mentioned. It is known that for two months I blockaded Bastia with a squadron : only fifty sacks of flour got into the town. At St. Fiorenzo and Calvi, for two months before nothing got in, and four French frigates could not get out, and are now ours. Yet my diligence is not mentioned; and others for keeping succours out of Calvi for a few summer months are handsomely mentioned. *Such things are.*

"I have got upon a subject near my heart, which is full when I think of the treatment I have received. Every man who had a considerable share in the reduction has got some place or other—I only am without reward. The taking of Corsica, like the sacking of St. Juan's, has cost me money. St. Juan's cost nearly £300; Corsica has cost me £500 and an eye, and a cut across my back; and my money I find cannot be repaid me. Nothing but my anxious endeavour to serve my country makes me bear up against it; but I sometimes am ready to give all up." [1]

At last, on the 13th and 14th of March, Nelson was in action with the French fleet, of superior force in guns and men, whose orders were to retake Corsica. How they were foiled in their expectations is told in the extracts from the log of the *Agamemnon*. On the eve of what might have been a desperate battle, and a great victory had a Hood or a Jervis been in the chief command, he wrote the following noble and feeling letter to his wife :—

"To Mrs. Nelson.

"*Agamemnon* at sea, *March* 10, 1795.

"We are just in sight of the French fleet, and a signal is out for a general chase. We have but little wind, and unfortunately the enemy are in shore of us; however, I hope the admiral will let us go on, and if the French do not skulk under their batteries, I trust we shall give a good account of them. Whatever may be my fate, I have no doubt in my own mind that my conduct will be such as will not bring a blush on the face of my friends. The lives of all are in the hands of Him who knows best whether to preserve mine or

---

[1] Despatches, vol. ii. p. 6.

not ; to His will do I resign myself. My character and good name are in my own keeping. Life with disgrace is dreadful. A glorious death is to be envied ; and if anything happens to me, recollect that death is a debt we must all pay, and whether now, or a few years hence, can be of little consequence. God bless you, and believe me ever your most faithful and affectionate husband,

"HORATIO NELSON."[1]

Lord Hotham's action, March 13-14, 1795 ; capture of *Ca Ira* 80, and *Sans Culotte* 74 ; and extracts from the log of the *Agamemnon* :—

"*March* 13*th*, at daylight.—Enemy's fleet in the S.W., about three or four leagues with fresh breezes. Signal for a general chase. At eight a.m., a French ship of the line carried away her main and foretopmasts (*Collision of* Ca Ira *with* La Victoire.) At a quarter past nine the *Inconstant* frigate (*Capt. Fremantle*) fired at the disabled ship, but, receiving many shot, was obliged to leave her. At ten a.m., tacked towards the disabled ship, and two others of the line. The disabled ship proved to be the *Ca Ira* of—

84 guns $\left\{ \begin{array}{l} 36 \ldots 24 \ldots 12 \text{ Pounders, French weight} \\ 42 \ldots 27 \ldots 14 \quad\quad, \quad\quad \text{English} \quad\quad, \end{array} \right\}$ 1,300 men.

Sans Culotte 120 guns, and the *Jean Barras* 74 guns. We could have reached the *Sans Culotte* by passing the *Ca Ira* to windward, but on looking round I saw no ship of the line within several miles to support me : the *Captain* was the nearest on our lee quarter. I then determined to direct my attention to *Ca Ira*, who at a quarter past ten was taken in tow by a frigate ; the *Sans Culotte* and *Jean Barras* keeping about gunshot distance on her weather-bow. At twenty minutes past ten the *Ca Ira* began firing her stern chasers. At half-past ten the *Inconstant* passed us to leeward, standing for the fleet. As we drew up with the enemy, so true did she fire her stern-guns, that not a shot missed some part of our ship, and latterly the masts were struck every shot, which obliged me to fire for a few minutes sooner than I intended, for it was my intention to have touched his stern before a shot was fired. But seeing plainly, from the situation of the two fleets, the impossibility of being supported, and in case of any accident happening to our masts the certainty of being severely cut up, I resolved to fire as soon as I thought we

---

[1] Despatches, vol. ii. p. 17.

had a certainty of hitting.   At a quarter-past eleven a.m., being
within one hundred yards of the *Ca Ira's* stern, I ordered the helm
to be put a-starboard, and the driver and after-sails to be braced up
and shivered, and as the ship fell off, gave her our whole broadside,
each gun double shotted.   Scarcely a shot appeared to miss.   The
instant all were fired, braced up our after-yards, put the helm a-port,
and stood after her again.   This manœuvre we practised till one p.m.,
never allowing *Ca Ira* to get a single gun from either side to fire on
us.   They attempted some of their after-guns, but all went far a-head
of us.   At this time the *Ca Ira* was a perfect wreck, her sails
hanging in tatters, mizen topmast, mizen topsail, and cross-jack yards
shot away.   At one p.m. the frigate hove in stays and got the *Ca Ira*
round.   As the frigate first, and the *Ca Ira* got their guns to bear,
each opened fire, and we passed within half-pistol shot.   As soon as
our after-guns ceased to bear, the ship was hove in stays, keeping as
she came round a constant fire, and the ship was worked with as much
exactness, as if she had been turning into Spithead.   On getting
round, I saw the *Sans Culotte*, who had before wore with many of the
enemy's ships, under our lee bow, and standing to pass to leeward
under top-gallant sails.   At half-past one p.m., the admiral made the
signal for the van-ships to join him.   I instantly bore away, and prepared to set all sails, but the enemy having saved their ship hauled
close to the wind, and opened their fire, but so distant as to do us no
harm ; not a shot, I believe, hitting.   Our sails and rigging were
very much cut, and many shot in our hull between wind and water,
but, wonderful, only seven men were wounded.   The enemy as they
passed our nearest ships opened their fire, but not a shot, that I saw,
reached any ship except the *Captain*, who had a few passed through
her sails." [1]

Again on the 14th, after describing in detail the movements of the fleets in the renewal of the action, and
the orders to the *Bedford* and *Captain* to come to close

[1] Note by Nelson : " I observed the guns of the *Ca Ira* to be much
elevated, doubtless laid for our rigging and distant shots, and when
she opened her fire in passing, the elevation not being altered, almost
every shot passed over us, very few striking the hull.   The captain of
the *Ca Ira* told Admiral Goodall and myself that we had killed and
wounded one hundred and ten men, and so cut his riggings to pieces
that it was impossible for him to get up topmasts " (Note, Despatches,
vol. ii. p. 14).

quarters, with the *Ca Ira* and the 74 that was towing her, the log states :—

"At twenty minutes past seven the *Britannia* hailed and ordered me to go to the assistance of the *Captain* and *Bedford*. Made all sail, *Captain* lying like a log on the water, all her sails and rigging shot away : Bedford on a wind on the leeward lack.—At eight a.m. the enemy's fleet began to pass our line to windward, and the *Ca Ira* and *Censeur* were on our lee side ; therefore, the *Illustrious, Courageux, Princess Royal*, and *Agamemnon* were obliged to fight on both sides of the ship. The enemy's fleet kept the southerly wind, which enabled them to keep their distances which was very great. From eight to ten engaging on both sides. About three-quarters past eight the *Illustrious* lost her main and mizen mast. At a quarter past nine, the *Courageux* lost her main and mizen masts. At twenty-five minutes to ten the *Ca Ira* lost all her masts and fired very little. At ten *Le Censeur* lost her main mast. At five minutes past ten both struck.

"Sent Lieut. George Andrews to board them, who hoisted English colours, and carried the captains, by order of Lord Hotham, on board the *Princess Royal* to Admiral Goodall. By computation the *Ca Ira* is supposed to have lost three hundred and fifty killed and wounded on both days, and *Le Censeur* about two hundred and fifty killed and wounded. From the lightness of the wind the enemy's fleet and our fleet were a very long time in passing, and it was past one p.m. before all firing ceased, at which time the enemy crowded all possible sail to the westward, our fleet laying with their heads to the S.E. and E." [1]

Nelson could not but be dissatisfied with such an inconclusive action. For the red-hot shot, which by the orders of the Directory the French ships fired, he had no fear. "I find," he wrote on the 21st of March, "nothing

[1] ENGLISH FLEET : *Captain* 74, *Bedford* 74, *Tancredi* 74, *Princess Royal* (Admiral Goodall) 90, *Agamemnon* 64, *Illustrious* 74, *Courageux* 74, *Britannia* 100 (Admiral Hotham), *Egmont* 74, *Windsor Castle* 90, *Diadem* 64, *St. George* 90, *Terrible* 74, *Fortitude* 74 = 1,090 guns, 7,560 men. FRENCH FLEET : *La Duquésne* 74, *Victoire* 80, *Guerrier* 74, *Conquerant* 74, *Mercure* 74, *Barras* 74, *Tonnant* 80, *Sans Culotte* 120, *Timoleon* 74, *Généreux* 74, *Censeur* 74, *Alcide* 74, *Souverain* 74, *Ca Ira* 80 = 1,174 guns, 16,900 men.

superior to the old mode of fighting. I only wish some of their ships will suffer by having such a furnace in their cock-pits, which will end such a diabolical practice." [1] A few days after he wrote to his father : —

"Sure it is that the enemy had no idea of our meeting them on the seas if it was possible to get into port, and so certain were they of our easy conquest, that the Mayor and all the Municipality of Bastia were on board the *Sans Culotte*, to resume their stations at that place—not that I am certain that Corsica is safe, if they undertake the expedition with proper spirit. . . . Had our good admiral have followed the blow, we should probably have done more, but the risk was thought too great. . . . Certain it is *Agamemnon* has given experience to her crew ; five times my ship has been engaged, three at sea, two against Bastia, three actions in boats, and two sieges ought to make us stand fire, but we are too far from home to be noticed. Our actions are not known beyond this country and our immediate friends." [2]

"TO MRS. NELSON.

"FIORENZO, *April* 1, 1795.

"I am absolutely, my dear Fanny, at this moment in the horrors, from our idling here, that the active enemy may send out two or three sail of the line, and some frigates to intercept our convoy, which is momentarily expected. In short, I wish to be Admiral, and in the command of the English Fleet ; I would very soon do much, or be ruined. My disposition cannot bear tame, slow measures. Sure I am, had I commanded our fleet on the 14th, that either the whole French Fleet should have graced my triumph, or I should have been in a confounded scrape. I went on board, Admiral Hotham, as soon as our firing grew slack in the van, and the *Ca Ira* and *Censeur* had struck, to propose to him leaving our two crippled ships, the two prizes, and four frigates, to themselves, and to pursue the enemy ; but he, much cooler than myself, said, 'We must be contented, we have done very well.' Now had we taken ten sail, and had allowed the eleventh to escape, when it had been possible to have got at her, I could never have called it well done. Goodall backed me ; I got him

---

[1] Extract from letter to William Locker, March 21, 1795 ; Despatches, vol. ii. p. 22.

[2] Extract from letter to his father, March 25, 1795 ; Despatches, vol. ii. p. 23.

to write to the admiral, but it would not do. We should have had such a day, as I believe the annals of England never produced. I verily think if the admiral can get hold of them once more, and he does but let us get close enough, we shall have the whole fleet. Nothing can stop the courage of English seamen.[1]

"I may venture to tell you, but as a secret, that I have a mistress given to me, no less a personage than the goddess Bellona ; so say the French verses made on me, and in them I am so covered with laurels, that you could hardly find my sallow face. At one period I am ' the dear Nelson,' ' the amiable Nelson,' ' the fiery Nelson.' However nonsensical these expressions are, they are better than censure, and we are all subject and open to flattery. The French admiral is to be tried, and some of the captains are under arrest ; it is reported that the captain of the *Sans Culotte* has run away. The Toulonese will not allow the French Fleet to enter their port, and make them remain in Hieres Bay, telling them to get out and execute their former orders, or never enter the ports of the Republic." [2]

The following letters from his father naturally find a place here, and a worthy conclusion to this chapter.

"BATH, *May* 5, 1795.

"I can now, my dear Horatio, address you in the language of our University, *Bene it optime fecisti ;* and do most heartily rejoice at your acquisition of a fresh, never-fading laurel obtained in a consciousness of having discharged the duties of your station, and by a religious sense of that over-ruling Providence who maketh all things work together for good to those who love him. It is said with confidence, that Lord Hood will not go to the Mediterranean : having reached St. Helen's he is returned to Spithead. This is the news of the day. God bless you ! Farewell ! "

---

[1] Lord Hood whilst at Spithead with a small squadron about to resume the command in the Mediterranean, remonstrated with the Admiralty on the inadequacy of the force on that Station, and was ordered to strike his flag. Sir John Jervis appointed, November, 1795. Sir W. Hamilton to Nelson : " I perceive that my old friend Hotham is not quite awake enough for such a command as that of the British Fleet in the Mediterranean, although he is the best creature imaginable" (Southey's " Life of Nelson "). On Hotham's retirement, Admiral Goodall also retired, annoyed at not being put in his place.

[2] Clarke and McArthur, vol i. p. 206.

On his appointment as Colonel of Marines [1] :—

[No date given, 1795.]

"DEAR HORATIO,—-I have this moment (on the King's birthday) received full authority to say, you are appointed one of the colonels of marines, vacated by the promotion to flags. God bless you with all the prosperity this pleasing and much-wished-for event can bring with it. It marks your public conduct as highly honourable, and worthy of notice."

On the arrival of Sir John Jervis this disheartening state of inactivity ceased, and Nelson, enjoying the full confidence of the new Commander-in-Chief, with a small detachment under his command, had the opportunity which he so ardently desired, for the exercise of his energy and ability in the field of his future triumphs.

[1] Jan. 4th, King's birthday, 1795.

THE BLOCKADE OF THE GENOESE
COAST.

CHAPTER VI.

THE BLOCKADE OF THE GENOESE COAST.

(1795.)

Neglect of the Fleet by the Admiralty—The *Agamemnon* chased by the French Fleet—Our little business—Struck Blockade of the Genoese Coast—Letter to Collingwood—The slowness of the Austrian Troops —Offer to be proposed for Parliament—Charge of connivance with the coasting vessels of the enemy—The defeat of the Austrians—A dilemma—Letters to his father and his wife—Admiral Sir John Jervis.

N uninteresting cruise about the Mediterranean ports filled up the two months that followed the actions of Lord Hotham's fleet. The English Fleet, from the dilatoriness of the Admiralty in sending reinforcements, was but little able to protect the traders, and almost daily expecting to be attacked by the far superior force of the enemy.

" We are put to sea," wrote Nelson to William Suckling, " not only as being more honourable, but also much safer than sulking in port. Nor do I think our very small fleet would be a very easy conquest; but all our zeal does not in the least justify the gross neglect of the new Admiralty Board. Lord Chatham was perhaps bad : in this fleet we find, from woful experience, that it is ten times worse. Our merchants are ruined for want of convoy, which it has never been in our power to grant. Had not our late action proved more distressing to the enemy than the Admiralty had a right to suppose, we should before this have been driven out of the Mediterranean. Every moment

I expect to see the enemy's fleet, for they must be as badly managed as ourselves, if they do not embrace the opportunity for any enterprise they may have in their heads." [1]

Again next day, he sent rather better news to his wife from off Leghorn :—

" We have been trying these two days past to get to the westward, to join our expected reinforcements from England, but the winds have been so contrary that we every day lost ground. Yesterday, to our surprise, our store-ships and victuallers from Gibraltar arrived in the fleet ; their escape from the enemy has been wonderful, and had we lost them, our game was up here. This I suppose has induced the admiral to bear up for this place, and by it we shall get the *Courageux* ready for sea." [2]

On June 8, 1795, Nelson applied to the Secretary of War for the allowance of the same pay for his services on shore at Calvi and Bastia, as would be made to a land officer of the same rank, *i.e.*, Brigadier-General. The reply was, " No pay has ever been issued under this direction, or to the knowledge of this office, to officers of the Navy serving with the Army on shore " (July 21, 1795). What an encouragement !

On the 7th of July the French Fleet chased Nelson in the *Agamemnon* from off Cape Dille Mille, where he had been detached with some frigates to co-operate with the Austrian General in the Reviera of Genoa, for twenty-four hours, till within sight of the English Fleet. For seven hours he seemed to be almost in the possession of the enemy, " but owing to the fickleness of the winds," he writes to William Locker, " in these seas at times was hard pressed ; but they being neither seamen nor officers, gave us many advantages." [3]

[1] To William Suckling, *Agamemnon* at sea, April 24, 1795. *Athenæum.* (Despatches, vol. ii. p. 32.)

[2] This made the fleet fourteen English and two Neapolitans. To Mrs. Nelson, Leghorn, April 25, 1795.

[3] Despatches, vol. ii. p. 49.

A week after he had a little brush with the French Fleet.

"*July* 14.   Yesterday we got sight of the French Fleet, our flyers were able to get near them, but not nearer than half-gun shot ; had the wind lasted ten minutes longer, the six ships would have been alongside six of the enemy.   Man commanded us, and a good man he is in every sense of the word.   I had every expectation of getting *Agamemnon* close alongside of an 80-gun ship, with a flag or broad pendant : but the west wind died away, and enabled them to reach their own coast, from which they were not more than eight or nine miles distant.   Rowley and myself were just again getting into close action, when the admiral made our signals to call us off.[1]   The *Alcide* 74, struck, but soon afterwards took fire, by a box of combustibles in her foretop, and she blew up : about two hundred French were saved by our boats.   In the morning I was certain of taking their whole fleet, latterly six sail.   I will say no ships behave better than ours, none worse than the French : but few men are killed, but our sails and rigging are a good deal cut up.   *Agamemnon*, with her usual good luck, has none killed, and only one badly wounded ; by chance, for I am sure they only fired high, they put several shot under water, which has kept [us] ever since at the pumps.   The enemy anchored at Frejas, and we are steering for Fiorenzo.

"HORATIO NELSON." [2]

Among his duties at this period was the blockade of the Genoese ports, a very ungrateful task.

"TO SIR GILBERT ELLIOT, VICEROY OF CORSICA.

"*Agamemnon*, LEGHORN, *July* 27, 1795.

"MY DEAR SIR,—A merchant of this place, . . . whose name I am confident you will keep secret, has just told me, and intends to tell the Consul that the gunpowder is sold out of the magazine at St. Fiorenzo. A vessel, he says, has just arrived which brought over two thousand barrels, and many others have brought small quantities.   He did not choose to disclose his informer's name, but I understand he was in the vessel.   As the information can do no harm if false, and a great deal of service if true, I think it right to send it to your Excellency.

---

[1] Because our ships had approached so near the shore.
[2] Despatches, vol. ii. p. 51.

" A gale of wind has blown me in here from off Genoa, on which coast I am stationed to co-operate with the Austrian Army, whose advanced posts are at Loano, twelve thousand men; the other part is in Vado, twenty thousand. A finer body of men I never saw, and the general seems inclined to go forward, if England will perform her part, which I hope she will; but the co-operation expected of us in the putting a stop to all supplies going to France, a measure Admiral Hotham may hesitate complying with. Mr. Trevor and Mr. Drake [1] have both wrote to him on the absolute necessity of the measure; in the meantime I have directed the squadron under my orders to detain all vessels, to whatever nation they may belong bound to France, or to any place occupied by the armies of France. This good effect has already resulted from this measure, that the Genoese are alarmed, and will be careful how they send their vessels to an almost certain capture. Insurance is not at present to be had; the capture of a Tuscan vessel or two will stop the Leghorn trade. The only fears that seem to me to strike England, are of the Barbary States; but, sir, is England to give up the almost certainty of finishing this war with honour, to fear of offence to such beings? Forbid it, Honour and every tie which can bind a great nation! If supplies are kept from France for six weeks, I am told the Austrian Army will be in Nice, which will be a great event for us, we having guaranteed the repossession of Nice to the King of Sardinia.

" A word for myself : the Colonelcy of Marines has been given me in a handsome manner, but, in good truth, I am almost worn out. I find my exertions have been beyond my strength. I have a complaint in my breast, which will probably bear me down; but, please God, if I see this campaign out, if *Agamemnon* does not go to England, I must, the medical people tell me, be on shore for a month or two, without thoughts of service." [2]

" From the vigorous measures I am taking with the Genoese, I am most unpopular here : I cannot, perhaps, with safety land at Genoa, but half measures will never do when I command. All war or all peace is my idea, and the old Austrian general is entirely of my way of thinking." [3]

---

[1] Mr. Drake was minister at Genoa, the Honourable John Trevor at Turin.

[2] From the Minto Papers ; Despatches, vol. ii. p. 61.

[3] To Rev. Mr. Nelson, Hillborough, July 29, 1795 ; Despatches, vol. ii. p. 63.

Nelson was now directed by Admiral Hotham to co-operate with the Austrian General De Vins in Vado Bay, in the Genoese territory. Whilst cruising off that port, he received intelligence of a French convoy with arms and ammunition, having arrived in the neighbouring Bay of Alassio, whither he at once proceeded on the 26th of August with his small squadron, and in less than an hour cut out nine ships, and destroyed two others, without the loss of a man, either killed or wounded. Had it not been that the town was defended by two thousand soldiers, he would have landed and attempted to destroy the magazines of ammunition and provisions. "His officer-like conduct," said Admiral Hotham in his public despatch, "upon this and indeed, upon every occasion when his services are called forth, reflects upon him the highest credit."

Of how he carried out his orders against Genoa, Nelson writes to Collingwood, a few days after the affair at Alassio.

"To Captain Collingwood.
"Vado Bay, *Aug.*, 31, 1795.

"My dear Coll.,—I cannot allow a ship to leave without a line for my old friend, who I shall rejoice to see; but I am afraid the admiral will not give me that pleasure at present. You are too old a Mediterranean man, that I can tell you nothing new about the country. My present command here is so far pleasant as it relieves me from the inactivity of our fleet, which is great indeed, as you will soon see. From the event of Spain making peace, which may be looked for, perhaps a war with that country; if so, their fleet (if no better than when our allies) will soon be done for. Reports here say, they mean to protect Genoese and other vessels from search by our cruisers, in the Gulf of Genoa. If so, the matter will soon be brought to issue; for I have given positive directions to search such vessels, denying the right of the Spaniard to dictate to us what ships we shall or shall not search. The Genoese are going, it is said, to carry a convoy with provisions to their towns in the Riviera of Genoa, in possession of the French Army. However cruel it may appear to deprive innocent people of provisions, yet policy will not allow it to be done; for if the inhabitants have plenty, so will the enemy, and, therefore, I have directed them to be brought into Vado. So far I have gone, and trust I have acted, and shall act, so as to merit approbation.   Our admiral, *entre nous*, has no political courage whatever, and is alarmed at the mention of any strong measure; but, in other respects, he is as good a man as can possibly be.

"I hope, my dear friend, you left Mrs. Collingwood well.   How many children have you?   Did you see Mrs. Montray lately?   Her dear amiable son was lost by serving under me.   I have a stone on board, which is to be erected in the Church of St. Fiorenzo, to his memory.   I hardly ever knew so amiable a young man.   Believe me, my dear Collingwood,

"Your most affectionate friend,
"HORATIO NELSON.

"Tell me a great deal."[1]

The difficulties and drawbacks of the service on which Nelson was employed, are described in the next letters to his wife, and the recognition of his exertions honourably acknowledged in the Sicilian Minister's letter as quoted by the admiral in the letter which Nelson wrote on September 29th to his father.

"To MRS. NELSON.

"VADO BAY, *Sept.* 15, 1795.

"I am not, Fanny, quite so well pleased as I expected with this army (the Austrian under General De Vins) which is slow beyond all description, and I begin to think, that the emperor is anxious to touch another £4,000,000 of English money.[2]   As for the German generals, war is their trade, and peace is ruin to them; therefore, we cannot expect that they should have any wish to finish the war. I have just made some propositions to the Austrian general, to spur him on, which I believe he would have been as well pleased had I omitted.   In short, I can hardly believe he means to go any further this winter.   I am now under sail on my way to Genoa, to consult

---

[1] In possession of the Hon. Mrs. Newnham Collingwood (Despatches, vol. ii. p. 77).

[2] By Convention of May 4, 1795, £4,600,000 was to be raised for the Emperor of Austria, who engaged to employ 200,000 men.

with our Minister on the inactivity of the Austrians ; and he must take some step to urge these people forward.   The small flotilla from Naples has just joined ; but the season is almost too late for their acting.   However, if they will act, I can find them plenty of employ- ment though I doubt their inclination.   I hope my dear father is as well as I sincerely pray he may be."

"To his Father.

"Leghorn, *Sept.* 29, 1795.

"My dear Father,—I am this moment receiving the pleasure of your letter of September 3rd, and should be glad, did circumstances so turn out, that I could get to England in the *Agamemnon*, for in no other way can I get home with honour or propriety ; and I must say, except being at home, I know no country so pleasant to serve in as this, or where my health is so good.   My command at Vado is honorary, though expensive, for all foreigners only consider our rank and not our pay.   I have the satisfaction to have received the handsomest testimony of conduct, and as I know you will partake with me that satisfaction, I send you a copy of the Minister's note to the admiral, viz., 'I cannot in justice to the abilities, judgment, and activity of Captain Nelson, omit mentioning to your Excellency, the very high opinion in which that officer is held by General De Vins, and the other Austrian generals ; and I have thought it my duty to transmit to his Majesty's Ministers at home, this handsome testimony which our allies bear to the zeal and good conduct of that officer, whom your Excellency was pleased to select to command the squadron co-operating with them.   This unprejudiced testimony is no less flattering to Captain Nelson than to your Excellency's dis- cernment in having made choice of him for this service.'

"I have nothing to write about, but myself, for none else attempt to do anything.   If our plan can be carried into execution, we shall take Nice, but much must be left to chance : the plan well laid is most likely, but never certain of success.   I came in here four days' past, and am now under sail for Vado.   Our fleet has arrived at Corsica from a cruise off Toulon, where they permitted six sail-of- the-line and eight frigates to escape out of Toulon, and I believe they have left the Mediterranean.   Having talked of myself, I have nothing more to add, except that Admiral Hotham is going to send six sail-of-the-line after the French ships escaped from Toulon, and supposed to be gone to the West Indies.   Josiah is well, never ill. Hoste has almost recovered his broken leg.   Parted with Frank

[Lepee his servant] for drunkenness, and, when so, mad. Never will keep a drunkard another hour. *Agamemnon* almost worn out, must go home. With best love to my wife." [1]

"To Mrs. Nelson.
"Vado Bay, *Oct.* 5, 1795.

" Nothing has occurred, since I wrote last, except the sailing of the French squadron from Genoa. As soon as they knew of my absence, they made a push, and I fear are all got off. Two of our frigates were seen firing at them; but I have not much expectation of their success. It was a near touch, for I came back the next morning, after they had sailed on the previous evening. I am vexed and disappointed; but the best-laid schemes, if obliged to be trusted to others, will sometimes fail. I must submit, and hope for better luck next time, yet a squadron of French ships would have so graced my triumph! In the opinion of the Genoese my squadron is constantly offending; so that it almost appears a trial between us, who shall be first tired, they of complaining, or me of answering them. However, my mind is fixed; and nothing they can say will make me alter my conduct towards them. . . . I have just received a very affectionate letter from H.R.H. the Duke of Clarence, and he appears to remember our long acquaintance with much satisfaction : one of his expressions is, 'I never part with a letter of yours, they are to me highly valuable!' He finds me unalterable, which I fancy he has not always done in those he has honoured with a preference." [2]

The following indignant letter to Lord Grenville, in defence of his brother captains and himself from a scandal circulated by the Austrians, marks the habitual eagerness of Nelson to defend not only his own character, but that of his brethren in the service.

This letter was due to a statement from Mr. Drake to Nelson that a report was circulated among the Allies to which the King of Sardinia had been induced to give credence, that the British cruisers connived with the enemy to permit coasting vessels to land their cargoes for the supply of the French Army in the Riviera of

---

[1] Despatches, vol. ii. pp. 89–90.
[2] Clarke and McArthur, Despatches, vol. ii. p. 92.

Genoa. According to Clarke and McArthur they had deemed it expedient to submit the statement through Viscountess Percival to Mr. Trevor, who was Minister at Turin during this time. His reply which they print, after stating as a fact that the French Army was most injuriously supplied by coasters notwithstanding the British cruisers, and that the supplies were smuggled at night, in consequence of the absence of light craft that could approach the shore, adds that he went to Milan to consult with Admiral Goodall and the Austrian General, and that they agreed that the only remedy was to get galleys and row-boats from Genoa or Civita Vecchia. In conclusion Mr. Trevor says, " I never saw the injurious paper in question ; from his ignorance of naval affairs, the Austrian Minister, without sufficiently attending to the case, easily listened to the misrepresentations that were made to him on the subject, and transmitted them to his Court ; whence or through Turin, they reached England. The accusation was general, and it does not appear that any names were mentioned ; the nature and channel of the information did not admit of any public refutation of it ; and Commodore Nelson's letter and Mr. Drake's answer, would have been more than sufficient to obliterate in a moment, any attention that might have been given to it by Government." [1]

> "LETTER TO LORD GRENVILLE,
>
> "FROM OFF GENOA ROAD, *Nov.* 23, 1795.
>
> "MY LORD,—Having received from Mr. Drake a copy of your lordship's letter to him of October 2nd, enclosing a paper highly reflecting on the honour of myself and other of His Majesty's officers employed on this coast under my orders, it well becomes me, as far as in my power lies, to wipe away this ignominious stain on our characters. I do, therefore, on behalf of myself and much injured

---

[1] Clarke and McArthur, vol. i. p. 224 ; Despatches, vol. ii. pp. 103–4, note.

brethren, demand that the person, whoever he may be, that wrote or gave that paper to your lordship, do fully and expressly bring home his charge ; which, as he states that this agreement is made by numbers of people on both sides, there can be no difficulty in doing. We dare him, my lord, to the proof. If he cannot, I do most humbly implore that His Majesty will be most graciously pleased to direct his Attorney-general to prosecute this infamous libeller in his Courts of Law ; and I likewise feel, that, without impropriety, I may on behalf of my brother officers demand the support of His Majesty's Ministers ; for, as, if true, no punishment can be too great for the traitors ; so, if false, none can be too heavy for the villain who has dared to allow his pen to write such a paper. Perhaps I ought to stop my letter now ; but I feel too much to rest easy for a moment, when the honour of the navy and our country is struck at through us, for if nine [ten] captains whom chance has thrown together, can instantly join together in such a traitorous measure, it is fair to conclude we are all bad.

" As this traitorous agreement could not be carried on but by the consent of all captains, if they were on the stations allotted them, and as they could only be drawn from these stations by orders from me, I do most fully acquit all my brother captains from such a combination, and have to request that I may be considered as the only responsible person for what is done under my command, if I approve of the conduct of those under my orders, which in this most public manner I beg to do ; for officers more alert, and more anxious for the good and honour of their king and country can scarcely ever fall to the lot of any commanding officer ; their names I place at the bottom of this letter.

" For myself, from my earliest youth I have been in the naval service, and in two wars have been in more than one hundred and forty skirmishes and battles, at sea and on shore ; have lost an eye and otherwise blood, in fighting the enemies of my king and country, and God knows, instead of riches, my little fortune has been diminished in the service ; but I shall not trouble your lordship further at present, than just to say—that at the close of this campaign, where I have had the pleasure to receive the approbation of the generals of the Allied Powers ; of his excellency, Mr. Drake, who has always been on the spot ; of Mr. Trevor, who has been at a distance ; when I expected and hoped from the representative of His Majesty's Ministers, that His Majesty would have most graciously condescended to have favourably noticed my earnest desire to serve him, and when, instead of all my fancied approbation, to receive an accusation of a most traitorous nature—it has almost been too much for me to bear. Conscious innocence, I hope, will support me.

> "I have the honour to be,
> > "My lord,
> > "Your lordship's most obedient, humble servant,
> > > > "Horatio Nelson.

"N.B.—Captains Fremantle, Hope, Cockburn, Hon. Charles Elphinstone, Shields, Middleton, Plampin, Brisbana, Thomas Elphintone, Macnamara." [1]

During this portion of his service Nelson appears to have received an invitation to bring him into Parliament —a matter, as far as I can discover, not before noticed by any of his biographers. From whom the offer was made is not known. It, however, came to nothing, and Nelson did not enter Parliament until he took his seat as a Viscount.

(No address.) "*Agamemnon*, Vado Bay, *Nov. 6*, 1795.

"Dear Sir,—I have just received your letter of September 29th, and will be open and sincere in my declaration, that I will not attempt to enter Parliament but in support of the real Whig interest — I mean the Portland interest, and I must know that those principles are truly acceptable to that party which you conceive would give me its support.

"My pretensions are only a long series of services performed for my country, and if that part of my country who may honour me with their confidence in Parliament think me an eligible person to serve them in the House of Commons, the same zeal shall manifest itself there as it has done so repeatedly in their service in action against the French. I have only to say that I have been more than one hundred times actually engaged in battle, at sea and on shore, against the French, since the commencement of this war, and that I have been twice wounded. If these gentlemen are satisfied, the Duke of Portland must be applied to through Lord Walpole and Lady Walpole; for, although I have so often seen the French shot,

---

[1] Autograph draft Nelson Papers, Despatches, vol. ii. p. 103.

yet truly, I have seen little of their money. I can have no doubt of Lord Hood's good wishes to serve me, and I will write to him on the subject ; nor will Admiral Cornwallis, I am confident, withhold his assistance. Lord Conway is my friend and acquaintance, and a more honourable man, I am confident, does not grace the navy of England ; therefore, if I am joined with him, the same Admiralty interest will support us both. If it is necessary that I should be in England, the Duke of Portland must make application for the *Agamemnon* to be ordered home ; but I should hope that, being now actually in the most active service in the Mediterranean, it will not be necessary (for I should much like a land voyage), therefore, if it be necessary I should hope *Agamemnon* will be ordered home. Thus, my dear sir, I have been plain, and cannot well be misunderstood,

> " Believe me ever
>> " Your most obliged, humble servant,
>>> " HORATIO NELSON." [1]

" To MRS. NELSON.

" *Dec.* 2, 1795.

" Lord Hood will have discovered that, from my last letter to him respecting the defeat of the Austrians, on the 23rd of November, the loss of Vado would consequently follow. Tell him the French had collected full a hundred sail of vessels, in case of failure to carry off their troops ; they had also ten or twelve gun-vessels, as many privateers, and a man-of-war brig. I described to the admiral the great service that the destruction of these vessels would be of, many of them being laden with corn, on which the French general had laid an embargo ; and as I had not force enough, I begged of the admiral, if he came to sea, to look at this fleet himself, offering if he would permit me the honour to lead the *Culloden* and *Courageux* to the attack, and with my then squadron of frigates to take or destroy the whole. I pretend not to say the Austrians would have not been beat, had not the gun-boats harassed them, for, on my conscience, I believe they would ; but I believe the French would not have attacked, had we destroyed all the vessels of war, transport, &c. The Austrians by all accounts did not stand firm. The French half-naked were determined to conquer or die, and had I not against my inclination been kept at Genoa, from eight to ten thousand men would have been taken prisoners, and amongst the number General de Vins himself.

---

[1] *The Athenæum*, Despatches, vol. ii. p. 94.

For the French plan, well-laid, was to possess a post in the road,[1] their people fled by, retreat it could not be called, for except a part of the army under General Wallis, of about ten thousand, it was 'the devil take the hindmost.' . . . The purser of the ship there (Vado) ran with the Austrians eighteen miles without stopping, the men without any arms whatever, officers without soldiers, women without assistance. Thus has ended my campaign. . . . Let the blame be where it may, I do not believe any party will seriously lay it at my door; and if they do, I am perfectly easy as to the consequences. I sincerely hope an inquiry may take place, the world would then know how hard I have fagged. The weather is intensely cold."

Ten days afterwards, Nelson in a letter to the father of his favourite pupil William Hoste, states the difficulty in which he was placed for want of a sufficient force to effectually watch so long a stretch of coast :—

"I was in a cleft stick," he writes, "if I quitted where I was at anchor, the French would have landed in the rear of the Austrian army, and the total defeat of that army must have been the consequence. If I remained at anchor the enemy's gun-boats in the general attack would harass the left wing of the Austrian army. Much against my inclination I took the plan of laying quiet, instead of attacking their gun-boats ; and most fortunate it has been for the army I did so, for eight or ten thousand men made their escape by the road I protected, and amongst them General de Vins himself. The Austrians will make the most of a want of naval force for all purposes. Admiral Hotham kept my squadron too small for its duty ; the moment Sir Hyde Parker took the command of the fleet, he reduced it to nothing—only one frigate and a brig, whereas I demanded two seventy-fours, and eight or ten frigates and sloops to ensure the safety of the army.

"However on inquiry, which I trust and sincerely hope will take place, on my account, it will turn out that the centre and right wing gave way, and that although it must have been very unpleasant to have a number of gun-boats firing on them, the left was the only part that was not defeated, but retreated in a body : whereas the others fled ; General de Vins, from ill-health, as he says, gave up the command in the middle of the battle, and from that moment not a

---

[1] At Genoa, but were prevented by Nelson being close to the port.

soldier stayed in his post, and many thousands ran away who had
never seen the enemy.   So much for my history." [1]

In this decision Nelson was confirmed by a letter of
Mr. Drake, of January 6, 1796, stating that by the
desire of the Imperial Chargé d'Affaires his presence
was required at Genoa, to prevent the French from
landing at Voltri, in the rear of the Austrian army, and
that he had written to Lord Grenville on the subject of
the Austrian complaints, and borne testimony to the
ability and zeal with which Nelson had acted despite the
unfortunate reduction of his squadron." [2]

Under what difficulties Nelson struggled, not only
with a squadron insufficient in number to keep a thorough
watch on the coast, but with the condition of his own
ship, may be judged from one fact.   When at the close
of this year the *Agamemnon* was refitted at Leghorn, it
was found that there was not a mast, yard, or sail, nor
any part of the rigging but was obliged to be repaired,
owing to the shot she had received, and that her hull
had been long repaired by cables served round.

But before the year closed the chief command had
changed.   On the 30th of November, Sir John Jervis
joined the fleet in St. Fiorenzo Bay, and Nelson at
once forwarded to him a full report of previous
occurrences.   He had now again a chief after his own
heart.

[1] To Rev. W. Hoste, December 12, 1795.   Despatches, vol. ii. p. 115.
[2] Clarke and McArthur, vol. i. p. 258 ; Despatches, vol. ii. note pp.
118–19.

NELSON AS A COMMODORE.

CHAPTER VII.

NELSON AS A COMMODORE.

(1796.)

His work in the Mediterranean—The distinguishing pendant—The King
of Spain's letter to the King of Naples—Fresh interview with Sir
John Jervis—The broad pendant—Capture of French ordnance
stores for the Siege of Mantua—Sale of Austrian prisoners of war
to the Spaniards—The Danish neutral—Nelson's reputation on his
station—His pecuniary position in 1796—Letters to his father and
his wife—The Mediterranean abandoned.

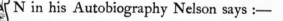N in his Autobiography Nelson says :—

"In 1796 the Commander-in-chief so much
approved of my conduct that he directed me to
wear a distinguishing pendant. In June I was
removed from the *Agamemnon* to the *Captain*, and
on the 11th of August had a captain appointed
under me. Between April and October, 1796, I was employed in the
blockade of Leghorn, taking Porto Ferrajo, the island of Caprea, and
finally in the evacuation of Bastia, when, having seen the troops in
safety to Porto Ferrajo, I joined the Admiral in St. Fiorenzo Bay, and
proceeded with him to Gibraltar ; whence, in December, I was sent
in *La Minerve* frigate, Captain George Cockburn, to Porto Ferrajo,
to bring down our naval stores, &c. On the passage we captured a
Spanish frigate, *La Sabina*, of 40 guns, 28 eighteen-pounders on her
main deck, as will appear by my letter."

With the opening of this eventful year, the prospect
of Spain throwing in her lot with the Government of

France, and thus, not only deserting Naples, but insuring an immense addition to the enemy's fleet in the Mediterranean, became more and more probable.

In October, 1795, Sir John Jervis had been appointed to the command of the Mediterranean Fleet, and before he left England gave to Earl Spencer, the then First Lord of the Admiralty, a paper in which were the following questions relative to the attitude of Spain. "Various pretences may be used by Spain to employ a squadron in the Mediterranean, such as conveying the Princess of Parma to Italy, protecting her trade, visiting her ports, particularly Port Mahon ; and under any of these pretexts a junction with the French at Toulon is very practicable. *Query*, What measures can be taken to defeat such a design? . . . In case," he adds in the second question, " such a junction is effected—which might give a very great superiority over His Majesty's ships—with evident signs of hostility on the part of Spain, what then is to be the conduct of the British Fleet ? " To these very pertinent questions Sir John *never* received a reply.[1]

Again, on Jan. 19, 1796, Sir John wrote to Admiral Man, who was in command of a detached squadron, that he was " without authentic intelligence of a hostile disposition on the part of Spain." In May, 1796, he complains to Mr. Drake " of the flagrant partiality shown by Spain to the French, in permitting the cruisers of the Republic to anchor in their ports, and to send out boats to capture unsuspecting, unarmed merchant ships." Again, in August, he warns Lord Spencer of " the lowering aspect with Spain." [2] And yet even then he was apparently without authentic information of the intentions of the Court of Spain. Yet, if the first paragraph in Nelson's last codicil to his will is founded

[1] Enclosed in letter to the Viceroy of Corsica. Tucker, vol. ii. p. 203.
[2] Tucker's " Lord St. Vincent," vol. i. p. 200.

on truth, in the year 1796 Lady Hamilton sent to the Ministry the letter which the King of Spain had written to his brother, the King of Naples, acquainting him of his intention to declare war against England, and the Ministry had sent out orders to Sir J. Jervis " to strike a stroke, if opportunity offered, against the arsenals of Spain or her fleets." It is difficult to reconcile these statements. Nelson, of course, believed what Lady Hamilton told him, but it is not unfair to doubt the accuracy of Lady Hamilton's statement.[1]

I begin the letters in this chapter with the following from his father, Jan. 4, 1796 :—

" The commencement of a new year calls on a father's tender and affectionate feelings to rejoice with you on the many extraordinary escapes you have experienced, which do evidence a Providential hand that has guarded you from impending dangers ; may that great and good Being still be your shield and defender. I have also further joy in perceiving these self-approving reflections which arise from a con-sciousness of having done all that the great trust in you could require,

---

[1] Mr. Cordy Jeffreson, in his late work on Lady Hamilton and Lord Nelson, has thrown serious doubts on the claim of the lady to having sent this letter at her own expense to the English Government (vol. i. chap. 18). The letter of September, 1796, says that writer, was by no means the first occasion on which the King of Spain informed his brother of Naples of his intention of withdrawing from the Coalition and join the French against England. He had so written on April 2, 1795, and on August 11th, in the same year, had written about the negotiation going on for peace between France and Spain. As a member of the Council all these letters must have been known to the Queen, and she could have no reason for picking the King's pocket of the September letter. The copy of the letter in the Morrison's MS. is certainly not in Lady Hamilton's handwriting, and the supposed endorsement of Sir William verifying it is, to my mind, very suspicious. The extracts which I have given from Sir J. Jervis's letters, seem to me to greatly increase the doubts of any such letter having been forwarded to the Government. If it was, the charge of gross negligence, in not having forwarded it to Jervis, lies on the Government, or on Sir John, in neither case likely. Another copy of the letter was sold in London lately. That Lady Hamilton paid £400 out of her own pocket has been thoroughly disproved by Mr. Jeffreson.

and this you must feel in the highest degree. May you, my dear son, add year to year, through a long life, with the indescribable delight that your heart condemns you not. It is difficult, within the narrow limits of an epistle, sufficiently to gratify a son who claims every mark of parental regard that language can express ; and little more than verbal expressions have ever been within the compass of my abilities, and my confined sphere of action to bestow.

"God has blessed me infinitely even beyond hope, by length of days, to see my posterity in possession of, what is more durable than riches or honours, a good name, an amiable disposition, upright conduct, and pure religion. These must be the supporters of public fame, and they will fight in its defence against envy and calumny. The almost daily proofs of your faithful observance of your various professional duties are pleasing compensations for your long absence. Every disappointment has its consolation, every storm its succeeding summer : and we bring this home immediately to ourselves. You are now in the very meridian of life, and have daily opportunities of growing rich in knowledge, of filling your honest and well-disposed heart with stores of good grain, which in time to come, when the mental powers shall decay, shall prove a treasure, and make good what time has stolen away. Old age is only made pleasant by happy reflections, and by reaping the harvest we have sown in youth. Be assured, my good son, I now regret to find that my stock in that respect is low. My education, situation in life, and opportunities of improvement have been all against me. But, thank God ! I still retain some sources of delight. My setting sun is clearer than when it was mid-day. My blessings are innumerable ; my wishes most abundantly fulfilled. God bless you ! and prosper all you undertake. Farewell ! "[1]

"To Mrs. Nelson.

"*Agamemnon*, St. Fiorenzo, *Jan.* 20, 1796.

"We were received not only with the greatest attention, but with much apparent friendship. Sir John Jervis's offer of either the *St. George* 90, or the *Zealous* 74, was declined, but with that respect and sense of obligation on my part which such handsome conduct demanded of me. I found the Admiral anxious to know many things, which I was a good deal surprised to find had not been communicated to him by others in the fleet ; and it would appear that he was so well satisfied with what is likely to happen, and the means of prevention

---

[1] Clarke and McArthur, vol. i. p. 374-5.

to be taken, that he had no reserve with me respecting his information and ideas of what is likely to be done. He concluded by asking me if I should have any objection to serve under him, with my flag. My answer was that if I were ordered to hoist my flag I should certainly be happy in serving under him, but if the *Agamemnon* were ordered to go home and my flag had not arrived, I should on many accounts wish to return to England; yet still, if the war continued, I should be very proud of the honour of hoisting my flag under his command; and I rather believe Sir John Jervis writes home this day that if the fleet is kept here my flag, on promotion, may be sent to the Mediterranean. The credit I derive from all these compliments must be satisfactory to you, and, should I remain until peace, which cannot be very long, you will, I sincerely hope, make your mind easy. Yet, sometimes, notwithstanding all I have said, I think my promotion will be announced, and that I shall have a land voyage; be it as it may, I shall take it easy. *Agamemnon* is just going to sea, and I can assure you that my health was never better than at this moment." [1]

" To the Same.

"GULF OF GENOA, *Jan.* 27, 1796.

" I sent you a line just as I was getting under sail from St. Fiorenzo. The fleet was not a little surprised at my leaving them so soon, and, I fancy, there was some degree of envy attached to the surprise, for one captain told me, ' You did just as you pleased, in Lord Hood's time, the same in Admiral Hotham's, and now again with Sir John Jervis; it makes no difference to you who is commander-in-chief.' I returned a pretty strong answer to this speech. My command here is to prevent any small number of men from making a descent on Italy. I hear no more of this promotion, and I sincerely hope they will put it off a little longer; unless, which I cannot well expect, they should send out my flag. My health was never better." [2]

" SIR J. JERVIS TO MR. DRAKE.

" *Feb.* 11, 1796.

" I am very happy to learn that Captain Nelson, whose zeal, activity, and enterprise cannot be surpassed, stands so high in your good opinion. I have only to lament the want of means to give him the command of a squadron equal to his merit." [3]

---

[1] Clarke and McArthur, vol. i. p. 255; Despatches, vol. ii. p. 124.
[2] Ibid., p. 257; Despatches, vol. ii. p. 126.
[3] Tucker's "St. Vincent," vol. i. p. 172.

" To Mrs. Nelson.

"*Feb.* 17, 1796.

" Time, my dear Fanny, will soon wear away, when we shall, I doubt not, possess a cottage of our own, and an ample income to live on, if not in luxury, at least in comfort. As yet I appear to stand well with Sir John Jervis, and it shall not be my fault if I don't continue to do so. My conduct has no mystery. I freely communicate my knowledge and observations, and only wish that whatever admiral I serve under may make proper use of it. God forbid I should have any other consideration on service than the good of my country. I am now sent to examine the state of the ships in Toulon ; their numbers we know full well, but the accounts of the state they are in are so contradictory as to leave us uncertain. Sir J. Jervis is at present inferior to the French ; they have built five sail-of-the-line since we left Toulon."

"*Feb.* 28.

" I am now on my way to Genoa, having been joined by the admiral on the 23rd, off Toulon. The French have thirteen sail-of-the-line and five frigates ready for sea, and four or five, which are in great forwardness, are fitting in the arsenal. Sir J. Jervis, by his manner, as I plainly perceive, does not wish me to leave this station. He seems, at present, to consider me more as an associate than a subordinate officer, for I am acting without orders. This may have its difficulties at a future day ; but I make none, knowing the uprightness of my intentions. He asked me if I had heard any more of my promotion. I told him, No. His answer was, ' You must have a larger ship, for we cannot spare you either as captain or admiral.' "[1]

In a letter to Mrs. Nelson, March 25, 1796, the following extract is given from Sir J. Jervis's letter on the conduct of Nelson on the Blockade of the Genoese Coast :—

" I have received by the *Blanche* your two letters of the 16th and 19th instant, together with the several enclosures and copies of your correspondence at Turin, Genoa, and Naples ; and I feel the greatest satisfaction in communicating this public testimony of my thorough approbation of your late conduct and recent correspondence."

In his private letter, Sir J. Jervis added :—

" No words can express the sense I entertain of every part of your

---

[1] Clarke and McArthur, vol. i. p. 257 ; Despatches, vol. ii. p. 127.

conduct, and I shall be very happy to manifest it in the most substantial manner; a distinguishing pendant you shall certainly wear,
and I will write to Lord Spencer about you; in short, there is nothing
within my grasp that I shall not be proud to confer on you." [1]

"GULF OF GENOA, *April* 24, 1796.

" You will be informed, from my last letters, that Sir J. Jervis has
such an opinion of my conduct that he is using every influence, both
public and private, with Lord Spencer, for my continuance on this
station; and I am certain you must feel the superior pleasure of
knowing that my integrity and plainness of conduct are the cause of
my being kept from you, to the receiving me as a person whom no
Commander-in-chief would keep under his flag.

"Sir John was a perfect stranger to me, therefore, I feel the more
flattered; and when I reflect that I have had the unbounded confidence of three Commanders-in-chief, I cannot but feel a conscious
pride, that I possess abilities. Rest assured, my dearest Fanny, of my
unbounded and steady affection, which, if possible, is increased by that
propriety of conduct which you pursue. While the war lasts I must
serve somewhere, and for health and nearness to England I know none
equal to this. In case Admiral Linzee returns, Sir J. Jervis informed
me that I am to hoist a broad pendant, with a captain under me, and
to command a division of the fleet." [2]

Memo. to Mr. Brame, British Consul at Genoa, about May 15, 1796 :—

" The papers from the Secretary of State I am astonished at, but
before I answer a word, I wish to receive, and officially, if it be
proper to communicate in that way with the Genoese Government,
which I think you told me it was not, a plain answer, ' Yes,' or ' No.'
Are all the batteries on the coast manned by and belonging to the
Genoese? Should the reply be ' Yes,' then I have a most heavy
complaint to make, and I doubt not that England is fully equal to
repel the insult which every day is offered to her flag. Should the
reply be, ' No,' they are in possession of the French, then of course
I shall consider it an enemy's coast. It may, however, be said, and

---

[1] Clarke and McArthur, vol. i. p. 264 ; Despatches, vol. ii. p. 140.
[2] Ibid., p. 276 ; Despatches, vol. ii. p. 161.

truly, ' The French have built batteries along the coast within shot of each other, but the Genoese have some fortresses which still remain in their possession, and yet we know that these batteries fire on the approach of any English ship, nor have we the means or power of preventing it. If an English ship comes into any Genoese ports or roads to the westward, we are certain she will be fired at and destroyed, unless she is able to batter down the fortifications; it must, therefore, be acknowledged that the Genoese ports to the westward are not neutral to the English! As this should be the language of the Secretary of State here, can he for a moment fancy that I will receive shot and shells from every part of the coast, and not consider it a hostile one? This, indeed, he may be assured of, that I never have, and never will, fire the first shot; but if shots are fired I will do my utmost to destroy the batteries firing at the English flag, although in doing this I shall guard, as much as possible, against injuring any individual Genoese, a nation which I respect on many accounts. The Secretary, however, must be sensible that the fire of cannon once opened is terrible to a town" (Clarke and McArthur, vol. i. p. 280; Despatches, vol. ii. p. 170).[1]

"To Admiral Sir J. Jervis.

Agamemnon, off Oneglia, *May* 31, 1796.

" Sir,—At two p.m. yesterday, seeing some vessels running along the shore, which I believed to be French, and knowing the great consequence of intercepting cannon and ordnance stores which I had information were expected from Toulon, to be landed at St. Pierre et Arena for the siege of Mantua, I made signal for general chase, when the vessels got close under a battery and anchored. Three o'clock *Mellager* and *Agamemnon* anchored; as soon after did the *Peteret* and *Speedy*. After a short resistance from the battery and the vessels we took possession of them. It is impossible I can do justice to the alacrity and gallantry ever conspicuous in my little squadron.'[2]

---

[1] In reply to complaints of the Genoese, especially that at Loano, he had knocked to pieces a large battery, and killed twenty-five French, and damaged the town. "The Genoese can prevent the French from firing; if they do, their towns are safe, if not, the acts rest with them" (To Sir J. Jervis, May 1, 1796; Despatches, vol. ii. p. 164; see Nelson's Answers, Despatches, p. 289.)

[2] The result was two vessels of war and five transports loaded with heavy ordnance, shot and shells, and entrenching tools. Note in *London Gazette*, July 16, 1796, from Sir J. Jervis, sending Nelson's letter

The following note shows how Nelson had done his work :—

"Prizes taken by Nelson's squadron between June 1, 1794, and June 1, 1796 :—There were forty-eight ships of various classes, the estimated value of which was £4,369 ; the realized, £2,405.

"This account to May 11, 1796, three years from my sailing from Spithead.—HORATIO NELSON."

"To Sir JOHN JERVIS.

"*June* 5, 1796.

"Two days after we took the vessel with Austrian troops on board, who had been made prisoners by the French, a boat came off to Captain Cockburn with a Genoese master, and the crew of the vessel and papers, to say, they were chartered by the Spanish Consul at Savona to carry these troops to Barcelona for the Swiss Regiment. I have examined some of the Austrians, who assert that they were marched by a guard to the vessel, and when on board a person gave them thirty sous each, and told them they were going to Spain, where they would find many of their comrades. The men declared it was against their inclination, and that they wished to return to their own service, or to serve with the English until there was an opportunity. Knowing, as I do, that the French absolutely sell them to the Spaniards, I have no scruple in keeping them, to be sent back to their own sovereign ; and if you, Sir, approve, I will discharge the Genoese vessel, and put the men, with Admiral Linzee's permission, into the *Mignonne*. They want a change of apparel, and a bed each, which if we get no work for, the German Government ought to provide ; they are as fine healthy-looking men as I ever saw, the oldest of the 152 is 34 years of age. Until we have an opportunity of sending them to General Beaulieu, I think they would add strength to our ships, five ships, thirty each ; that is submitted with deference to your better judgment. . . . I have written so fully by *Egmont*, which I hope will be with you to-morrow, that I shall not venture to urge my request, viz., that you would contrive that I may still serve you. I may have been impertinent in suggesting so many ways by which I might still

---

to Admiralty: "Their Lordships are so fully acquainted with the vigilance and enterprise of Commodore Nelson, that I forbear to repeat his merits on this occasion."

remain, but do not, Sir, imagine, that I meant anything by my propositions, than what an anxious disposition pointed out." [1]

Sir J. Jervis thus alluded to these disgraceful proceedings in a letter to Mr. Jackson, Secretary to the Legation at Turin, dated *Victory*, off Toulon, August 15, 1796 :—

" From a Swiss dealer in human flesh the demand made upon me to deliver up 152 Austrian Grenadiers, serving on board His Majesty's Fleet under my command, is natural enough ; but that a Spaniard, who is a noble creature, should join in such a demand, I must confess astonishes me ; and I can only account for it by the Chevalier Camano being ignorant that the persons in question were prisoners of war in the last affair with General Beaulieu, and are not deserters, and they were most basely sold by the French Commissaries in the Western Riviera of Genoa, to the vile crimps who recruit for the foreign regiments in the service of Spain. It is high time a stop should be put to this abominable traffic, a million times more disgraceful than the African slave trade ; and I trust the strong remonstrances about to be made by the Court of Vienna to the Court of Madrid will produce the desired effect." [2]

" To Mrs. Nelson.

Captain at Sea, *June* 13, 1796.

" You will see, my dear Fanny, by the date of this letter, that I have at last left poor old *Agamemnon*. Whether it is right or wrong, time must determine. I have remained in a state of uncertainty for a week, and had the corn ships, which were momentarily expected from Naples, arrived, I should have sailed for England. The admiral has on every occasion behaved with the greatest attention to me ; and if I am to serve, it is better I should serve in this country, where I am known and respected, than to take my chance of being sent home, and ordered to another station. All *Agamemnon's* officers are changed, except Suckling and the Master, who has a wife and large family. Suckling wishes, as his elder brother is dead, to return. I do not believe any one person in the world has a better heart than he has, or

---

[1] Clarke and McArthur, vol. i. p. 289 ; Despatches, vol. ii. p. 182.

[2] Tucker's " Earl St. Vincent," vol. i. p. 201 ; Note to Despatches, vol. ii. p. 182.

would do more real good, if Providence ordains that he should be master of the Wootton Estates." [1]

On the 28th of June, the French took possession of Leghorn, and Nelson was ordered to blockade the port (Notice to Consuls, July 7th). Porto Ferrajo and Elba were occupied by troops under Nelson's orders, July 10th, to prevent easy access to Corsica.

"To Sir J. Jervis.

"*July* 18, 1796.

"Dear Sir,—I hope his Holiness the Pope may yet wage war against the French. I have never heard that he has been in actual hostility against them. The blockade of Leghorn is complete, not a vessel can go in or come out without my permission. Yesterday a Dane came out laden with oil and wine for Genoa. I told him he must return, or I would send him to Corsica. His answer wás, ' I am a neutral, and you may take me, but I will not return.' I, therefore, took possession, and intended giving him to a Corsican privateer; when in about two hours, he begged I would allow him to return ! On this I sent him back with a letter to the Danish consul, whence the following is an extract : ' Respect for the Danish flag, and humanity to the owners of this vessel compel me to return her into their possession, and not to proceed to those extremities which the laws of Nations allow in case of a declared blockade of a port.' This, I am satisfied, was a trial of what I intended ; for, he said, all the neutrals were determined to come out. If we are firm, the Grand Duke (Tuscany) will sorely repent his advances to the French ; his repeated proclamations to the people to be quiet, have given time to the French to lay powder under all the works ; and in case of disturbance they say, ' Up shall go all the works.' Cannon are pointed from the walls to every street, and all the cannon and mortars are mounted ; the famous brass gun is on the Mole head, and also a mortar. The Grand Duke declares he yet hopes the Directory will order Buonaparte to leave Leghorn ; but I believe the French now wish to get into fortified towns, to prolong the campaign." [2]

---

[1] Clarke and McArthur, vol. i. p. 290; Despatches, vol. ii. p. 184.
[2] Ibid., p. 300 ; Despatches, vol. ii. p. 216–7.

" To Mrs. Nelson.

" *August 2, 1796.*

" Had all my actions, dearest Fanny, been gazetted, not one fortnight would have passed during the whole war without a letter from me ; *one day or other I will have a long Gazette to myself :* I feel that such an opportunity will be given me. I cannot, if in the field of glory, be kept out of sight. Probably my services may be forgotten by the great, by the time I get home ; but my mind will not forget, nor cease to feel a degree of consolation and applause superior to undeserved rewards. Wherever there is anything to be done, there Providence is sure to direct my steps. Credit must be given to me in spite of envy. Even the French respect me ; their Minister at Genoa in answering a note of mine, when returning some wearing apparel that had been taken, said, ' Your nation, Sir, and mine, are made to show examples of generosity as well as valour to all the people of the earth.' I will also relate another anecdote, all vanity to myself, but you will partake of it. A person sent me a letter, and directed it as follows, ' Horatio Nelson, Genoa.' On being asked how he could direct it in such a manner, his answer was, in a large party, ' Sir, there is but one " Horatio Nelson " in the world.' The letter came immediately. At Genoa, where I have stopped all their trade, I am beloved and respected both by the Senate and lower order. If any man is fearful of his vessel being stopped, he comes and asks me ; if I give him a paper, or say, ' All is right,' he is contented. I am known throughout Italy ; not a kingdom, or state, where my name will be forgotten. This is my Gazette.

" Lord Spencer has expressed his sincere desire to Sir J. Jervis to give me my flag. You will ask me when I shall come home ? I believe when either an honourable peace is made, or a Spanish war, which may draw our fleet out of the Mediterranean. God knows I shall come to you not a sixpence richer than when I set out. I had a letter a few days since from H.R.H. the Duke of Clarence, assuring me of his unalterable friendship. With kindest love to my father, believe me, your most affectionate husband,

" Horatio Nelson." [1]

" To his Brother.

" *Captain,* between Bastia and Leghorn, *August 18th.*
" My dear Brother,—I have very great pleasure in receiving a

---

[1] Clarke and McArthur, vol. i. p. 304 ; Despatches, vol. ii. p. 230.

letter from you, and I have only to beg that you will write more frequently.   I laugh at your fancying my being able to buy, at least, Tofts ; and don't be uneasy when I assure you that if I have saved my ship pay, the Marine I throw in, I shall be content; but I verily believe it will not be the case.   It is true I have taken numbers of prizes, but I have always shared with my squadron, none of whom have I ever received a sixpence from ; or had so many vessels in sight, that they ran away with the greater part.   I believe had I trusted to my own good fortune and enterprising spirit, I might have been able to think of Tofts, but it gives me not a moment's concern. Happy, happy shall I be to return to a little, but neat cottage.   However, now I am a real commodore, with a captain under me, I shall share for all prizes whoever is the taker.   A Spanish galleon taken now in this country will be a capital stroke."

"To Sir J. Jervis.

"*August* 5, 1796.

"I have also permitted, by the desire of Mr. North, some goods to pass, and the American tribute to the Dey of Algiers.   The Dey's Lord of the Bedchamber, or some such great man, has been on board my ship ; he was highly pleased with my entertainment of him, and declared he would supply us with bullocks of 600 lbs. each, for ten Spanish dollars ; he was never tired of looking about him.

"I must relate an anecdote : I asked him why he would not make peace with the Genoese and Neapolitans, for they would pay the Dey ?   His answer was, 'If we make peace with every one, what is the Dey to do with his ships ? '   What a reason for carrying on a naval war !   but has our Minister a better one at present ? " [1]

"To his Father.

"*Captain, August* 19, 1796.

"My dear Father,—Your most affectionate letter of July 4th gave me infinite pleasure, and I assure you no small part of the satisfaction I feel in doing my duty, is knowing the pleasure it will give you and my dear wife.   As to rewards, I think it very possible those who are on the spot will get them, whilst we who fag at a distance are forgot.   The *last* service is always the best, for it is natural. This gentleman had a victory two years ago, the fruits of which we

[1] Clarke and McArthur, vol. i. p. 306 ; Despatches, vol. ii. p. 235.

enjoyed, and perhaps have lost again. The other is on the spot to receive his reward before the newer object presents itself. But all cannot be employed at home, and half the rewards are useless. God forbid I should ever lose myself so much as to be knighted. Fame says we are to have a Spanish war in this country. The only consequence it can be to us may be the necessary evacuation of Corsica, and that our fleet will draw down the Mediterranean. The Dons will suffer in every way for their folly, if they are really so foolhardy as to go to war to please the French. I am now an established commodore, having a captain appointed to the ship; therefore, my professional rise is regular and honourable. My brother William thinks I have been making a fortune, but I have assured him to the contrary." [1]

On the 20th of September Nelson fell in with a Spanish frigate on his way from Capraja to Leghorn, and brought it to, sending a letter on board asking its captain to tell him " on his honour, whether he knew that there was war or peace between England and Spain." The captain of the frigate (*La Vengeance*) replied that when he left Carthagena, he had heard nothing extraordinary, and of no declaration of war or any defensive alliance with France, and wished to refer to the two courts the question of his being allowed to enter Leghorn. In his reply, Nelson, saying " that it was not possible for him to desire a Spanish officer to do what he considered in the smallest degree dishonourable," gave him the alternative offer of accompanying him to Bastia, to know the truth from the Viceroy. " Should you refuse," added Nelson, " this most reasonable request, the fatal consequences must rest with you ; and I must do my duty in using force." The Spaniard again repeated his story, and in the end, Nelson, having got so much information out of him, replied, " If you pledge your word of honour that the harmony between our two courts is uninterrupted, on giving me your honour that you will proceed direct to Spain, I allow you to proceed;" and so the Spaniard went back to Carthagena.

Of this amusing incident, Nelson gives the following account to his Commander-in-chief:—

"To Admiral Sir J. Jervis.

"*Captain* at Sea, *Sept.* 21, 1796.

"Sir,—Yesterday morning I saw a Spanish frigate coming from the southward, who when he raised our hull, hauled her wind to the eastward. In about one hour after this she bore down to us, and I sent on board the letter No. 1; on which the letters to No. 6 passed between us. As to permitting him to go into Leghorn, that was out of the question; but I chose to have a good deal of communication with him, that I might draw my final opinion if it was war when he sailed, which I am certain it was not.[1] The second captain who came on board, admitted that an English ship was detained at Carthagena, but that it was in consequence of several Spanish ships having been detained by the English, particularly in Corsica, and that Lord Bute had made representations on the subject. On the other hand, his circuitous route through the Straits of Bonifacio, wishing to get into Leghorn from the southward, led me to fancy he had cause for not wishing to meet any English ships of war [then stating that from the letters he had received, announcing the treaty with France, but no actual declaration of war]. Thus, circumstanced, I thought it most proper not to take him (although I own my fingers itched for it), which I hope you will approve of. The Don is not aware that it is this question that was working in my mind, but that it was that I wanted him to go to Bastia, to know from the Viceroy whether I might allow him to go in to Leghorn, and that I would force him to go to Bastia to have his answer before I would allow him to return to Spain.

"I am, sir,
"Your obedient servant,
"Horatio Nelson."

On the signature of the treaty between Spain and France, August 19, 1796, the Government sent orders to Sir

---

[1] The alliance between France and Spain was signed on the 19th of August, but war was not declared until October.

J. Jervis to arrange for the evacuation of Corsica, and
the retreat of his fleet down the Mediterranean.   On the
25th of September, Sir J. Jervis sent orders to Nelson to
co-operate with the Viceroy for that purpose without
delay, and it was accomplished by the 19th of October, and
the troops, stores, &c., conveyed to Porto Ferrajo, Elba.
On the 20th the Spanish Fleet, thirty-eight sail-of-the-line
and ten frigates, was abreast of Cape Corse ; on the 21st
a despatch for the garrison to remain, if not embarked,
was received by Sir J. Jervis—too late.   In a letter to
Earl Spencer, Nov. 11th, Sir J. Jervis wrote—" I consider
it a great blessing that the evacuation of Corsica had taken
place before I had received the orders to maintain the
Viceroy in the sovereignty of it, which could not have
been for any length of time, as the moment the enemy
landed in force, every man in the interior of the island
could have taken part with him, and there was not a
tenable part in it." [1]

" To Mrs. Nelson.

" About *Oct.* 17, 1796.

"We are all preparing to leave the Mediterranean, a measure
which I cannot approve.   They at home do not know what this fleet
is capable of performing; anything and everything.   Much as I shall
rejoice to see England, I lament our present orders in sackcloth
and ashes, so dishonourable to the dignity of England, whose fleets
are equal to meet the world in arms ; and of all fleets I ever saw, I
never beheld one in point of officers and men equal to Sir J. Jervis's,
who is a commander-in-chief equal to lead them to glory." [2]

In a letter of Sir J. Jervis to Earl Spencer, Oct. 23rd, he
relates how, on the Corsicans being told of the evacuation,
the Government of the island was wrested from the Viceroy, and a council of thirty appointed, and that when a

---

[1] Tucker's " St. Vincent," vol. i. p. 239.
[2] Clarke and McArthur, vol. i. p. 329; Despatches, vol. ii. p. 290.

gale temporarily blew the transports off the coast, they insisted that an equal number of Corsicans and British troops should mount guard on the citadel and batteries of Bastia, and refused to let the Viceroy send a message to the Corsican generals in the French service at Leghorn, as they would send a deputation themselves. " Happily, at this most interesting period, Commodore Nelson arrived in the *Diadem*, and by the firm tone he held, soon reduced these gentlemen to order, and quiet submission to the embarkation. . . . By the unwearied labour of Commodore Nelson, and those under his command, everything was embarked on the 19th, and he sailed to Porto Ferrajo at midnight."

On Nov. 2, 1796, the English Fleet sailed from Mortella Bay and arrived at Gibraltar, leaving the Mediterranean to the mercy of the Allied squadrons. Before, however, the fleet finally left the mouth of the Mediterranean, Nelson was sent with two frigates to remove all the valuable stores from Porto Ferrajo. " He alone," says Captain Jurien de la Gravière, " was capable of fulfilling this mission, and of penetrating fearlessly to the furthest part of the Mediterranean, notwithstanding the squadrons that were cruising about that vast sea abandoned by England to the united flags of France and Castile." [1]   On his way Nelson fell in with a Spanish frigate.

On his way from Gibraltar with the *Blanche* frigate (the 19th of December), Nelson, whose pendant was in the *La Minerve* frigate, fell in with the *La Sabina* and *Ceres*, Spanish frigates, and at once brought the former to action with his own ship. The result was that after a very severe action, in which the Spanish ship lost 164 men killed and wounded, she struck, and the Spanish captain, Don Jacobo Stuart, gave up his sword to Nelson on the quarter-deck

[1] Vol. i. p. 142.

of *La Minerve*. Soon after three Spanish ships, two of them line-of-battle and the frigate *Ceres* which had escaped from the *Blanche*, gave chase to *La Minerve* and the prize which had hoisted English colours, and took her ; they then pursued the *La Minerve*, which, with difficulty through good seamanship, escaped. In the following letter to his brother William we hear Nelson's graphic account of this hard-fought action :—

"*La Minerve*, PORTO FERRAJO, *Jan.* 13, 1797.

"MY DEAR BROTHER,—Although I can tell you nothing more than my public letters will of our actions, yet I feel you will like to receive a private one, merely if it contains only, ' We are well,' which is literally all I can write, for what is past the papers will tell—what is to come, I must not. However, if self-approbation is a comfort, which I readily admit, I am receiving inexpressible pleasure to be received in the way I ever have been in this country, and particularly since our last business. You love particulars : therefore, for your *private* journal, I shall relate some circumstances which are most flattering to me, and our action stands the foremost of any in this war.

"When I hailed the Don, and told him, 'This is an English frigate,' and demanded his surrender or I would fire into him, his answer was noble, and such as became the illustrious family from which he is descended, 'This is a Spanish frigate, and you may begin as soon as you please.' I have no idea of a closer or sharper battle ; the force to a gun the same, and nearly the same number of men, we having 250 (*La Sabina*, 286). I asked him several times to surrender during the action, but his answer was, 'No, sir ; not whilst I have the means of fighting left !' When only himself of all the officers were left alive, he hailed and said he could fight no more, and begged me I would stop the firing. The next frigate was *La Ceres* of 40 guns, which did not choose to fight much; not a mast, yard, or sail, or rope but is knocked to pieces. Main and mizen masts with mainyard are new, and every shroud and rope in the ship, foremast and foreyard, are fished.

"On my arrival here it was a ball night, and being attended by the captains, was received in due form by the general, and one particular tune was played ; the second was ' Rule Britannia.' From Italy I am loaded with compliments—it is true these are given on the spot ; what England may think I know not. *We* are at a distance. In about a week I shall be at sea, and it is very probable you will soon hear of another action, for I am very much inclined to make the Dons repent for this war" (Despatches, vol. ii. p. 326). [1]

Nelson's letter on releasing Don Jacobo :—

" To Admiral Don Juan Marino.

" Sir,—I cannot allow Don Jacobo[2] to return to you without expressing my admiration of his gallant conduct.   To you who have seen the state of his ship, it is needless to mention the impossibility of her longer defence.   I have lost many brave men ; but in our masts I was most fortunate, or probably I should have had the honour of your acquaintance.   But it pleased God to order it otherwise, for which I am thankful.   I have endeavoured to make Don Jacobo's captivity as easy as possible, and I rely on your generosity for reciprocal treatment towards my brave officers and men.

" I am, &c.,

" Horatio Nelson." [3]

Having done his duty at Porto Ferrajo, Nelson returned to the appointed rendezvous off Cape St. Vincent.

[1] Loss of *Minerve* in action, 7 killed and 34 wounded, 4 missing in prize, which did not surrender until her main and foremast went by the board.

[2] Don Jacobo Stuart was a descendant of the Duke of Berwick, son of James II.

[3] Harrison's " Nelson," vol. i. p. 150.

THE BATTLE OF ST. VINCENT.

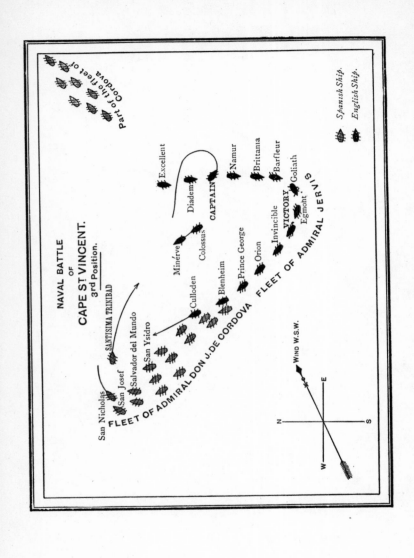

NAVAL BATTLE
OF
CAPE ST VINCENT.
3rd Position.

Part of the fleet of Cordova

Excellent

Diadem

CAPTAIN

Namur

Brittania

Barfleur

Goliath

VICTORY

Egmont

Invincible

Orion

Prince George

Blenheim

Culloden

Minerve

Colossus

SANTISIMA TRINIDAD

San Nicholas

San Josef

Salvador del Mundo

San Ysidro

FLEET OF ADMIRAL DON J. DE CORDOVA

FLEET OF ADMIRAL JERVIS

Spanish Ship.

English Ship.

WIND W.S.W.

N

E

S

W

CHAPTER VIII.

THE BATTLE OF ST. VINCENT.

(1797.)

The Battle of St. Vincent—Nelson's own account—Letters from Collingwood, Prince William Henry—His father and his wife—Jervis's error
of tactics—Rear-Admiral—Knight of the Bath—Blockade of Cadiz
and the Spanish Fleet—Capture of the Spanish gunboat—Nelson's
life saved by John Sykes—The cost of a Knighthood of the Bath
and coat-of-arms.

N the 16th of December, 1796, Sir J.
Jervis sailed for Lisbon with his fleet,
now, by a series of accidents, reduced
to ten sail-of-the-line, where he remained
until the 18th of January, 1797, when
he left for the rendezvous which he had
appointed off Cape St. Vincent. On
the 6th of February, a reinforcement of six ships-of-the-
line reached him there, and with fifteen sail-of-the-line
and four frigates he there awaited the Allied squadrons.
On the 12th, Nelson in the *Minerve* brought the news
that the Spanish Fleet had been seen two days before in
the Straits ; and on the 13th, the look-out ships of both
squadrons reported the enemy by signal at the same
time.

" The Spaniards," says his gallant French biographer, "who knew
nothing of the reinforcement of Jervis's squadron, and felt confident
in their immense superiority of numbers, neglected to close up their
order of sailing during the night, and continued in a state of dis-

persion. Little ambitious of closing with the English squadron, they imagined that it would never venture to act on the offensive ; but Jervis, on the contrary, intended to fight. He knew how important a victory would be to England at this moment ; and he calculated on this victory from the labours he had bestowed for two years upon the improvement of his squadron." [1]

"The 14th of February," continues our author, "a day fatal to the navy of Spain, broke dark and hazy upon the two fleets—towards the east the coast of Portugal showed dimly through the fog, with its rocky cliffs and the lofty Sierras of Monchique, commanding the Bay of Lagos. The English frigates sent forward to reconnoitre the enemy, only reported as yet six Spanish ships, and a thick mist shrouded both squadrons. However, as the sun rose above the horizon, the mist which had enveloped them rolled off in fleecy clouds, driven before the breeze, or spirally ascended through the masts, to disperse in the atmosphere. At nine o'clock, twenty sail of Spaniards had been counted from the masthead of the *Victory*, and at eleven the English frigates reported twenty-five. Owing to the loose manner in which they had sailed during the night, the Spanish ships now found themselves divided into two groups. Admiral Jervis determined to profit by this fault, and prepared to attack one of the divisions. The one composed of nineteen ships formed the main body of the fleet ; the other, only consisting of six, had fallen to lee-ward during the night, and was the first seen by the British ships. Both carried all sail to effect a junction imprudently delayed. Towards the interval which still separated the two masses of the enemy's fleet, but which was momentarily narrowing, the British squadron advanced in a single line. Such was the exciting scene presented for some hours by the two fleets ; but the Spanish admiral, seeing that if he continued on the same course he would not clear the whole of the British squadron, tacked the moment the British van approached him. Hardly had *Cordova* tacked when Jervis made the signal to *Culloden* (the leading ship of the English van) to do the same, and to lead the fleet after the sixteen ships which were standing on the larboard tack. The ships between the *Culloden* and the *Victory* followed the *Culloden* movement, and followed in succession by the centre ranged up along-side the Spanish Fleet.

"But though by this movement, in time the whole of the English ships might have been ranged side by side with Spanish ships, and an old-fashioned battle in two lines fought with some success, it was

---

[1] Jurien de la Gravière, vol. i. p. 148.

Nelson's disregard, or rather anticipation of orders, that caused the great success. Seeing that the Spanish admiral led his line so as to pass on the rear of the English Fleet. But Nelson," continues the author, " who had re-hoisted his broad pendant on the *Captain*, commanded by Captain Miller, was the third ship of the rear division, and watched the fate of the day. He had astern of him only the *Excellent* 74, Captain Collingwood, and a small sixty-four, the *Diadem. Cordova's* movement was scarce commenced when Nelson, guessing its object, saw that he would not have time to inform Admiral Jervis and receive his orders; there was not, in fact, an instant to lose if this movement of the Spanish Fleet was to be opposed. Nelson quitted his station without hesitation, and wearing his ship, passed between the *Excellent* and the *Diadem*, who continued their course, and placed himself across the bows of the *Santissima Trinidad*. Thus he stopped the way against her, obliged her to haul to the wind, and threw her back upon the English advanced ships. A part of that advanced squadron then passed to leeward of the Spanish ships, to prevent a further attempt to that which Nelson had defeated, and the other part, led by the *Victory*, ranged along the Spanish line to windward, and placed *Cordova's* rear ships between two fires.''

How Nelson fared in his desperate manœuvre will be best told in his own words :—

" A few remarks relative to myself in the *Captain*, in which my pendant was flying on the most glorious Valentine's Day, 1797.

" On Feb. 13, at six p.m., shifted my pendant from *La Minerve* frigate to the *Captain*.

Valentine's Day, at daylight, signal to prepare for battle : at ten, saw some strange ships standing across the van of our fleet, on the larboard tack, which was sailing in two divisions, eight in the weather, seven in the lee, on the starboard tack. About eleven, signal to form line as most convenient. At twenty-five past eleven the action commenced in the van, then passing through the enemy's line. About one a.m., the *Captain* having passed the sternmost of the enemy's ships, which formed their van, consisting of seventeen sail-of-the-line, and perceiving the Spanish Fleet to bear up before the wind, evidently with the intention of forming their line, going large—joining their separated divisions—or flying from us ; to prevent either of their schemes from taking effect, I ordered the ship to be wore, and passing between the *Diadem* and the *Excellent*, at ten minutes past one o'clock, I was in close action with the van, and, of course, leeward of the Spanish Fleet. The ships which I know were the *Santa Trinidad, San Josef, Salvador del Mando, San Nicolas, San Isidoro,* another first-rate and seventy-four, names unknown. I was immediately joined and most ably supported by the *Culloden*, Captain Troubridge. The Spanish Fleet, from not wishing, I suppose, to have a decisive battle, hauled to the wind on the larboard tack, which brought the ships above-mentioned to be the leewardmost ships in their fleet. For an hour the *Culloden* and *Captain* supported this apparently, but not in reality, unequal contest, when the *Blenheim*, passing to windward of us and ahead, eased us a little. By this time the *Salvador del Mondo* and *San Isidoro* dropped astern, and were fired into in a masterly style by the *Excellent*, Captain Collingwood, who compelled them to hoist English colours, when, disdaining the parade of taking possession of beaten enemies, he most gallantly pushed up to save his old friend and messmate, who was apparently in a critical situation, the *Blenheim* having fallen to leeward, and the *Culloden* crippled and astern, the *Captain* at this time being actually fired upon by three first-rates, and the *San Nicolas* and seventy-four, about pistol-shot from the *San Nicolas*. The *Excellent* ranged up, with every sail set, and hauling up his mainsail just astern, passed within ten feet of the *San Nicolas*, giving her a most awful and tremendous fire. The *San Nicolas* luffing up, the *San Josef* fell on board of her, and the *Excellent* passing on to the *Santa Trinidad*, the *Captain* resumed her situation abreast of them, close alongside.

"At this time the *Captain*, having lost her foretopmast, not a sail, shroud, or rope standing, the wheel shot away, and incapable of further service in the line or in chase, I directed Captain Miller to put the helm a-starboard, and calling for boarders ordered them to board.

"The soldiers of the 69th Regiment, with an alacrity which will ever do them credit, with Lieutenant Pierson, of the same regiment, were amongst the foremost on this service. The first man who jumped into the enemy's mizen chains was Captain Berry, late my first lieutenant. He was supported from our spritsail yard ; and a soldier of the 69th Regiment, having broken the upper quarter gallery window, jumped in, followed by myself and others, as fast as possible. I found the cabin doors fastened, and the Spanish officers fired their pistols at us through the windows, but having broken open the doors, the soldiers fired, and the Spanish brigadier (commodore with a distinguishing pendant) fell as retreating to the quarter-deck. Having pushed on the quarter-deck, I found Captain Berry in possession of the poop, and the Spanish ensign hauling down. The *San Josef* at this moment fired muskets and pistols from the admiral's stern-gallery. Our seamen were in full possession of every part. About seven of my men were killed and some few wounded, and about twenty Spaniards. Having placed sentinels at the different ladders, and ordered Captain Miller to push more men into the *San Nicolas,* I directed my brave fellows to board the first-rate, which was done in a moment. When I got into her main-chains, a Spanish officer came on the quarter-deck, without arms, and said the ship surrendered. From this welcome information, it was not long before I was on the quarter-deck, when the Spanish captain, with a bended knee, presented me, his sword, and told me the admiral was dying with his wounds below. I gave him my hand, and desired him to call to the officers and ship's crew that the ship had surrendered, which he did; and on the quarter-deck of a Spanish first-rate, extravagant as the story may seem, did I receive the swords of the vanquished Spaniards, which as I received I gave to William Fearney, one of my bargemen, who placed them with the greatest *sang froid* under his arm. I was surrounded by Captain Berry, Lieutenant Pierson, 67th Regiment, John Sykes, John Thompson, Francis Cook, and William Fearney, all old *Agamemnons,* and several other brave men, seamen and soldiers. Thus fell these ships. The *Victory,* passing, saluted us with three cheers, as did every ship in the fleet. The *Minerve* sent a boat for me, and I hoisted my pendant on board her, directing Captain Cockburn to put me on board the first uninjured ship-of-the-line, which was done, and I hoisted my pendant in the *Irresistible;* but the day was too far advanced to venture on taking possession of the *Santa Trinidad,* although she had long ceased to resist, as it must have brought on a night action with a still superior fleet. At dusk I went on board the *Victory,* when the admiral received me on the quarter-deck, and having embraced me, said he could not sufficiently thank me, and used every kind expression which could not fail to make me happy.[1] On my return to the *Irresistible* my bruises were looked to, and found but trifling, and a few days made me as well as ever.

"N.B.—There is a saying in the fleet too flattering for me to omit telling, viz., 'NELSON'S PATENT BRIDGE FOR BOARDING FIRST-RATES,' alluding to my passing over an enemy's 80-gun ship ; and another of a sailor's taking my hand on board the *San Josef,* saying he might

---

[1] He returned the Spanish Rear Admiral's sword to Nelson, which he had so bravely won. This Nelson afterwards presented to the Corporation of Norwich, in whose custody it still remains.

not soon have such another place to do it in, and assuring me that he was heartily glad to see me." [1]

The following account, showing Sir J. Jervis's error and Nelson's fortunate correction of it, is so clearly given by a late critic that the most unprofessional reader can understand it :—

"If the reader will imagine Sir J. Jervis's fleet in a line, standing down from the right hand upper corner of this page, towards the left hand lower corner, with Nelson in the rear of the line and the upper corner of the page ; if he will suppose the Spanish Fleet, in some confusion, passing to the right of the English towards the upper corner of the page, which the English Fleet are leaving behind them, he will be fully able to realize the whole tactical question involved. The fleets are passing each other, and only a scattered and ineffectual fire can be maintained in consequence. If the motion is continued, the ships will pass one another altogether, and there will be no real battle. Troubridge, near the bottom of the page, in the leading ship—*Culloden*—is so well aware of the situation, and so confident that a certain signal from Jervis, who is in the middle of the page, ought not to be delayed a moment, that he has prepared and ready for instant display. The delay—minutes really, but seeming hours—continues. Nelson sees that the opportunity is rapidly vanishing. Presently Jervis makes the signal, 'Tack in succession,' which Troubridge, fully prepared, instantly repeats. But, however it might have been earlier, this is the wrong signal now, and Nelson is keenly sensible of the fact. The method of obeying it would be this. Troubridge, in the leading ship, not now very far from the rear ships of the Spaniards, would turn round to the right, and, with the Spanish ships on his left hand, would steer with them to the top of the page. The next English ship behind the *Culloden* would not turn round at the same time as she did, but would stand on, and turn only when she reached the spot near the bottom of the page, where Troubridge had turned. Every following ship was to do likewise, and none should turn till she reached near the bottom of the page. The results, obviously, would have been that only a few of the head-most ships could have got into action with a very few of the rear ships of the Spaniards. Nelson, it was clear, could not join in the fight at

---

[1] Despatches, vol. ii. p. 344-7.

all, but, worse than that, the Spaniards would certainly escape. His resolution was instantly taken, and he threw himself, in entire disobedience of the signal, into the heart of the enemy where he was. The tactical error of Sir J. Jervis, which Nelson—terribly to his chief's humiliation—thus boldly corrected, had been the display of a wrong signal at a vital moment. Had Jervis made ' Tack together,' or ' Wear together,' instead of those which he did, the Spanish Fleet would have been annihilated, for every English ship would then have turned round where she was, and would have brought her opponent to close action. Unquestionably Nelson would have used either of these signals ; it did not require high intellectual effort, nor even genius. But it required singleness of mind and purpose—a clear vision of that which was immediately in view, and no thought of any kind beyond it.[1]

Satisfied as Nelson was with the reception which he met with from Sir J. Jervis on the deck of the *Victory*, he not unnaturally felt that his great service was overlooked in Sir John's official account of the victory. In that the only captain mentioned was Sir Robert Calder, "whose able assistance," wrote his chief, "greatly contributed to the public service." Sir Robert, however, is less favourably known in history by his envious remark to Sir John, " that Nelson's act was that of disobedience to orders," and the rebuff that he met with, " I saw it, but if ever you commit such a breach of orders I will forgive you also." It will be seen how, before the day of Trafalgar, Nelson did his best—even at the cost of weakening his fleet—to enable Calder to obtain witnesses in his own favour, and proceed without delay to England to meet the charge that lay against him of not having done his duty in his engagement with the Allied fleet. Jealousy of his professional brethren was unknown to Nelson. The following letters that came to him after the great event was known must have been a con-

[1] *Edinburgh Review*, October, 1886, pp. 365-6.

solation for his neglect in the official despatch of his chief [1] :—

                              "*Excellent*, Febuary 15, 1797.

" MY DEAR GOOD FRIEND,—First let me congratulate you on the success of yesterday, on the brilliancy it attached to the British Navy, and the humility it must cause to its enemies ; and then let me congratulate my dear commodore on the distinguished part which he ever takes when the honour and interest of his country are at stake. It added very much to the satisfaction which I felt in thumping the Spaniards that I released you a little. The highest rewards are due to you and *Culloden ;* you formed the plan of attack—we were only accessories to the Don's rain ; for, had they got on the other tack, they would have sooner joined, and the business would have been less complete. We have come off pretty well, considering ; eleven killed and fourteen wounded. You saw the four-decker going off this morning to Cadiz—she should have come to Lagos, to make the thing better, but we could not brace our yards up to get nearer. I beg my compliments to Captain Martin ; I think he was at Jamaica when we were.

    " I am ever, my dear friend, affectionately yours,

                              " C. COLLINGWOOD." [2]

Nelson had not waited for Collingwood's letter to acknowledge the succour he had received from his old comrade. On the morning after the victory he wrote to Collingwood :—

" MY DEAREST FRIEND,—' A friend in need is a friend indeed' was never more truly verified than by your most noble and gallant conduct yesterday in sparing the *Captain* from further loss ; and I beg, both as a public officer and a friend, you will accept my most sincere thanks. I have not failed, by letter to the admiral, to represent the services of the *Excellent*."

———————

[1] In his letter to Lord Hugh Seymour, February 17, 1797, Sir John excuses his omission on the plea " that he preferred Sir G. Wallis's style," that he had taken, sunk, burnt, or destroyed of the enemy, as per margin (Tucker's " St. Vincent," vol. i.).

[2] Collingwood Correspondence, 5th edition, vol. i. p. 55.

Letter from Mrs. Nelson :—

"*Feb.* 23, 1797.

"MY DEAREST HUSBAND,—Yesterday's *Gazette* authorizes our good father and myself to congratulate you on your being a Flag officer. May it please God your fame and successes continue to increase under this promotion. I never saw anything elevate your father equal to this. He repeated with pleasure the last words your good uncle (Captain Maurice Suckling) told him, 'that he would live to see you an admiral.'"

Again, in reply to one from him of February 16, 1797 :—

"*March* 11, 1797.

"MY DEAREST HUSBAND,—Yesterday I received your letter of February 16th. Thank God you are well and Josiah. My anxiety was far beyond my powers of expression. Mr. Nelson and Captain Locker behaved humanely and attentive to me. They wrote immediately, Captain Locker assuring me you were perfectly well, and Maurice begging me not to believe idle reports, the *Gazette* saying you were slightly wounded. Altogether, my dearest husband, my sufferings were great. Lady Saumarez came running to tell me she had letters from her husband—all this was on this day week. He speaks generously and manly about you, and concluded by saying, 'Commodore Nelson's conduct is above praise. You were universally the subject of conversation.'"

Mrs. Nelson then described the polite speeches made to her, and thus naturally expressed her alarm about the *boarding*.

"I shall not be myself till I hear from you again. What can I attempt to say to you about boarding? You have been most wonderfully protected : you have done desperate actions enough. Now may I—indeed I do—beg that you never board again. *Leave it for captains.* How rejoiced Jo must have been to have seen you, although it was but an absence of two months. To-morrow is our wedding day, when it gave me a dear husband, my child the best of fathers. I hope he will deserve all the blessings Providence has bestowed upon him. Do come home this summer or in the autumn. It is said a change in Administration would certainly have taken place, had not this wonderful and fortunate victory have taken place. Admiral Parker had written the *Captain* and *Culloden* bore the brunt of the action. This instant I have a letter from Lord Hood, telling me Sir R. Calder was gone to Portsmouth. Thank you, my dearest husband, a thousand times for your letter of February 22nd. God bless and protect you, and my Jo—crown all your endeavours with success, and grant us a happy meeting. I can bear all my extreme good fortune.

" Your affectionate wife,

"FRANCES H. NELSON."[1]

Again, in a letter of March 20th :—

" I sincerely hope, my dear husband, that all these wonderful and desperate actions—such as boarding ships you will leave to others. With the protection of a Supreme Being, you have acquired a character, or name, which all hands agree cannot be greater : therefore, rest satisfied. What does Josiah say to all this ? he is seasoned."[2]

Of Nelson's letters to his wife of the 18th and 22nd of February, to which the letter from her previously quoted is the reply, there do not appear to be any copies extant, On the 28th of that month we have a letter from him, when at Lisbon with the prizes, and on the eve of his starting for the commencement of the blockade in Cadiz, of the enemy so lately defeated off Cape St. Vincent— gratitude to Providence and anxiety for his venerable father's wants are the ruling thoughts of the victor's mind.

"TO MRS. NELSON.

" *Irresistible*, LISBON, *Feb.* 28, 1797.

" We got up here with our prizes this afternoon ; the more I think of my late action, the more I am astonished ; it absolutely appears

---

[1] Sir James Saumarez commanded the *Orion* in the battle. The news of the battle reached London, *March 3rd*. Nelson had been made Rear-Admiral before this, *i.e.*, *February 20th*. The nominal value of Spanish prizes taken from August 10th was £437,500 in which he had a flag officer's share. Mr. Clarke Russell is in error in stating that Nelson's promotion was given on account of his services at the Battle of St. Vincent (" Nelson," Putnams, New York, p. 76.)

[2] Nelson Papers ; Despatches, vol. ii. pp. 358-9, notes.

a dream. The *Santissima Trinidad* of four decks, lost five hundred
killed and wounded ; and had not my ship been so cut up, I would
have had her; but it is well, thank God for it. As for myself, I
assure you, I never was better, and rich in the praises of every man
from the highest to the lowest in the fleet. The Spanish war will
give us a cottage and a piece of ground, which is all I want. I shall
come one day or other laughing back, when we will retire from the
busy scenes of life. I do not, however, mean to be a hermit ; the
Dons will give us a little money.

"If my father should at any time wish for any part that is in my
agent's hands, I beg he will always take it, for that would give more
real pleasure than buying house or land. I go to sea the day after
to-morrow in this ship with a squadron to be off Cadiz, consisting of
Orion, Irresistible, &c. Sir J. Jervis has spread the frigates ; and I
shall return by the time the fleet is ready for sea." [1]

From his father, :—

"MY DEAR REAR-ADMIRAL,—I thank my God with all the power
of a grateful soul for the mercies He has most graciously bestowed on
me, in preserving you amidst the imminent perils which so lately
threatened your life at every moment ; and amongst other innumerable blessings I must not forget the bounty of Heaven in granting you
a mind that rejoices in the practice of those eminent virtues which
form great and good characters. Not only my few acquaintance here,
but the people in general meet me at every corner with such handsome
words, that I was obliged to retire from the public eye. A wise
moralist has observed that even bliss can rise but to a certain pitch,
and this has been verified in me. The height of glory to which your
professional judgment, united with a proper degree of bravery, guarded
by Providence, has raised you, few sons, my dear child, attain to, and
fewer fathers live to see. Tears of joy have involuntarily trickled
down my furrowed cheeks. Who can stand the force of such general
congratulation ? The name and services of Nelson have sounded
through the city of Bath, from the common ballad-singer to the
public theatre. Joy sparkles in every eye, and desponding Britain
draws her sable veil and smiles. It gives me inward satisfaction to
know, that the laurels you have wreathed sprung from those principles
and religious truth which alone constitute the hero ; but though a

---

[1] Clarke and McArthur, vol. i. p. 355 ; Despatches, vol. ii. p. 358.

civic crown is all you at present reap, it is to the mind of inestimable value, and I have no doubt will one day bear a golden apple : that field of glory in which you have been so conspicuous is still open." [1]

From the Duke of Clarence :—

"RICHMOND, *March* 13, 1797.

"DEAR NELSON,—I am, believe me, very happy to own myself in the wrong, and in future to acknowledge that the British Fleet, when *well* disciplined, *well* officered, and *nobly* commanded, *can* beat *any* number of *Spaniards*. I rejoice, my good friend, with all my heart, at the splendid victory Jervis and his fine fellows have gained over the Dons. Your conduct has been, as usual, meritorious, and you really need not have been wounded to complete your fame : for amongst all ranks of people your character has *long* been established. I am happy to inform you that his Majesty has expressed himself in the most gracious manner about you ; and it is but justice to Spencer, though I hate him, to say that in his speech he did you the credit you so amply merited. You, my dear friend, have long known my sentiments about Jervis, and I am happy they coincide with yours : the action and its result speak for themselves, and must give every Englishman sincere pleasure—more particularly to those who belong to the British Navy, and have the happiness, as I have, of possessing intimate friends in that gallant fleet. I am very sorry to see by the Returns that you are wounded, and still more so by your silence, as I am alarmed that you have severely suffered : for I am persuaded otherwise, after such an event, so glorious to the British Navy, you would certainly have written to one who is attached to the Service, and particularly interested in your welfare. My best wishes for your health and happiness attend you, and ever believe me, yours sincerely,

"WILLIAM." [2]

"FROM THE SAME.

"*April* 30, 1797.

"You, my good friend, conclude your last letter by saying you are a *gallant fleet*. Gracious God ! what a difference in this country. The ships at Spithead for a whole week in a perfect condition of mutiny—the men commanding their officers, and a Parliament con-

---

[1] Clarke and McArthur, vol. i. p. 524.
[2] Despatches, vol. ii. p. 386 note.

sisting of delegates from each ship-of-the-line sitting all that time on board the *Queen Charlotte*, and issuing orders to his Majesty's fleet. I hope, though I have not a good opinion of Lord Spencer, that the Admiralty have acted with discretion.   The King, with the advice of his Ministers, has very properly pardoned the seamen and marines. A squadron has proceeded to sea, and discipline is once more restored in the British Navy, but the mutiny has spread to Portsmouth and still rages there.   The business, of course, must come before Parliament; therefore, till the investigation, I shall say no more.   But paint to yourself the fleet at Spithead during a war for a whole week in a complete state of mutiny, and the necessity for the pardon for the whole from the sovereign.   As for Ireland, that country is in a state of rebellion ; therefore, the worst consequences from the *now necessary* want of discipline, would arise in the sister kingdom, should the French seriously turn their thoughts to the invasion of Ireland. Pardon my gloom ; but I have a very great stake in this country, and a family of young children to protect.   In all situations, I am yours sincerely,   "WILLIAM." [1]

Though the actual loss of the Spaniards in the battle of St. Vincent was limited to four sail-of-the-line — the *Salvador del Mundo* and the *San Isidoro*, besides the *San Josef* 112 and the *San Nicolas* 80, which had been taken by Nelson—so thoroughly disheartened were they, that the fleet, still numbering over twenty most powerful ships, took refuge in Spanish ports, only to be blockaded by the victorious English.   To their defeated admiral the Spanish Government showed most unjust severity. Don Jose de Cordova, notwithstanding his brave defence of the *Santissima Trinidad*, was broke and expelled the service, and his flag-officer as well as six captains of his fleet shared his disgrace.   To the victors honours were given with no stinted hand by the grateful Government at home.   Sir John Jervis became Earl St Vincent, and Nelson was afraid that the honour of a baronetcy, usually offered on such occasions to the junior flag officer, would be offered to him.   This, by the help

[1] Despatches, vol. ii. pp. 387–8 note.

of his good friend, the Viceroy of Corsica, it will be seen by the following letter, he barely escaped. His very reasonable wish was to be a Knight of the Bath.

According to Colonel Drinkwater (whose account of the action which he had witnessed from the *Lively* sloop is well known), Nelson plainly expressed his wishes in the following conversation which the Colonel had with him, immediately after the battle :—

"I then adverted to the honours that must attend such distinguished services. ' The Admiral,' I observed, ' will of course be made a peer, and his seconds in command noticed accordingly. ' As for you, Commodore,' I continued, ' they will make you a baronet.' The word was scarcely uttered, when, placing his hand on my arm, and looking me most expressively in the face, he said, ' No, no; if they want to mark my services it must not be done in that manner.' ' Oh,' I said, interrupting him, ' you wish to be made a Knight of the Bath ?' for I could not imagine that his ambition, at that time, led him to expect a peerage. My supposition proved to be correct, for he instantly answered me, ' Yes ; if my services have been of any value, let them be noticed in a way that the public may know me and them.' " [1]

His reasonable objection to a baronetcy was forcibly put to Sir Gilbert Elliot, the late Viceroy of Corsica, in the following letter :—

" *Irresistible, Feb.* 17, 1797.

" You will now, I am sure, think me an odd man, but still I hope you will agree with me in opinion, and if you can be instrumental in keeping back what I expect will happen, it will be an additional obligation, for very far is it from my disposition to hold light the honours of the Crown ; but I conceive to take hereditary honours without a fortune to support the dignity, is to lower that honour it would be my pride to support in proper splendour.

" On the 1st of June, 12th of April (Lord Howe 1794, Lord Rodney 1782), and other glorious days, baronetage was bestowed on the junior flag-officers ; this honour is what I dread, for the reasons

[1] Colonel Drinkwater's Narrative, pp. 83–8.

before given, which I wish a friend to urge for me to Lord
Spencer, or such other of his Majesty's Ministers as are supposed
to advise the Crown. There are other honours which die with the
possessor, and I should be proud to accept, if my efforts are thought
worthy of the favour of my King." [1]

By Sir Gilbert's intervention with Mr. Pitt, the offer
of a baronetcy was changed to that of the Order of the
Bath ; as Nelson wrote to his wife :—

"To Mrs. Nelson.

"*April,* 1797.

"Though we can afford no more than a cottage — yet, with a
contented mind, my dearest Fanny, my chains, medals, and ribbons
are all sufficient. We must be contented with a little, and the
cottage near Norwich, or any other place you like better, will, I
assure you, satisfy me. Do not mention this mark of the Royal
favour to any one except my father. Be assured, whether my letters
are long or short, yet still that my heart is entirely with you. With
love to my father, believe me your most affectionate husband.[2]

"Horatio Nelson."

In writing to his brother William on the 6th of April,
Nelson said :—

"I beg you will thank all our friends for their kind congratulations ;
and I must be delighted, when, from the King to the peasant, all are
willing to do me honour. But I will partake of nothing but what
shall include Collingwood and Troubridge. We are the only three
ships who made great exertions on that glorious day ; the others did
their duty, and some not exactly to my satisfaction. We ought to
have had the *Santissima Trinidad* and the *Soberano* 74. They belonged to us by conquest, and only wanted some good fellows to get
alongside of them, and they were ours. But it is well, and for that
reason we do not like to say much.

"Sir John Jervis is not quite contented, but says nothing publicly.
An anecdote in the action is honourable to the admiral, and to
Troubridge and myself. Calder (the first captain of the *Victory*)

---

[1] Minto Papers, Despatches, vol. ii. p. 350.
[2] See Letter of Lord Spencer, March 17, 1797, appointment not
gazetted till May 27th.

said, ' Sir, the *Captain* and *Culloden* are separated from the fleet, and unsupported ; shall we recall them ? ' ' I will not have them re-called.   I put my faith in these ships : it is a disgrace that they are unsupported and separated.' "

In the blockade of the fugitive Spanish squadron in Cadiz, which Lord St. Vincent established before the end of March, Nelson bore a very active part.   For a month he was detached to secure the safety of the garrison of Elba ; but by the 24th of May he had rejoined his chief, and was put in command of the in-shore squadron, hoisting his flag on the *Theseus*.   In the performance of this duty his personal courage was conspicuous.   In the first attempt to force out from the harbour the Spanish Fleet—amounting to twenty-eight sail-of-the-line —the attacking force was met on the part of the Spaniards by a great number of mortar gunboats, and large armed launches, in hopes of cutting off the *Thunder* bomb; but so vigorous was Nelson's attack on them that they fled in the greatest disorder, and took refuge under the batteries.   In this service Nelson was for a time in eminent peril.   The commandant of the Spanish gun-boats, in an armed launch carrying twenty-six men, laid himself aboard Nelson's barge, in which besides Captain Fremantle he had only his ten bargemen.   In the des-perate hand-to-hand encounter that ensued, " his faith-ful follower, John Sykes, twice saved Nelson's life, by parrying blows that were aimed at him, and at last actually interposed his own head to receive the blows of a Spanish sabre, which he could not by any other means avert."   Notwithstanding the great disproportion of numbers, eighteen of the enemy were killed and all the rest wounded, and the barge taken.   Nelson would have asked for a lieutenancy for Sykes if he had served long enough.   " His manner and conduct were so entirely above his situation that nature certainly intended him for a gentleman; but though he recovered from the dangerous wound, he did not live to profit by the gratitude and friendship of his commander." That the devotion of John Sykes was shared by the whole ship's company of the *Theseus* was shown in a paper dropped on her quarter-deck, a fortnight before :—

" To Mrs. Nelson.

" *June* 15, 1797.

" A few nights ago a paper was dropped on the quarter-deck, of which this is a copy: 'Success attend Admiral Nelson ! God bless Captain Miller ! We thank them for the officers they have placed over us. We are happy and comfortable, and will shed every drop of blood in our veins to support them, and the name of the *Theseus* shall be immortalized as high as the *Captain's* ship's company.' " [1]

In reporting this perilous affair to the Admiralty on the 5th of July, Lord St. Vincent did full justice to Nelson's conspicuous gallantry. "The rear-admiral," wrote his chief, "who is always present in the most arduous enterprises, with the assistance of some other barges, boarded and carried two of the enemy's gunboats and a large launch belonging to one of the ships of war, with the commandant of the flotilla. Rear-Admiral Nelson's acts speak for themselves; any praise of mine would fall very far short of his merit."

On the night when this despatch was written Nelson again bombarded Cadiz with such effect that the Spanish admirals in their flag-ships with eight more sail-of-the-line warped with great precipitation out of the range of the shells. This service was accomplished with but trifling loss on our side. Again on the 8th he had arranged for another attack under his own direction; but the wind blew so strong down the bay that he could not get

[1] His ship at the battle of St. Vincent.

the bomb-vessels up to the point of attack in time.　On the 15th he was despatched to the ill-fated attempt on Santa Cruz.

The following letters of this period show Nelson's kindness of heart for his fellow-workers :—

"I send you the state of the *Swiftsure ;* even the sight of the two poor men in irons on board her has affected me more than I can express; if Mr. Weir (physician to the fleet) would look at them, I should be glad.　The youth may, I hope, be saved, as he has intervals of sense, his countenance is most interesting.　If any mode can be devised for sending him home, I will with pleasure pay fifty pounds to place him in some proper place for his recovery; the other I fear is too old."[1]

Again :—

"*June* 10, 1797.

"My dear Sir,—I hope for the poor men's sakes, that they are imposing on me ; but depend upon it, that God Almighty has afflicted them with the most dreadful of all diseases.　They don't sham ; indeed you will find I am not mistaken, and all the commissioners in the world cannot convince me of it.　For what purpose can these poor wretches attempt to destroy themselves ?　For what purpose can one of them have spoken to me as rationally as any person could do ?　Do let Mr. Weir look at them ; I am sure he will think with me, from the order to represent those objects who are unfit for service, I could not do otherwise than I did ; but if you think I have said too much, pray curtail my report.　But I will get to pleasanter subjects.　I am forming a ladder for the escalade, which when finished I will send to the *Ville de Paris* (Sir J. Jervis's flagship), that we may have as many as twenty at least.　Ten hours shall make me either conqueror or defeat me.　I long to be at work, for I begin to think these fellows will not soon come out, at least not while negotiations are going on."[2]

By his promotion to be a Knight of the Bath, at that

---

[1] To Sir J. Jervis, June 9 ; 1797, Clarke and McArthur, vol. ii. p. 16 ; Despatches, vol. ii. p. 393.

[2] Clarke and McArthur, vol. ii. p. 17 ; Despatches, vol. ii. p. 395.

time before the subsequent division of the order in the form we now have it, Nelson was entitled to supporters to the family arms, hence the following correspondence with which I close this chapter. In the list of fees, most of them to servants of the Royal Household, of the most absurd kind, given in the Appendix, it will be seen that Nelson was wise in refusing at the outset to be saddled by such a payment for enjoying the bounty of his sovereign, an abominable tax on hard-earned merit :—

" To MRS. NELSON.

" *June 29*, 1797.

" I have to thank many friends for their kind congratulations, and have had a long letter and genealogy from the *York Herald*, Mr. Naylor, whom I have referred to my brother Maurice. I have sent my brother my supporters, crest, and motto : on one side a sailor properly habited, holding in his hand the broad pendant on a staff, and trampling on a Spanish flag ; on the other side the British lion tearing the Spanish flag, the remnants hanging down, and the flag in tatters. Motto what my brother William suggested, turned into English, ' Faith and work.' " [1]

To G. Naylor, Esq., *York Herald*, auto. in possession of W. Woods, Esq., *Lanc. Herald* :—

" SIR,—I am honoured with your letter of May 29th, relative to my pedigree ; and I have desired my brother to deliver to you this letter, and to arrange such matters as are proper with you. As Government have always, I believe, on occasions like the present paid all fees of office, installation, &c., I expect they will do so on the present occasion, for I cannot think of being at one sixpence of expense ; but my brother will express my sentiments fully on this head, and I have the honour to be, &c., [2]

" H. N."

---

[1] Clarke and McArthur, vol. ii. p. 21 ; Despatches, vol. ii. p. 399–400. note.

[2] Despatches, vol. ii. p. 400. The claim made eventually was for more than £400. See Appendix. In those days there was only one class in the Order, that of K.B.

SANTA CRUZ—TENERIFFE.

CHAPTER IX.

S*ANTA CRUZ—TENERIFFE.*

(1797.)

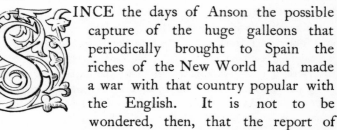INCE the days of Anson the possible
capture of the huge galleons that
periodically brought to Spain the
riches of the New World had made
a war with that country popular with
the English. It is not to be
wondered, then, that the report of
the Viceroy of Mexico having evaded the English
frigates that kept watch from the Straits of Gibraltar
to Cape St. Vincent, from the day that Cordova and
his fleet fled to Cadiz, had put into Santa Cruz, in the
island of Teneriffe, should lead such daring spirits as
those of Nelson and Troubridge to project an expedition
for the capture of the riches supposed to be in that port.
In 1657 Admiral Blake had succeeded in a similar project
—a precedent far too tempting to the daring mind of

Nelson. Though, instead of the Viceroy of Mexico's fleet, only one ship of any value had reached Santa Cruz, the capture of that town, and the consequent submission of the whole island, would undoubtedly have been a severe blow to the Spanish Government, coming so soon after the day of St. Vincent, and might have had the effect on which Nelson calculated in his first communication to his chief, and, had the expedition been as powerful by land as by sea, as he proposed, might have been brought to a successful issue.

In a letter to Sir J. Jervis, April 15, 1797, Nelson gives his masterly views of the practicability of an attack on Santa Cruz, Teneriffe, where the Viceroy of Mexico and one of the galleons were believed to be anchored.

" April 12, 1797.

" MY DEAR SIR,—Troubridge talked to me last night about the Viceroy at Teneriffe. Since I first believed it was possible that his Excellency might have gone there, I have endeavoured to make myself master of the situation and means of approach by sea and land. I shall begin by sea.

" The Spanish ships generally moor with two cables to the sea, and four cables from their sterns to the shore ; therefore, although we might get to be masters of them, should the wind not come off the shore, it does not appear certain we should succeed so completly as we might wish. As to any opposition, except from natural impediments, I should not think it would avail. I do not reckon myself equal to Blake ; but if I recollect right, he was more obliged to the wind coming off the land than to any exertions of his own ; fortune favoured the gallant attempt, and may do so again. But it becomes my duty to state all the difficulties, as you have done me the honour to desire me to enter on the subject.

" The approach by sea to the anchoring place is under very high land, passing three valleys; therefore the wind is either in from the sea, or squally with calms from the mountains. Sometimes in a night a ship may get in with the land wind and moderate weather. So much for the sea attack, which, if you approve, I am ready and willing to look at or to carry into execution. But now comes my plan, which could not fail of success, would immortalize the undertakers, ruin

Spain, and has every prospect of raising our country to a higher pitch of wealth than she ever yet attained ; but here soldiers must be consulted, and I know from experience, excepting General O'Hara, they have not the same boldness in undertaking a political measure that we have. We look to the benefit of our country, and risk our fame every day to serve her ; a soldier obeys his orders, and no more. By saying soldiers should be consulted, you will guess I mean the army of 3,700 men from Elba, with cannon, mortars, and every implement now embarked ; they would do the business in three days, probably much less. I will undertake with a very small squadron to do the naval part. The shore, though not very easy of access, is so steep that the transports may run in, and land the army in one day. The water is conveyed to the town in wooden troughs ; this supply cut off would probably induce a very speedy surrender ; good terms for the town, private property secured to the islanders, and only the delivery of public stores and foreign merchandise demanded, with threats of utter destruction if one gun is fired. In short, the business could not miscarry."

"Now it comes for me to discover what might induce General de Burgh to act in this business. All the risk and responsibility must rest with you. A fair representation should also be made by you of the great national advantages that would arise to our country, and of the ruin that our success would occasion to Spain. Your opinion besides should be stated, of the superior advantages a fortnight thus employed would be to the Army, to what they could do in Portugal ; and that of the six or seven millions sterling the army would have one half. If this sum were thrown into circulation in England, what might not be done ? It would secure an honourable peace, with innumerable other blessings. It has long occupied my thoughts. Should General de Burgh not choose to act, after having all those blessings for our country stated to him, which are almost put into our hands, we must look to General O'Hara. The Royals, about six hundred, are in the fleet, with artillery sufficient for the purpose. You have the power of stopping the store-ships ; one thousand more men would still insure the business, for Teneriffe never was besieged ; therefore the hills that cover the town are not fortified to resist any attempt of taking them by storm ; the rest must follow—a fleet of ships and money to reward the victors. But I know with you, and I can lay my hand on my heart and say the same : it is the honour and prosperity of our country that we wish to extend.

"I am, &c.,
"Horatio Nelson."

From the not unnatural objection of the commander of
the land forces to deviate from the orders he had received,
no troops were available for the expedition, and Nelson
was left to attempt the venture with only such soldiers as
were serving as marines on board his squadron, and with
the blue jackets who could be spared from the ships.
Besides this serious difficulty, it was probable that the
treasure brought to Santa Cruz in the one vessel would
have been landed and stored in the town, and to be
obtained only by a vigorous attack on its defences and
defenders.   Still, Nelson felt that the attempt should be
made, and with four line-of-battle ships, three frigates,
and the ill-fated *Fox* cutter, essayed the enterprise.
How the expedition fared is best told in his own
words :

"On Friday, the 21st instant (July) I directed to be embarked on
Seahorse, Terpsichore, and *Emerald* frigates one thousand men (including
250 marines under the command of Captain Thomas Oldfield), the
whole commanded by Captain Troubridge, attended by all the boats
of the squadron, scaling ladders, and every implement which I thought
necessary for the success of the enterprise.   I directed that the boats
should land in the night, between the fort on the north-east side of
the Bay of Santa Cruz and the town, and endeavour to make themselves masters of that fort, which done, to send in my summons, the
liberal terms of which I am confident you will approve.

"Although the frigates approached within three miles of the place
of debarkation by twelve o'clock, yet from the unforeseen circumstance
of a strong gale of wind in the offing, and a strong current against
them in shore, they did not approach within a mile of the landing
place when the day dawned, which discovered to the Spaniards our
force and intentions.   On my approach with the line-of-battle ships,
Captains Troubridge and Bowen, with Captain Oldfield of the
Marines, came on board to consult with me what was best to be done,
and were of opinion, if they could possess the heights over the fort
above mentioned, that it could be stormed, to which I gave my assent,
and directed the line-of-battle ships to batter the fort, in order to
create a diversion ; but this was found impracticable, not being able

to get nearer the shore than three miles, from a calm and contrary current, nor could our men possess themselves of the heights, as the enemy had taken possession of them, and seemed as anxious to retain, &c., as we were to get them. Thus foiled in my original plan, I considered it for the honour of my King and country not to give over the attempt to possess ourselves of the town, that our enemies might be convinced there is nothing that Englishmen are not equal to; and confident in the bravery of those who would be employed in the service, I embarked every person from the shore on 22nd at night.

"On the 24th I got the ships to an anchor about two miles to the northward of the town, and made every show for a disposition of attacking the heights, which appeared to answer the end, from the great number of people they had placed on them. The *Leander*, Captain Thomson, joined this afternoon, and her Marines were added to the force before appointed, and Captain Thompson also volunteered his services.

"At eleven at night the boats of the squadron, containing between six and seven hundred men, one hundred and eighty on board the *Fox* cutter, and about seventy or eighty men in a boat we had taken the night before, proceeded towards the town. The divisions of the boats conducted by all the captains, except Fremantle and Bowen, who attended with me to regulate and lead the way to the attack; every captain being acquainted that the landing was to be made on the Mole, from whence they were to proceed as fast as possible to the Great Square, where they were to form, and proceed on such service, as might be found necessary. We were not discovered till within half-gun-shot of the landing-place, when I directed the boats to cast off from each other, give an hurrah, and push for the shore.

"A fire of thirty or forty pieces of cannon, with musketry, from one end of the town to the other, opened upon us, but nothing could stop the intrepidity of the captains leading the divisions. Unfortunately, the greatest part of the boats did not see the Mole, but went on shore through a raging surf, which stove all the boats to the left of it.

"For the details of the proceedings, I send a copy of Captain Troubridge's account to me, and I cannot but express my admiration of the firmness with which he and his brave associates supported the honour of the British flag.

"Captains Fremantle, Bowen, and myself, with four or five boats, stormed the Mole, although opposed apparently by four hundred or five hundred men, took possession of it, and spiked the guns; but such a heavy fire of musketry and grape shot was kept up from the citadel and houses on the Mole, that we could not advance, and we were all nearly killed or wounded.

"The *Fox* cutter, in rowing towards the town, received a shot under water from one of the enemy's distant batteries, immediately sank, and Lieut. Gibson, her commander, with ninety-seven men were drowned.

"I must not omit to acquaint you of the satisfaction I received from the conduct of Lieut. Baynes, of the Royal Artillery, not only from the ardour with which he undertook every service, and also from his professional skill." [1]

In the log of the *Theseus,* the desperate attack made by the men in the boats is thus given, almost in the terms of Troubridge's letter :—

"Captains Troubridge, Hood, Miller, and Waller landed with part of the boats, just to the southward of the Citadel, passing through a raging surf, which stove all the boats, and wet all the ammunition. Notwithstanding these difficulties they pushed over the enemy's line wall and batteries, and formed in the great square of the town, about eighty marines, eighty pikemen, and one hundred and eighty small-armed seamen (total three hundred and forty), where they took possession of a convent, from whence they marched against the citadel, but found it far beyond their power to take. At daylight, from prisoners taken, Captain Troubridge found there were eight thousand Spaniards in arms, and one hundred French, with five field-pieces, assembled at the entrance of the town, and seeing the impossibility of getting any assistance from the ships, at seven o'clock he sent Captain Hood with a message to the governor, that if he should be allowed, freely and without molestation, to embark his people at the Mole head, taking off such boats as were not stove, and that the governor should find others to carry off the people, the squadron before the town would not molest it. The governor told Captain Hood he thought they ought to surrender as prisoners of war, to which he replied that Captain Troubridge had directed him to say that if the terms he had offered were not accepted in five minutes, he would set the town on fire and attack the Spaniards at the point of the bayonet, on which the governor instantly closed with the terms, when Captain Troubridge and his party marched, with British colours

---

[1] Despatches, vol. ii. p. 425.

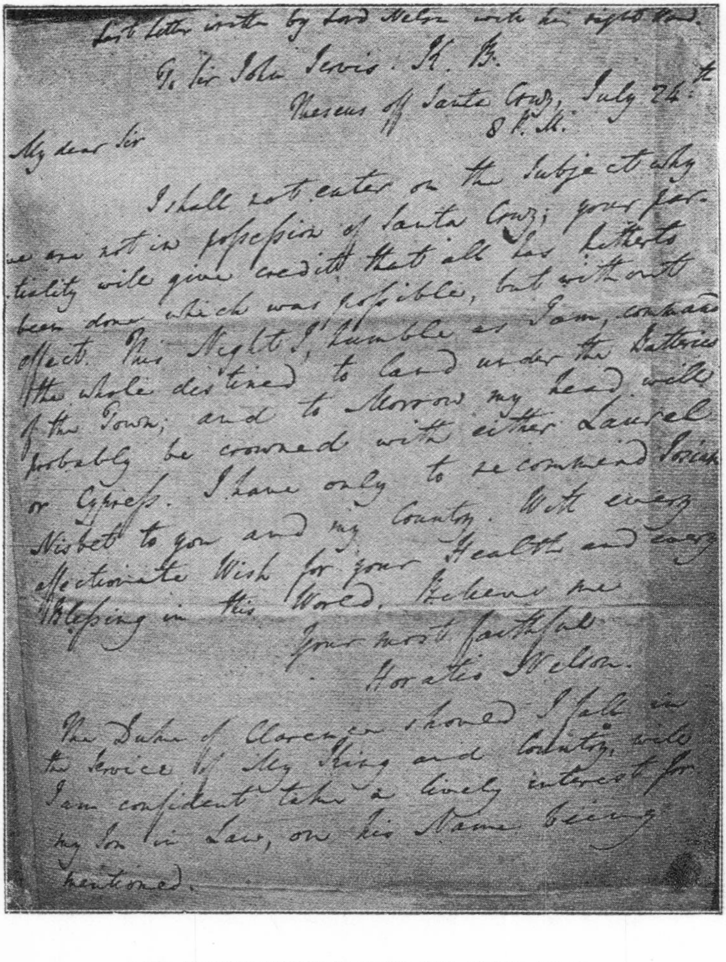
Last Letter wrote by Lord Nelson with his right hand.

To Sir John Jervis. K. B.

Theseus off Santa Cruz, July 24th
8 P. M.

My dear Sir

I shall not enter on the subject why we are not in possession of Santa Cruz; your partiality will give credit that all has hitherto been done which was possible, but without effect. This Night I, humble as I am, command the whole destined to land under the Batteries of the Town; and to Morrow my head will probably be crowned with either Laurel or Cypress. I have only to recommend Josiah Nisbet to you and my Country. With every affectionate Wish for your Health and every Blessing in this World, Believe me

Your most faithful
Horatio Nelson.

The Duke of Clarence should I fall in the service of my King and Country, will I am confident take a lively interest for my Son in Law, on his Name being mentioned.

LAST LETTER WRITTEN WITH HIS RIGHT HAND.

flying, to the Mole, where they embarked in such of our boats as were not stove, the Spaniards finding others to carry them to their ships. And here it is right that we should notice the generous and noble conduct of Don Juan Antonio Gutierres, the Spanish governor. The moment the terms were agreed to he directed our wounded men to be received into the hospitals, and all our people to be supplied with the best provisions that could be procured, and made it known that the ships were at liberty to send on shore and purchase whatever refreshments they were in want of during the time they might lie off the island " (Despatches, vol. ii. pp. 432–3).[1]

When foiled " in his first attempt on the 23rd, Nelson re-embarked his men, got the ships to anchor about two miles to the north of the town, and made a show as if it was intended to attack the heights." Before, however, preparing to renew the attack, he wrote to his chief the following letter, the last, probably, which he wrote with his right hand, of which I insert a facsimile :—

"I shall not enter on the subject why we are not in possession of Santa Cruz. Your partiality will give credit that all has hitherto been done which was possible, but without effect. This night I, humble as I am, command the whole destined to land under the batteries of the town, and to-morrow my head will probably be crowned with laurel or cyprus. I have only to recommend Josiah Nisbet to you and my country. The Duke of Clarence, should I fall, will, I am confident, take a lively interest for my son-in-law, on his name being mentioned."

It is related by Southey that :—

"Perfectly aware how desperate a service this was likely to prove, before he left the *Theseus* he called Lieutenant Nisbet, who had the watch on deck, into the cabin, that he might assist in arranging and burning his mother's letters. Perceiving that the young man was armed he earnestly begged him to remain behind. 'Should we both fall, Josiah,' said he, 'what would become of your poor mother? The care of the *Theseus* falls to you ; stay, therefore, and take charge

---

[1] The total loss was 44 killed (7 officers), 105 wounded (5 officers), 97 drowned, 5 missing=246.

of her.' Nisbet replied, 'Sir, the ship must take care of herself; I will go with you to-night, if I never go again.' . . . In act of stepping out of the boat Nelson received a shot through the right elbow and fell; but as he fell he caught the sword, which he had just drawn, in his left hand, determined never to part with it while he lived, for it had belonged to his uncle, Captain Suckling, and he valued it like a relic. Nisbet, who was close to him, placed him at the bottom of the boat, and laid his hat over the shattered arm, lest the sight of the blood, which gushed out in great abundance, should increase his faintness. He then examined the wound, and taking some silk handkerchiefs from his neck, bound them tightly over the lacerated vessels. One of his bargemen, Lovel, tore his shirt into shreds and made a sling with them for the broken limb. They then collected five other seamen, by whose assistance they succeeded at length in getting the boat afloat, for it had grounded with the falling tide. Nisbet took one of the oars, and ordered the steersman to go close under the guns of the battery, that they might be safe from the tremendous fire. Hearing his voice, Nelson roused himself and desired to be lifted up that he might look about him. Nisbet raised him up, but nothing could be seen except the firing of the guns on shore, and what could be discerned by their flashes upon the stormy sea. In a few minutes a general shriek was heard from the crew of the *Fox*, which had received a shot under water, and went down. Ninety-seven men were lost in her; eighty-three were saved, many by Nelson himself, whose exertions on this occasion greatly increased the pain and danger of his wound. The first ship which the boat could reach was the *Seahorse*, but nothing could induce him to go on board, though he was assured that if they attempted to row to another ship it might be at the risk of his life. 'I had rather suffer death,' he replied, 'than alarm Mrs. Fremantle by letting her see me in this state, when I can give her no tidings whatever of her husband.' They pushed on for the *Theseus*. When they came alongside he peremptorily refused all assistance in getting on board, so impatient was he that the boat should return in hopes that it might save a few more from the *Fox*. He desired to have only a single rope thrown over the side, which he twisted round his left hand, saying, 'Let me alone; I have yet my legs and one arm. Tell the surgeon to hasten and get his instruments. I know I must lose my right arm; so the sooner it is off the better.' The spirit he displayed in jumping up the ship's side astonished everybody." [1]

---

[1] Southey's "Life of Nelson," reprint Morley's edition (Routledge), 1886, p. 106 *et seq.*

Such was Nelson ever—no thought about himself—
every thought for others. In his despatch it will be
noticed he made no notice of his severe wound. How
severely he felt it, as in all probability removing him from
active service, was shown in his letter to Sir J. Jervis on
the 27th, the first written with his left hand, and that of
the 10th of August, as well as to his letter to his wife,
written at intervals from the 9th to the 16th of that
month, which are now quoted.[1]

" To Sir J. Jervis.

" Theseus, July 27, 1797.

" My dear Sir,—I am become a burthen to my friends, and useless
to my country ; but by my letter wrote on the 24th, you will perceive
my anxiety for the promotion of my son-in-law, Josiah Nisbet.
When I leave your command I become dead to the world ; I go hence,
and am no more seen. If from poor Bowen's loss you think proper to
oblige me, I rest confident you will do it : the boy is under obligations
to me, but he repaid me by bringing me from the Mole of Santa
Cruz. I hope you will be able to give me a frigate to convey the
remains of my carcase to England. God bless you, my dear Sir, and
believe me, &c.,

" Horatio Nelson.

" You will excuse this scrawl, considering it is my first attempt."

Again, August 10th :—

" My dear Sir,—I rejoice at being once more in sight of your flag,

---

[1] He afterwards allowed Andrew Webb, in 1805, a sergeant of the 15th
Foot, an annuity of £5 for his services on that occasion, and when passing through Salisbury in his progress after the Peace of Amiens, he
recognized, in the enthusiastic crowd, a man who had assisted at the
amputation of his arm ; he beckoned him out of the crowd, shook hands
with him, and made him a present in remembrance of his services on
that occasion, The man, it was said at the time, took from his bosom
a piece of lace, which he had torn from the sleeve of the amputated limb,
saying he had preserved it and would preserve it to the last moment
in memory of his old commander. The first of these notes is taken
from Archibald Duncan's " Life of Nelson," London, 1805, p. 52. The
other anecdote is well known.

and with your permission will come on board the *Ville de Paris*, and pay you my respects. If the *Emerald* has joined you know my wishes. A left-handed admiral will never again be considered useful ; therefore the sooner I get to my very humble cottage the better, to make room for a better man to serve the State ; but whatever be my lot, believe me, with the most sincere affection, ever your most faithful,

"H. N." [1]

" To Mrs. Nelson.

" *August* 9 (to 16), 1797.

" My dearest Fanny,—I am so confident of your affection that I feel the pleasure you will receive will be equal, whether my letter is wrote by my right hand or left. It was the chance of war, and I have great reason to be thankful ; and I know that it will add much to your pleasure in finding that Josiah, under God's providence, was principally instrumental in saving my life. As to my health, it never was better ; and now I hope soon to return to you ; and my country, I trust, will not allow me any longer to linger in want of that pecuniary assistance which I have been fighting all the war to preserve to her. But I shall not be surprised to be neglected and forgot, as probably I shall no longer be considered useful. However, I shall feel rich if I enjoy your affection. The cottage is now more necessary than ever. You will see by the papers Lieutenant Weatherhead is gone. Poor fellow, he lived four days after he was shot. I shall not close this letter till I join the fleet, which seems distant, for it's been calm these three days' past. I am fortunate in having a good surgeon on board ; in short, I am much more recovered than (I) could have expected. I beg neither you or my father will think much of this mishap, my mind has been long made up to such an event. God bless you, and believe me your affectionate husband,

" H. N.

" *August* 18th.

" Just joined the fleet perfectly well, and shall be with you perhaps as soon as this letter. Good Earl St. Vincent has made Josiah a master and commander. I shall come to Bath the moment permission comes from the Admiralty for me to strike my flag. Sir Peter feels himself authorized to give me leave of absence, when the first you hear of me will be at the door. God bless you and my father, and ever believe me," &c., &c.

Despatches, vol. ii. pp. 434-5.

On the 1st of Sept., Nelson arrived at Spithead in the *Seahorse*, and obtaining permission to go on shore for the recovery of his wounds joined his wife at Bath. There in the care of the local surgeons he remained for a short time, with scarcely any intermission of pain day or night, and then he removed to London for the better advice of the London surgeons. During three months of pain he thus remained, his wife having acquired sufficient resolution to dress his wound herself, until at last the ligature, formed according to the practice of French surgeons of silk instead of waxed thread, came away, and from that time the wound began to heal, and he had every prospect of being restored to health.

" One night," it is related, " that during this state of acute suffering, when Nelson was lodging in Bond Street, and had retired early to bed in the hope of getting some rest from laudanum, the love and respect felt for him was shown by the crowd who were calling on all persons to illuminate for Duncan's victory at Camperdown. When they were told that Nelson lay there in bed, the foremost of them replied, ' You shall hear no more of us to night.' The word was passed from crowd to crowd, and the house was not molested again."

It was during his residence at Bath that the following letters passed :—

" LADY NELSON TO HER UNCLE MR. SUCKLING.

" BATH, *Sept.* 6, 1797.

" MY DEAR SIR,—I beg you will accept the united thanks of my dear husband and myself for your kind inquiries, and truly friendly invitation to your house, which we would have accepted had it not been for the necessity of my husband's arm being dressed every day by a surgeon. We propose being in London the middle of next week. I have written to Mr. M. Nelson to take us a lodging, and as soon as my husband can do without a surgeon, we will spend some time with you. Earl Spencer has written a handsome letter, and is to be in town next week. My husband's spirits are very good, although he suffers a great deal of pain—the arm taken off very high, near the shoulder. Opium procures him rest, and last night he was pretty quiet. The Corporation have handsomely congratulated him on his safe arrival. Such a letter from Lord Hood—it does him honour, and I have forgotten the ill-treatment of former years my good man received from him. Everything which concerns my husband I know you feel interested in, therefore shall not make any excuse for what I have told you." [1]

From the Duke of Clarence :—

" To Sir Horatio Nelson, K.B.

" Dover, *Sept.* 7, 1797.

" Dear Sir,—I congratulate you with all my heart upon your safe arrival at last, covered with honours and glory. As an old friend, I cannot but lament the severe loss you have sustained in losing your right arm. I hope your health is good, and that you are gone, as I am informed, more for the purpose of joining Lady Nelson than for the re-establishment of a constitution in which I am doubly interested, both as a friend and as one who is anxious to see the country have restored to her a brave and excellent officer. Excuse my anxiety, as it proceeds from friendship and admiration of your public character, and I must request you will allow Lady Nelson to write to me how you are, and when you will be able to be in London, that I may be the first to shake you by the hand. My best wishes and compliments attend you and Lady Nelson, and ever believe me, Dear Sir, yours sincerely,

" William." [2]

Nelson's reply, Sept. 7, 1797 :—

" Sir,—I trust your Royal Highness will attribute my not having sent a letter since my arrival to its true cause—viz., the not being now a ready writer. I feel confident of your sorrow for my accident ; but I assure your Royal Highness, that not a scrap of that ardour with which I have served our King has been shot away.

" I am, &c.,

"Horatio Nelson." [3]

---

[1] *Athenæum*, Despatches, vol. ii. p. 440, note.
[2] Auto. Nelson Papers ; Despatches, vol. ii. p. 441.
[3] Clarke and McArthur, vol. ii. p. 45 ; Despatches, vol. ii. p. 441.

"To Sir A. S. Hamond.

"*Sept.* 8, 1797.

"Success covers a multitude of blunders, and the want of it hides the greatest gallantry and good conduct. You will see by my journal the first attack on the 21st under Troubridge completely failed; and it was the 25th before it could be again attacked which gave four days for collecting a force to oppose us. Had I been with the first party, I have reason to believe complete success would have crowned our endeavours. My pride suffered; and I felt the second attack was a forlorn hope, yet the honour of our country called for the attack, and that I should command it. I never expected to return, and am thankful. I shall not go to town till the 20th, or my arm is well; I suffer a good deal of pain owing to a cold falling on it." [1]

In order to qualify himself for the pension of nominally a £1,000, which it was now proposed to confer on him, Nelson had to send a memorial to his sovereign in which his numerous services were set out :—

"To the King's Most Excellent Majesty, the memorial of Sir Horatio Nelson, K.B., and Rear Admiral in your Majesty's Fleet—humbly sheweth—

"That during the present war, your memorialist has been in four actions with the fleets of the enemy; viz., on the 13th and 14th of March, 1795, on the 13th of July, and on the 14th of February, 1797 ; in three actions with frigates ; in six engagements against batteries ; in ten actions in boats in cutting out of harbours, in destroying vessels, and in taking three towns. Your memorialist has also served on shore with the army four months, and commanded the batteries at the sieges of Bastia and Calvi.

"That during the war he has assisted at the capture of seven sail-of-the-line, six frigates, four corvettes, and eleven privateers of different sizes, and destroyed near fifty sail of merchant vessels ; and your memorialist has actually been engaged against the enemy upwards of one hundred and fifty times.

"In which service your memorialist has lost his right eye and arm, and been severely wounded and bruised in his body. All which

---

[1] Quoted as printed in Professor Laughton's "Nelson's Letters and Despatches," p. 130.

services and wounds your memorialist most humbly submits to your Majesty's most gracious consideration."

To Lord St. Vincent he wrote on this subject on the 6th of October :—

"Lord Spencer says my pension will be the same as those for the 1st of June, £712, with the deductions. My poor arm continues quite as it was, the ligature still fast to the nerve, and very painful at times. The moment I am cured I shall offer myself for service ; and if you continue to hold your opinion of me, shall press to return with all the zeal, although not with the personal ability I had formerly."[1]

It, perhaps, may be remembered how Wellington after all his great victories failed to obtain a living, from the Chancellor of his day, for the army-chaplain who had served with his army throughout the Peninsular Campaign. The following letters show how Nelson fared with Lord Loughborough, the then Chancellor, in his application for his brother :—

"To THE RT. HONBLE. THE LORD CHANCELLOR.

"141, BOND STREET, *Oct.* 12, 1797.

"MY LORD,—In addressing a letter to you some persons may think me wrong, and I ought to have the interference of a friend; but feeling a conviction that if what I ask is proper for you to grant that I require, on the present occasion, no interest but your own opinion of my endeavours to serve the State. I, therefore, enclose my request [to give his youngest brother one of the livings held by his father, on his resignation of it], which, if your lordship has the goodness to comply with, will be a small provision for the youngest son of my venerable father, and a resting obligation conferred upon

"Your obedient servant,

"HORATIO NELSON."

Lord Loughborough's reply :—

"SIR,—You have judged perfectly right in the mode of application to me. Any interference would have much diminished the satis-

---

[1] Laughton, pp. 130–131.

faction I feel in acknowledging the perfect propriety of your request, and the just title your great services have gained to every mark of attention which, in the exercise of a public duty, it is in my power to express.

"Yours,

"LOUGHBOROUGH." [1]

As soon as he felt that his health was re-established, Nelson sent the following request to the minister of the parish church :—

"An officer desires to return thanks to Almighty God for his perfect recovery from a severe wound, and also for the many mercies bestowed upon him.

"*December* 8, 1797.   (For next Sunday)." [2]

"Not having been in England till now since he lost his eye," says Southey, "he went to receive a year's pay as smart money, but could not obtain payment because he had neglected to bring a certificate from a surgeon that the sight was actually destroyed. A little irritated that this form should be insisted on, because, though the fact was not apparent, he thought it was sufficiently notorious, he procured a certificate at the same time for the loss of his arm, saying they might as well doubt one as the other. This put him in good humour with himself, and with the clerk who had offended him. On his return to the office, the clerk finding it was only the annual pay of a captain observed he thought it had been more. 'Oh,' replied Nelson, 'this is only for an eye. In a few days I shall come for an arm, and in a little longer, God knows, most probably for a leg.' Accordingly, he soon afterwards went, and with perfect good humour exhibited the certificate for the loss of his arm." [3]

Before the close of the year he received the following characteristic letter from his venerable father :—

"BATH, *Dec.*, 1797.

"MY DEAR HORATIO,—I cannot sufficiently extol the praises of that all good and gracious Providence which has been your protector from

---

[1] Nelson Papers ; Despatches, vol. ii. p. 450, note.

[2] Fac-simile in possession of the family of Rev. Greville, then minister of St. George's, Hanover Square (Despatches, vol. ii. p. 455). Now in that of Sir W. A. Fraser, Bart.

[3] Southey's "Life of Nelson," p. 112.

such innumerable perils.   Your peculiar preservation Providence
has ordained, for great and wise purposes.   He evidently gives His
Angels charge concerning thee.   I have lived long and seen many
days, in the small sphere that it has been my lot to move, and I
regard you, my good son, as a rare instance of personal merit
rewarded with self-earned laurels.   You once stood alone ; and had
you fallen no hand was near to raise you.   May I, O God ! have
regarded that blessing as properly as from frail man could be
expected.   I ought to have addressed a letter to my good Lady
Nelson, but I rely on her kindness in excusing the indolence of an
old, infirm father ; she knows she may depend on me in all places
and all seasons, to act with affectionate kindness to her and you.

" EDMUND NELSON." [1]

Remarking on the memorial to the King, just quoted,
his gallant French biographer truly says, " In these
various engagements he had lost his right eye and arm ;
but his country, to borrow the words of George III., *had
still something to expect from him.*   Nelson, in fact,
burned with the desire of avenging the defeat at
Teneriffe.   He had impatiently endured his long absence
from the theatre of the war, and would long since have
joined the fleet off Cadiz, if the Admiralty had not
retained him to command the reinforcements that were
to be sent to Admiral Jervis." [2]

His offer of renewed service was gladly accepted by

---

[1] Clarke and McArthur, vol. ii. p. 68.   I take this opportunity of
expressing my regret that *Mr. Clarke Russell* has thought fit to make
the following remarks on these letters of Nelson's venerable father to his
son during his dangerous career.   " He " (his father) " was a man of a
heavy cast of piety, ponderous in opinion and sentiment, constantly
pursuing his son with unnecessary admonitions, and taxing the gravity
of posterity by a style of correspondence curiously in keeping with the
well-like pews, the Georgian wigs, and the drowsing, insipid, hour-
and-a-half sermons of the days of Porteous and Hurd " (p. 2).   Such
reflections and admonitions are no doubt little to the taste of some men
of the present day.   These letters truly represent the religious opinion
of their date, and were ever welcome to his illustrious son.   I only regret
that more of them have not been preserved.

[2] De la Gravière.   Plunkett, vol. i. p. 195.

the Admiralty ; there was apparently no other delay than that of waiting for the new ship—the *Foudroyant*—expected to be launched in the January of the next year, and commissioned in the February ; and that event was after all not to be waited for.   In writing to Captain Berry on the 8th of December, whose marriage was expected, Nelson said, " If you mean to marry, I would recommend your doing it speedily, or the to-be Mrs. Berry will have very little of your company ; for I am well, and you may expect to be called for every hour. We shall probably be at sea before the *Foudroyant* is launched.   Our ship is at Chatham, a seventy-four, and she will be choicely manned.   This may not happen, but it stands so to-day." [1]   Still the year found him at home, when it closed.

[1] Laughton, p. 131.

THE BATTLE OF THE NILE.

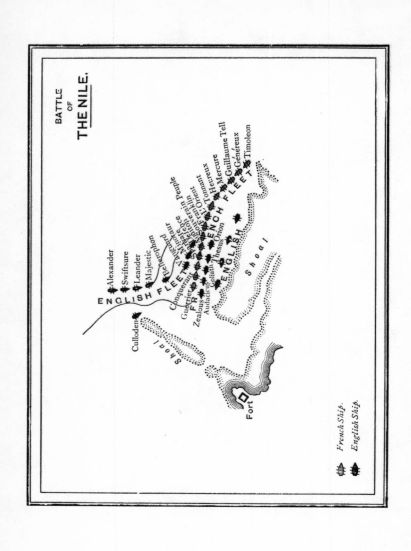

BATTLE
OF
THE NILE.

French Ship.
English Ship.

CHAPTER X.

THE BATTLE OF THE NILE.

(1798.)

Autobiography—The French expedition to Egypt—Secret instructions to Lord St. Vincent—Nelson's appointment to the detached squadron —The *Vanguard* dismasted in the storm—His letter to his wife— Conduct of the government of Sardinia—The chase up and down the Mediterranean after Buonaparte—The watering at Syracuse— The Queen of Naples and Lady Hamilton—Nelson's instructions to his captains during the chase—The Battle of the Nile—Incidents in the battle—The *Minotaur* and *L'Aquilon*—The burning of *L'Orient* —The wrecks of the French fleet in the bay—St. Vincent's energy in repairing the English ships.

N his Autobiography Nelson gives the following very brief record of his services in this eventful year :—

"On the 19th of December, 1797, the *Vanguard* was commissioned for my flag-ship. On the 1st of April, 1798, I sailed with a convoy from Spithead ; at the back of the (Isle of) Wight, the wind coming to the westward, I was obliged to put back to St. Helen's, and finally sailed on the 9th of April, carrying a convoy to Oporto and Cadiz. I joined Earl St. Vincent off Cadiz on April 29th ; on the 30th I was ordered to the Mediterranean. I refer to the printed Narrative of my proceedings to the close of the Battle of the Nile."

At the moment when Nelson joined the fleet of Lord St. Vincent off Cadiz, the British Consul at Leghorn informed that Admiral that the French Government had already assembled near four hundred sail in the ports of

Provence and Italy ; and that this fleet, under the escort
of the ships which were being fitted out with the utmost
haste, could readily convey forty thousand soldiers to Sicily
or Malta, perhaps even to Egypt. " For my own part,"
added the Consul, " I do not look upon the latter destination as improbable. The late Empress of Russia, Catherine
II., had conceived a similar project ; and if the French have
the intention, on landing in Egypt, of joining Tippoo
Saib to overthrow the English powers in India, it will not
be the risk of losing half their army in the desert that
will deter them." [1]   Such was the first rumour of the expedition of Buonaparte for the conquest of Egypt, and
consequently the possession of the shortest highway to
India.

On the receipt of this warning, Lord St. Vincent at
once, on the 2nd of May, despatched Nelson with the
Vanguard, Orion, and *Alexander*, line-of-battle ships, and
four frigates, and a corvette to cruise along the coasts of
Provence and the Gulf of Genoa, to discover if possible
the real destination of this formidable expedition.

On May 19th, the day on which Nelson sailed, Lord St.
Vincent received secret orders to detach a squadron of
twelve sail-of-the-line and frigates under some discreet
officer to proceed in quest of the armament that had sailed
from Toulon, to keep at sea as long as their provisions
would last or they could get fresh supplies from friendly
ports, and these failing to rejoin his fleet.   In a private
letter of same date, Lord Spencer wrote, " If you determine
to send a detachment, I think it almost unnecessary to
suggest to you the propriety of putting it under the
command of Sir H. Nelson, whose acquaintance with that
part of the world, as well as his activity and disposition,
seem to qualify him in a peculiar manner for that service."

[1] De la Gravière, vol. i. p. 187.

His seniors in the fleet did their worst to prevent his appointment. Hence, on June 22nd, Lord St. Vincent writes to Nelson :—

" Sir W. Parker and Sir John Orde (who were senior to Nelson) have written strong remonstrances against your commanding a detached squadron instead of them. I did all I could to prevent it consistently with my situation, but there is a faction fraught with all manner of ill to you, that unfortunately for the two Baronets domin'd over any argument or influence I could use. They will both be sent home the moment their letters arrive."

" The Duke of Clarence," says Sir Edward Berry, in a letter to Lord Nelson, dated London, Dec. 30, 1798—

" desired I would tell you from him that it was the *King that sent you* with the squadron up the Mediterranean, and formed the whole plan. *I believe it seriously.*" [1]

Before the information of his appointment to this command could reach Nelson, who was cruizing off the coast of Provence, Buonaparte with the French Fleet had sailed from Toulon on the 20th of May, as Nelson's little squadron had been put in imminent peril by a gale from the north-east, that drove it from the coast, almost entirely dismasted his own ship, separated him from his frigates, and severely injured the rest of his squadron. With what resignation he bore this serious disappointment we learn from the following letter to his wife :—

" *Vanguard*, ISLAND OF ST. PETER'S, SARDINIA, *May* 24, 1798.

" MY DEAREST FANNY,—I ought not to call what has happened to the *Vanguard* by the cold name of accident : I believe firmly, that it was the Almighty's goodness, to check my consummate vanity. I hope it has made me a better officer, as I feel confident it has made me a better man. I kiss with all humility the Rod.

---

[1] It is stated in Tucker's "St. Vincent" (vol. i. p. 349), that Sir Gilbert Elliot called on Lord Spencer, and advised the appointment of Nelson, and that Lord Spencer said that there was no chance of any other person being thought of. (Letters from Lord Minto to Nelson, April 25, 1798.)

" Figure to yourself a vain man, on Sunday evening at sunset, walking in his cabin with his squadron around him, who looked up to their chief to lead them to glory, and in whom the chief placed the firmest reliance, that the proudest ships, in equal numbers belonging to France, would have lowered their flags ; and a very rich prize lying by him.   Figure to yourself this proud, conceited man, when the sun rose on Monday morning, his ship dismasted, his fleet dispersed, and himself in such distress, that the meanest frigate out of France would have been a very unwelcome guest.   But it has pleased Almighty God to bring us into a safe port, where although we are refused the rights of humanity, yet the *Vanguard* will in two days get to sea again, as an English man-of-war.

" The exertions of Sir James Saumerez, in the *Orion*, and Captain A. Ball in the *Alexander*, have been wonderful ; if the ship had been in England, months would have been taken to send her to sea ; here my operations will not be delayed four days, and I shall join the rest of my fleet on the rendezvous.

" If this letter gets to you, be so good as to write a line to Lord Spencer, telling him the *Vanguard* is fitted tolerably for sea, and that what has happened will not retard my operations.   We are all in health and good humour ; tell Lady Saumerez, Sir James never was in better health.   With kind love to my father, believe me ever your affectionate husband,

" Horatio Nelson." [1]

" To His Excellency the Viceroy of Sardinia.

" His Britannic Majesty's ship *Vanguard*.   At
anchor off the Island of St. Peter's,
" *May* 26, 1798.

" Sir,—Having by a gale of wind sustained some trifling damage, I anchored a small part of his Majesty's Fleet, under my orders, off this island, and was surprised to hear, by an officer sent by the gover-

---

[1] Despatches, vol. iii. p. 17 ; from copy in possession of Mr. Conway, and another copy in Nelson Papers.—Captain Berry, in his letter to his wife, writes, " In four days the *Vanguard* was again cruizing after the enemy on their own coast ! with a maintopmast for a foremast, and a topgallant mast for a topmast ; consequently everything else reduced in proportion.   By our superiority of sailing with other ships, we find the loss trifling to what it would have been to the generality of ships.   With such perseverance you will say we deserve success " (Despatches, vol. iii. p. 19, note).

nor, that admittance was to be refused to the flag of his Britannic Majesty into this port. When I reflect that my most gracious sovereign is the oldest (I believe), and certainly the most faithful Ally which his Majesty of Sardinia ever had, I could feel the sorrow which it must been to his Majesty to have given such an order, and also for your Excellency, who has to direct its execution. I cannot but look at Afric's shore, where the followers of Mahomet are performing the part of the good Samaritan, which I look for in vain at St. Peter's, where it is said the Christian religion is professed. May I request the favour of your Excellency to forward one letter for his Britannic Majesty's Minister at Turin, and the other for his Britannic Majesty's Consul at Leghorn. May God Almighty bless your Excellency, is the sincere wish of your most obedient servant,

" Horatio Nelson." [1]

Five days later he wrote to Earl St. Vincent, May 31, 1798 :—

" My dear Lord,—My pride was too great for man ; but I trust my friends will think I bore the chastisement like a man. It has pleased God to assist us with his favour, and here I am again off Toulon,

" I am, &c.,
" H. N." [2]

On the morning of the day when Nelson's squadron had been driven out to sea, Buonaparte, with a fleet of seventy-two ships of war sailed from the roads of Toulon, hove off Genoa, passed the extremity of Corsica at the time when Nelson was anchored in the Bay of San Pietro, coasted Sardinia, on the 9th of June made the Maltese islands, and within three days reduced the old home of the Knights of St. John of Jerusalem to the French Republic. Rapidly refitting his flag-ship with makeshift

---

[1] Despatches, vol. iii. p. 21.

[2] Clarke and McArthur, vol. ii. p. 90 ; Despatches, vol. ii. p. 23. Ever thoughtful for those who did good service, he made a special recommendation of Morrison, the carpenter of the *Alexander*, for his work in refitting the *Vanguard*.

masts, on the 31st of May, Nelson sailed from San
Pietro, and soon found himself off Toulon.   There he
learnt the departure of the expedition, but was unable to
procure any information of its destination.   He returned,
therefore, off Corsica, seriously weakened by the absence
of his frigates, that ought to have awaited him at the
appointed rendezvous.   Captain Hope, the senior in
command, however, having seen the *Vanguard* dismasted,
and persuaded himself that she would steer for some
English port, gave up the rendezvous and went to seek
him elsewhere.   "I thought," said Nelson, when he
heard the reason, "that Captain Hope knew his admiral
better."   On the 5th of June the *Mutine* brig brought
the news of the coming of the reinforcement, and next
day Troubridge brought up the eleven ships that were
to form the squadron of the victors of the Nile.

"Then," writes his French biographer, "began the chase, indefati-
gably carried on for nearly two months, in search of the French Expedition.   The secret of the expedition had been well kept, and except
the hint conveyed in the Consul's letter to Lord St. Vincent, there
was no hint of Egypt being its destination.   Naples, Sicily, the Morea,
Portugal, and even Ireland had been thought of, and Egypt was the
only destination mentioned in the instructions from the Admiralty.
Amidst so many different suppositions," continues his French biographer,
"Nelson could only rely upon his own judgment ; and it must be
admitted that in tracking the French squadron, he showed from the first
as much sagacity as activity.   The day on which Malta capitulated,
he doubled the southern extremity of Corsica, and sent to reconnoitre
the great bay of Telamon, opposite the Isle of Elba, a point which he
had long considered well adapted for a landing in Italy.   The Bay
of Telamon was empty, the French had not been seen there.   Con-
tinuing his route along the coast of Tuscany, Nelson, on the 17th of
June, presented himself in the Bay of Naples, and there learnt that
the French Fleet had gone to Malta.   Burning with impatience, he
passed the Faro of Messina, on the 20th of June, steered for Malta,
which island the French Fleet had left two days before, after taking
possession of it.   From the report of a Ragusan ship that had passed

through the convoy, he learnt that the French leaving Malta with a
north-west wind, had been seen to the eastward of that island running before the wind. Combining this news with some more certain
particulars from Sir William Hamilton, he no longer doubted that
Egypt was the destination of Boney's fleet. Always prompt in his
decisions, he carried a press of sail, and without seeking further intelligence, steered directly for Alexandria. On the 28th of June he was
off that town ; but no French ship had been seen there ; and Nelson
himself carried the first news of the danger which threatened Egypt.
At the sight of the empty harbour, Nelson's vexation was extreme ;
he lost all confidence in the reasons which had allured him so far
from Sicily ; and imagining that island already invaded by a French
army, he determined to retrace his steps without anchoring, or taking
a moment's rest. His activity served him ill this time, because if he
had waited a single day, he would have seen our fleet come to him.
In order to return to Sicily, it was necessary to beat against the contrary winds, which always prevail at that season, and while he set off
towards the coast of Caramania in his first tack, beyond the track of
our squadron, the latter, delayed in its voyage by the immense convoy
which accompanied it, found, in consequence of this fortunate hind-
rance, the roads of Alexandria without defence, and effected the landing of the troops on the deserted beach of Marabout." [1]

From this devious and disheartening chase, Nelson returned to Sicilian waters, in need of a fresh supply of
water before he could renew it. To ensure this, it was
absolutely necessary that he should take his fleet into the
port of Syracuse, from which he was, by the treaty that
had been made between France and Naples, debarred from
entering with more than a few ships at a time. Lying off
Syracuse, we are told by the biographer who drew his
information from Lady Hamilton, he sent Troubridge as
his envoy to Naples to obtain a remission of this clause,
which, according to this writer's statement, Lady Hamilton persuaded, or rather almost forced, the Queen to issue
before it was too late. Of the truth of this romantic
story I entertain the same doubts as Professor Laughton.
If Lady Hamilton is to be believed, she extracted from

[1] Jurien de la Gravière, vol. i. p. 206–8.

the Queen a letter, commanding the Governor at Syracuse on her own authority, to admit Nelson's fleet to victual and water, in despite of the existing treaty between Naples and France. To this, we are told, on the authority of a *fac-simile* of the following reply in Nelson's handwriting of the date of July 22, 1798 :—

"My dear Friends,—Thanks to your exertions, we have victualled and watered ; and surely, watering at the Fountain of Arethusa, we must have victory. We shall sail by the first breeze, and be assured I will return either crowned with laurels or covered with cypress."

Besides this letter being in direct contradiction to one from Nelson of the same date to Sir William Hamilton, in which he expresses his astonishment at his exclusion from the Syracusian ports, and his expectation that private orders were to have been given for his free admission, of Troubridge's Mission to Naples to get such a letter, "history," as Mr. Jeffreson pointedly says, "has no cognizance." From the following letter in the second volume of the "Private Correspondence" at Cricket, it would seem that Troubridge left Naples on the 17th of the previous month, and no trace of his return is found in Miss Knight's very full journal of the events at Naples during that period :—

"*June* 17, 1798.

"My dear Admiral,—I wrote in a hurry as Capt. T. cannot stay a moment. God bless you and send you victorious. See you bring back Buonaparte with you. Pray send Capt. Hardy out to us, for I shall have a fever with anxiety. The Queen desires to say everything that is kind, and bids me say with her whole heart and soul she wishes you victory. God bless you, my dear sir ; I will not say how glad I shall be to see you, indeed, I cannot describe to you my feeling in your being so near us.

"Ever, dear sir,

"Your obliged and faithful

"Emma Hamilton."

In her journal Miss Knight speaks of the anxiety they were in at Naples to hear of their success, " as we knew that they had touched at Syracuse, and we hoped that they might follow the directions they would probably receive there, for the Sicilians, an acute people and sworn enemies of the French, were the most likely to obtain correct information as to the movements of the latter " (vol. i. 108, 109), referring evidently to information as to the course taken by the French, but not to any private orders for an infraction of the treaty. The next entry in the journal is of the arrival of the *Mutine* with Captain Capel and the despatches ; and the only reference made by Nelson is in the letter of October, 1798, " I have experienced the ability and activity of Troubridge's mind and body ; it was Troubridge that equipped the squadron so soon at Syracuse—it was Troubridge whom I left as myself at Naples to watch movements." These duties evidently refer to the part played by Troubridge at Naples after the Battle of the Nile. It is to be regretted that no diary or letters of Troubridge now exist recording his part in the momentous events immediately preceding the Battle of the Nile.[1]

Still, that some private order was sent is very probable, and I presume is referred to in the following letter, without place or date, written at the foot of the same page in the " Private Correspondence " at Cricket St. Thomas, as the one of June 17th just cited :—

" DEAR SIR,—I send you a letter I have received this moment from the Queen. *Kiss* it, and send it to me back by (name illegible, but looks like Bowen), as I am bound not to give any of her letters.

" EMMA."

---

[1] Letter from Mrs. Herbert Jones, May 22, 1889, referring me to these extracts, and to the absence of such a diary, &c., and adding : " It is certain that Troubridge felt gratitude to Lady H. (*vide* his letter to her October, 1798), but I fail to find any definite confirmation of handing him the secret order."

This is all the evidence bearing on this disputed point that has as yet been discovered, and it fails to make me believe in the authenticity of the "Fountain of Arethusa" letter.

It will be sufficient now to note that he obtained the indispensable supply, and started again in pursuit of the enemy. It must, however, be borne in mind that by his original instructions from Lord St. Vincent, dated May 21st, he was ordered " to consider and treat as hostile ports within the Mediterranean (those of Sardinia excepted) when provisions, or other articles you may be in want of, and which they may be enabled to furnish, shall be refused." And, again, in the additional instructions of the same date, he is informed " that the Lords expect that he will receive a favourable neutrality from Tuscany and the Two Sicilies," and that, " in any event, you are to extract whatever you want from the territories of the Duke of Tuscany, *the King of the Two Sicilies*, the Ottoman Empire, Malta, and the *ci-devant* Venetian dominions now belonging to the Emperor of Germany." It is clear, therefore, that his demand of water at Syracuse could not be resisted, and could be pleaded by the authorities as a compulsory, and not a culpable, evasion of the treaty. Still, it may be that Nelson, in his care for the Neapolitan crown, would prefer a permission to exacting it by force, and that the Queen of Naples from her known feelings of hatred to the French would have been glad to obtain it for the English Fleet. Anyhow, the necessary supply was obtained, and the chase was renewed.

Whilst apparently he was hesitating whether to compel the authorities of Syracuse to give him the necessary supply, or waiting for some permission from the Neapolitan Court, Nelson wrote the following brief letter to his wife :—

"To Lady Nelson.

"Syracuse, *July* 20, 1798.

"I have not been able to find the French Fleet, to my great mortification, or the event I scarcely doubt. We have been off Malta, to
Alexandria in Egypt, Syria, into Asia, and are returned without
success. However, no person will say that has been for want of
activity. I yet live in hopes of meeting these fellows ; but it would
have been my delight to have tried Buonaparte on a wind, for he
commands the fleet as well as the army. Glory is my object, and
that alone. God Almighty bless you.

"Horatio Nelson."

The long and weary days of the chase were not thrown
away by Nelson ; as Sir Edward Berry relates, he never
lost an opportunity of consulting with his captains on the
operations that might be found advisable, and prepared a
plan suitable to varied circumstances in friendly consultation with his " Band of Brothers."

"The admiral," writes Captain Berry in his narrative, "had, and
it appeared most justly, the highest opinion of, and placed the firmest
reliance on, the valour and conduct of every captain in his squadron.
It had been his practice during the whole of his cruise, whenever the
weather and circumstances would permit, to have his captains on
board the *Vanguard*, where he would fully develop to them his own
ideas of the different and best modes of attack, and such plans as he
proposed to execute upon falling in with the enemy, whatever their
situation or position might be, by day or by night. There was no
possible position in which they could be found that he did not take
into his calculation, and for the most advantageous attack of which
he had digested and arranged the best possible disposition of the force
which he commanded. With the masterly ideas of their admiral,
therefore, on the subject of naval tactics, every one of the captains
of his squadron was most thoroughly acquainted ; and on surveying
the situation of the enemy, they could ascertain with precision what
were the ideas and intentions of their commander, without the aid
of any further instructions ; by which means signals became almost
unnecessary. Much time was saved, and the attention of every captain could almost undistractedly be paid to the conduct of his own

particular ship, a circumstance from which, upon this occasion, the
advantages to the general service were almost incalculable.

" It cannot here be thought irrelevant to give some idea of what
were the plans which Admiral Nelson had formed, and which he
explained to his captains with such perspicuity as to render his ideas
completely their own. To the naval service, at least, they must
prove not only interesting, but useful. Had he fallen in with the French
Fleet at sea, that he might make the best impression upon any part of
it that should appear to be the most vulnerable, or the most eligible
for attack, he divided his force into three sub-squadrons, viz. :—

Vanguard	*Orion*	*Culloden*
Minotaur	*Goliath*	*Theseus*
Leander	*Majestic*	*Alexander*
Audacious	*Bellerophon*	*Swiftsure*
Defence		
Zealous		

" Two of these sub-squadrons were to attack the ships of war,
while the third was to pursue the transports, and to sink and destroy
as many as it could.

" The destination of the French armament was involved no doubt
in uncertainty ; but it forcibly struck the admiral, that, as it was
commanded by the man whom the French had dignified with the title
of the Conqueror of Italy, and as he had with him a very large body
of troops, an expedition had been planned which the land force might
execute without the aid of their fleet, should the transports be permitted to make their escape, and reach in safety their place of rendezvous. It therefore became a material consideration with the admiral
so to arrange his force as at once to engage the whole attention of their
ships of war, and at the same time materially to annoy and injure
their convoy. It will be fully admitted, from the subsequent information which had been received on the subject, that the ideas of the
admiral upon this occasion were perfectly just, and that the plan
which he had arranged was the most likely to frustrate the design of
the enemy.

" It is almost unnecessary to explain his projected mode of attack
at anchor, as that was minutely and precisely executed in the action
which we now come to describe. These plans, however, were formed
two months before an opportunity presented itself of executing any of
them, and the advantage now was that they were familiar to the
understanding of every captain in the fleet." [1]

---

[1] Despatches, vol. iii. p. 48 note. " Authentic Narrative of the Proceedings of his Majesty's Squadron under the Command of Rear-Admiral

Captain Berry's narrative continued :—

" We saw the Pharos of Alexandria at noon on the 1st of August. The *Alexander* and *Swiftsure* had been detached ahead on the preceding evening to reconnoitre the ports of Alexandria, while the body of the squadron kept in the offing. The enemy's fleet was first discovered by the *Zealous*, Captain Hood, who immediately communicated by signal, the number of ships, sixteen, lying at anchor in line-of-battle in a bay on the larboard bow, which was afterwards discovered to be Aboukir Bay. The admiral hauled his wind that instant, a movement which was immediately observed and followed by the whole squadron, and at the same time he recalled the *Alexander* and the *Swiftsure*. The wind was at this time N.N.W., and blew what seamen call a top-gallant breeze. The admiral made signal to prepare for battle, as it was his intention to attack the enemy's van and centre, as they lay at anchor, and according to the plan before developed. His idea, in this disposition of his force, was, first to secure the victory, and then make the most of it according to circumstances. A bower cable of each ship was immediately got abaft, and bent forward. We continued carrying sail and standing in for the enemy's fleet in a close line of battle. As all the officers of our squadron were totally unacquainted with Aboukir Bay, each ship kept sounding as she stood in. The enemy appeared to be moored in a strong and compact line of battle, close in with the shore, their line describing an obtuse angle in its form, flanked by numerous gunboats, four frigates, and a battery of guns and mortars, on an island in their van. This situation of the enemy seemed to secure to them decided advantages, as they had nothing to attend to but their artillery, in the superior skill in the use of which the French so much pride themselves, and to which their splendid series of land victories are in a great measure to be imputed.

" The position of the enemy presented the most formidable obstacles; but the admiral viewed these with the eye of a seamen determined on attack, and it instantly struck his eager and penetrating mind, *that where there was room for an enemy's ship to swing, there was room for one of ours to anchor*. No further signal was necessary than those which had already been made. The admiral's designs were as fully known to his whole squadron as was his determination to

---

Sir Horatio Nelson, from its sailing from Gibraltar to the Conclusion of the Battle of the Nile," 3rd edit., 1798; first published in the *True Briton* and *Sun* newspapers.

conquer or perish in the attempt. The *Goliath* and *Zealous* [1] had the honour to lead inside, and to receive the first fire from the van ships of the enemy, as well as from the batteries and gun-boats with which their van was strengthened. These two ships with the *Orion*, *Audacious*, and *Theseus*, took their station inside the enemy's line and were immediately in close action. The *Vanguard* anchored the first on the outer side of the enemy, and was opposed within half-pistol shot by *Le Spartiate*, the third in the enemy's line. In standing in our leading ships were unavoidably obliged to receive into their bows the whole fire of the broadsides of the French line, until they could take their respective stations : and it is but justice to observe, that the enemy received us with great firmness and deliberation, no colours having been hoisted on either side till our van-ships were within half-gun shot. At this time the necessary number of our men were employed aloft furling sails, and on deck in hauling the braces, &c., preparatory to our casting anchor. As soon as this took place, a most animated fire was opened from the *Vanguard,* which ship covered the approach of those in the rear. The *Minotaur, Defence, Bellerophon, Majestic, Swiftsure,* and *Alexander,* came up in succession, and, passing within hail of the *Vanguard,* took their respective stations opposed to the enemy's line. All our ships anchored by the stern, by which the British line was inverted from van to rear. Captain Thompson of the *Leander,* 50 guns, with a degree of skill and intrepidity highly honourable to his professional character, advanced towards the enemy's line on the outside, and most judiciously dropped his anchor athwart hawse of *Le Franklin,* raking her with great success; the shot from the *Leander's* broadside which passed that ship all striking *L'Orient,* the flag-ship of the French commander-in-chief."

Captain Berry then describes how the action commenced about half-past six and that by seven total darkness came on, our ships all hoisting signal lights by the admiral's signal—how in twelve minutes the van-

[1] Previous to the attack on the French line, the admiral hailed Captain Hood of the *Zealous*, to inquire if he thought there was sufficient depth of water for our ships between the enemy and the shore ? Captain Hood said " he did not know, but with the admiral's permission he would lead in and try. The *Goliath*, however, being the fastest sailer, and having the start, first gained the post of honour. (Duncan's " Nelson" p. 99, note.)

ship, *Le Guerrier* surrendered, the *Conquerant* and *Le Spartiate* within ten minutes after, and *L'Aquilon* and *Le Peuple Souverain* were taken possession of by half-past eight.   "Captain Berry," he then continues :—

"At that hour, sent Lieutenant Galway, of the *Vanguard*, with a party of marines to take possession of *Le Spartiate*, who returned with the French captain's sword, which the captain immediately delivered to the admiral who was then below in consequence of the severe wound which he had received in the head during the heat of the attack.   At this moment, it appeared that the victory had already declared in our favour ; for although *L'Orient, L'Henreux*, and *Le Tounant* were not taken possession of, they were considered as completely in our power.   At ten minutes after nine a fire was observed on board *L'Orient*, the French admiral's ship, which seemed to proceed from the after-part of the cabin, and which increased with great rapidity, presently involving the whole after-part of the ship in flames, This circumstance Captain Berry immediately communicated to the admiral, who though suffering severely from his wound, came up on deck, where the first consideration that struck his mind was concern for the danger of so many lives, to save as many as possible, of whom he ordered Captain Berry to make every practicable exertion.   A boat, the only one that could swim was instantly despatched from the *Vanguard*, and other ships that were in a condition to do so immediately followed the example, by which means from the best possible information, the lives of about seventy Frenchmen were saved.   The light thrown by the fire of *L'Orient* upon the surrounding objects, enabled us to see with more certainty the situation of the two fleets, the colours of both being distinguishable.   The cannonading was partially kept up to leeward of the centre till about ten o'clock, when *L'Orient* blew up with a tremendous explosion.   An awful pause and death-like silence for about three minutes ensued, when the wreck of the masts, yards, &c., which had been carried to a vast height, fell down into the water, and on board the surrounding ships. A port-fire from *L'Orient* fell into the main-yard of the *Alexander*, the fire occasioned by which was, however, extinguished in about two minutes by the active exertions of Captain Ball.   After this awful scene, the firing was re-commenced with the ships to leeward of the centre, till twenty minutes past ten, when there was a total cessation of firing for about ten minutes ; after which it was revived till about three in the morning, when it again ceased.

"Although it is natural to suppose that the time and attention of the admiral, and all the officers of his squadron, were fully employed in repairing damages sustained by their own ships, and in securing these of the enemy, which their valour had subdued, yet the mind of that great and good man felt the strongest emotions of the most pious gratitude to the Supreme Being for the signal success which, by His Divine favour, had crowned his endeavours in the cause of his country; and, in consequence, on the mornirg of the 2nd, he issued the following Memorandum to the different captains of his squadron :—

"' *Almighty God having blessed his Majesty's Arms with Victory, the Admiral intends returning Public Thanksgiving for the same at two o'clock this day; and he recommends every ship doing the same as soon as convenient.* "'HORATIO NELSON.'

"At two o'clock accordingly on that day, public service was performed on the quarter-deck of the *Vanguard* by the Rev. Mr. Comyn, the other ships following the example of the admiral, though perhaps not all at the same time. This solemn act of gratitude seemed to make a very deep impression on several of the prisoners, both officers and men, some of the former of whom remarked, 'that it was no wonder that we should preserve such order and discipline, when we could impress the minds of our men with such sentiments after a victory so great, and at a moment of such seeming confusion.' On the same day, the following Memorandum was issued to all the ships, expressive of the admiral's sentiments of the noble exertions of the different officers and men of his squadron :—

"*Vanguard*, OFF THE MOUTH OF THE NILE, *August* 2, 1798.
"' *The Admiral most heartily congratulates the Captains, Officers, Seamen, and Marines of the Squadron he has the honour to command, on the event of the late action; and he desires they will accept his sincere and cordial thanks for their very gallant behaviour in this glorious Battle. It must strike forcibly every British seaman, how superior their conduct is, when in discipline and good order, to the riotous behaviour of lawless Frenchmen.*
"' *The Squadron may be assured the Admiral will not fail, with his despatches, to represent their truly meritorious conduct in the strongest terms to the Commander-in-chief.* "'HORATIO NELSON.'"

"To LORD ST. VINCENT.

"*Vanguard*, OFF THE MOUTH OF THE NILE, *August* 2, 1798.
"MY LORD,—Almighty God has blessed his Majesty's arms in the

late battle, by a great victory over the fleet of the enemy, who I attacked at sunset on the 1st of August in a strong line of battle, for defending the entrance of the Bay (of shoals) flanked by numerous gunboats, four frigates, and a battery of guns and mortars on an island in their van : but nothing could withstand the squadron your lordship did me the honour to place under my command. Their high state of discipline is well known to you, and with the judgment of the captains, together with their valour, and that of the officers and men of every description, it was absolutely irresistible. Could anything more from my pen add to the character of the captains I would write it with pleasure.

"I have to regret the loss of Captain Westcott, of the *Majestic*, who was killed early in the action ; but the ship was continued to be so well fought by her first-lieutenant, Mr. Cuthbert, that I have given him an order to command her till your lordship's pleasure is known.

"The ships of the enemy, all but their two rear ships, are nearly dismasted ; and those two, with two frigates, I am sorry to say, made their escape ; nor was it, I assure you, in my power to prevent them. Captain Hood most handsomely endeavoured to do it, but I had no ship in a condition to support the *Zealous*, and I was obliged to call her in.

"The support and assistance I have received from Captain Berry, cannot be sufficiently expressed. I was wounded in the head, and obliged to be carried off the deck ; but the service suffered no loss by that event ; Captain Berry was fully equal to the important service then going on, and to him I must beg to refer you for every information relative to this victory. He will present you with the flag of the second in command, that of the commander-in-chief, being burnt in *L'Orient*." [1]

I have given Captain Berry's narrative as the only apparently authorized description of this eventful day, though aware that it is too rhetorical to be strictly

[1] The lists enclosed in this despatch showed that 16 officers, 150 seamen, and 46 marines, were killed ; and 37 officers, 562 seamen and 78 marines wounded—total, 896.

The result of the victory was eight men-of-war taken, two (*L'Orient* and *Le Timoleon*) burnt ; two (*Le Guillaume Tell* and *Le Généreux*) escaped, with two frigates, and one frigate (*L'Artemise*) burnt, and another (*La Serieuse*) dismasted and sunk.

accurate in describing the tactical aims of Nelson at the Battle of the Nile. To Lord Howe alone did Nelson ever detail the action, and in that letter he made no claim to having ordered the movement of the first of his ships on the inside of the enemy's line :—

"To Lord Howe.

"Palermo, *Jan.* 8, 1799.

" My Lord,—It was only this moment that I had the invaluable approbation of the great, the immortal Lord Howe—an honour the most flattering a sea-officer could receive, as it comes from the first and greatest sea-officer the world ever produced. I had the happiness to command a Band of Brothers : therefore night was my advantage. Each knew his duty, and I was sure each would feel for a French ship. By attacking the enemy's van and centre, the wind blowing directly along their line, I was enabled to throw what force I pleased on a few ships. This plan my friends readily conceived by the signals (for which we are principally, if not entirely, indebted to your lordship), and we always kept a superior force to the enemy. At twenty-eight minutes past six, the sun in the horizon, the firing commenced. At five minutes past ten, when *L'Orient* blew up, having burnt seventy minutes, the six van ships had surrendered. I then pressed further towards the rear; and had it pleased God that I had not been wounded and stone blind, there cannot be a doubt but every ship would have been in our possession. But here let it not be supposed that any officer is to blame. No; on my honour, I am satisfied each did his very best. I have never before, my lord, detailed the action to any one ; but I should have thought it wrong to have kept it from one who is our great master of tactics and bravery.
" Nelson." [1]

Commenting on this letter, written before Nelson had seen Berry's narrative, our Edinburgh Reviewer justly remarks :—

" So that Nelson's efforts at the Nile were moral and not intellectual. It is true he made the exact signals, and the only signals, which the calmest reflection after the event tells us were necessary. 'Prepare

---

[1] Prof. Laughton, p. 180.

to anchor by the stern,' and ' Attack the enemy's van and centre ' ;
and that if we wish to credit him with profundity, we may do so as far
as these signals go. But such orders were not the result of profundity,
they were the children of simplicity and directness. The two things
most plain were, that the French rear might be left out of action, and
incapable, and that anchoring by the stern was sure to save many
English lives. The genius was not in the intellectual depth which
dictated such orders, but in the moral simplicity and directness which
trusted to them, and went straight on when the sun was going down,
and when the whole design had been, so to speak, got up on the spur
of the moment. The genius lay in the absence of hesitation, and the
impossibility of conceiving that there was any cause for hesitation or
delay. And it was precisely the same quality which made Nelson
the year before decline to fight a routine battle in the *Captain* at St.
Vincent." [1]

Realizing the vital importance of this victory, so
entirely isolating the French army in Egypt, to our
Indian possessions then hardly established, on the 9th
of August Nelson wrote a despatch to the Governor
of Bombay, detailing the landing of the French troops
and the destruction of their fleet, which he sent by
Lieutenant Duval, of the *Zealous*, overland, by the same
route as has been so repeatedly proposed for the Euphrates
Valley Railway. Landing at Scanderoon, and taking the
route by Aleppo and Bagdad, the bearer of this important
despatch reached Bombay in sixty-five days :—

"As I have Buonaparte despatches before me," writes Nelson,
"which I took yesterday, I speak positively. He says, 'I am now
going to send off to take Suez and Damietta.' Alexandria, both town
and shipping, are so distressed for provisions, which they can only get
from the Nile by water, that I cannot guess the good success which
may attend my holding our present position, for Buonaparte writes his
distress for stores, artillery, things for their hospital, &c., is great. All
useful communication is at end between Alexandria and Cairo : you
may be assured I shall remain here as long as possible. Buonaparte
had never yet to contend with an English officer ; and I shall make
him respect us.'"

_____

[1] *Edinburgh Review*, pp. 367–8.

The following anecdotes of Lord Nelson were given to the author in the year 1851, by his father-in-law, the late Captain John Forbes, of Winkfield Place, Berks, who was a midshipman in the *Minotaur* at the Battle of the Nile :—

"The writer of this was on board the *Minotaur*, and begs to hand down an anecdote which he believes has never appeared in public. Lord Nelson during the action sent a boat to the *Minotaur* to require the presence of Captain Louis on board the *Vanguard*. He said, 'Louis, I am wounded, and know not to what extent, but your support has prevented me from being obliged to haul out of the line, and I thank you from my soul.

"In various letters afterwards Lord Nelson repeated his thanks. The *Aquilon* was the ship the *Minotaur* was opposed to, and after the fight I happened to be on board of her. The first captain was killed. I asked the second captain how it was that as we approached they did not fire at us? He said, 'After we got within a certain distance they ceased, reserving their broadside until we should anchor, and when swinging, they meant to rake us; instead of which,' he said, 'you anchored by the stern, and the first broadside you gave us killed the post-captain and destroyed every battery but the lower deck, where the carnage was very great.' Some days subsequent to the battle the *Aquilon* was set fire to. We hailed the *Minotaur* to state the fact, who made signal to that effect, upon which the *Vanguard* threw out signal for the fleet to send their boats, which was quickly done, but, to the astonishment of the Frenchmen, the boats of the *Vanguard* had their crews with a brace of pistols and a cutlass with each man. On inquiry they found Lord Nelson's orders were to take out the English and leave the French to extinguish the fire he had no doubt they had created. This was soon done, and no more complaints were made of fire subsequently." [1]

In the Rev. Cooper Willyam's "Voyage up the Mediterranean" (chaplain of the *Swiftsure*), it is said that in a conference held with some French officers and Captain Hallowell, on board the *Swiftsure*, the British

[1] See "Life of Lord Nelson," by the author, published by the Society for Promoting Christian Knowledge, 1851.

were accused of having unfairly used some combustible missiles at the Battle of the Nile, upon which the captain ordered Mr. Parr, the gunner, to bring up some balls, and to tell them where he had obtained them. To the confusion of the Frenchmen he stated them to have been taken from the *Spartiate*, one of the ships captured on the 1st of August. Experiments were now made with them. One tried was a fire-ball, the composition of which was not known, but as it did not explode it was thrown into the water, where it continued to burn, pouring forth a black pitchy matter, until the shell in which it was contained was completely emptied. Another ball exploded on being set fire to, and had nigh proved dangerous to those who were around.[1]

A short time before the expedition to Minorca sailed, and while the equipment was causing the severest exertion to every department within the fortress of Gibraltar, Sir J. Saumarez, with the disabled ships and the prizes in the Battle of the Nile, arrived, amid the shouts and cheers from all ranks assembled to greet them. But though the spectacle was a proud one to the community, it was serious to the civil department, for Lord St. Vincent ordered the repairs of the whole to be taken in hand immediately :—

" It did not take long to patch up the prizes for merely a voyage to Lisbon ; but then followed the more substantial repairs of the captors, for though they were such battered ships, Lord St. Vincent, to the surprise of every one, announced that it was his intention to restore them all to perfect worthiness at Gibraltar. . . . While he exulted in this splendid naval victory, he further saw how important it was to England that Europe should see that Lord Nelson had smashed the French Fleet so easily, that it was not necessary to send a single British ship off the station to repair damages.

" The state of the *Bellerophon* was a serious difficulty. From her

---

[1] Quoted in Pettigrew's " Nelson," vol. i. p. 131.

gallant struggle with *L'Orient* she was so injured that it was commonly said you could drive a post-chaise through her, and her captain (Darby) and some of his officers grumbled at the notion of being sent to sea to be drowned for their exertions at the Nile. St. Vincent persevered, and by relating a dream he pretended to have had, in which he was told all these complaints, and thought he was sitting at a courtmartial, at which Darby's sword was on the table, somewhat calmed the captain's fears. Still, however, Darby maintained that it was impossible to do the work. 'As it is,' he said, 'we are short here of artificers ; but it would take a shipload of carpenters to fish her masts and make her hull seaworthy.' 'Nevertheless,' replied St. Vincent, ' I think it will come to pass.'

" A day or two afterwards, on Captain Darby's visiting the dockyard, his ears were astonished by an unusual clatter of calkers and carpenters from his own ship. Lord St. Vincent had despatched a brig to the fleet off Cadiz for two shipwrights from every line-ofbattle ship, and now, having reached the yard before the captain greeted him, when he approached the *Bellerophon*, ' Well, Darby, half my prophecy is fulfilled ; the shipload of carpenters are arrived, and I foretell the *Bellerophon* will go out of the Mole on the appointed day. Still Captain Darby was sceptical : the hold was unstowed, the mizenmast ashore, the repairs yet to be given to the hull considerable : but the admiral repeated his prognostication, and they separated. Efforts were redoubled by yet more and more artificers, and on the morning fixed for the *Bellerophon's* departure, while at breakfast with his lordship, Darby's attention was arrested by a gun from the flagship. ' That gun, my dear Darby, is the signal for the boats to assist in towing out the *Bellerophon*.' ' But the mizenmast, my lord, is not yet shipped, and the rigging not yet received from the dockyard.' ' That will be alongside as soon as the ship is anchored in the Bay ; there's another gun for you, my dear Darby.' And the guns continued firing till the ship's lashings were cast off, and the chief's prophecy fulfilled to the letter." [1]

----

[1] Tucker, vol. i. p. 371 *et seq.*

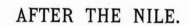

AFTER THE NILE.

NELSON WEARING THE CHELLINCK, BY GUZZANDI.

CHAPTER XI.

AFTER THE NILE.

(1798-1800.)

Autobiography—Arrival of the news of the victory—The Cardinal of
York and the news—Arrival of Nelson at Naples and his state of
health—His reception by the King and the people—Letters to his
father and his wife—The bird and relics in Nelson's cabin—The
New Coalition—The advance of the Neapolitan army to Rome—
Capture of Leghorn and blockade of Malta—Cowardice of Neapolitan officers, and incapability or treachery of Mack—Secret flight of
the Royal Family from Naples to Palermo—Nelson and Lord Keith—
Return to Naples—Ruffo's treaty with the rebels annulled—The life
and death of Carraciolo—Capture of *Le Généreux* and *Le Guillaume
Tell*—The last of the French Fleet at Aboukir Bay—Nelson and Sir
Sidney Smith—Letter from the First Lord Auckland—Strikes his
flag and prepares to reach England through Germany—His reception
in England.

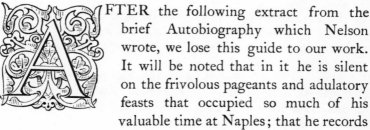FTER the following extract from the
brief Autobiography which Nelson
wrote, we lose this guide to our work.
It will be noted that in it he is silent
on the frivolous pageants and adulatory
feasts that occupied so much of his
valuable time at Naples; that he records
in the driest terms his share in the secret flight of the
King and his family, and not a word is said about the
incident of Carraciolo's fate or the successes with which his
expedition's against Capua and Gaieta were crowned:
The concluding paragraph of the Autobiography ought

to be the monitor and guide of every naval officer.
Let them never forget Hoste's signal at the battle of
Lissa, " REMEMBER NELSON," and Nelson's own advice,
" GO THOU AND DO LIKEWISE." [1]

"On the 22nd of September, 1798, I arrived at Naples, and was
received as a deliverer by the King, Queen, and the whole kingdom.
October 12th the blockade of Malta took place, which has continued
without intermission to this day (October 13, 1799). On the 21st of
December, 1798, his Sicilian Majesty and family embarked in the
Vanguard, and were carried to Palermo in Sicily. In March, 1799, I
arranged a plan for taking the islands in the Bay of Naples, and for
supporting the Royalists who were making head in the kingdom. This
plan succeeded in every part. In May I shifted my flag, being promoted
to be Rear Admiral of the Red to the *Foudroyant*, and was obliged to
be on my guard against the French Fleet. In June and July, 1799, I
went to Naples, and, as his Sicilian Majesty is pleased to say, re-
conquered his kingdom, and placed him on his throne. On the 9th
of August I brought back his Sicilian Majesty to Palermo, having
been upwards of four weeks on board the *Foudroyant*.

"On the 13th his Sicilian Majesty presented me with a sword
magnificently enriched with diamonds, the title of Duke of Bronte,
and annexed to it the feud of Bronte, supposed to be worth £3,000
per annum. On the arrival of the Russian Squadron at Naples
I directed Commodore Troubridge to go with the squadron, and
blockade closely Civita Vecchia, and to offer to the French most
favourable conditions if they would evacuate Rome and Civita
Vecchia; which the French general, Grenier, complied with, and
they were signed on board the *Culloden*, when a prophecy, made to
me on my arrival at Naples, was fulfilled, viz., *that I should take Rome
with my ships.*"

"Thus may be exemplified by my Life that perseverance in my
profession will most probably meet its reward. Without having any
inheritance, or being fortunate in prize money, I have received all the
honours of my profession, been created a Peer of Great Britain, and I
may say to the reader :

"'GO THOU AND DO LIKEWISE.'

" NELSON.

" *October* 15, 1799, Port Mahon."

_____

[1] The Autobiography, September, 1798, to October 15, 1799.

Previously to the arrival at Naples of the news of the victory of the Nile, great was the anxiety of the Court and its friends.   On the 4th of June Sir William Hamilton had told them " at a grand dinner, that he had received from Lord St. Vincent a letter, informing him that a squadron under Nelson was coming to the Mediterranean to protect our allies."   " The impatience of our naval heroes to discover the French Fleet," adds Miss Knight, " was scarcely greater than that which we felt to hear of their success.   We knew that they had touched at Syracuse, and we hoped that they might follow the directions they might probably receive there ; for the Sicilians, an acute people and sworn enemies of the French, were the most likely to obtain correct information of the movements of the latter."   At last their suspense was relieved, when the *Mutine*, Captain Hoste, arrived in the Bay with Captain Capel and Nelson's despatches on board.[1]

One of the earliest to hear the great news was the last of the Stuarts :—

"Cardinal York was then at Naples, having fled from Rome to avoid falling into the hands of the French.   Sir W. Hamilton, on his return from the palace, met him in his carriage, called to the Cardinal's coachman to stop, and, getting out of his own carriage, went to the Cardinal's, and said, 'I beg pardon of your Eminence for stopping your carriage, but I am sure you will be glad to hear the good news I have to communicate.'

"The Cardinal, rather surprised, said, 'Pray, sir, to whom have I the honour of speaking ?'

"'To Sir W. Hamilton.'

"'Oh, to the British Minister.   I am much obliged to you.   What is the news ?'

"Sir William then gave an account of the victory as succinctly as he could.   The Cardinal, agitated, rejoiced, said, 'But may we depend on the truth of this great affair ?   There are so many false reports.' Sir William then introduced Captain Capel, saying, 'This gentleman, a brother of Lord Essex, was in the action, and is going home imme-

---

[1] Miss Cornelia Knight's Journal, vol. i. pp. 105, 108–10.

diately with the despatches.' ' In that case, sir,' said the Cardinal to Captain Capel, 'when you arrive in England, do me the favour to say that no man rejoices more sincerely than I do in the success and glory of the British Navy.' " [1]

Close on the heels of the *Mutine* came the *Culloden* and *Alexander*, with Troubridge and Ball, and on the 22nd of September Nelson in the *Vanguard* came in— " Very weak in body and mind from my cough and fever." Pitiable was Nelson's account of his illness :—

" On the day Hoste left me," he wrote to Lord St. Vincent, " I · was taken with a fever which has very nearly done my business; for eighteen hours my life was thought to be past hope ; I am now up, but very weak in body and mind from my cough and this fever. I never expect, my lord, to see your face again ; it may please God that this battle will be the finish to that fever of anxiety which I have endured from the middle of June ; but be that as pleases His goodness—I am resigned to His will." [2]

How Nelson was received by King, Court, and people, has been told with elaboration by all his previous biographers, with all its dangerous flattery to a man so naturally vain as the Hero of the Nile. Following out my plan of letting Nelson tell his own tale as far as it is possible, I insert his letters to Lady Nelson and his venerable father relating to the events of this time :—

" To Lady Nelson.

" About *September* 25, 1798.

" The poor wretched *Vanguard* arrived here on the 22nd of September. I must endeavour to convey to you something of what passed; but if it was so affecting to those who were only united to me by bonds of friendship, what must it be to my dearest wife, my friend, my everything which is most dear to me in this world ? Sir William and Lady Hamilton came out to sea, attended by numerous

---

[1] Miss Knight's Journal, vol. i. pp. 112–13.
[2] Clarke and McArthur, vol. ii. p. 100 ; Despatches, vol. iii. p. 128.

boats with emblems, &c. They, my most respectable friends, had really been laid up and seriously ill, first from anxiety, and then from joy. It was imprudently told Lady Hamilton in a moment, and the effect was like a shot; she fell apparently dead, and is not yet perfectly recovered from severe bruises. Alongside came my honoured friends. The scene in the boat was terribly affecting; up flew her ladyship, and exclaiming, 'God, is it possible?' she fell into my arm more dead than alive. Tears, however, soon set matters to rights, when alongside came the King. The scene was in its way as interesting. He took me by the hand, calling me his 'Deliverer and Preserver,' with every other expression of kindness. In short, all Naples calls me 'Nostro Liberatore;' my greeting from the lower classes was truly affecting. I hope some day to have the pleasure of introducing you to Lady Hamilton; she is one of the best of women in this world; she is an honour to her sex. Her kindness, with Sir William's, to me is more than I can express; I am in their house, and I may tell you that it required all the kindness of my friends to set me up. Lady Hamilton intends writing to you. May God Almighty bless you, and give us in due time a happy meeting.[1]

"H. N."[2]

"TO HIS FATHER.

"*Sept.* 25, 1798.

"MY DEAR FATHER,—I have to thank you for your two affectionate letters from Round Wood, and if the place and neighbourhood are not so pleasant as could be wished, I trust my country will enable me to choose a comfortable resting-place. The Almighty has blessed my exertions for the happiness of mankind, and I am daily receiving the thanks and prayers of Turks and Christians. In short, I am placed by Providence in that situation, that all my caution will be necessary to prevent vanity showing itself superior to my gratitude and thankfulness. The hand of God has visibly pressed on the French, it was not in the power of man to gain such a victory. In their Sicilian Majesties' thanks and congratulations are the following lines : 'History, either ancient or modern, does not record such a battle. You have saved us, sir, by this most glorious action, which, superior to any battle fought at sea, has this most glorious and important consequence—of being to all Europe, I repeat it, of the highest

---

[1] I defer to a future chapter my remarks on the life Nelson is accused of living with the Hamiltons abroad or at home, chap. xix.

[2] Clarke and McArthur, vol. ii. p. 101 ; Despatches, vol. iii. p. 130.

advantage.' The whole letter, being in the same strain, is enough to make me vain. My head is quite healed, and, if it were necessary, I could not at present leave Italy, who looks up to me as, under God, its protector. May God Almighty bless you, my dear father, is the affectionate wish of your dutiful son, "H. N." [1]

It was after this that his venerable father wrote to Mr. Allott, who was afterwards Dean of Raphoe, the interesting letter of which, by the kindness of Earl Nelson, I am able to insert a facsimile.[2] Again he writes to his wife :—

"To Lady Nelson.

"*Sept.* 28, 1798.

" The preparations of Lady Hamilton for celebrating my birthday to-morrow are enough to fill me with vanity. Every ribbon, every button, has Nelson, &c. The whole service is marked 'H. N., glorious 1st of August.' Songs and sonetti are numerous beyond what I ever could deserve. I send the additional verse to 'God save the King,' as I know you will sing it with pleasure. I cannot move on foot, or in a carriage, for the kindness of the populace ; but good Lady H. preserves all the papers as the highest treat for you. The Queen yesterday, being still ill, sent her favourite son to visit and bring me a letter from her of gratitude and thanks. Miserable accounts of *Le Guillaume Tell.*[3] I trust Almighty God will yet put her into the hands of our King. His all-powerful hand has gone with us to the battle, protected us, and still continues destroying unbelievers. All glory be to God ! The more I think, the more I hear, the greater is my astonishment at the extent and good consequences of our victory."[4]

---

[1] Despatches, vol. i. p. 131.

[2] For a copy see Appendix.

[3] The *Guillaume Tell* (80) encountered the *Leander* (50) in which Captain Berry was taking home Nelson's despatch of the battle. He had, however, wisely sent a duplicate overland by Captain Capel. On the surrender of the *Leander* in this unequal contest, the French crew treated Captains Berry and Thompson with the utmost cruelty, stripping them of everything valuable, even the doctor of his case of instruments. On the captain of *Le Généreux* being appealed to by Captain Berry, his only reply was the French sailors are all thieves.

[4] Clarke and McArthur, vol. ii. p. 102 ; Despatches, vol. iii. pp. 134-5.

" To Lady Nelson.

" *Oct.* 1 to 6, 1798.

" Our time here is actively employed; and between business and
what is called pleasure, I am not my own master for five minutes.
The combined kind attention of Sir W. and Lady Hamilton must ever
make you and I love them, they are deserving of the admiration of
all the world. The Grand Signor has ordered me a valuable diamond.
If it were worth a million, my pleasure would be to see it in your
possession. My pride is being your husband, the son of my dear
father, and in having Sir William and Lady Hamilton for my friends.
While these approve of my conduct, I shall not feel or regard the
envy of thousands. Could I, my dearest Fanny, tell you half the
honours which are shown me here, not a ream of paper would hold
it. On my birthday eighty people dined at Sir W. Hamilton's, and
one thousand seven hundred and forty came to a ball, where eight
hundred supped. A rostral column is erected under a magnificent
canopy, never, Lady H. says, to come down while they remain in
Naples. A little circumstance has also happened, which does honour
to the King of Naples, and is not unpleasant to me. I went to view
the magnificent manufactory of china. After admiring all the fine
things, sufficient to seduce the money out of my pocket, I came to
some busts in china of all the Royal Family. These I immediately
ordered. When I wanted to pay for them, I was informed that the
King had directed whatever I chose should be delivered free of all
cost; it was handsome in the King.

" Yours, &c.,

" H. N."

The following letter contains the first indication of
mental irritability, due probably to the severe wound in
the head at the battle of the Nile :—

" To Lady Nelson.

" Naples, *Dec.* 11, 1798.

" I have not received a line from England since October 1st.
Lord St. Vincent is in no hurry to oblige me now, in short, I am an
envied man, but better that than to be a pitied one. Never mind; it
is my present intention to leave this country in May. The poor Queen
has again made me promise not to quit her and her family until
brighter prospects appear than do at present. The King is with the
army, and she is sole Regent. Lady Hamilton's goodness forces me

15

out at noon for an hour. What can I say of her and Sir W.'s attention to me? They are, in fact, with the exception of you and my
good father, the dearest friends I have in this world. I live as Sir
William's son in the house, and my glory is as dear to them as their
own; in short, I am under such obligations as I can never repay, but
with eternal gratitude. The improvement made in Josiah by Lady
H. is wonderful; your obligations and mine are infinite on that score;
not but Josiah's heart is as good and as humane as ever was covered
by a human breast. God bless him; I love him dearly, with all his
roughness." [1]

I must find room for the following anecdote, told by
Miss Knight, and her account of the relics in Nelson's
cabin. Speaking of the King's visit to the *Vanguard*
she says :—

" The King afterwards sat down with us to a handsome breakfast,
at which I remarked a little bird hopping about on the table. This
bird had come on board the *Vanguard* the evening before the action,
and had remained in her ever since. The Admiral's cabin was its
chief residence, but it was fed and petted by all who came near it,
for sailors regard the arrival of a bird as a promise of victory. It flew
away, I believe, soon after their ship reached Naples. . . . A carving
in wood of an immense three-coloured plume of feathers, which
ornamented the cap of the figure of *William Tell*, when the ship
struck to the *Foudroyant;* four muskets taken on board the *San Josef*
by Nelson at the battle of St. Vincent; and the flagstaff of *L'Orient*,
saved from the flames when that ship was blown up at the battle of
the Nile, formed the chief ornaments of his cabin." [2]

The pageants and festivities at Naples were but short-
lived. The victory of the Nile afforded the long-wished-
for opportunity for a new coalition against France. Her
most successful general with his army was locked up in
Egypt, and had Nelson had his way that army, at least,
would never have left it save as prisoners of war. Austria
was the first to take advantage of the crisis to declare war;

[1] Despatches, vol. iii. p. 194.
[2] Vol. i. p. 116, 146–7.

THE SICILIAN MEDAL—REVERSE—THE RECOVERY OF NAPLES.

THE SICILIAN MEDAL—OBVERSE—KING FERDINAND.

Russia was preparing to join the new coalition with a powerful army under Suwarrow, and England, as before, ready with her liberal subsidies. After many doubts and hesitations, influenced by the plain-spoken advice of Nelson, the King of Naples at length joined the Coalition with an army of eighty thousand men, good to look at, but unreliable, under the Austrian general, Mack, subsequently too well known for the cowardly or treacherous capitulation of Ulmn. In Mack, who could not travel without his six carriages, Nelson had no confidence. For his part in the war, he pressed the blockade of Malta, and the capture of Leghorn ; and then, after the surrender of the French garrison of Gozo, leaving Ball in command, returned to Naples, where for a brief space the success of the war was believed in. The King of Naples with his army had entered Rome, but a French corps still held a strong post in the Roman states, against which the Austrian general, Mack, advanced with a far superior force. Treachery aided by cowardice, proved fatal to the Neapolitan soldiers. A total defeat ensued, in which cannon, baggage, and stores were lost, and though the loss of men was but trifling, the army fled in confusion. The story of the failure is told by Nelson in the following letter to Lord Spencer :—

"NAPLES, *Dec.* 11, 1798.

" The Neapolitan officers have not lost much honour, for God knows they had but little to lose ; but they lost all they had. Mack has supplicated the king to sabre every man who ran from Cività Castellana to Rome. He has, we hear, torn off the epaulettes of some of these scoundrels and placed them on good sergeants. I will, as briefly as I can, state the position of the army, and its lost honour, for defeat they had none. The right wing of nineteen thousand men, under General St. Philip and Michaux (who ran away at Toulon) were to take post between Ancona and Rome, to cut off supplies and communication. Near Fermi they fell in with the enemy, about three thousand. After a little firing, St. Philip advanced to the

French general, and returning to his men, said, 'I no longer command you,' and was going off to the enemy. A sergeant said, 'You are a traitor; what! have you been talking to the enemy?' St. Philip replied, 'I no longer command you.' 'Then you are an enemy,' and, levelling his musket, shot St. Philip through the right arm. However, the enemy advanced; he was amongst them. Michaux ran away, as did all the infantry, and had it not been for the good conduct of two regiments of cavalry, would have been destroyed. So great was their panic, that cannon, tents, baggage, and military chests, all were left to the French. Could you credit, but it is true, that this loss has been sustained with the death of only forty men. The French lost many by the cavalry, and having got the good things, did not run after an army three times their number. Some ran thirty miles to Pessaro. The peasantry took up arms— even the women—to defend their country. However, the runaways are not only collected, but advanced to Arcoti, which they took from the French, cutting open the gates with hatchets. It is said they have a good general—Cetto, a Neapolitan prince—and I hope will be ashamed of their former conduct. General Michaux is bringing a prisoner to Naples.

"This failure has thrown Mack backward. It was the intention of the general to surround Città Castellana. Chevalier Saxe advanced to Viterbó, General Melch (?) to Fermi, and Mack with the main body, finding his communications not open with Fermi, retreated to Città Castellana. In his route he was attacked from an entrenchment of the enemy, which it was necessary to carry. Finding his troops backwards, he dismounted, and attempted to rally them, but they left their general and basely fled. The natural consequence was he was sorely wounded, but saved by some gallant cavalry, and carried off by the bravery of a coachman, and is safe, poor fellow, at Rome, and hopes are entertained of his recovery. The fugitives fled to Rome, fancying the French at their heels, who never moved from their entrenchment, which was carried by another party of troops under General Dumas. It is reported that the King stripped the Prince di Taranto, Duc di Trani, of his uniform, and disgraced him. He commanded under Saxe, and fled among the first to Rome. 'Tis for the traitorous and cowardly conduct of these scoundrels that the great Queen is miserable, knowing not who to trust. The French Minister and his Legation went off by sea yesterday.[1]   "NELSON."

---

[1] Despatches, vol. iii. p. 195.

Every fresh courier brought news from the army of a like character, whilst in Naples some new treachery was being daily found out. The safety of the Royal family was not to be risked, now that the King had returned to Naples. Everything, therefore, was arranged for a secret flight. The chief property of the royal house and most of the valuable collection of Sir W. Hamilton were conveyed to the boats of the English Squadron, through a tunnel that ran to the shore from the palace ; and on the night of the 21st of December the whole Royal family and the Hamiltons were received by Nelson on the *Vanguard.*[1] For two days the English and Neapolitan ships were busy taking off refugees and their property, and then the fleet sailed for Sicily, and, after encountering a violent storm on the 26th, the fugitives were landed at Palermo. The Neapolitan army had practically disappeared, and though the Lazzaroni of Naples fought nobly in defence of their city, by the middle of January the French were in possession of the capital.

On January 29, 1799, the Parthenopœan Republic was proclaimed by the French general, and joined by some of the confidential servants of the fugitive king, as well as by some of the higher nobility.

Until the middle of June, Nelson kept watch and ward over Sicily and the Royal family, only leaving the Bay of Palermo for the station of Maritimo, when warned by Lord Keith of the escape of a French squadron from Brest and its entry into the Mediterranean, presumably in Lord Keith's opinion for the reduction of Minorca. In the danger of Minorca, Nelson did not believe. In his view Sicily was in danger, and go to Minorca he would

[1] Whether these arrangements were mainly, if not entirely, due to Lady Hamilton, as she claimed, it is not within my province to discuss ; the question has been threshed out by Mr. Cordy Jeffreson in his late publications, " Nelson and Lady Hamilton," and " the Queen of Naples and Lady Hamilton."

not. He was content to recall Troubridge and the ships of the line from Naples, leaving the *Seahorse* frigate and a bomb-vessel to co-operate with the Royalist army, which Cardinal Ruffo had gathered from the wilds of Calabria. On the 20th of June, however, Nelson received a despatch from Lord Keith, which induced him to return to Palermo from his cruise off Maritimo, and persuade the King to return with the fleet to Naples, whither it was supposed the French Fleet had gone.

On his voyage to Naples, Nelson received the intelligence that a treaty with the rebels had been made by Cardinal Ruffo for the surrender of the Castles of Uovo and Nuovo, which he denounced as "infamous" only from the report, and declared that " he could not permit them to embark or quit those places. They must surrender themselves to his Majesty's royal mercy." [1]

What had occurred in Naples during Nelson's absence, and his cruelly misrepresented action in the annulling of Ruffo's treaty, and the condemnation of Count Carraciolo, cannot be more clearly or more correctly told than in the words of Mr. John Paget, in his articles published in " Blackwood " (March and April) in 1860, from which, with the permission of my old friend, I extract the following :— [2]

"The King had fled to Palermo. It is hardly possible to say that any government at all existed in Naples. The French had evacuated the city. The Republican insurgents had been defeated. The castles of St. Elmo, Uovo, and Nuovo, were, however, still garrisoned by the French, and many of the principal Neapolitan insurgents had taken refuge within their walls. The Royalist forces, under the

---

[1] Nelson to Cardinal Ruffo, June 24, Despatches, vol. iii. pp. 384–6.
[2] The truth about Carraciolo and the treaty had been previously partly told by Commander Mills in a pamphlet, now hardly to be found except in the British Museum. It was not, however, until 1860 that Mr. Paget made the whole question plain and popular in " Blackwood." These articles are now reprinted in " Paradoxes and Puzzles," 1874.

command of Cardinal Ruffo, *whose orders from the King were express not to treat with rebels*, were engaged in an attempt to reduce these castles. Nelson, with the English Fleet, was at sea on the look-out for the French Fleet. One frigate (the *Seahorse*) and a bomb were left in the Bay of Naples, under the command of Captain Foote, with orders to co-operate with the land forces. On the 19th of June, to his great surprise, Captain Foote received a letter from Cardinal Ruffo, requesting him to suspend hostilities against the castles, as a negotiation had taken place. After some remonstrance on the part of Captain Foote, and correspondence with Cardinal Ruffo, whose fidelity was, to say the least, gravely suspected ; Captain Foote received from the Cardinal the plan of capitulation already signed by him, with a request to the captain that he would affix his name. He did this, believing that Ruffo had the royal authority, returning it to the Cardinal with a protest. A formal capitulation was signed in a similar manner on the 23rd. It was in direct contravention of the orders Cardinal Ruffo had received. It provided, in substance, that the garrisons should march out with all the honours of war ; that all persons in the forts, and all prisoners taken by the king's troops, should remain unmolested in Naples, or if they preferred, should be freely conveyed in vessels, to be provided by the King, to Toulon, and there landed and set at liberty. It was also provided that the evacuation of the forts should not take place until the moment of embarkation.

"On the next day, the 24th, before any step had been taken to carry the capitulation into effect, Nelson, with a powerful squadron, entered the bay. He instantly signalled the *Seahorse* to haul down the flag of truce. On the following day, the 25th, he sent a declaration that 'he would not permit the rebellious subjects of his Sicilian Majesty to embark or quit those places. They must surrender to his Majesty's royal mercy.' On the 26th, Nelson took possession of the Castles of Uovo and Nuovo, '*the garrisons and other persons quitting them with full knowledge that the terms of the capitulation would not be carried into execution.*' They were detained as prisoners until the arrival of the King, on the 10th of July, when they were given up to the Neapolitan Government." [1]

---

[1] By the laws of war and nations was Nelson justified in annulling the capitulation ? Yes ; because entered into by persons who exceeded their instructions and acted beyond their powers. [See Marten's " Precis du droit des gens," 54 ii. c. ii. sec. 48 ; do. Klüber, ii. 75, sec. 276. Nelson Despatches, vol. iii. p. 496.] Mr. Paget cites the case of the capitulation of Marshal Gouvion St. Cyr, when blockaded in Dresden after Leipsig

" It was not for him," writes Mr. Paget, " to determine whether
the course adopted by the Government at home was wise or not.   To
him the French were enemies, and the insurgent Neapolitans rebels
and traitors.   The King was an ally to be faithfully served—a guest
to be loyally protected.   The Queen was the sister of the murdered
Marie Antoinette, to whose service he was bound by all the laws of
chivalry and honour.   With these feelings can we be surprised that
when he learned that Ruffo, in direct violation of the orders of his
sovereign, had granted favourable terms to the traitors with whom he
was expressly forbidden to treat, and that a British officer had unwil-
lingly affixed his name to what he felt to be an ' infamous ' capitulation, he instantly exercised his powers as commander-in-chief, and
annulled the disgraceful instrument."

Mr. Fox, on the capitulation at Naples on February 3,
1800, on motion for address thanking his Majesty for
refusing to negotiate with the French Republic, said that
" after the capitulation of the castles of Uovo and Nuovo,
contrary to its terms, the rebels were plundered, numbers
of them thrown into dungeons, and some notwithstanding
the British guarantee."   A division approving the address
was taken at the close of Fox's speech, and no reply was
then made to these charges.   Nelson having heard of this,
on the 9th of May, 1800, wrote as follows to A.
Davison :— [1]

" MALTA, *May* 9, 1800.

" MY DEAR SIR,—Mr. Fox having in the House of Commons, in
February, made an accusation against somebody for what he calls a
breach of a treaty with rebels, which had been entered into with a
British officer, and having used language unbecoming either the
wisdom of a senator, or the politeness of a gentleman, or an Englishman, who ought ever to suppose that his Majesty's officers would
always act with honour and openness in all their transactions; and as

---

by Count Klenau, which was annulled by Prince Schwarzenberg after the
troops had marched on their way to France as far as Allerberg (" Histoire
abregie des Traites de Paix," par Koch, ix. 310).   Similar case at Dantzig
in 1813.
    [1] Also to Mr. A. Stephens, author of "History of the Wars of the
French Revolution."   Clarke and McArthur, vol. ii. p. 182, note.

the whole affairs of the kingdom of Naples were at the time alluded to absolutely placed in my hands,—it is I who am called upon to explain my conduct, and, therefore, send you my observations on the infamous armistice entered into by the Cardinal; and on his refusal to send in a joint declaration to the French and rebels, I sent in my note, on which the rebels came out of the castles *as they ought*, and as I hope all those who are false to their King and country will, *to be hanged*, or otherwise disposed of as their sovereign thought proper. The terms granted by Captain Foote, of the *Seahorse*, at Castel-à-Mare, were all strictly complied with, the rebels having surrendered before my arrival. There has been nothing promised by a British officer that his Sicilian Majesty has not complied with, even in disobedience to his orders to the Cardinal.

" Bronte Nelson of the Nile.

" Show these papers to Mr. Rose or some other, and if thought right you will put them in the paper." [1]

Among those who took refuge with the rebels in the castles of Uovo and Nuovo was Count Carraciolo, a cadet of a noble family, and one of the pupils in the Naval Academy which Sir J. Acton established in Naples in 1780. Entering the naval service of his country he eventually, about 1790, became a Commodore, and served with credit with the English Fleet in the Mediterranean, thus becoming acquainted with Nelson and his officers. In 1798, he commanded the Neapolitan vessels that aided in the removal of the Royal family to Sicily, and remained at Palermo in the king's service until the Parthenopœan Republic issued an edict forfeiting the estates of those who did not return to Naples. On obtaining leave of the King to return to save the confiscation of his property, he was warned by him to keep clear of the republicans. According to his own story, however, he was compelled to take service with the Republic, and for a time Troubridge, who was in command off Naples, believed him. On the 1st of May, 1799, Troubridge entertained a far

---

[1] Despatches, Appendix, vol. iii. p. 510.

different opinion of the Count. " I am now satisfied," he
wrote, " that Carraciolo is a Jacobin. He came in the
gunboats to Castel-à-Mare himself, and spirited up the
Jacobins."[1]   " Yesterday," writes Captain James Oswald,
of the *Perseus*, bomb vessel to Nelson, May 20, 1799,
" he harangued the sailors and promised to give up to
them Procida and Ischia to military plunder as soon as
they could get possession of them, using every exertion
since the British ships left the bay to get out the frigate
and corvette."[2]   On the 26th of May, Captain Foote
wrote, " Carraciolo threatens a second attack with a considerable addition of force ; " and on the 11th of June he
writes, " Carraciolo's gunboats have for some time been
firing at the town of Annunciata and the adjacent
houses."[3]   On the approach of Ruffo's forces he took
refuge in one of the castles of Uovo and Nuovo, but
before the surrender quitted it and fled to the mountains.
Here he was in a double danger from brigands and the
vengeance of the Royalists. A reward was offered for
his capture, and on the 29th of June he was seized in a
cave in the Calabrian Mountains, brought bound on board
the *Foudroyant*, and put in charge of Lieutenant Parsons,
the signal lieutenant of the flagship. " He was," says
Parsons, " a thick set man of apparent strength, but
haggard with misery and want."[4]   By the order of
Captain Hardy his arms were unbound and food offered
to him.

On the 29th Nelson issued his order for a court-martial
on the prisoner, composed of officers of the Neapolitan
service, Captain Thurn to be the president, to be held on
board the *Foudroyant*.   What evidence was given of

[1] Despatches, vol. iii. p. 358.
[2] Clarke and McArthur, vol. ii. pp. 248–9.
[3] Despatches, vol. iii. p. 499.
[4] " Nelson Reminiscences," p. 3.   He was not the old man he professed
to be, his real age being about forty-two years.

Carraciolo's actions there is no record. There could not, however, have been any difficulty in proving his late acts of war on the Royalist forces. His defence, according to Lieutenant Parsons, was a recriminatory attack on the King, and the excuse that he had been compelled to join the revolutionary party to save his patrimonial property from confiscation. When he had once given the order for the trial, Nelson studiously refused to see any one but his own officers, and when the verdict of guilty—the only one that could be—was given, he refused to listen to any applications for a respite or a new trial. At five o'clock on the day of his trial Carraciolo was hung at the yard-arm of his own frigate. With this event Lady Hamilton had nothing whatever to do. With Sir William she was on board the flagship, but beyond acting as interpreter between Nelson and Cardinal Ruffo, she had no part in the events in the Bay of Naples. As for the stories told by Southey, and in more detail by Brenton, and repeated by Brougham and Allison, that she instigated and was present at the execution, and, according to Brenton, said to Nelson, " Bronte, let us go and see the fellow hung "— they were all false. Even if it were not sufficient to note that the gift and title of Bronte were not given till some-time after this event, or that it was asserted that John Mitford's denial of it is unreliable (as one writer has asserted) because he was a poor man lodging over a potato - dealer's shop, the evidence of Sir Francis Augustus Collier, who was on board the *Foudroyant*, is decisive that it was an arrant falsehood. The late Lord Northwich, too, told Mr. Mulready that he very well remembered being at dinner in Nelson's cabin, with the Hamiltons, when he heard the gun fired for Car-raciolo's execution.[1]

---

[1] How far the Queen of Naples was concerned in the matter, I leave to her latest biographer, Mr. Jeffreson. It is only fair, however, to quote

Though the castles of Uovo and Nuovo had been surrendered, those of St. Elmo, Capua, and Gaeta still remained in the hands of the French. To Troubridge the capture of these strong places was committed, and right well did he do the work, and prove himself as good a general by land as a captain by sea. " General Koehler," Nelson said in a letter to the Duke of Clarence, " does not approve of such irregular proceedings as naval officers attacking and defending fortifications. We have but one idea—to get close alongside. None but a sailor would have placed a battery only 180 yards from the Castle of St. Elmo : a soldier must have gone according to art-and-the Z Z way. My brave Troubridge went straight on, for we had no time to spare." By such tactics St. Elmo and Capua fell to Troubridge, and Gaeta surrendered to Captain Louis in the *Minotaur*. By the same bold plans, shortly after, the Franciscan friar's prophecy, that Nelson would take Rome with his ships, was fulfilled, when Louis rowed up the Tiber in his barge, hoisted the English flag on the Capitol, and acted for a time as governor of the city. The following letter to the Pope refers to this curious incident :—

" To His Holiness the Pope.

" LEGHORN, *June* 24, 1800.

" HOLY FATHER,—As an individual, who from his public situation has had an opportunity of using his utmost exertions to assist in bringing about the happy event of your Holiness's return to Rome, I presume to offer my most sincere congratulations on this occasion ; and with my most fervent wishes and prayers that your residence may be blessed with health and every comfort this world can afford.

" Your Holiness will, I am sure, forgive my mentioning a circum-

---

from her letter to Nelson of July 2nd, the following sentence, " I have seen also the sad and merited end of the unfortunate and mad-brained Carraciolo. I am sensible how much your excellent heart must have suffered."

stance which, although at the time it was spoken appeared impossible, yet the fact did happen.   Father McCormick, a friar, coming to the house of Sir W. Hamilton, in September, 1798, to congratulate me on the Battle of the Nile, said, ' What you have done is great, but you will do a greater thing—you will take Rome with your ships.' Although I do not believe that the father had the gift of prophecy, yet his guess was so extraordinary, and has turned out so exactly, that I could not, on my conscience, avoid telling your Holiness of it.   I will now only trespass on your time by assuring your Holiness with what respect I am, your obedient servant,

" BRONTE NELSON OF THE NILE." [1]

It was during these events that Nelson received orders from Lord Keith to " send such of his ships as he could spare off the Island of Minorca to wait his orders." Nelson's reply was an unhesitating refusal :—

" I have," he wrote to Lord Keith, " to acknowledge the receipt of your lordship's orders of June 27th, and as soon as the safety of his Sicilian Majesty's kingdom is secured, I shall lose not one moment in making the detachment you are pleased to order.   At present, under God's providence, the safety of his Sicilian Majesty and his speedy restoration to his kingdom depends on this fleet; and the confidence inspired even by the appearance of our ships before this city is beyond all belief; and I have no scruple in declaring my opinion that should any event draw us from this kingdom, that if the French remain in any part of it, disturbances will again arise, for all order having been completely overturned, it must take a thorough cleansing, and some little time to restore tranquillity." [2]

On the 19th of July came a peremptory note from Lord Keith, dated the 9th, to which Nelson replied :—

" That unless the French are at least drove from Capua, I think it not right to obey your lordship's order for sending down any part of the squadron under my orders   I am perfectly aware of the conse-quences of disobeying the orders of my commander-in-chief; but as

---

[1] Despatches, vol. iv. p. 259.
[2] Lord Keith to Nelson, June 27th; Nelson to Lord Keith, July 18, 1799 ; and Lord Keith to Nelson, July 9th.

I believe the safety of the Kingdom of Naples depends at the present moment on my detaining my squadron, I have no scruple in deciding that it is better to save the kingdom of Naples and risk Minorca, than to risk the kingdom of Naples to save Minorca." [1]

On the same day he wrote to Lord Spencer and the Duke of Clarence :—

"To Lord Spencer.

"*Foudroyant, July* 19, 1799.

"My Lord,—You will easily conceive my feelings at the order this day received here from Lord Keith; but my mind, your lordship will know by my letter sent by Lieutenant Parkinson, and Mr. Silvester, was perfectly prepared for the order ; and more than ever is my mind made up that, at this moment, I will not part with a single ship, as I cannot do that without drawing one hundred and twenty men from each ship at the siege of Capua, where an army has gone this day. I am fully aware of the act I have committed : but sensible of my loyal intentions, I am prepared for any fate which may await my disobedience. Capua and Gaeta will soon fall ; and the moment the scoundrels of French are out of this kingdom, I shall send eight or nine ships-of-the-line to Minorca. I have done what I thought right ; others may think differently ; but it will be my consolation that I have gained a kingdom, seated a faithful ally of his Majesty firmly on his throne, and restored happiness to millions. Do not think, my dear lord, that my opinion is formed from the arrangements of any one. *No ;* be it good or be it bad, it is all my own. It is natural that I should wish the decision of the Admiralty and my commander-in-chief as speedily as possible. To obtain the former, I beg your lordship's interest with the Board ; and in all events I shall consider myself to be your lordships, &c., &c.,

"Nelson." [2]

"To the Duke of Clarence.

"About *July* 19, 1799.

"You will have heard, Sir, and conversation will naturally arise upon it, that I have disobeyed Lord Keith's orders in not sending or going down with the squadron under my command ; but, by not doing it, I have been, with God's blessing, the principal means of placing a good man and a faithful ally of your Royal father on his

---

[1] To Lord Keith, July 19th.   [2] Despatches, vol. iii. pp. 408–9.

throne, and securing peace to these two kingdoms.   I am well aware
of the consequences of disobeying my orders ; but as I have ofter.
before risked my life for the good cause, so I with cheerfulness did
my commission ; for, although a military tribunal may think me
criminal, the world will approve of my conduct.   I regard not my
own safety, when the honour of my gracious King is at stake.   The
Almighty has in this war blessed my endeavours beyond my most
sanguine expectations, and never more than in the entire expulsion of
the French thieves from the kingdom of Naples.

" I am, &c.,

" NELSON."

In Malta the French still held possession, thanks to the
disgraceful neglect of the troops under Ball, who were
half starving and suffering from disease and hunger.   The
expedition from Minorca was delayed for lack of money
and supplies.   " The cause," said Nelson, " cannot stand
still for want of a little money.   If nobody will pay it,
I will sell Bronte and the Emperor of Russia's box."
The expedition at last started, and was like to have been
starved had not Ball seized the Neapolitan corn-ships at
Girgenti.

In the beginning of February, 1800, Nelson sailed for
Malta, and on his way fell in with and captured one of
his antagonists at the Nile, *Le Généreux,* part of a
squadron bound for the relief of the French garrison in
Malta.   Of this battle Lieut. Parsons gives the following
graphic account in his " Reminiscences."   Lord Nelson, it
is reported, when he heard the news, said, "She knew that
she belonged to us, and her conscience would not let her
stay away any longer." [1]

" ' Deck there !   The stranger is evidently a man-of-war.'

" ' She is a line-of-battle ship, my Lord, and going large on the
starboard tack.'

------

[1] Miss Knight, vol. ii. p. 287.   Was not this said by him of *Le Guillaume
Tell,* of which he only heard the news, and was not at her capture as he
was at that of *Le Généreux ?*

" 'Ah! an enemy, Mr. Haines. I pray God it may be *Le Généreux*. The signal for a general chase, Sir Ed'ard (addressed to Sir Edward Berry). Make the *Foudroyant* fly.'

" Thus spoke Nelson ; and every exertion that emulation could inspire was used to crowd the canvas, the *Northumberland* taking the lead, with the flag-ship close on her quarter.

" ' This will not do, Sir Ed'ard ; it is certainly *Le Généreux*, and to my flag-ship she can alone surrender. Sir Ed'ard, we must, we shall beat the *Northumberland.*'

" ' I will do my utmost, my Lord ; get the engine to work on the sails—hang butts of water to the stays—pipe the hammocks down, and each man place shot in them—slack the stays, knock up the wedges, and give the masts play—start off the water, Mr. James, and pump ship. The *Foudroyant* is drawing ahead, and at last takes the lead in the chase. The Admiral is working his fin (the stump of his right arm), do not cross his hawse, I advise you.'

" The advice was good, for at that moment Nelson opened furiously on the quarter-master at the cones.

" ' I'll knock you off your perch, you rascal, if you are so in-attentive. Sir Ed'ard, send your best quarter-master to the weather-wheel.'

" ' A strange sail a-head of the chase,' called out the look-out man.

" ' Youngster to the mast-head. What ! going without your glass, and be d——d to you ? Let me know what she is immediately.'

" ' A sloop of war or frigate, my Lord,' shouted the young signal midshipman.

" ' Demand her number.'

" ' The *Success*, my Lord.'

" ' Captain Peard, signal to cut off the flying enemy—great odds though—thirty-two small guns to eighty large ones.'

" ' The *Success* has hove to, athwart hawse of the *Généreux*, and is firing her larboard broadside. The Frenchman has hoisted his tri-colour.'

" ' Bravo. *Success at her again.*'

" ' She has wore round, my Lord, and firing her starboard broad-side. It has winged her—her flying kites are flying away altogether. The enemy is close on the *Success*, who must receive her tremendous broadside. The *Généreux* opens her fire on her little enemy, and every person stands aghast, afraid of the consequences. The smoke clears away, and there is the *Success*, crippled, it is true, but bull-dog-like, bearing up after the enemy.'

" ' Signal for *Success* to discontinue action, and come under my stern,' said Lord Nelson, 'she has done well for her size.   Try a shot from the lower deck at her, Sir Ed'ard.'

" 'It goes over her.'

" 'Beat to quarters, and fire coolly and deliberately at her masts and yards.'

" *Le Généreux* at this moment opened fire on the *Foudroyant*, and a shot passed through the mizen staysail, when Lord Nelson, patting one of the youngsters on the head, asked him jocularly how he relished the music ; and observing something like alarm depicted on his countenance, consoled him with the information, that Charles XII. ran away from the first shot he heard, though afterwards he was called 'The Great,' and deservedly from his bravery.   'I therefore,' said Lord Nelson, ' hope much from you in the future.'

" The *Northumberland* now opened her fire, and the tri-coloured ensign came down, amid the thunder of the English cannon.   A signal to discontinue firing was accordingly made, and Sir Edward Berry ordered to board the prize.   Very shortly Lieut. Parsons says he returned with Rear-Admiral Perée's sword, who he stated was dying on his quarter deck, with the loss of both legs ; shot off by the raking broadsides of the little *Success*.   This unfortunate Frenchman was under the imputation of having broken his parole, and was considered lucky in having redeemed his honour by dying in battle." [1]

One line-of-battle ship, *Le Guillaume Tell*, and two frigates alone remained of the fleet that fought at Aboukir.   The *Guillaume Tell*, closely watched in Valetta harbour, attempted to make her escape, and was encountered by the British squadron.   How she, the last of the ships-of-the-line that escaped from the Nile, was taken is best told in the letters of Captain Sir Edward Berry and Nelson.

" SIR EDWARD BERRY TO NELSON.

" *Foudroyant, March* 30, 1800.

" MY DEAR LORD,—I had but one wish this morning—it was for you.   After a most gallent defence *Le Guillaume Tell* surrendered.   She is completely dismasted.   The *Foudroyant's* lower masts and main-top-mast are standing, but every roll I expect them to go over the

---

[1] Lieut. Parson's " Nelsonian Reminiscences."

side, they are so much shattered.   I was slightly hurt in the foot, and
I fear about forty men badly wounded, besides the killed, which you
shall know hereafter.

"All hands behaved as you could have wished.   How we prayed
for you, God knows, and your sincere and faithful friend,
" E. BERRY.

"Love to all.   Pray send this to my wife, or write the Admiralty.
Within hail before I fired."

Nelson's reply :—

" PALERMO (*April*) 5, 1800.

"MY DEAR BERRY,—I am sensible of your kindness in wishing my
presence at the finish of the Egyptian Fleet, but I have no cause of
sorrow.   The thing could not be better done, and I would not for all
the world rob you of one particle of your well-earned laurels.   Thank
kindly all my brave friends in the *Foudroyant* : and whatever fate awaits
me, my attachment to them will never cease but with my life.   I hope
the *Foudroyant* will be able to come here to carry us first to Malta,
and from thence, taking the Queen of Naples to Leghorn, proceed
with us at least to Gibraltar, if not to England.   My task is done, my
health is lost, and the orders of the great Earl St. Vincent are completely fulfilled—thanks, ten thousand thanks, to my brave friends !
"Ever, my dear Berry, your sincere and affectionate friend,
"BRONTE NELSON OF THE NILE."

Nelson's letter to Evan Nepean, Esq., Admiralty :—

"PALERMO, *April* 4, 1800.

"SIR,—I have no official reports ; but I have letters from Commodore Troubridge, Captain Dixon, and Sir Edward Berry, telling me
of the capture of the *William Tell*, on the morn of the 30th of March,
after a gallant defence of three hours.   The *Lion* and the *Foudroyant*
lost each forty killed and wounded ; the French ship is dismasted ; the
French Admiral Decrès wounded ; the *Foudroyant* much shattered.
I send Sir E. Berry's hasty note.   Thus, owing to my brave friends,
is the entire capture and destruction of the French Mediterranean
Fleet to be attributed, and my orders from the great Earl St. Vincent
fulfilled.   Captain Blackwood of the *Penelope*, and Captain Long of
the *Vincejo* have the greatest merit.   My task is done, my health
finished, and, probably, my retreat for ever fixed, unless another
French Fleet should be placed for me to look after.
"BRONTE NELSON OF THE NILE."

In the end only one of the frigates escaped capture, the other being taken in an attempt to escape from Valetta harbour before the surrender of Malta to our forces.

With a brief account of one more incident—the correspondence between Nelson and Sir Sidney Smith, the future victor at Acre—this chapter must be closed. At the close of the year 1798, Nelson was naturally irritated with the claim made by Sir Sidney Smith, to assume an independent command off Alexandria, and, without so much as a request to him, take under his orders the squadron under Captain Hood, which Nelson had left to blockade that port. This annoyance due, we must hope, to Sir Sidney having misread his orders from home, was increased by the error of the Government in appointing him as joint ambassador at Constantinople with his brother Spencer.

" I do feel, for I am a man," wrote Nelson to Lord St. Vincent, now happily returned to his former command, "that it is impossible for me to serve in these seas with the squadron under a junior officer. Could I have thought it !—and from Earl Spencer. Never, never, was I so astonished as your letter made me. As soon as I can get hold of Troubridge, I shall send him to Egypt to endeavour to destroy the ships in Alexandria. If it can be done, Troubridge will do it. The Swedish knight writes Sir William, that he shall go to Egypt, and take Captain Hood and his squadron under his command. The knight forgets the respect due to his superior officer. He has no orders from you to take any ships from my command ; but it is all of a piece ? Is it to be borne ? Pray grant me permission to retire, and I hope the *Vanguard* will be allowed to convey me and my friends, Sir W. and Lady Hamilton, to England. God bless you, my lord, and believe me your most affectionate friend,

" NELSON."

Lord St. Vincent's reply was all that Nelson could have wished from his commander and friend. St. Vincent had been equally astonished with Nelson at the letter of the

Swedish knight, and had sent him peremptory orders to place himself immediately under Nelson's command.

"For the sake of your country," added St. Vincent, "and the existence of its power in the Levant, moderate your feelings, and continue in your command. . . . The sensations you must have gone through before and after your departure from Naples, must have been very trying ; nevertheless, I trust the greatness of your mind will keep the body, and that you will not think of abandoning the Royal family you have by your firmness and address preserved from the fate of their late Royal relations of France. Employ Sir Sidney Smith in any manner you think proper ; knowing your magnanimity, I am sure you will mortify him as little as possible, consistently with what is due to the great characters, senior to him on the list, and his superiors in every sense of the word. God bless you, my dear lord ; be assured no man loves and esteems you more truly than your very affectionate St. Vincent."[1]

Again, on the 8th of March, Nelson writes to St. Vincent, how he is puzzled to know whether Sir Sidney writes to him as a Minister or as a captain in the navy, and—

"As the latter," he adds, "they [his Letters] are highly indecent to write to an officer of my rank. You will agree with me, that the manner of saying the same thing makes it proper or otherwise ; but Sir Sidney's dictatorial way of writing is what I never before met with."

On the same day he wrote to Sir Sidney, requiring him

"Whenever he had ministerial affairs to communicate, that it be done jointly with your respectable brother, and not mix naval business with the other." "A representative may dictate to an admiral—a captain of a man-of-war would be censured for the same thing." "Not a ship more than the service requires shall be kept away on any particular station, and that number must be left to my judgment, as an admiral commanding the squadron detached by the commander-in-chief to the extent of the Black Sea."

[1] Despatches, vol. iii. pp. 315–6, note.

Though thus compelled to abate his pretensions of dealing with the ships of Nelson's squadron, Sir Sidney also, without seeking the leave or advice of Nelson, issued a passport in his own name, allowing ships and men to pass from Alexandria to France. "Now," wrote Nelson to Sir Sidney on the 18th of March, "as this is in direct opposition to my opinion, which is, never to suffer any one individual Frenchman to quit Egypt, I must, therefore, strictly charge and command you never to give any ship or man leave to quit Egypt."

Though thus decided in his rebuke of Sir Sidney's attempt to exercise an independent command, no one was more ready than Nelson to acknowledge his "truly meritorious and wonderful exertions" on the coast of Syria. Hence it was that when the news arrived of the rescue of Acre through Sir Sidney's exertions, he wrote to him the following letter of congratulation and justification of his previous conduct :—

"To Sir Sidney Smith.

"*August* 20, 1799.

"My dear Sir,—I have received, with the truest satisfaction, all your very interesting letters to 16th of July. The immense fatigue you have had in defending Acre against such a chosen army of French villains, headed by that arch-villain Bonaparte, has never been exceeded, and the bravery shown by you and your brave companions, is such as to merit every encomium which all the civilized world can bestow. As an individual and an admiral, will you accept my feeble tribute of praise and admiration, and make them acceptable to all those under your command.

Be assured, my dear Sir Sidney, of my perfect esteem and regard, and do not let any one persuade you to the contrary. But my character is, that I will not suffer the smallest tittle of my command to be taken from me ; but with pleasure I give way to my friends, among whom I beg you will allow me to consider you, and that I am, with truest esteem and affection, your faithful humble servant,

"Nelson."

Nelson's stay in the Mediterranean was now drawing to a close. He was ill in body, and dissatisfied in mind at having been passed over for Lord Keith in the Mediterranean command. On the 10th of June, 1800, he sailed with the Queen and her children, now eager to escape to Vienna, for the harbour of Leghorn, where they stayed a month ; and then on the 13th of July struck his flag, and prepared for a journey through Germany to England.

Whilst on this portion of his life, I add the following letter from the first Lord Auckland, to a brother of Sir Sidney Smith, which I found pasted in the cover of a " Life of Lord Nelson, by a Captain in the Navy," published in 1805, in the possession of Earl Nelson :—

" EDEN FARM, *Sept. 29th.*

" MY DEAR SIR,—Lord Nelson's [Letters ?] are creditable both to him and Sir Sydney (*sic* in the MS.), and very deserving to make a part of Sir Sydney's family archives. But for that purpose it is necessary that he should establish a family, which may never happen, if he should persist in the pursuit of broken bones, pestilence, and all the pains of body and vexations of mind that are to be found on the coasts of Judæa and of Egypt.

" By the by, I am no admirer of the Dukedom of Bronte :—the title of Thunderer from so helpless an idiot as the King of Naples is not half so flattering as the Barony of Nelson of the Nile from George the Third.

" We most heartily lament the domestic affliction to which Mrs. Smith and you continue to experience,

" I am, my dear Sir,

" Most sincerely yours,

" AUCKLAND."

On the 6th of November, 1800, after passing through Germany with the Hamiltons,[1] Nelson landed at Yarmouth. He had been absent from England for three years of almost ceaseless toil, which had told severely on his delicate

---

[1] I have, *post* Chapter XIX., dealt with the scandalous report circulated by Mrs. French of the conduct of Nelson and the Hamiltons at Dresden.

frame. His reception in his native land was worthy of
his great acts. As soon as he landed, the populace who
had assembled in crowds, took the horses out of his
carriage and drew him to his house. The municipal
authorities presented him with the freedom of their
ancient borough, and in procession went with him to the
grand old church for a service of thanksgiving. The
military in the town paraded before his hotel, and all the
day and evening up till midnight, music and volleys of fire-
arms kept up the excitement, whilst in the harbour all
the ships flew their colours. Two days after he left for
London, stopping on his way at the old parsonage in the
hopes of meeting his venerable father, who had gone to
Lady Nelson's in London, and eventually meeting him
there with his wife.

The next day—Lord Mayor's Day—he was invited to
a banquet, and again as he joined the procession to
Guildhall, the people took out his horses and dragged his
carriage thither, the whole route being lined with a shout-
ing crowd, and the windows filled with excited spectators.
At the civic feast he was presented with a valuable sword,
on the handle of which the figure of a crocodile appears
emblematic of the grand event off the mouth of the Nile.
Nelson's reply to the address of the Chamberlain on the
presentation of the sword, which he held in his left hand,
was admirably brief. " It is," he said, " with the greatest
pride and satisfaction I receive from the honourable Court
this testimony of their approbation of my conduct ; and
with this very sword (taking it in his hand), I hope soon
to aid in reducing our implacable and inveterate enemy
to proper and due limits—without which this country can
neither hope for, nor expect, a solid, honourable, and
permanent peace."

COPENHAGEN.

CHAPTER XII.

COPENHAGEN.

(1801.)

England and the Northern Coalition—The navies of the Northern
Powers—Nelson's flag removed to the *St. George* from the *San
Josef*—The Expedition to the Baltic—Delay in sailing—Letters to
Troubridge and St. Vincent—Ignorance of the plan of the expedi-
tion—Sail at last—Nelson's plan for the attack on the Danes—
Parker's indecision and delays—Loss of valuable time—The scene
of the battle—Danish defences—Nelson's account of the action—
Signal No. 30—The letters to the Danes—The truce and its results
—Further hesitation of Parker—At last in the Baltic—Recall of
Parker and appointment of Nelson—The cruise to Revel—Anger of
the Russians—Pahlen's letter and subsequent apology—No more
fighting—Nelson and his fleet—Commodores and contractors—The
infringement of the armistice—Resigns his command—Takes leave
of the fleet.

N the beginning of the year 1801,
when Nelson was returning to London,
his prophecy, that "England, after
beginning this war with all Europe
on her side, will end it with all Europe
against her," was fulfilled. The claim
of the English "to search vessels be-
longing to neutral powers in times of war," was denied
by these powers; and the northern Courts—Denmark and
Sweden — putting themselves under the protection of
Russia, formed an armed neutrality to resist it. Masters
of the sea, the English ignored this demand, and brought
the question to the brink of an issue by the capture, in

July, 1800, of a Danish merchantman, which had refused to allow her cargo to be searched for goods contraband of war. The situation demanded immediate action on the part of England :—

"On the one side," writes M. Jurien de la Gravière, "the systematic energy of France directed the military force of Prussia and the maritime resources of Spain against Great Britain ; on the other, the morbid activity of the great Catherine's fantastic successor closed the Continent against the English from the Neva to the Elbe. If anything could have lessened the importance of the last coalition, it was the singular coincidence by which the sovereign powers of the northern thrones had fallen into such eccentric hands. Christian VII. of Denmark had fallen into imbecility ; but there at least the Prince Royal afterwards Frederick VI., son of the unfortunate Matilda, sister of George III., had taken the reins of government with a firm hand. Gustavus IV. of Sweden was subject to frequent fits of temporary insanity ; and the Emperor of Russia, by his chivalrous maxims and his versatile and absurd policy, betrayed the madman under the cloak of the despot." [1]

According to the information at our Admiralty, these three powers could put to sea more than one hundred and twenty line-of-battle ships. In reality, their effective force in the northern seas did not exceed fifty men-of-war, of whom the eleven of Sweden and ten of Denmark were ready for sea, and capable of being manned with efficient crews and commanded by experienced officers. Still could the fleets of the three powers have effected a junction, they might have proved difficult antagonists in such a dangerous sea as the Baltic. To prevent this junction was the object of the Baltic Expedition, a project initiated by Earl Spencer and continued by Lord St. Vincent, who, in February, 1801, succeeded him as First Lord of the Admiralty.

On the 17th of January, 1801, Nelson, as a vice-

---

[1] Capt. Jurien de la Gravière, vol. ii. p. 78.

admiral, had hoisted his flag in the *San Josef*, 112 guns, his former prize at the battle of St. Vincent. He had hoped to have been sent to replace Lord Keith in the Mediterranean, but in the interim joined the Channel Fleet under Lord St. Vincent, and on his removal to the Admiralty was placed under Sir Hyde Parker for the Baltic Expedition.

The fleet now preparing mustered twenty-one line-of-battle ships and three flag officers. Sir Hyde Parker in the *London*, Nelson in the *St. George*, and Admiral Graves in the *Defiance*; and to meet the difficulties of the navigation in the Danish seas, five ships of sixty-four guns and two of fifty were added to the eleven seventy-fours; these, with some frigates, fire-ships, bombs, and small craft, made up the total of fifty-three sail, with a corps of soldiers of the 49th Regiment, two companies of Carabineers, and a detachment of Artillery.

In February, 1801, therefore, Nelson shifted his flag to the *St. George*, as a more suitable ship for the proposed service, and at once became anxious for the sailing of the expedition. "Time," as he once said to General William Twiss, "Time is everything: five minutes make the difference between a victory and a defeat." [1] Apparently at this time he wrote the following letter to Troubridge, now one of the Junior Lords of the Admiralty :—

"Aye, my dear Troubridge, had you been here to-day you would have thought, had the *Pilot* arrived a fortnight hence, there would have been time enough. *Fame* says *we* are to sail on the 20th, and I believe it, unless you pack us off. I was in hopes that Sir Hyde would have had a degree of confidence, but no appearance of it. I know he has from Nepean the plan of the fortifications of the New Islands off Copenhagen and the intended station of some Danish ship. I have, be assured, no other desire of knowing anything than that I may the better execute the service, but I have no right to know, and

---

[1] Despatches, vol iv. p. 290, note. Ex relatione E. Sartees, Esq.

do not say a word of it to Lord St. Vincent, for he may think me very impertinent in endeavouring to dive into the plans of my commander-in-chief, but the water being clear, I can see the *bottom* with half an eye. I begged Domet [1] only to use the *St. George* and we would do anything. The *Squirrel* will be refitted in two hours to-morrow from a list of complaints of two sides of paper. The Gun Brigs are in wretched order, but they will get on. Poor Domet seemed in a pack of troubles. Get rid of us, my dear friend, and we shall not be tempted to lay abed till eleven o'clock. If the Earl would give Josiah a ship in greater forwardness, and send him abroad, it would be an act of kindness. I feel all your kindness, but perhaps I am now unfit to command, my only ambition is to obey. I have no wish ungratified in the service, so you may say, but I told you I was *unhappy*." [2]

It was not, however, until the beginning of March that Nelson could sail for the appointed rendezvous in Yarmouth Roads, when he wrote the following despairing letter to Lord St. Vincent :—

"*March* 2nd.

"Getting under sail. I am always happy when my conduct meets your approbation ; whilst I remain in the service my utmost exertions shall be called forth ; for although, I own, I have met with more honour and rewards than ever my most sanguine ideas led me to expect, yet I am so circumstanced that probably this expedition will be the last service ever performed by your obliged and affectionate friend,

"BRONTE AND NELSON."

St. Vincent's reply :—

" Be assured, my dear lord, that every public act of your life has been the subject of my admiration, which I should have sooner declared, but that I was appalled by the last sentence of your letter ; for God's sake, do not suffer yourself to be carried away by a sudden

---

[1] Sir Hyde Parker's captain, and captain of the fleet.

[2] I am indebted to the kindness of Mrs. Herbert Jones, of King's Lynn, and the proprieters of *The Century* Company, New York, for the liberty of using this and the following letters of Nelson to Troubridge, originally published in *The Century* magazine of November, 1888.

impulse. With many thanks for the spur you have given to the movement of the ships at Spithead, believe me, &c.,

"St. Vincent." [1]

When, after a long and rough passage, he reached the
rendezvous early in March, still the hesitation of Sir
Hyde Parker again increased his anxiety for action :—

"*St. George, March* 11, 1801.

"My dear Troubridge,—It is not that I care what support I may
have as far as relates to myself, but the *glorious* support I am to have
marks *me ;* but let jealousy, cabal, and art conspire to do their worst,
the *St. George* is and shall be fit for battle. I will trust to myself
alone, and Hardy will support me. Far, far, very far from good
health, this conduct will and shall rouse me for the moment, but we
cannot get off. My information is, I dare say, better than yours.
The *London* was unmoored when the signal was made to prepare for
sea, but now she is safely *moor'd.* I shall trouble you to forward any
letters to me and from me to my friends, and ever believe me your
most affectionate

"Nelson and Bronte.

"You will make —— very happy by getting him a ship to go
abroad. Hardy has been on board of Domet, who told Hardy to tell
me he did not order the form of Battle. By that, he sees as I do.
Captain Otway has not been on board all yesterday or to-day. Domet
hopes to sail to-morrow."

Again on the same day he wrote to Troubridge :—

"*St. George, March* 11, 1801.

"My dear Troubridge,—The signal is made to prepare to unmoor
at twelve o'clock, but I think, the wind being S.S.E., and very dirty,
that our chief may defer it. If it rains a little the wind will fly to
the westward. Now we can have no desire for staying, for her ladyship is gone, and the *Ball* for Friday knocked up by yours and the
earl's unpoliteness, to send gentlemen to sea instead of dancing with
white gloves. I will only say as yet I know not that we are
even going to the Baltic, except from the newspapers, and at sea I
cannot go out of my ship but with serious inconvenience. I could

---

[1] Clarke and McArthur, vol. ii. p. 258 ; Despatches, vol. iv. 290–1,
note.

say much, but patience.   I shall knock down my bulkheads throughout the ship, and then, let what will happen the *St. George*—she has only to trust to herself—will be prepared.   Remember me to the earl, and believe me, your affectionate friend,

"   NELSON AND BRONTE.

"Every day and hour shows me Hardy's work.   Captain Thesiger is not so active as Parker."

It was Captain Thesiger who carried the famous letter from Nelson to the Danes in the heat of the battle, when serving as aide-de-camp to Nelson on the *St. George*. After serving for two years in the Russian Navy, he had lately left it in consequence of the extraordinary conduct of the Emperor Paul.[1]

At length, on the 12th of March, the fleet sailed, and on the 13th, when off the Naze of Norway, Nelson wrote a letter to Troubridge, dated 13th and 16th, the latter portion of which I give :—

"*March* 16th.

"I am yet all in the dark, and am not sure we are bound to the Baltic. Reports says (and I only make my remarks from reports) that we are to anchor this side Cronenburgh to give time for negotiation.   I earnestly hope this is not true, for I wish for peace with Denmark, and therefore am clearly of opinion that to show our fleet off Copenhagen would, if in the least wavering, almost ensure it, for I think that the Danish Minister would be a hardy man to put his name to a paper which in a few minutes would, I trust, involve his master's navy, and I hope his capital, in flames.   But as I am not in the *secret*, and feel I have a right to speak out, not in the fleet certainly, but in England and to England, my ideas are to get up the Cattegat as soon as possible (we are now standing on a wind at W.S.W. moderate weather, off the Naze), to send a flag of truce, if such is necessary, to Cronen-

---

[1] See letter to Lord St. Helen's, Ambassador at St. Petersburg, May 22nd.   Despatches, vol. iv. p. 380.   He was the uncle of the late Lord Chelmsford, better known as Sir Frederick Thesiger, and for his conduct in the Russian Navy against the Swedes received the Cross of St. George from the Empress Catherine ; he was only a commander in our navy, and served as a volunteer in Nelson's fleet ; posted in 1801, and died 1805 ; agent for prisoners of war at Portsmouth.

burg to say that I should pass the Castle, and that if they did not fire at me, I should not at them. The despatches, if any, for our Minister at Copenhagen, at the same time to be sent. I should certainly pass the Castle whether they fired or not, and send the same message to Copenhagen till negotiation was over. Being off that city, I could prevent all additional preparation from being carried on or any more gunboats &c. placed outside, whilst I should prepare everything, and the moment the Danish Minister said WAR, he should have enough of it, but he would say peace, and save his honour with his new friends. Thus we should have peace with Denmark to a certainty either by *fair* or *foul* means, but I may be all wrong and the measures pursuing never better. I wish they may, but I doubt. Bold measures from ministers and speedily executed, meet my ideas. If you were here just to look at us ! I had heard of the manœuvres off Ushant, but ours beat all ever seen. Would it were all over, I am really sick of it. With my kind respects to the Earl, believe me, ever your affectionate and faithful

"NELSON AND BRONTE.

"*March* 17, 1801."[1]

As yet Nelson had only a vague report of the plans of Sir Hyde Parker :—

"I have not yet seen my Commander-in-Chief," he wrote to Davison, on the 16th of March, "and have had no official communication whatever. All I have gathered of first plans I disapprove most exceedingly ; honour may arise from them, good cannot. I hear we are likely to anchor outside Cronenburg Castle instead of Copenhagen, which would give weight to our negotiation : a Danish Minister would think twice before he would put his name to war with England, when the next moment he would probably see his master's fleet in flames, and his capital in ruins ; but 'out of sight out of mind,' is an old saying. The Dane should see our flag waving every moment he lifted up his head."[2]

On the 22nd the Admiralty instructions reached Sir Hyde Parker to enter the Baltic and seize the Russian Fleet at Revel, if the negotiations with Denmark turned out favourably, and if those with Sweden were also satis-

[1] Letters to Troubridge, *Century* magazine.
[2] Despatches, vol. iv. p. 246 ; Nelson sometimes writes "Krouberg," the Danish form of spelling : I have kept to the English form.

factory to protect that power from the enmity of Russia. On the 24th, Mr. Vansittart, our envoy, returned to the fleet, then off the point of Elsinore, with the intelligence that our offers to the Danes had been rejected, and the expedition must proceed. On the previous day Nelson had been on board the flagship in consultation with his chief, and the next day wrote the following letter to Sir Hyde Parker, with his advice how the duty now certain to be imposed on the fleet should be done :—

"MY DEAR SIR HYDE,—The conversation we had yesterday has naturally, from its importance, been the subject of my thoughts, and the more I have reflected the more I am confirmed in opinion, that not a moment should be lost in attacking the enemy ; they will every day and hour be stronger ; we never shall be so good a match for them as at this moment. The only consideration in my mind is how to get at them with the least risk of our ships. By Mr. Vansittart's account, their state of preparation exceeds what he conceives our Government thought possible, and that the Danish Government is hostile to us in the greatest possible degree. Therefore, here you are, with almost the safety, certainly the honour of England more entrusted to you, than ever fell to the lot of a British officer. On your decision depends whether our country shall be degraded in the eyes of Europe, or whether she shall rear her head higher than ever; again, do I repeat, never did out country depend so much on the success of any fleet as on this. How best to honour our country, and abate the pride of her enemies by defeating their schemes, must be the subject of your deepest consideration as Commander-in-chief, and if what I offer can be the least useful in forming your decision, you are most heartily welcome.

"I shall begin with supposing you are determined to enter by the passage of the Sound, as there are those who think if you leave that passage, that the Danish Fleet may sail from Copenhagen and join the the Dutch or French. I own I have no fears on that subject ; for it is not likely that whilst their capital is menaced with an attack, nine thousand of their best men would be sent out of the kingdom. I suppose that some danger may arise amongst our masts and yards ; yet, perhaps, there will not be one of them but could be made serviceable again. You are now about Cronenburg ; if the wind be fair, and you determine to attack the ships and the Crown Islands, you must expect the natural issue of such a battle—ships crippled, and perhaps one or two lost; for the wind which carries you in will most probably not bring out a crippled ship. This mode I call taking the bull by the horns. It, however, will not prevent the Revel ships, or Swedes, from joining the Danes; and to prevent this taking effect, is, in my humble opinion, a measure absolutely necessary—and still to attack Copenhagen. Two modes are in my view: one to pass Cronenburg, taking the risk of damage, and to pass up the deepest and straightest channel above the Middle Grounds; and coming down the Garbar or King's Channel, to attack their floating batteries, &c., &c., as we find it convenient. It must have the effect of preventing a junction between the Russians, Swedes, and Danes, and may give us an opportunity of bombarding Copenhagen. I am also pretty certain that a passage could be found to the northward of Saltholm for all our ships; perhaps it might be necessary to warp a short distance in the very narrow part.

"Should this mode be ineligible, the passage of the Belt, I have no doubt, would be accomplished in four or five days, and then the attack by Drajin could be carried into effect, and the junction with the Russians prevented, with every probability of success against the Danish floating batteries. What effect a bombardment would have I am not called upon to give an opinion; but think that the way would be cleared by the trial. Supposing us through the Belt with the wind full westerly, would it not be possible to either go with the fleet, or detach ten ships of three and two decks, with one bomb and two fire-ships, to Revel, to destroy the Russian squadron at that place? I do not see the great risk of such a detachment, and with the remainder to attempt the business at Copenhagen. The measure may be thought bold, but I am of opinion the boldest measures are the safest; and our country demands a most vigorous exertion of her force, directed with judgment.

"In supporting you, my dear Sir Hyde, through the arduous and important task you have undertaken, no exertion of head or heart shall be wanting from your most obedient and faithful servant,

"NELSON AND BRONTE."[1]

To enable my readers to understand the value of this advice, I now give Captain Jurien de la Gravière's very clear description of the scene of the impending action:—

"Better to appreciate this new exploit of the English Navy, it is necessary to have a clear idea of the obstacles of all sorts which the very nature of the scene of operations would present to the designs of

---

[1] Despatches, vol. iv. pp. 295-98.

the Admiralty. Three passages—the Sound, the Great and Little Belt—
are the channels which form the entrance from the German Ocean
to the Baltic, and connect these two dangerous seas, separated from
each other only by that narrow country which, under the name of
Jutland, stretches northward from the mouth of the Elbe to the fifty-
eighth degree of latitude. To penetrate into the Baltic, therefore, it
is necessary, in the first place, to double the northern points of Jutland, by sailing through the Channel where shipwrecks are so
frequent, and which bears the name of *Skagerack*. Then to steer
southwards through the Cattegat to where the islands of Zealand and
Funen seem to fill up the space which separates Jutland and Sweden
for one of the three passages. Of these three one is almost impracticable—the Little Belt—a narrow and intricate channel formed by
nature between the Isle of Funen and the coast of Jutland. The
Great Belt, a sinous strait, which separates the Isle of Funen and the
Isle of Zealand and enters the Baltic after a course of fifty leagues,
presenting difficulties which at that time the English could not surmount. The third passage, called the Sound, that between the island
of Zealand on which Copenhagen is built, and the southern extremity
of Sweden, is the easiest and most frequented. It was long regarded
as the key of the Baltic. On the coast of Zealand is the Castle of
Kronenberg ; a palace, fortress, and state prison command the
entrance. This castle is distant from the coast of Sweden about
three miles, and partly shuts out the view of the town of Elsinore.
The Island of Hueen, with its whitish cliffs, occupies the middle
channel, which rapidly enlarges below Elsinore. In the distance,
and twenty-two miles from Kronenberg, may be seen the lofty steeples
of Copenhagen and the low islands of Saltholm and Anag, the first
nearer Sweden, the second united to the capital of Denmark by long
bridges. Beyond these two islands the Sound opens into the Baltic.

"Near the island of Saltholm, on the coast of Sweden, opposite
Copenhagen, stands the town of Malmo. Between these two towns,
distant from each other about fifteen miles, the Island of Saltholm
forms two straits : one separating from Malmo, the other between
Saltholm and the meadow land of Anag, united, as we have said, to
the city of Copenhagen. This last strait is itself divided in two by a
shoal three miles long, called the Middel Grund, on which there are
only two fathom and a half. This is the Danish pass of Thermopylæ.
The western passage, called the King's, is compressed between the
port of Copenhagen, to which it forms an outer road and the Middel
Grund ; the eastern passage separates that shoal from the Isle of Saltholm, and is called the Outer Channel. Both run north and south,

and are practicable for the largest ships ; but the channel where they unite, beyond the Middel Grund, is shoaled, and a line-of-battle ship to get through must be lightened.   Rapid currents, generally following the direction of the wind, make this intricate navigation still more dangerous." [1]

To add to these natural difficulties, the Danes had taken advantage of the unfortunate delay of the expedition to increase the natural defences of their capital.   In addition to the Trekonner battery, with its sixty-nine guns, defending the entrance to the King's Channel from the north end and the inner harbour, two old line-of-battle ships were placed to further guard the fleet.

" It was only, then," continues our author, " from the south end, therefore, of the ' King's Channel' that Copenhagen could be attacked, and even on that side there were formidable obstacles, for the Danes had covered the face of the town with a long line of hulks and old ships, carrying 628 guns and 4,849 men.   That line-of-battle anchored about a quarter of a mile in advance of the batteries of the town left a space of half a mile between it and the Middel Grund, with an average depth of five or six fathoms.   If these first defences should be destroyed, the threat of a bombardment might probably overcome the resistance of Denmark ; but the first and greatest difficulty was to get through the King's passage." [2]

The reports of the Danish defences at Cronenberg and Copenhagen, brought by Mr. Vansittart and the pilots who accompanied him, induced the Commander-in-chief to turn back on the 26th, and attempt the passage by the Great Belt.   After, however, sailing for a few leagues along the coast of Zealand, the plan was suddenly changed, and the fleet came back to its anchorage off the entrance of the Sound.   This fortunate change, we are told by Captain Stewart, whose account of the battle is so well known, was due " partly

---

[1] "The Last Naval War," Jurien de la Gravière, vol. ii. pp. 87–90.

[2] Ibid., vol. ii. p. 91. M. J. de la Gravière as a foreigner uses the Danish spelling of the proper names ; apparently " Anag" is the island of " Armager," see Nelson's letter to Addington, p. 256.

to the suggestions of Captain George Murray of the
Edgar, who was to have led through this intricate passage,
but chiefly at the instigation of Lord Nelson, who went
on board the *London* at ten a.m." According to the writer
of a memoir of Sir Robert Waller Otway, who at that
time was on board the *London,* it was due to his urgent
advice that the route by the Sound was at last selected
by Sir Hyde. " On Captain Otway being sent to apprise
Lord Nelson of the reasons, Nelson exclaimed, ' I don't
care by which passage we go, so that we fight them.' He
determined to return with Captain Otway to the Commander-in-chief, and, in consequence of the wind blowing
fresh, was hoisted out in one of the boats ; and on his
arrival on board the *London,* everything was finally
arranged agreeably." [1] Still, however, Sir Hyde Parker
hesitated, delaying in order to send a message to the
Governor of Cronenberg to inquire whether he had
orders to oppose the passage of the fleet. His answer
might have been expected : " He had nothing to do with
politics, but could not suffer a fleet of which he did not
know the intentions to approach the guns of Cronenberg."
Three days more were thus lost, and it was not until the
30th that the fleet finally weighed,[2] Nelson leading the
van in the *Elephant* 74, a lighter ship than the *St. George,*
Parker leading the centre, and Admiral Graves the rear.
On that day Nelson wrote to Troubridge :—

" *March* 30th, six o'clock in the morning.

"We are now standing for Cronenberg ; the van is formed in a
compact line, and old Stricker, for that is the Governor's name, had

---

[1] Ralfe's " Naval Biography " ; Despatches, vol. iv. p. 301, note.

[2] It is related by Mr. Ferguson, the surgeon of the *Elephant,* that the
necessary soundings down the outer channel were made under Nelson's
own eye. " I could only admire," he said, " when I saw the first man in
all the world spend the hours of the day and night in the boats, and
wonder, when the light showed me a path marked by buoys which was
trackless the preceding evening " (Reported by Harrison, vol. ii. p. 291).

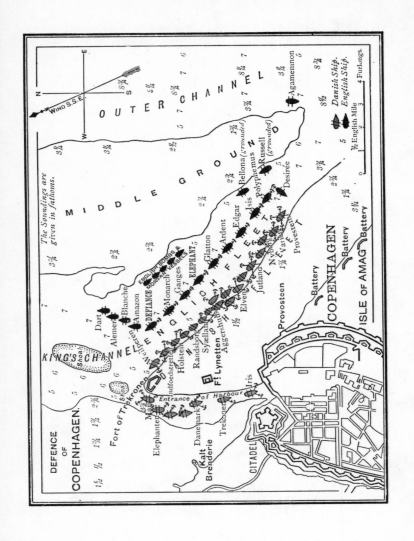

better take care we don't *strike* his head off. I hope we shall mend on board the *London*, but I now pity Sir Hyde and Domet; they both, I fancy wish themselves elsewhere. You may depend on every exertion of mine to keep up harmony. For the rest the spirit of the fleet will make all difficulty from enemies appear as nothing. I do not think I ever saw more true a desire to distinguish themselves in my life. I have more to tell you if ever we meet. With kindest regards to the Earl,

"Believe me,

"Ever your affectionate

"NELSON AND BRONTE."

"On the back of this letter is written the following list of the line :—

Monarch.	*Polephemus.*	
Bellona.	*Agamemnon.*	
Elephant.	*Defence.*	Lord Nelson's Division." [1]
Ardent.	*Russell.*	
Isis.	*Glatton.*	

Pursuing the plan of allowing Nelson, as far as possible, to tell his own story, I give his official report to Sir Hyde Parker of this most severe action. It will be noted that in this account he speaks very little of himself, but does not allow the meritorious acts of his comrades to escape unnoticed. As in the case of Troubridge at the Nile, he specially vindicates those captains, who had the misfortune to get on shore in making the difficult passage to the battle ground, from the slightest blame, and recognizes the value of their services when thus debarred from joining in the terrible *mêlée :—*

"To VICE-ADMIRAL SIR HYDE PARKER.

"*Elephant*, OFF COPENHAGEN, *April* 3, 1801.

"SIR,—In obedience to your directions to report the proceedings of the squadron named in the margin,[2] which you did me the honour to place under my command, I beg leave to inform you that, having,

---

[1] *Century* magazine.

[2] *Elephant, Defiance, Monarch, Bellona, Edgar, Russell, Ganges, Glatton, Isis, Agamemnon, Polyphemus, Ardent;* frigates *Amazon, Desiree, Blanche, Alcmene,* four sloops, two fire-ships, and seven bombs.

by the assistance of that able officer, Captain Rion, and the unremitting exertions of Captain Brisbane, and the masters of the *Amazon*
and *Cruiser* in particular, buoyed the channel of the Outer Deep and
the position of the Middle Ground, the squadron passed in safety,
and anchored off Draco the evening of the first, and that yesterday
morning I made signal for the squadron to weigh, and to engage the
Danish line, consisting of six sail-of-the-line, eleven floating batteries,
mounting from 26 twenty-four-pounders to 18 eighteen-pounders, and
one bomb-ship, besides schooner gun-vessels. These were supported
by the Crown Islands, mounting eighty-eight cannon, and four sail-
of-the-line moored in the harbour's mouth, and some batteries on the
Island of Anak.

"The bomb-ship and schooner gun-vessels made their escape. The
other seventeen sail are sunk, burnt, or taken, being the whole of the
Danish line to the southward of the Crown Islands, after a battle of
four hours.

"From the very intricate navigation the *Bellona* and *Russell*
unfortunately grounded, but, although not in the situation assigned
them, yet so placed as to be of great service. The *Agamemnon* could
not weather the shoals of the Middle Ground, and was obliged to
anchor, but not the smallest blame can be attached to Captain
Faircourt. It was an event to which all the ships were liable.
These accidents prevented the extension of our line by the three
ships before mentioned, who would, I am confident, have silenced the
the Crown Islands, the two outer ships in the harbour's mouth, and
prevented the heavy loss in the *Monarch* and *Defiance*, and which
unhappily threw the gallant and good Captain Rion (to whom I had
given the command of the frigates and sloops named in the margin to
assist in the attack of the ships at the harbour's mouth) under a very
heavy fire. The consequence has been the death of Captain Rion
and many brave officers and men in the frigates and sloops.

"The Bombs were directed and took their stations abreast of the
Elephant, and threw some shell into the Arsenal. Captain Rose, who
volunteered his services to direct the gun-brigs, did everything that
was possible to get them forward, but the current was too strong for
them to be of service in the action ; but not the less merit is due to
Captain Rose, and, I believe, all the officers and crews of the gun-brigs
for their exertions.

"The boats of these ships of the fleet who were not ordered on the
attack, afforded every assistance ; and the officers and men who were
in them merit my warmest approbation.

"The *Desiree* took her position in raking the southernmost Danish ship-of-the-line, and performed the greatest service. The action began at five minutes past ten—the van led by Captain George Murray, of the *Edgar*, who set a noble example of intrepidity, which was as well followed up by every captain, officer, and man in the squadron.

"It is my duty to state to you the high and distinguished merit and gallantry of Rear-Admiral Graves. To Captain Foley, who permitted me the honour of hoisting my flag in the *Elephant*, I feel under the greatest obligations ; his advice was necessary on many and important occasions during the battle. I beg leave to express how much I feel indebted to every captain, officer, and man for their zeal and distinguished bravery on this occasion. The Honourable Colonel Stewart did me the favour to be on board the *Elephant* ; and himself, with every officer and soldier under his orders, shared with pleasure the toils and dangers of the day.

"The loss in such a battle has necessarily been heavy.[1] Amongst other brave officers and men who were killed, I have with sorrow to place the name of Captain Moss of the *Monarch*, who has left a wife and six children to lament his loss. Among the wounded, that of Sir Thomas Boulden Thompson of the *Bellona*.

"I have the honour to be, &c.,

"Nelson and Bronte."

I now add Colonel Stewart's account of how Nelson acted when the signal of recall was made by Parker.

"About one p.m., when," says Colonel Stewart, "the contest in general, though from the relaxed state of the enemy's fire, it might might not have given much room for apprehension as to the result, had not declared itself on either side, Sir Hyde Parker made

"Signal No. 30.

"Lord Nelson was at this time, as he had been during the whole action, walking the starboard side of the quarter-deck ; sometimes much animated, at others heroically fine in his observations. A shot through the mainmast knocked a few splinters about us. He observed to me with a smile, 'It is warm work, and this day may be the last of any of us at a moment ; ' and then stopping short at the gangway, he used an expression never to be erased from my memory, and said with emotion, 'I would not be elsewhere for thousands.' When the signal No. 30 (cease firing) was made, the signal lieutenant reported it to

---

[1] The total loss was 29 officers and 234 men=263 killed ; and wounded : Officers, 48 ; men, 641 =680. Total, 943. Despatches, vol. iv. p. 313, *et seq.*

him. He continued his walk, and did not appear to take notice of it. The lieutenant, meeting his lordship at the next turn, asked ' whether he should repeat it.' Lord Nelson answered ' No ; acknowledge it.' On the officer returning to the poop, his lordship called after him, ' Is No. 16 still hoisted ? ' The lieutenant answering in the affirmative, Lord Nelson said, ' Mind you keep it so.' He now walked the deck considerably agitated, which was always known by his moving the stump of his right arm. After a turn or two, he said to me in a quick manner, ' Do you know what's shown on board the commander-in-chief, No. 30 ? ' On asking him what that meant, he answered, ' Why, to leave off action.' ' Leave off action,' he repeated, and then added with a shrug, ' Now, damn me if I do ! ' He also observed, I believe, to Captain Foley, ' I have only one eye—I have a right to be blind sometimes,' and then with an archness peculiar to his character, putting the glasses to his blind eye, he exclaimed, ' I really do not see the signal.' [1]

" Still, therefore, the battle raged. ' At two p.m. the greater part of the Danish line ceased to fire, some of the lighter ships were adrift, and the carnage on board the enemy, who reinforced their crews from the shore, was dreadful. The taking possession of such ships as had struck, was, however, attended with difficulty ; partly by reason of the batteries on Anak Island protecting them, and partly because an irregular fire was made on our boats, as they approached, from the ships themselves. The *Danebrog* (the ship directly opposed to the *Elephant*)

---

[1] Colonel Stewart's narrative, Despatches, vol. iv. pp. 308–9. The reason for this signal has been much canvassed. Southey and James state that it was " under a mistaken judgment, but from a disinterested and generous feeling, fearing that the squadron would be defeated, the wind and current preventing his bringing his own division to its assistance. The fire, he said, was too hot for Nelson to oppose, a retreat, he thought, must be made. He was aware of the consequences to his own personal reputation ; but it would be cowardly in him to leave Nelson to bear the whole shame of the failure, if shame it should be deemed." The truth, it is believed, was that Nelson had before arranged that he might, in his discretion, neglect the signal. In the biography of the Rev. A. J. Scott, Lord Nelson's chaplain, who acted as Secretary of Legation, in the negotiations with the Danes, it is said, " The simple version of this circumstance is, that it had been arranged between the admirals, that if it should appear that the ships which were engaged were suffering too severely, the signal for retreat should be made, to give Lord Nelson the option of retiring, if he thought fit." (" Life of Dr. Scott," p. 70). " Foley was probably in the secret, and Nelson's pantomime was probably a joke, such as he sometimes was guilty of " (Laughton, p. 256, note).

acted in this manner, and fired at our boats, although that ship was on fire and had struck.' A renewed attack on her by the *Elephant* and *Glatton*, in a quarter of an hour, silenced her, and she was seen, as the smoke cleared, drifting away in flames. Such of the crew as survived throwing themselves from the port-holes. At half-past three she blew up. Before the *Danebrog* blew up, when the whole line astern of the *Elephant* had struck, and the action was practically over, Nelson lost all patience at the firing of the Anak batteries, and the way in which his boats were repulsed from the sides of the prizes. 'I must send on shore,' he said, 'and stop this irregular proceeding, or send in our fire-ships to burn them.' He then retired to the stern gallery and wrote the well-known letter to the Crown Prince, which was taken on shore by Sir F. Thesiger."

"To the Brothers of Englishmen, the Danes.

"Lord Nelson has directions to spare Denmark, when no longer resisting ; but if the firing is continued on the part of Denmark, Lord Nelson will be obliged to set on fire all the floating batteries he has taken, without having the power of saving the brave Danes who have defended them.

"Dated on board His Britannic Majesty's ship *Elephant*, Copenhagen Roads, *April* 2, 1801,

"Nelson and Bronte."[1]

"To the Government of Denmark.

"*Elephant, April* 2, 1801.

"Lord Nelson's object in sending on shore a flag of truce is humanity. He therefore consents that hostilities shall cease till Lord Nelson can take his prisoners out of the prizes, and he consents to land all the wounded Danes, and to burn or remove his prizes. Lord Nelson, with humble duty to his Royal Highness, begs leave to say that he will ever esteem it the greatest victory he ever gained, if this flag of truce may be the forerunner of a lasting and happy union between his Most Gracious Sovereign and his Majesty the King of Denmark.

"Nelson and Bronte."

The Crown Prince knew too well the situation of his fleet, to consent to such a further demand of

---

[1] It is generally said that Nelson refused to wafer this letter, and sent for a candle and wax to seal it, lest it should be thought that he was anxious for the result of this appeal.

sacrifices from his brave people, to reject Nelson's first
letter. He at once ordered the firing to cease, and sent
his adjutant-general, Lindholm, on board the *Elephant*
to ask simply what was the object of Lord Nelson's letter.
The second letter just given was Nelson's reply. From
the *Elephant*, Lindholm went to Sir Hyde's flagship,
which was some four miles' distant, soon after followed by
Nelson himself ; and arrangements were at once made for
Nelson to go on shore and meet the Crown Prince, to
arrange the terms of the truce. In the meantime, whilst
the boats of Sir Hyde's division assisted to tow the prizes
out of gunshot and to get the grounded ships afloat,
Nelson's squadron sailed out of the King's Channel,
passing under the guns of the Trekonner battery, and
joined the rest of the fleet. That evening Nelson,
accompanied by Hardy and Fremantle landed,[1] and
commenced the negotiation. " I do not hope much," he
wrote to the Prime Minister that night, " as it appears
clearly to me that Denmark would at this moment renounce her alliance to be friendly with us, if the fear of
Russia was not the preponderating consideration." For
five days the discussion continued, protracted by the

---

[1] Two very different accounts of Nelson's reception on his landing are
on record. According to Mr. Addington in his speech on the vote of
thanks, " Lord Nelson was received by a brave and generous people—for
brave they had shown themselves in their defence, and generous in the
oblivion of their loss—with the loudest and most general acclamations."
Mr. Carr in his " Northern Summer" says : " Upon Nelson's arrival at
the quay, he found a carriage sent to him by Mr. D., a merchant of high
respectability, the confusion being too great to enable the prince to send
one of the royal carriages ; in the former the admiral proceeded to the
palace in the Octagon, through crowds of people whose fury was rising
to frenzy, and amongst whom his person was in more imminent danger
than even from the cannon of the block ships ; but nothing could shake
the soul of such a man. Arrived at the palace, he calmly descended
from the carriage amidst the murmurs and groans of the enraged con-
course, which not even the presence of the Danish officers who accompanied him could restrain." Quoted in note, Despatches, vol. iv. p. 169.
[Such florid writing is not trustworthy.]

attempts of Bernstorff, the Prime Minister, to obtain leave to give notice to the Swedish Fleet, which had at last put to sea, and to afford the Russians, still detained in the port of Revel, time to place their ships in safety in Carlscrona or Cronstadt. During this interval Sir Hyde destroyed the prizes that were not worth keeping, and advanced his bombs into the King's Channel, whilst the Danes, on their side, threw up new defences, and both parties made ready for a renewal of. hostilities. It was at this moment that the Danes received the news of the murder of the mad Emperor Paul, and the intelligence that his successor had no inclination for a war with the British. On the 9th, therefore, a truce for fourteen weeks was signed by Nelson and the Crown Prince, and ratified by the Commander-in-chief. During its continuance the British ships had free passage through the King's Channel, and were to be supplied with provisions. Nelson's letter to Mr. Addington describes the value of his successful negotiation.

"To the Right Honble. Henry Addington.

"*St. George, April* 9, 1801.

"My dear Sir,—A negotiator is certainly out of my line, but being thrown into it, I have endeavoured to acquit myself as well as I was able, and in such a manner as I hope will not entirely merit your disapprobation. If it unfortunately does, I have only to request that I may be permitted to retire, which my state of health and inconvenience from my loss of limb has long rendered necessary. I trust you will take into consideration all the circumstances which have presented themselves to my view. 1st. We beat the Danes. 2nd. We wish to make them feel we are their real friends, therefore have spared their town, which we can always set on fire ; and I do not think if we burnt Copenhagen it would have the effect of attaching them to us; on the contrary, they would hate us. 3rd. They understand perfectly that we are at war with them for their Treaty of Armed Neutrality made last year. 4th. We have made them suspend the operations of that treaty. 5th. It has given our fleet free scope to act against Russia and Sweden, 6th, which we never should have done, although Copenhagen would have been burnt, for Sir Hyde Parker was determined not to leave Denmark hostile in his rear. Our passage over the grounds might have been very seriously interrupted by the batteries near Draco. 7th. Every reinforcement, even a cutter, can join us without molestation, and also provisions, stores, &c. 8th. Great Britain is left with the stake of the Danish property in her hands, her colonies, &c., if she refuses peace. 9th. The hands of Denmark are tied up ; ours are free to act against her confederate allies. 10th. Although we might have burnt the city, I have my doubts whether we could their ships. They lay this way :—

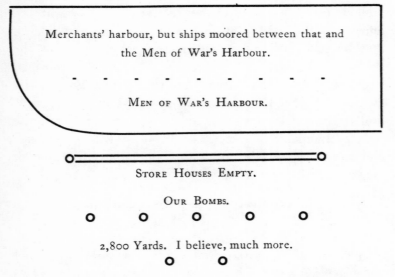

Merchants' harbour, but ships moored between that and the Men of War's Harbour.

MEN OF WAR'S HARBOUR.

STORE HOUSES EMPTY.

OUR BOMBS.

2,800 Yards. I believe, much more.

" Therefore, our shells have only the width of a line-of-battle ship, and every ship must be separately burnt, for they have plenty of room to haul any ship on fire clear of the others. All these considerations weighed deeply in my mind ; added to which, having shown that it was not because we feared fighting them that we negotiated, but for the cause of humanity, and the wish to conciliate their affections ; all these matters have affected my mind, nor shall I have a moment's rest till I know, at least, that I am not thought to have done mischief. After we had forced the expression of the suspension of the Treaty of Armed Neutrality, a point very difficult for fear of Russia, I said to the Prince, 'Now, sir, this is settled, suppose we write peace instead of armistice,' to which he replied, 'that he should be happy to have a peace, but he must bring it about slowly, so as not to make new wars.' We talked whether some method could not be thought of to prevent the mortifications to which ships of war with convoys were liable, by being stopped ; to which I answered I thought that might be very easily. I did not enter further on the subject with him, although I did to his Adjutant-general of the fleet, Lindholm, who seems much in his confidence. My idea is, that no convoys shall be granted to any vessels bound to ports at war with us ; that if any such convoy is granted, that it shall be considered as an act of hostility ; and that if any vessel under convoy proceeds to an enemy of England's port, that the owner shall lose the value of his ship and cargo, and the master be severely punished. On these foundations I would build a foundation against future disputes; but all these matters I leave to wiser heads, and shall only assure you that I am truly, with the greatest respect, your most faithful and obedient servant,

"NELSON AND BRONTE."

" I have the pleasure to tell you Count Bernstoff was too ill to make me a visit yesterday. I had sent him a message to leave off his ministerial duplicity, and to recollect he had now British admirals to deal with, who came with their hearts in their hands. I hate the fellow. Colonel Stewart, a very fine gallant man, will give you every information." [1]

On the same day he wrote to his old commander and friend :—

"ADMIRAL THE EARL ST. VINCENT.

"*St. George, April* 9, 1801.

" Just returned from getting the Armistice ratified. I am tired to death. No man but those on the spot can tell what I have gone through and do suffer. I make no scruple in saying, that I would have been at Revel fourteen days ago; that without this Armistice the fleet would never have gone but by order of the Admiralty ; and with it, I dare say, we shall not go this week. I wanted Sir Hyde to let me at least go and cruise off Carlscrona, to prevent the Revel ships from getting in. I said I would not go to Revel to take any of those laurels which I am sure he would reap there. Think for me, my dear lord, and if I have deserved well, let me retire ; if ill, for heaven's sake supersede me, for I cannot exist in this state.

" I am, &c.,

" NELSON AND BRONTE." [2]

---

[1] Despatches, vol. iv. pp. 339–41. [2] Ibid., vol. iv. p. 341.

In a subsequent private letter to Mr. Addington, Nelson gives his reasons for the Truce and the Armistice.

" To the Right Honble. Henry Addington.
" Copenhagen.

" My dearest Friend,—As both my friends and enemies seem not to know why I sent on shore the flag of truce—the former, many of them thought it a *ruse de guerre*, and not quite justifiable ; the latter, I believe, attributed it to a desire to have no more fighting, and few, very few, to the cause that I felt, and which I trust in God I shall maintain to the last moment, *humanity*. I know it must to the world be proved, and therefore I will suppose you all the world to me. First, no ship was on shore near the Crown batteries, or anywhere else, within reach of the shore, when my flag of truce went on shore. The Crown batteries and the batteries on Armager and the Dockyard were firing at us, one half of their shot necessarily striking the ships that had surrendered, and our fire did the same, and worse, for the surrendered ships had four of them got close together, and it was a massacre. This caused my Note. It was a sight which no real man could have enjoyed. I felt when the Danes became my prisoners, I became their protector ; and if that had not been a sufficient reason, the moment of a complete victory was surely the proper time to make an opening with the nation we had been fighting with.

" When the truce was settled, and full possession taken of our prizes, the ships were ordered, except two, to proceed to join Sir Hyde Parker, and in performing this service, the *Elephant* and the *Defiance* grounded on the Middle Ground. I give you, verbatim, an answer to a part of a letter from a person in high rank (Adjutant-General Lindholm) about the Prince Royal, which will bear testimony to the truth of my assertions. ' As to your lordship's motives for sending a flag of truce to our government, it never can be misconstrued ; and your subsequent conduct has sufficiently shown that humanity is always the companion of true valour. You have done more. You have shown yourself a friend of the re-establishment of peace and good harmony between this country and Great Britain.'

" Much having been said relative to the bad terms of the Armistice made with Denmark, I wish to observe, first, that the Armistice was only intended (to be) a military one, and that all political subjects were left to the discussion of the ministers of the two powers. Peace, Denmark could not in the moment make with you, she would lose all her possessions, except the island of Zealand, and that also the moment the frost set in ; therefore, there was no damage we could do her equal to the loss of everything. Our destruction would have been Copenhagen and her fleet ; then we had done our worst, and not much nearer being friends. By the Armistice we tied the arms of Denmark for four months from assisting our enemies and her allies, whilst we had every part of Denmark and its provinces to give us everything we wanted. Great Britain was left the power of taking Danish possessions and ships in all parts of the world, whilst we had locked up the Danish navy, and put the key in our pocket; time was afforded the two countries to arrange matters on an amicable footing ; besides, to say the truth, I look upon the Northern League to be like a tree, of which Paul was the trunk, and Sweden and Denmark the branches. If I can get at the trunk and hew it down, the branches fall of course ; but I may lop the branches, and yet not be able to fell the tree, and my power must be weakest when its greatest strength is required. If we could have cut up the Russian Fleet, that was my object. Denmark and Sweden deserved whipping, but Paul deserved punishment. I own I consider it as a wise measure, and I wish my reputation to stand upon its merits." [1]

Still again Sir Hyde did not move, sorely to the disgust of Nelson. "At length having sent the *Holstein* (the only prize that he had not burnt) to England, with the *Monarch* and *Iris*, in charge of the wounded ; he decided to lighten his ships by putting the guns out of most of them into merchant vessels, and attempt the passage into the Baltic over the banks between Anag and Saltholm. On the 12th, this was effected by sixteen sail-of-the-line, which were steered for Bornholm, just too late to surprise the Swedish Fleet that had taken refuge in Carlscrona. Thither Sir Hyde proceeded, and on the 23rd received a letter from Count Pahlen, informing him of Paul's death, and the wish of his successor to renew friendly relations." [2] Returning to Kioge Bay below Copenhagen,

---

[1] From the Sidmouth Papers. Despatches, vol. iv. p. 360, 361.

[2] Captain Jurien de la Gravière, vol. ii. p. 119. Anag, Armager, and Anak, spelt differently by different authorities, refer to same island.

Sir Hyde found orders for him to return home and hand over the command to Nelson. With this decision of the Admiralty, Nelson could not be surprised. Sir Hyde Parker, good officer as he was, was clearly not the man for the situation. The next letters speak Nelson's mind :—

"To Earl St. Vincent.

"*May* 5, 1801.

"I am, in truth, unable to hold the very honourable station you have conferred upon me. Admiral Graves also is so ill, as to keep his bed. I know not the purpose exactly of Fremantle's mission (Capt. F. sent with a communication to the Russian Government). If Sir Hyde were gone, I would now be under sail, leave six sail-of-the-line off Bornholm to watch the Swedes, and to cover our communication, and go to Revel, where I should at least, if not too late, prevent the junction of the two squadrons ; that I shall never suffer. I will have all the English shipping and property restored ; but I will do nothing violently ; neither commit my country, nor suffer Russia to mix the affairs of Denmark and Sweden with the detention of our ships. Should I meet the Revel squadron, I shall make them stay with me until all our English ships join ; for we must not joke. As the business will be settled in a fortnight, I must entreat that some person may come out to take this command." [1]

"To the Right Honble. H. Addington.

"*St. George, May* 5, 1801.

"My dear Sir,—I am very much flattered by your truly kind letter, and also for the kind expressions you were so good as to send me by Colonel Stewart. I am sorry that the Armistice is only approved under *all* considerations. Now I own myself of opinion that every part of the *all* was to the advantage of our King and country ; I stated many reasons for thinking it advantageous. We knew not of the death of Paul (March 24th), or of the change of sentiments of the Court of Prussia, if her sentiments are changed. My object was to get to Revel before the frost broke up at Cronstadt, that the twelve sail-of-the-line might be destroyed. I shall now go there as a friend, but the two fleets shall not form a junction, if not already accomplished, unless my orders permit it. My health is gone, and although

---

[1] Despatches, vol. iv. p. 354.

I should be happy to try and hold out a month or six weeks longer, yet death is no respecter of persons.   I own at present, I should not wish to die a natural death ; but to the last believe me, my dear sir, your most obliged,

" NELSON AND BRONTE." [1]

Nelson acted at once.   On the 7th of May he wrote to Mr. Addington that the fleet had sailed on the previous day, and that it was his intention to leave a detachment off Bornholm, whilst with eleven sail-of-the-line he showed himself in the Gulf of Finland, " in such a manner, as I trust will be taken as a compliment by the Emperor of Russia, and at the same time, with the precaution, that if the whole Russian Empire were hostile to us, their lordships may be perfectly at ease for the safety of the squadron, in spite of all the power of Russia." [2]   Thanks to Sir Hyde's delays, Nelson was too late, the Russian Squadron in Revel had escaped to Cronstadt nine days before he arrived off the bay.   Feeling safe about their fleet, the Russian Government professed to regard this visit as " incompatible with the earnest wish expressed by the British Government for the re-establishment of harmony between the two governments "—Count Pahlen adding, that " he had his Majesty's commands to tell him that the only proof of the sincerity of his intentions was the prompt withdrawal of his fleet, and that no negotiations could take place as long as a naval force remained in sight of the fortifications." [3]   This letter was quite unwarranted, and, Nelson truly said, " would never have been written, had the Russian fleet been still in Revel."   He had " not even entered the outer Bay of Revel without the consent of the Governor and the Admiral " (he had received and returned friendly salutes).   " My conduct, I feel, is so

[1] Sidmouth Papers ; Despatches, vol. iv. p. 355.
[2] Despatches, vol. iv. p. 358
[3] Count Pahlen's letter to Nelson, St. Petersburg, May 13th ; Despatches, vol. iv. p. 371, note.

entirely different to what your Excellency has expressed
in your letter, that I have only to regret, that my desire
to pay a marked attention to his Imperial Majesty has
been so entirely misunderstood.   That being the case, I
shall sail immediately into the Baltic." [1]   Though it was
night, the fleet sailed away at once.   An ample apology
came on the 26th of May from Count Pahlen :—

"A. S. E.   My Lord Nelson Bronte.

"St. Petersbourg le 6 *Mai*, 1801.

" Je regrette vivement, My Lord, que vôtre lettre précédente ait
produit un mésentendu, mais celui qui councit comme vous les loix
d' l'honneur et de la vraie dignité ne peut en être surpris.   Sa Majesté
Imperiale me charge demander à votre excellence qu'elle charmee de
faire connaisance personelle du héros du Nile, et devoir à sa cour,
si vous instructions vous permittent dequitter la flotte et d'aborder
avec un seul Vaisseux dans un des nos Ports." [2]

" The lugger which brought this letter to Nelson off
Rostock, on leaving the fleet fired a salute, an act which
implies much more in the Russian service than in many
others.   Lord Nelson observed to his secretary, on his
return from the shore, ' Did you hear that little fellow
salute.   Well, now, there is peace with Russia depend on
it, our jaunt to Revel was not so bad after all.' " [3]

" The keeping of his fleet continually on the alert," says Colonel
Stewart, " and thus amply furnishing it with fresh provisions, were
the objects of his lordship's unremitting care ; and to this may, in a
great measure, be ascribed the uniform good health and discipline
which prevailed.   Another point to which he gave nearly equal
attention was his economy of the resources of the fleet in regard to
stores ; their consumption was as remarkable for their smallness in the
Baltic as it was in the fleet afterwards under his command in the
Mediterranean.   His hour of rising was four or five o'clock, and of
going to rest about ten, breakfast was never later than six, and

---

[1] Nelson's reply May 16th; Despatches, vol. ii. p. 371.
[2] Despatches, vol. iv. p. 393, note.
[3] Colonel Stewart's narrative.

generally nearer five o'clock. A midshipman or two were always of the party; and I have known him send during the middle watch to invite the little fellows to breakfast with him when relieved. At table with them he would enter into all their boyish tricks, and be the most youthful of the party. At dinner he invariably had every officer of his ship in turn. The whole ordinary business of the fleet was invariably despatched, as it had been by Lord St. Vincent, before eight o'clock. The great command of time which Nelson thus gave himself, and the alertness which this example imparted throughout the whole fleet, can only be understood by those who witnessed it or knew the value of early hours. . . . At Rostock not an hour was lost in procuring fresh provisions for the fleet. The greatest veneration was here shown to the name of Nelson; and some distant towns of Mecklenberg sent even deputations with their public books of record, to have his name written in them by himself. Boats were constantly rowing round his flagship, the *St. George*, with persons of respectability, anxious to catch a sight of this illustrious man. He did not again land while in the Baltic; his health was not good, and his mind was not at ease; with him mind and health invariably sympathized." [1]

How he made his captains see to the provisioning of their ships is amusingly described by Nelson in the following letter to Captain George Murray, of the 1st of June :—

"MY DEAR MURRAY,—Although you like to be a commodore, I find you have no inclination to be a contractor. Now, as I find no honest men but commodores, you must necessarily, if you will be a commodore, become a contractor. Myself and Hardy are contractors; Lord Henry (Paulet, captain of the *Defence*) is just established a commodore and a contractor; only I charge you, being a brother contractor, not to let the world know how much you make by it! Be that as it may, ever believe me, my dear Murray, your obliged and faithful friend,

"NELSON AND BRONTE.

"Graves has the Red Ribbon, I a Viscount." [2]

"As soon as the treaty was signed," writes his French

---

[1] Colonel Stewart's Narrative.
[2] Despatches, vol. iv. p. 399.

biographer, " Nelson dreaded the impression it would produce in England, feeling himself that it was the seal of imperfect success ; and yet the Baltic Expedition will always be regarded by seamen as his highest claim to glory. He alone could have displayed such daring and perseverance. He alone could have faced the immense difficulties of this enterprise, and triumphed over them. When, in 1807, England, after the Treaty of Tilsit, resolved upon another attack on Copenhagen, twenty-five sail-of-the-line, forty frigates, and a land force of twenty-seven thousand men were employed to accomplish what Nelson undertook with twelve ships." [1]

In England, it will be remembered, the truce was only confirmed " under *all* circumstances," and though the honour of a Viscountcy, and the resettlement of the Barony of Nelson on the descendants of his father was granted, no medal was given for the hardest earned victory, and no recognition of his services was offered by the Corporation of London, who had before said to him, " You bring victories, we will find honours." By the leader of the Danish defence, who had so precipitately deserted his flagship, the *Danebrog*, in the heat of the engagement, the idea of a truce was misrepresented as an escape from an impending defeat, and the terms of the Armistice were steadily infringed or evaded by the Danes.

Nelson wrote to Lord St. Vincent from Kioge Bay, on June 14th, as follows :—

" I hope the reply of the Admiralty to my letter of this day will be clear and explicit whether the commander-in-chief is at liberty to hold language becoming a British admiral ? which very probably, if I am here, will break the Armistice, and set Copenhagen in a blaze. I see everything that is dirty and mean going on, and the Prince

---

[1] Captain Jurien de la Gravière, vol. ii. p. 117.

Royal at the head of it ; but your astonishment will cease when I assure (you) that a French Republican officer, in his uniform, feathers, &c., is always with his Royal Highness. The measure is so indelicate towards England that you will not be surprised if everything which is sacred amongst nations of honour should be broken. The Armistice, except their ships being absolutely hauled out, has been totally disregarded. Ships have been manned, guns taken on board, floating batteries prepared ; and except hauling out and completing their rigging, everything has been done in defiance of the treaty. I do not, under our present circumstances, feel myself at liberty to pass over the Grounds with a part of the fleet ; but the moment I receive an assurance that the business with Russia is settled, I shall pass into Copenhagen Roads with all the fleet, except eight sail-of-the-line to watch the Swedes until they are settled. My heart burns, my lord, at seeing the word of a Prince, nearly allied to our good King, so falsified ; but his conduct is such that he will lose his kingdom if he goes on, for Jacobins rule in Denmark. I have made no representations yet, as it would be useless to do so until I have power of correction. All I beg in the name of the future commander-in-chief is, that the orders may be clear; for enough is done to break twenty treaties, if it should be wished, or to make the Prince Royal and his republican companion humble themselves before British generosity.

"I am, &c.,

"BRONTE AND NELSON." [1]

In the end the pacific attitude of the new Czar of Russia cured all difficulties, and thanks to Nelson's firmness the Northern Coalition collapsed. And now, "the fighting being over in the North Sea," as Nelson wrote, he was daily more and more anxious to be relieved from his arduous duties—fighting, not negotiation, was his *forte.* At last the difficulty was got over in the selection of a successor, by the appointment of Vice-Admiral Pole ; and on the 19th of June, refusing to weaken the fleet by requiring a frigate, he left the Baltic in a small brig, and, after a trying passage, landed at Yarmouth on the 18th of July. Before he left Nelson took leave of his comrades in the following noble memorandum :—

" Lord Nelson has been obliged, from the late very bad state of his health, to apply to the Lords Commissioners of the Admiralty for leave to return to England, which their lordships have been pleased to comply with. But Lord Nelson cannot allow himself to leave the fleet without expressing to the admirals, captains, officers, and men how sensibly he has felt, and does feel, all their kindness to him, and also how nobly and honourably they have supported him in the hour of battle, and the readiness which they have shown to maintain the honour of their King and country on many occasions which have offered ; and had more opportunities presented themselves, Lord Nelson is firmly persuaded, they would have added more to the glory of their country.

" Lord Nelson cannot but observe, with the highest satisfaction which can fill the breast of a British admiral, that with the exception (of the conduct of the officers of two gunbrigs and a bomb), out of eighteen thousand of which the fleet is composed, not a complaint has been made of any officer or man in it ; and he cannot but remark that the extraordinary health of the fleet, under the blessing of Almighty God, is to be attributed to the great regularity, exact discipline, and cheerful obedience of every individual of the fleet.

" The Vice-Admiral assures them that he will not fail to represent to the Lords Commissioners of the Admiralty their highly praiseworthy conduct ; and if it pleases God that the Vice-Admiral should recover his health, he will feel proud, on some future day, to go with them in pursuit of further glory, and to assist in making the name of our King and country beloved and respected by the world.

" St. George, Kioge Bay, June 18, 1801." [1]

---

[1] Letter Book, Despatches, vol. iv. p. 420.

THE BOULOGNE FLOTILLA.

MERTON PLACE, SURREY.

THE RESIDENCE OF LORD NELSON.

CHAPTER XIII.

THE BOULOGNE FLOTILLA.

(1801-2.)

The armaments for the invasion of England—The Boulogne Flotilla—
Nelson appointed to defend the Coast—His plan for the defence of
London—Attack on the Boulogne Flotilla, August 4th—The Sea
Fencibles—Second attack and failure, August 15th—Nelson's dis-
tress at his losses—The boy midshipmen and dear young Parker
—His attention and anxiety for Parker, and grief at his death—
Blackmail—Attempt to intimidate Nelson—Correspondence with
his father—Last letter from his father before his death—The Peace
of Amiens—Return to Merton.

ELSON'S services were again impera-
tively demanded. After a brief rest
at Merton, the residence which he had
so lately purchased, he was called
upon to meet the threatened invasion
of England, by the flotillas of Buonaparte—he obeyed the call of duty.

"Buonaparte," says his French biographer, "delivered from all
anxiety on the side of the continent by the treaty of Luneville, conceived the idea of transporting his legions to the British soil, and also
threatened to conduct those soldiers who had twice conquered Italy to
London. The port of Boulogne was to be the rendezvous of the
enormous flotilla which he had ordered to be built in all the ports of
the Channel. The invasion of England by means of gunboats and
flat-boats had long been a favourite plan of the First Consul: he had
suggested it in 1797 ; now adopted it in 1801, and three years later
raised it to gigantic proportions. In the month of July, nine divisions
of gunboats, and the troops they could embark, were assembled under

Admiral La Touche Treville. It was not, it is true, the first time that
the threat of invasion alarmed England ; but never had it appeared so
close at hand. The Addington Ministry, therefore, could not slight
the public agitation, and the Admiralty deferred to the popular will,
by appointing Nelson, on the 24th of July, to command the squadron
of defence assembled between Orfordness and Beachy Head." [1]

Broken though he was in health from the winds of
the North Sea, and feeling himself by no means suited to
such a post, Nelson left his home at Merton, and on the
27th of July hoisted his flag on the *Unite* frigate at
Sheerness. Two days before he sent the following observations on the defence of the Thames to the Admiralty,
showing how he grasped the whole situation—tracing
boldly with a master-hand the general outlines of his
plan, purposely omitting the details.

"Besides the stationed ships at the different ports between the
North Foreland and Orfordness, as many gun vessels as can be spared
from the very necessary protection of the coast of Sussex and Kent to
the westward of Dover, should be collected, for this part of the coast
must be seriously attended to ; for supposing London the object of
surprise, I am of opinion that the enemy's object *ought* to be the
getting on shore as speedily as possible, for the dangers of a navigation of forty-eight hours, appear to me to be an insurmountable
objection to the rowing from Boulogne to the coast of Essex. It is,
therefore, most probable (for it is certainly proper to believe the
French are coming to attack London, and, therefore, to be prepared)
that from Boulogne, Calais, and even Havre, the enemy will try to
land in Sussex or the lower part of Kent, and from Dunkirk, Ostend,
and the other parts of Flanders, to land on the coast of Essex or
Suffolk ; for I own myself of opinion that, the object being to get on
shore somewhere within one hundred miles of London, as speedily as
possible, that the flats at the mouth of the Thames will not be the
only place necessary to attend to ; added to this, the enemy will
create a powerful diversion by the sailing of the combined fleet, and
the either sailing, or creating such an appearance of sailing, of the
Dutch Fleet, as will prevent Admiral Dickson (commander-in-chief

in the North Sea) from sending anything off from the great Dutch ports, whilst the smaller ports will send forth its flotilla—viz., Flushing, &c., &c. It must be pretty well ascertained what number of small vessels are in each port.

"I will suppose that forty thousand men are destined for this attack, or rather surprise of London ; twenty thousand will land on the west side of Dover, sixty or seventy miles from London, and the same number on the east side : they are too knowing to let us have but one point of alarm for London. Supposing two hundred craft collected at Boulogne, &c., they are supposed equal to carry twenty thousand men. In very calm weather they might row over, supposing no impediment, in twelve hours ; at the same instant by telegraph the same number of troops would be rowed out of Dunkirk, Ostend, &c., &c. These are the two great objects to attend to from Dover and the Downs, and perhaps one of the small ports to the westward. Boulogne (which I call the central point of the western attack) must be attended to. If it is calm when the enemy row out, all our vessels and boats appointed to watch them must get into the Channel and meet them as soon as possible ; if not strong enough for the attack they must watch, and keep them company till a favourable opportunity offers. If a breeze springs up, our ships are to deal *destruction*, no delicacy can be observed on this occasion. But should it remain calm, and our flotilla not fancy itself strong enough to attack the enemy on their passage, the moment they begin to touch our shore, strong or weak, our flotilla of boats must attack as much of the enemy's flotilla as they are able—say only one half or two-thirds ; it will create a most powerful diversion, for the bows of our flotilla will be opposed to their unarmed sterns, and the courage of Britains will never, I believe, allow one Frenchman to leave the beach. A great number of Deal and Dover boats to be on board our vessels, off the port of Boulogne to give notice of the direction taken by the enemy. If it is calm, vessels in the Channel can make signals of intelligence to our shores, from the North Foreland to Orfordness, and even as far as Solebay, not an improbable place, about seventy or eighty miles from London."

Then after noticing the positions for the different flotillas and floating batteries, and that " the moment of the enemy's movement from Boulogne is to be considered as the movement from Dunkirk," Nelson thus concludes his valuable paper :—

"Whenever the enemy's flotilla can be seen our divisions are to unite, but not intermix, and to be ready to execute such orders as may be deemed necessary, or as indispensable services may require. For this purpose, men of such confidence in each other should be looked for, that (as far as human foresight can go) no little jealousy may creep into any man's mind, but to be all animated with the same desire of preventing the descent of the enemy on our coasts. Stationary floating batteries are not, from any apparent advantage, to be moved, for the tide may prevent their resuming the very important stations assigned them : they are on no account to be supposed neglected, even should the enemy surround them, for they may rely on support, and reflect, that perhaps their gallant conduct may prevent the mischievous designs of the enemy.

"Whatever plans may be adopted, the moment the enemy touch our coasts, be it where it may, they are to be attacked by every man afloat or on shore. This must be perfectly understood. *Never fear the event.*

"The flat-boats can probably be manned (partly at least) by the Sea Fencibles (the number and fixed places of whom I am entirely ignorant of), but the flat-boats they may man to be in grand and sub-divisions, commanded by their own captains and lieutenants as far as possible. The number of the boats is well known to me, as also the other means of defence in small craft; but I am clearly of opinion that a proportion of the small force should be kept to watch the flat-boats from Boulogne, and the others in the way I have presumed to suggest.

"These are offered as merely the rude ideas of the moment, and are only meant as a sea plan of defence of the City of London ; but I believe other ports may likewise be menaced, if the Brest Fleet, and those from Rochfort and Holland put to sea ; although I feel confident that the fleets of the enemy will meet the same fate which has always attended them, yet their sailing will facilitate the coming over of their flotilla, as they will naturally suppose our attention will be called only to the fleets." [1]

It would have been well had this carefully considered plan of defence not have been deviated from. On the 4th of August, however, whether from orders from the Admiralty or from the temptation offered by La Touche Treville forming a large portion of his vessels outside the

[1] Despatches, vol. iv. pp. 325-7.

harbour of Boulogne, Nelson attacked them where they lay, and with but little loss sunk five of them, drove others on shore, and showed the enemy, as he wrote to the Admiralty and the Duke of Clarence that "they could not with impunity come outside their ports." [1]   In his letter to the squadron, he said, after expressing his satisfaction at the manner in which the bomb vessels had been placed—

"The Commander-in-chief cannot avoid noting the great zeal and desire to attack the enemy in a closer and different combat, which manifested itself in all ranks of persons, and which Lord Nelson would gladly have given scope to, had the attempt at this moment been proper ; but the officers and others may rely that an early opportunity shall be given them for showing their judgment and their bravery." [2]

The Sea Fencibles—volunteer corps composed of residents in the coast towns, and seafaring men, and fishermen—were by no means so ready to leave their homes and their boats, as Nelson expected.   On the 6th of August, therefore, he wrote the following appeal to their patriotism :—

"I am authorized to assure the Fencibles and other seafaring men who may come forward on this occasion, that they shall not be sent off the coast of the kingdom ; shall be kept as near their homes as the nature of the service will admit ; and that the moment the alarm of the threatened invasion is over that every man shall be returned to their own homes ; and also, that during their continuance on board ship, that as much attention as is possible shall be paid to their reasonable wants.   And I flatter myself that at the moment when all the volunteer corps in the kingdom are come forward to defend our land, that the seamen will not be slow to defend our own proper element, and maintain as pure as our glorious ancestors have transmitted it to us, the undoubted right to the sovereignty of the

---

[1] Letters to E. Nepean and the Duke of Clarence, August 4th.   Despatches, vol. iv. p. 441.

[2] Despatches, vol. iv. p. 442.

Narrow Seas, on which no Frenchman has yet *dared* to sail with impunity. Our country looks to its sea defence, and let it not be disappointed." [1]

With the Sea Fencibles Nelson was sadly disappointed.

" Not one Sea Fencible," he wrote to Sir E. Berry at a subsequent date, " has come forth either from Kent or Sussex. The establishment of them was originally bad ; for no man liable to be impressed should have been enrolled unless they had large families." [2]

" The early opportunity," which he promised to afford to his officers and men, " to show their judgment and bravery," proved a more disastrous failure than that of the 4th of August. On the 15th he prepared for a far more serious one, with more than fifty vessels of all sizes, to take or destroy the French Flotilla, still anchored outside the port of Boulogne. By a spy, or the foolish chattering of the newspapers of the day, La Touche Treville had been fully warned of the impending attack, and made good use of his time. Not only were the various vessels securely anchored by chains, and actually chained together, and high boarding nettings fastened on every one of them, but detachments of soldiers were added to the usual crews, and extra batteries erected bearing on the attacking party. Of these additional defences, Nelson had no information. I give his own account of the sad failure :—

" To Evan Nepean, Esq., Admiralty.
" *Medusa*, off Boulogne, *August* 16, 1801.
" Sir,—Having deemed it proper to attempt bringing off the enemy's flotilla, moored in front of Boulogne, I directed the attack to be made in four divisions : seventeen boats for boarders, under the command of Captains Somerville, Cotgrave, Jones, and Parker, and a division of howitzer boats, under Captain Conn. The boats put off

---

[1] Despatches, vol. iv. p. 444.   [2] Ibid., vol. iv. p. 482.

from the *Medusa*, at half-past eleven o'clock last night, in the best possible order, and before one o'clock this morning the firing began, and I had, from the judgment of the officers, and the zeal and gallantry of every man, the most perfect confidence of complete success ; but the darkness of the night, with the tide at half-tide, separated the divisions, and from all not arriving at the same happy moment with Captain Parker is to be attributed the failure of success. But I beg to be perfectly understood that not the smallest blame attaches itself to any person ; for although the divisions did not arrive together, yet each (except the fourth division, which could not get up before day) made a successful attack on that part of the enemy they fell in with, and actually took possession of many brigs and flats, and cut their cables ; but many of them being aground, and the moment of the battle's ceasing on board of them, the vessels were filled with volleys of musketry, the enemy being perfectly regardless of their own men, who must have suffered equally with us. It was, therefore, impossible to remain on board, even to burn them ; but allow me to say, who have seen much service in war, that more determined, persevering courage, I never witnessed, and that nothing but the impossibility of being successful could have prevented me from congratulating their lordships. But although, in value, the loss of such gallant and good men is incalculable, yet, in point of numbers, it has fallen short of my expectations. I must also beg to state that greater zeal and ardent desire to distinguish themselves by an attack on the enemy was never shown than by all the captains, officers, and crews of all descriptions under my command." [1]

To Lord St. Vincent he wrote :—

" I am sorry to tell you that I have not succeeded in bringing out or destroying the enemy's flotilla, moored in the mouth of the harbour of Boulogne. The most astonishing bravery was evinced by many of our officers and men, and Captains Somerville, Cotgrave, and Parker exerted themselves to the utmost. We have lost many brave officers and men : upwards of one hundred killed and wounded. Dear little Parker, his thigh much shattered ; I have fears for his life. Langford shot through the leg. The loss has been heavy, and the object was great. The flotilla, brigs and flats, were moored by the

---

[1] Four officers and 40 men killed ; 14 officers and 114 men wounded. Despatches, vol. iv. p. 466.

bottom to the shore, and to each other by chains ; therefore, although several of them were carried, yet the heavy fire of musketry from the shore which overlooked them, forced our people to leave them, without being able, as I am told, to set them on fire. No person can be blamed for sending them to the attack but myself ; I knew the difficulty of the undertaking, therefore I ventured to ask your opinion." [1]

"It is not given to us to command success," replied St. Vincent : "your lordship and the gallant officers and men under your orders, most certainly deserve it ; and I cannot sufficiently express my admiration of the zeal and persevering courage with which this gallant enterprise was followed up, lamenting most sincerely the loss sustained in it. The manner in which the enemy's flotilla was made fast to the ground and to each other could not have been foreseen." [2]

Nelson's distress at the failure of the attempt and the death of the two brave young midshipmen, and the wounds of Parker and Langford, was most acute.

"I own," he wrote to Lord St. Vincent, "I shall never bring myself again to allow any attack to go forward where I am not personally concerned ; my mind suffers much more than if I had a leg shot off in this late business. I am writing between poor Parker and Langford, therefore I must beg great indulgences. Only believe that I will do my utmost. I am ready to assist the good cause, and have no other view in my mind. Had our force arrived, as I intended, 'twas not all the chains in France that could have prevented our folks from bringing off the whole of the vessels. . . . Dear Parker I fear is in a bad way." [3]

In a letter to Lady Hamilton he writes :—

"I have this morning been attending the funeral of two young mids : a Mr. Gore, cousin of Captain Gore, and a Mr. Bristow—one nineteen, the other seventeen years of age. Last night (17th August) I was all the evening in the hospital, seeing that all was done for the comfort of the poor fellows. I am going on board. . . . I shall come in the morning to see Parker." [4]

---

[1] Despatches, vol. iv. p. 464.   [2] Ibid., vol. iv. p. 471.
[3] Ibid., vol. iv. p. 470.   [4] Ibid., vol. iv. p. 473.

"To Dr. Baird.

"*Amazon, September* 20, 1801.

"My dear Doctor,—Your kind letter has given me hopes of my dear Parker : he is my child, for I found him in distress. I am prepared for the worst, although I still hope. Pray tell me as often as you can. Would I could be useful, I would come on shore and nurse him. I rely on your abilities, and if his life is to be spared, that you, under the blessing of God, are fully equal to be the instrument. Say everything which is kind to Mrs. Parker, and if my Parker remembers me say, ‵God bless him,’ and do you believe me your much obliged and thankful friend,

"Nelson and Bronte." [1]

Again he writes to Davison :—

"You will join me in my affliction for the fate of dear, good little Parker. Yesterday, at two in the afternoon, I was with him, so were Lady Hamilton, Dr. William and Mrs. Nelson (Dr. Nelson's wife); he was so well that I was for the first moment sanguine in my hopes of his recovery ; at ten o'clock the great artery burst, and he is now at death's door. You will judge our feelings." [2]

Next day he had a more encouraging letter from Dr. Baird, which he forwarded to Lady Hamilton. "You will (see)," he wrote, "Parker is treated like an infant. Poor fellow ! I trust he will get well, and take possession of his room at the Farm." [3] Day after day these anxious letters continue, as Parker seemed to rally so much, that on the 24th, Nelson wrote to Dr. Baird that he hoped to be allowed to see my son Parker ; to you I shall always think I owe his life." [4] The rally, however, proved deceptive. On the 27th, Parker—"A happy release." "I feel," he wrote to Dr. Baird, "all has been done which was possible ; God's will be done. I beg that his hair may be cut off and given to me ; it shall remain

[1] Despatches, vol. iv. p. 491.
[2] Ibid., vol. iv. pp. 493-5-7.
[3] Ibid., vol. iv. pp. 493-5-7.
[4] Ibid., vol. iv. pp. 493-5-7.

and be buried with me. What must the poor father feel when he is gone ? " [1]

The following letter to Lord St. Vincent, of September 27th, closes this affecting incident :—

"The scene, my lord, with our dear Parker is closed for ever ; and I am sure your good heart will participate in our grief, both as a public and a private loss ; not a creature living was ever more deserving of our affections. Every action of his life, from Sir John Orde to the moment of his death, showed innocence, joined to a firm mind in keeping the road of honour, however it might appear incompatible with his interest ; his conduct in Orde's business won my regard. When he was abandoned by the world, your heart had begun to yearn towards him—how well he deserved my love and affection his actions have shown. His father, in his advanced age, looked forward for assistance to this good son. Pensions, I know, have sometimes been granted to the parents of those who have lost their lives in the service of their king and country. All will agree, none fell more nobly than dear Parker ; and none ever resigned their life into the hands of their Creator with more resignation to the Divine Will than our Parker. I trust much to your friendship to recommend his father's case to the kind consideration of the King. I fear his loss has made a wound in my heart which time will scarcely heal. But God is good, and we must all die. I am, &c.,

"NELSON AND BRONTE." [2]

It was not to be expected that those scribes who seek to make a living by threatening to insert libellous comments in the journals of the day, on the great men of their time, should spare Nelson. With the exception, however, of the exaggerated accounts of his life in Palermo and Naples, circulated by Jacobin writers and the letters (at that time unpublished) of Mrs. St. George,

---

[1] Despatches, vol. iv. pp. 493–5–7.

[2] Nelson, who was one of the mourners, was visibly affected during the ceremony ; Admiral Lutwidge and many captains and officers of both services also attended. See "Naval Chronicle," vol. vi. p. 341. Despatches, vol. iv. p. 495. It is said by Mr. C. Russell that on the Admiralty refusing to pay for Parker's funeral, Nelson did so.

of the character of his journey through Europe after the victory of the Nile, he had escaped their attempts to levy blackmail.   The failure of his attack on the Boulogne Flotilla, however, offered an occasion for intimidation too tempting to be overlooked.

In September, 1801, Lord Nelson received a paper entitled " Remarks of a Seaman on the Attack at Boulogne," containing severe strictures on his official despatch, to which was added, " Should Lord Nelson wish the enclosed not to be inserted in the newspapers, he will please to *enclose by return of post a bank note for* £100, to Mr. Hill, to be left at the Post Office till called for."   To this Nelson replied :—

> " *Amazon*, Downs, *September* 6, 1801.
>
> " Mr. Hill,—Very likely I am unfit for my present command, and whenever Government change me, I hope they will find no difficulty in selecting an officer of greater abilities ; but you will, I trust, be punished for threatening my character.   But I have not been brought up in the school of fear, and therefore care not wha you do.   I defy you and your malice.
>
> " Nelson and Bronte."

Mr. Hill's letter he forwarded to the Admiralty.

> " To Evan Nepean, Esq., Admiralty.
>
> " *September* 6.
>
> " Sir,—I send you a paper, and a note at the bottom.   I have answered Mr. Hill's note, and it will be in London on Tuesday morning.   If their Lordships think it proper to save me from such letters, they will please to send proper people to take up whoever comes for Mr. Hill's letter.   I have franked it with the following direction :—
>
> " Mr. Hill.
> " To be left at the post-office till called for.
> " I am, sir, your most obedient servant,
> " Nelson and Bronte." [1]

---

[1] Despatches, vol. iv. p. 485.

"*September* 10, 1801.

"A man a few days ago sent me a letter demanding a bank note of £100, or he would abuse me in the papers ; I sent it, of course, to Nepean ; the porter who went to the post-office for my answer has been taken up, but he knew not his employer, and probably never will be caught." [1]

Nelson, willing as ever to do his duty, realized the unfitness of this "boat business" being entrusted to one in his position. Hence the following letter :—

"This boat business must be over," wrote Nelson to St. Vincent at the end of September. "It may be a part of a great plan of invasion, but can never be the only one; therefore, as our ships cannot act any more lying off the French coast, I own I do not think it is now a command for a vice-admiral. Turn it in your mind. It is not that I want to get a more lucrative situation—far from it. I do not know if the Mediterranean were vacant to-morrow that I am equal to undertake it. You will forgive me if I have said too much. They are my feelings, which for several years you have allowed me to throw before you, not in an impertinent manner, but with all the respect due to your great character and exalted situation." [2]

Before, however, he was, as he hoped, relieved, he determined to try to have his revenge on his enemy by sending a fire-brig to attempt the destruction of the flotilla.[3] Whilst, however, arranging to carry out this plan he received the news of the negotiations of M. Otto that eventually led to the so-called Peace of Amiens, and by the 24th of October was back at Merton.

The following letters from and to his father will serve to complete this chapter :—

"MY DEAR HOR.,—However distant our firesides may be, yet winds waft quickly intelligence of every kind, and with others it is probable

---

[1] To A. Davison, September 14, 1801 ; Despatches, vol. iv. p. 489.
[2] Despatches, vol. iv. p. 500.
[3] Letter most secret, October 1st; Despatches, vol. iv. p. 500.

you may have heard a rumour that I am not quite so stout now as two years ago. It is a truth and lately, a severe, and in some instances an unexpected attack has pulled me much lower than usual, and has left a complete old man, in every point answering the poet's description of that last stage of human life. However, some principal stamina still are apparently sound. I am rallying, and perhaps shall enjoy another summer's sun, and have amongst other blessings that of seeing you. But any of the publick, of which you are a part, is not for me to expect. I well remember that upon my receiving a wound you promised to heal it by giving me another daughter; indeed you have; Lady N.'s kindness as a friend, a nurse, a daughter, I want words to express. Your brother William is still without a stall and sits uneasy.

" Pray God bless you,

" Excuse me,

" Adieu.

" *February* 24, 1800.   " EDMUND NELSON." [1]

" BURNHAM, *October* 8, 1801.

" MY DEAR HORATIO,—Upon the happy return of peace, I may, with a little variation, address you in the words of an apostle, and say, You have fought a good fight. You have finished your military career with glory and honour; henceforth there is laid up for you much happiness, subject, indeed, in this present time to uncertainty, but in a future state immutable and incorruptible.

" As a public character I could be acquainted only with what was made public respecting you. Now in a private station possibly you may tell me where it is likely your general place of residence may be, so that sometimes we may have mutual happiness in each other, notwithstanding the severe reproaches I feel from an anonymous letter for my conduct to you, which is such, it seems, as will totally separate us. This is unexpected indeed. Most likely the winter may be too cold for me to continue here, and I mean to spend it between Bath and London. If Lady Nelson is in a hired house and by herself, gratitude requires that I should sometimes be with her, if it is likely to be of any comfort to her. Everywhere age and my many infirmities are very troublesome, and require every mark of respect. At present I am in the Parsonage; it is warm and comfortable. I am quite by myself, except the gentleman who takes care of the churches. He is a worthy, sensible, sober man, and, as far as rests with him, makes me very happy. I cannot do any public duty, nor even walk

---

[1] In the second volume of Private Correspondence at Cricket.

to the next house.   But, my dearest son, here is still room enough to give you a warm and a joyful and affectionate reception, if you could find an inclination to look once more at me in Burnham Parsonage. I pray God to continue His blessings in all stations, places, and undertakings.

" EDMUND NELSON."

Lord Nelson's memorandum for reply to this letter is as follows :—

" I am thinking of writing my poor old father to this effect : that I shall live at Merton with Sir W. and Lady Hamilton ; that a warm room for him and a cheerful society will always be happy to receive him ; that nothing in *my conduct* could ever cause a separation of a moment between me and him, for that I had all the respect and love which a son could bear towards a good father ; that going to Burnham was impossible, as my duty, even if I was inclined, would not permit it ; that, as to anonymous letters, they made no impression where they did not fit, and that I should ever conduct myself towards him as his dutiful son.   " N. AND B."

To Lady Hamilton, communicating the above, he writes :—

" Tell me, my friend, do you approve ?   If he remains at Burnham he will die, and I am sure he will not stay at Somerset Street (Lady N.'s residence).   Pray let him come to your care at Merton.   Your kindness will keep him alive, for you have a kind soul." [1]

From his father :—

" HILLBOROUGH, November 2, 1801.

" MY DEAR HORATIO,—I have to acknowledge many kind and polite invitations from yourself and Lady Hamilton to visit Merton, which it is my intention to accept before my winter residence commences at Bath.   My journey to London is very slow, not only from infirmities, but by necessary and pleasing visits with my children, whose kindnesses are a *cordial for age* such as few parents can boast of. After finishing some necessary business in town, if convenient to your

---

[1] Pettigrew, vol. ii. pp. 210–11.

family, I shall, with the highest gratification a fond parent can receive, pass a time with you.   I am, with all proper regard to the family at Merton,

"Yours most affectionately,

"EDMUND NELSON." [1]

His father visited Lord Nelson at Merton, and upon his return to Bath wrote the following letter :—

"BATH, *December* 5, 1801.

"My DEAR HORATIO,—The affectionate and kind manner in which you received and entertained me at Merton must have excited all those parental feelings which none but fond parents know ; and having seen you safe through the perils which infancy, childhood, and even early years of manhood are exposed to, how must I rejoice to see so few impediments to as much felicity as falls to the share of mortals.   What you possess, my good son, take care of ; what you may still want, consult your own good sense in which way it can be attained.   Strive for honours and riches that will not fade, but will profit in good time of need.   Excuse my anxiety for what I esteem your real good.

"My journey here was cold, yet safe ; arrived last night and met with a kind and warm reception from your good sister and her indulgent husband.   Am now going to a warm lodging in 10, New King Street.   Though tired with scrawling, yet must add my best thanks to Sir W. and Lady Hamilton for their very many civilities to me. Your sister and Mr. M.'s best regards as ever with you.

"*December, Friday.*   "EDMUND NELSON."

"*December* 13, 1801.

"My DEAR HORATIO,—The little addition you are likely to make to your landed property will, I hope, bring some further pleasure and domestic comfort, such as the real comfort of a private and independent life must consist of, and every event which you are so good as to communicate to me, which is likely to increase your happiness, adds a prop to my declining life, and the little incidents, even of a difference, which Lady Hamilton politely communicates to me are at all times very acceptable.   You sister's daily care in watching my infirmities and rendering them as easy as in her power

---

[1] Pettigrew, vol. ii. p. 232.

l feel with delight. She is, as usual, cheerful, often regretting not
having been able to see you, and even still she and Mr. Matcham
meditate a vist to Merton for a day or two, to wait upon Lady
Hamilton and yourself, if the weather is tolerably good, and she
herself can prudently undertake such a journey five or six weeks
hence, when the bairns are all returned to their several academies.
The box came safe, as did the plaid—very handsome. Lady
Hamilton will accept my thanks for her care about it, to whom,
with Sir William, present my respects, as also to the whole party.

> " I am, my dear,
> " Your affectionate father,
> " EDMUND NELSON."

" By enclosing a letter now and then I would not infringe upon
your privilege."

" MY DEAR HORATIO,—From an old man you will accept the old-
fashioned language at the approaching happy season, which is, I wish
you a Merry Christmas and a Happy New Year. For multiplied
favour Lady Hamilton has my respectful thanks.

> " E. N."

With these letters the correspondence with his father
ceases. It is said by one biographer that his father had
proposed coming to them at Merton in May had he lived.
Paralysis and asthma closed his long life in the previous
month.

THE CHASE TO THE WEST INDIES.

Victory in Quarantine
Augt. 19th 1805

My Dear Brother

By a letter from Lady
Hamilton I find you are in Norfolk
and by Horace's letter I see he belongs
to Cambridge You will have heard
of our arrival but I know you would
like better to have it under my hand
James so but what is very off the letters
for going to the West Indies and even with
the anxiety. We must not talk of Sir
Robt. Calder's battle I might not have so much
with my small force if I had fell in with
them you would probably have been a
Lord before this for I know they meant
to make a dead set at the Victory

Hardy is I am sorry to say very unwell
give my kind love to Mrs. Nelson &
Horace, kind regards to the Archdeacon
Mr. Rolfe and our other friends
and be assured I am ever your most
affectionate Brother
Nelson & Bronte

LETTER SHOWING NELSON'S LEFT-HANDED WRITING.

CHAPTER XIV.

THE CHASE TO THE WEST INDIES.

(1803–1805.)

Rupture of the Peace of Amiens—Result of the Naval War to 1802—
Nelson watching Toulon—Readiness for any service—Deserters to
the Spaniards—Nelson and La Touche Treville—Care for the health
of the fleet—The enemy at sea—Passage of the Straits of Bonifacio
—Cruise about the Mediterranean—To Egypt and back to Toulon—
Campbell's information—To the West Indies after Villeneuve—
Nelson's own account of the chase—Misled by Brereton's letter—
Return towards home—The story of a privateer—Two years less ten
days on board ship—Collingwood's suggestion—Joins the Channel
Fleet—At Spithead—Merton.

HE so-called Peace of Amiens, which
was signed on the 25th of March,
1802, had but a short life. In the
mind of Buonaparte it was simply one
of those truces which the great Greek
comedian described as " smelling of
pitch and naval preparations." He
required breathing time, and thanks to the determination
of the British Cabinet, that was but short. That he did
not intend it to be permanent was evident from his acts on
the Continent, even whilst the negotiations for the peace
were in progress, when he became Dictator of the Cisal-
pine Republic. When it was concluded he sent an army
into Switzerland, and treated with little courtesy the mild
remonstrance of the British Government. Then came
the formal annexation of Piedmont to the French

Republic, and the refusal to withdraw his troops from
Holland. The British Government replied with a vote
for one hundred and twenty thousand troops and fifty
thousand sailors and marines. Buonaparte treated these
measures as menaces. From the moment that he heard of
the King's speech, calling for increased forces, he had been
preparing for an invasion of England, and made the non-
surrender of Malta to the Knights of the Order—which
had really no practical existence—as the ground of his
quarrel. On the 18th of May, 1803, war was declared.
France was crowded with English visitors, and on the
plea that two French vessels had been captured before
that date, Buonaparte arrested ten thousand English
travellers, never to be released from captivity until his
fall in 1814. England was of one mind. With one
mind and one spirit every class bound themselves together
to aid in the defence of the honour of their country.
Money was voted without stint, and from end to end of
the kingdom volunteers came forward in such numbers
that it was impossible for some time to furnish them with
arms.

Such was the reply of England to the new threat of
invasion. What were Buonaparte's naval forces, by the
aid of which alone it could hope to succeed?

"By prodigious efforts," says our French authority, "England
had raised her navy to 189 sail-of-the-line, whilst that of France
hardly contained thirty-six. In this augmentation of the English
navy, fifty line-of-battle ships captured from France or her allies
formed a considerable proportion ; and, nevertheless, this number
comprised but a part of the losses that we had incurred in this
unfortunate war, for these losses amounted to fifty-three sail-of-
the-line on the part of France, eighteen on that of Holland, ten taken
from Spain, and two from Denmark. In comparison of these eighty-
five captured or destroyed, the loss to the English Fleet was not worth
mentioning. From 1793 to 1802, England had only lost twenty
ships, fifteen of which had been destroyed by accidents, and only five

had fallen into the hands of the enemy. Such was the deplorable balance of this great war. Had the guerilla sort of warfare, so often urged upon the Directory, produced more favourable results? We had changed the general disposition and employment of our naval forces more than once during these lengthened hostilities, but we had never changed the internal organization of our ships. In spite of these fatal oversights, the devotion of our sailors had not always been fruitless. Nevertheless, notwithstanding some glorious triumphs, fortune had not seconded our hopes on this new battle-ground. After having dragged our allies into this fatal course, and given to the enemy's cruisers 184 frigates, 224 brigs or corvettes, 958 privateers, 6,200 merchant ships, by the dispersion of our forces, after having seen the Government compelled to forbid privateering, we found ourselves overwhelmed, but not instructed by so many disasters." [1]

No time was lost in England; by the 1st of June, 1803, sixty-six ships were watching the French coasts. Cornwallis was off Brest; Collingwood in the Bay of Biscay; Keith in the Channel; and Nelson off Toulon, again on his favourite scene of operations.

On hoisting his flag on the *Victory*, he wrote :—

" To St. Vincent.

" *May* 18, 3 p.m.

" My dear Lord,—As the *Victory* will be ready, Captain Sutton tells me, to sail on Friday morning (and I am trying to make it to-morrow night), I have on many accounts thought it best to hoist my flag on her. If Admiral Cornwallis wants her—which is very improbable according to what I have heard—but if he does I shall remove nothing from the frigate but my cot, and therefore, be gone in five minutes. You may rely, my dear lord, that nothing shall be left undone by me, by a vigorous and active exertion of the force under my command, to bring about a happy peace."

" *May* 19, 1803.

" If the devil stands at the door the *Victory* shall sail to-morrow forenoon." [2]

---

[1] Jurien de la Gravière, vol. ii. p. 146.
[2] Despatches, vol. v. p. 667.

" *Portsmouth, May* 20*th.* Such was the anxiety of Lord Nelson to embark, that yesterday, to every one who spoke to him of his sailing, he said, 'I cannot go before to-morrow, and that is an age.' This morning, about ten o'clock, his lordship went off in a heavy shower of rain, and sailed with a northerly wind." [1]

On the 9th of July, 1803, Nelson wrote to Mr. Addington :—

" I joined our fleet yesterday. With the casual absence of one or two ships, we shall be always seven sail-of-the-line ; and as the French have at least seven—I believe nine—nearly ready, we are in hopes that Bonaparte may be angry and order them out, which I have no doubt will put our ships in high feather ; for I never knew any wants after a victory, although we are always full of them before." [2]

During the tedious days of the blockade of Toulon, Nelson heard of the savage murder of Chief Justice Kilwarden in Dublin by some of the wretched followers of Emmet, and with his usual promptitude and unselfishness offered his services to the Government in any capacity which they might deem advisable. All for King and country, and no thought of self.

" To Right Honble. Lord Addington.

" *Victory,* off Toulon, *August* 25, 1803.

" My dear Sir,—By a vessel spoke with from Marseilles, it was with real sorrow that I read his Majesty's message of July 28th, on the occasion of the horrid murder of Lord Kilwarden in Dublin. The unanimity of all good subjects will, I trust, soon bring the rebels to justice, and certainly the more danger the more necessary for us to put ourselves forward. I assure you that I wish I only knew how I could serve my country more effectually than in my present command. I attach no value to the high rank I at present hold, and if any, even the lowest, situation is thought to be fittest for me in these times, I should feel prouder to be placed (there) than in any elevation of rank ; all I ask is to be allowed to be one of the men to be placed in the breach to defend my King and country. I have but one arm, it is true, but,

---

[1] " Naval Chronicles," vol. ix. p. 421.
[2] Laughton, p. 311.

believe me, my heart is in the right trim—therefore, only consider how I can be best employed. But I trust, my dear Sir, that you know me, therefore I will not say more, for I fear it would be suspected that I arrogate to myself more merit than I believe will be found in nine hundred and ninety-nine of every one thousand in the United Kingdom. These lines have involuntarily flowed from my pen as they have done from my heart : pardon the effusion. I took the pen for a different subject." [1]

The letter then continues about his orders to chase a small squadron from Marseilles intended for Corsica and Sardinia.

For four months Nelson kept watch and ward over the French Fleet in Toulon, not indeed to prevent their coming out, but by showing at times a smaller force, hoping to entice them to venture a battle with his small fleet. The real nature of his watch of Toulon was naïvely told by Nelson in his letter to the Lord Mayor of London, on receiving the congratulations of the City on "the blockade" in the following letter :—

"To the Lord Mayor of London.
"*Victory, August* 1, 1804.

"My Lord,—I am honoured with your lordship's letter transmitting me the resolution of the Corporation of London, thanking me as commanding the fleet blockading Toulon. . . . I beg to inform your lordship that the port of Toulon has never been blockaded by me— quite the reverse—every opportunity has been offered the enemy to put to sea, for it is there that we hope to realize the hopes and expectations of our country, and I trust that they will not be disappointed."

When the approach of the winter and want of water compelled him to seek a port to recruit and refit, still retaining his old prejudice against Malta, he, in spite of easterly winds, sought a large bay in the straits of Bonifacio, sheltered by the Maddallena Islands, and capable of receiving his squadron. Thence, extending his frigates

[1] Despatches, vol. v. pp. 177–8.

as far as Toulon, he kept the French Fleet in sight, prepared as soon as he should know of its venturing out to give chase to it.

During these tedious months of watching, the Spaniards, only hesitating to declare war with us until they persuaded themselves that they were prepared, carried on a regular system of trying to induce our sailors and marines to desert, and compelled Nelson with his accustomed kindness to issue to them the following warning :—

"To the respective Captains, &c., of his Majesty's ships on the Mediterranean Station.

"*Victory*, off Toulon, *September* 13, 1803.

"When British seamen and marines so far degrade themselves in time of war, as to desert from the service of their own country and enter into that of Spain ; when they leave one shilling a day, and plenty of the best provisions, with every comfort that can be thought of for them—for twopence a day, black bread, horse beans, and stinking oil for their food—when British seamen and marines turn Spanish soldiers, I blush for them ; they forfeit in their own opinion, I am sure, that character of love of their country which foreigners are taught to admire. A Briton to put himself under the lash of a Frenchman or Spaniard must be more degrading to any man of spirit than any punishment I can inflict on their bodies. I shall leave the punishment to their own feelings, which, if they have any, and are still Englishmen, must be very great. But as they thought proper to abandon voluntarily their wives, fathers, mothers, and every endearing tie, and also all prospect of returning to their native country, I shall make them remain out of that country, which they do not wish to see, and allow others, who love their country, and are attached to their families to return in their stead. And as they have also thought proper to resign all their pay, I shall take care that it is not returned to them, nor their ' R ' taken off, but it shall be noted against them, 'Deserted to the Spaniards,' or 'Entered as Spanish soldiers,' as the case was.

"Nelson Bronte."

"The above memorandum respecting the desertion of British seamen or marines to be read to the respective companies of all ships and vessels under my command ; and copies thereof to be stuck up

in the most public places of the ships, in order that the magnitude of
the crime may be properly impressed on their minds.

" NELSON BRONTE." [1]

Finding, after he reached the Maddallena Straits, that
these desertions continued, Nelson spoke plainly in
another memorandum of November 7th :—

" Lord Nelson is sorry to find that notwithstanding his forgiveness
of the men who deserted to Spain, it has failed to have its proper
effect, and that there still are men who so far forget their duty to their
King and country as to desert the service at a time when every man
in England is in arms to defend it against the French. Therefore,
Lord Nelson desires that it may be perfectly understood, that if any
man be so infamous as to desert from the service in future, he will not
only be brought to a court martial, but, that, if the sentence be death,
it will most assuredly be carried out."

Who the detractor was, who is referred to in the
following letter, it is, perhaps, as well that I have failed
to discover. The indignant reply is all-sufficient.

" *Victory*, OFF TOULON, *Oct.* 14, 1803.

MY DEAR ——,—Your letter of July 21st came to me in the
Childers, Sir William Bolton, and I assure you that I feel very much
obliged by your kind hint, but I do not believe one word of your
information ; malicious liars are travelling about doing evil. If he
comes out here I shall be heartily glad to see him. I *well* know his
reasons for coming out ; and even ——, was he an ill-disposed man,
could that hurt me ? Can my mind be turned against my King by any
beings on the earth ? Besides, what is there to find out here ? Only
what he knows, and what every man in England and the fleet knows—
that I will fight the French Fleet the moment I can get at them. I
have no plans to divulge ; and if I had, I should not put it in any
man's power to give information. In *finis*, I believe the gentleman to
be as loyal and attached to the King and country as you or I am ; if he
is not, why do not the Ministry take him up ? My dear ——, some
backbiting rascals are, in our towns, pulling us to pieces : you, I, him.
and others. I shall close by my old expression—they be ——." [2]

---

[1] Despatches, vol. v. p. 201-2.
[2] Ibid., vol. v. p. 241, from " Naval Chronicles " vol. xxxix. p. 131.

From the Straits of Bonifacio Nelson continued to watch Toulon for another year, a short cruise to Algiers, in the hopes of compelling the Dey by a show of force to yield in the matter of our Consul, alone interfering with this tedious task. At Toulon La Touche Treville, who had foiled Nelson's attempt at Boulogne, was now in command—a vigilant officer, constant in his endeavours to improve the discipline of his fleet, and keen in irritating Nelson by venturing out of his harbour with now a portion, again the whole of his squadron, but always returning when the English Fleet drew near, and threatening to stop his "popping out and in." During one of these feints, La Touche Treville persuaded himself that Nelson had run away in fear of him, and wrote the following letter of June 15, 1804, describing his exploits in terms which intensely irritated Nelson, and caused the following correspondence on his part :—

> " ABORD DU *Bucentance*, EN RADE DU TOULON,
>
>   " *Le* 26 *Prairial an* 12.
>
> " GENERAL,—Jai l'honneur de vous rendre compte de la sortie de toute l'escadre à mes ordres. Sur l'avis que j'avais reçu que plusiers corsaires Anglais infestaient la côte et les Iles d'Hieres, je donnai l'ordre, il a trois jours, aux frigates *l'Incoruptible* et *la Syrêne*, et le brick *le Furet*, de se rendre dans la baie d'Hieres. Le vent d'est ayant contrairées, elles mouillèront sous le chateau de Porquereles. Hier Matin, les enemies en eurent connaisance. Vers midi, ils detacheront deux frigates et un vaisseau, qui enterent par la grande passe, dans l'intention de couper la retraite à nos frigates. Du moment ou je m' aperçus de sa maneuvre, je fis signal d'appereiller a loute l'escadre ; ce qui fut executé. En 14 minutes tout etait sous voiles, et je fis porter sui l'ennemi pour lui couper le chemin de la petite passe, et dans le dessein de l'y suivre, s'il avait tenté d'y passer ; mais l'Amiral Anglais ne tarda pas à renoncer à son projet, rappela son vaisseau et les deux frigates engagés dans les iles et prit chasse. Je l'ai poursaivi jusqu'a la nuit ; il courait au sud-est, Le Matin, au jour, je n'en ai eu aucune connaissance. Je vous salue avec respect,
>
>   " LA TOUCHE TREVILLE."

This letter was found in the post-office, Malta, by Dr Lambton Este, and forwarded by him to Lord Nelson.[1]

"To HIS BROTHER.

"*Victory, August* 9, 1804.

"P.S.—You will have seen Monsieur La Touche's letter, of how he chased me, and how I ran. I keep it; and by God, if I take him he shall *Eat* it."[2]

"To ALEX. DAVISON.

"*Victory, August* 9, 1804.

"I am expecting Monsieur La Touche (as he has wrote a letter that I ran away) to come out of his nest. The whole history was too contemptible for my notice, but I have thought it right, not upon my own account, but for the satisfaction of the Admiralty, &c., &c., to send a copy of the *Victory's* Log; for if my character for *not* running away is not fixed by this time, it is not worth my trouble to put the world right at my time of life; and if any Englishman has believed for one moment the story, I may, to my friend say, without fear of being thought arrogant, that they do not deserve to have me serve them; but I have kept Monsieur La Touche's letter, and if I take him, I shall ever never see him, or if I do, *make him eat* his letter—perhaps sovereign contempt is the best."[3]

"To WM. MARSDEN, ESQ., ADMIRALTY.

"*Victory* AT SEA, *August* 12, 1804.

"SIR,—Although I most certainly never thought of writing a line upon Monsieur La Touche's having cut a caper a few miles outside of Toulon, on the 14th of June, where he well knew I could not get at him without placing the ships under the batteries which surround the port, and that had I attacked him in that position he could retire into his secure nest whenever he pleased, yet as that gentleman has thought proper to write a letter stating that the fleet under my command ran away, and that he pursued it, perhaps it may be thought necessary for me to say something. But I do assure you, Sir, that I do not know what to say, except by a flat contradiction; for, if my character is not established by this time for not being apt to run away, it is not worth my time to attempt to put the world right. It is not, therefore, I do assure their lordships, with any such intention that I stain my paper with a vaunting man's name, and, therefore, I shall only state that the

---

[1] Despatches, vol. vi. p. 131, note.   [2] Ibid., vol. vi. p. 147.
[3] Ibid., vol. vi. p. 148.

fleet which I have the honour and happiness to command is in the highest state of discipline, good order, good humour, and good health, and that the united wishes of all are, I am sure, to meet Monsieur La Touche at sea; then I ought not to doubt that I should be able to write a letter equally satisfactory to my King, my country, and myself. I send you a copy of the ship's log [which I have never seen till this day. I observe that so little was thought of Monsieur La Touche's return to Toulon harbour more than any other time, that it is not even noticed, *although by the bearings at Noon and Latitude, that we were but four Miles outside the Port* where he was snug at anchor, and that at one o'clock we attempted to get at the *Swiftsure*, which was the only ship outside the harbour [1]].

" NELSON AND BRONTE." [2]

Nelson wrote to Sir A. J. Ball, on October 4, 1804, as follows :—

" No admiral has hoisted his flag in the room of La Touche—he is gone, and all his lies with him. The French papers say he died in consequence of walking so often up to the signal port upon Sepat, to watch us. I always pronounced that would be his death." [3]

During this period, thanks to the care and foresight of Nelson, the fleet was in the best of health ; not so the admiral himself, who would gladly have been relieved for a time, yet held on in hopes that the French Fleet would yet come out and face him. Of his unremitting care of

[1] Autograph Draught.

[2] French Fleet under Monsieur La Touche—8 sail-of-the-line, 6 frigates, 2 frigates and a brig in Hieres Bay, who joined in the night. British Fleet—5 sail-of-the-line and 2 frigates, one of which, the *Excellent* 74, and 2 frigates, did not join till the middle of the night, having been sent into Hieres Bay.

From 6.10 to 7.28 p.m. the British formed in line to receive Monsieur La Touche, maintopsail to mast.

The movements of the squadron on the evening of the 14th of June, 1804 :—

Laying to
$$\begin{cases} \text{5.43 P.M.} & \text{Prepared for Battle.} \\ \text{5.49 } \text{,,} & \text{Recalled } \textit{Excellent.} \\ \text{6.10 } \text{,,} & \text{Formed line of Battle.} \end{cases}$$

7.28. Came to the Windward together on the larboard tack. 7.45. Tacked together. 7.59. Formed order of sailing. (Despatches, vol. vi. p. 150.)

[3] Despatches, vol. vi. p. 214.

the health of his fleet, the despatches furnish some interesting examples. The smallest details that could promote
the health of the sailors were not above his care. In one
letter we find him pointing out the way in which the
vegetables, the pork and beef were to be tested before they
were received and distributed among the crews. Again
he is writing to the commissioners of the Admiralty on
the flannel shirts that had been sent out, " These flannel
shirts being made five or six inches too short," he wrote,
" exposed the men to sudden chills, so he proposed to give
them to the boys. These shirts, five or six inches longer,
would be one of the best things yet introduced into the
navy, and would perhaps save the lives of more than one
good sailor." One more instance of his sedulous care of
his sailors :—

" I am sure your lordships will see the justness of the case as plain
as I do. Each man was allowed a pint of oatmeal on certain days ;
but as it was found that generally a man could not get a pint of dry
oatmeal down his throat, and, I suppose, thinking it no longer necessary
to prevent this saving to the purser, half a pint of oatmeal was issued
instead of a pint, and in lieu of the other half pint, a proportion of
molasses ; it has sometimes occurred in the Channel Fleet, that no
molasses could be procured, nor was any allowance made for such
temporary omissions. In the West Indies, cocoa and sugar are
allowed ; in the Channel, I hear, tea and sugar. In the Mediterranean
we have no molasses, nor any substitute ; nor is our want of molasses
temporary, but lasting. I beg, therefore, to call their lordships'
attention to this circumstance ; and to propose, that when molasses
cannot be obtained, a proportion of sugar should be mixed with the
oatmeal, in lieu of molasses, and if sugar cannot be obtained, the men
having no substitute in lieu, should be paid the saving, as in all other
species of provisions. It is not necessary to enter more at large on
subject ; their lordships' wisdom will direct their proceedings." [1]

At length, at the close of 1804, Spain declared war
with England, justifying her conduct on the ground of

[1] To the Secretary of the Admiralty, Sept. 22, 1804 ; Clarke and
McArthur, pp. 68-9.

the capture of four Spanish frigates on the 5th of October
by the frigate squadron of Captain More.   On the 5th of
March, 1805, Spain took the field.   At this juncture,
Villeneuve took the command at Toulon in consequence
of La Touch Treville's early death.   As far as taking
troops, saddles and horses on board, every preparation
for an expedition was made, but still his fleet lingered in
harbour, though if he has been rightly reported, he told
his men, " There is nothing about an English Fleet that
should frighten you ; their ships are worn out by a two
years' blockade."   He little knew " what had been effected
by the salutary and daily labours of a life at sea under a
good chief."

"A first essay," writes Jurien de la Gravière, "was destined to
establish the immense difference which cannot but exist between a fleet
inured to labour, and another just escaped from the idleness of a port.
On Jan. 19, 1805, Nelson was at anchor in Agincourt Roads, where
two of his frigates, the *Active* and *Seahorse*, appeared at the entrance
of the Straits of Bonifacio under a press of sail, with the long-expected
signal, ' The enemy is at sea.'   It was three o'clock in the afternoon
when they anchored near the *Victory*, and at half-past four the English
Fleet was under sail.   It becomes dark there about five o'clock at that
time of the year; the wind was blowing strong from the westward,
and the fleet could not work to windward against it.   So that it was
necessary to go through one of the eastern passages which open into
the Tuscan Sea.   Though it was now completely dark, Nelson took
the lead in the *Victory*, and resolved to conduct his eleven ships-of-the-
line between the rocks of Biscia, and the north-east extremity of
Sardinia.   This passage, whose breadth does not exceed a quarter of
a mile, has never since been attempted by any fleet.   The English
squadron cleared it ; formed in a single line ahead.   Each ship
showing a light astern, to guide the one which followed." [1]

From the direction in which he was informed that the
French Fleet was sailing, Nelson persuaded himself that
the easternmost point of Sardinia was their object.   Thither

[1] " The Last Naval War," p. 148–9.

he sailed at once, only to be disappointed of hearing any news of the enemy. From the signs of the weather, Nelson foresaw the approach of a storm, and prepared for it.

"Better acquainted than anybody with the seas in which he then was, he knew how with sudden violence the heaviest gales commence in the Mediterranean, and expecting to meet the enemy, he did not wish to risk doing so with ships already disabled. The tempest, which Nelson had foreseen, burst out the next morning, and found the English squadron under close-reefed sails, ready to defy the fury of the squalls which succeeded each other without interruption until the 23rd of January."[1]

Unprepared for such weather, Villeneuve had put back to Toulon, with loss, but as yet Nelson knew it not. He had heard of a French line-of-battle ship having taken refuge at Ajaccio, but was still determined to sail to Egypt. "If the enemy have put back crippled," he wrote to the Admiralty, "I could never overtake them, and therefore I could not do any harm in going to the eastward ; and if the enemy are gone to the eastward, I am right." [2]

On the 29th of January, therefore, he beat through the straits of Messina, and some days later was off the coast of Egypt. There were no signs of the French. On the 8th of February, therefore, he sailed back to Malta and Toulon. According to his French biographer, on the 8th of February, Nelson wrote again to the Admiralty, justifying his sailing to Egypt.

"Had I even known the injury sustained by one French ship, I could not forget the character of Buonaparte. I know that in the orders given by him on the banks of the Seine, neither wind nor weather would be considered, and indeed, in my opinion, though

---

[1] "The Last Naval War," p. 170.
[2] To Mr. Marsden, 29th Jan.

there had been three or four French ships disabled, that was no reason for delaying an important expedition." [1]

Until the 10th of April, Nelson kept cruising about the French and Italian coasts, and though Villeneuve sailed a second time from Toulon on the 29th of March, it was not until the middle of April that he had any certain news that the French squadron had left the Mediterranean. Nelson at once made for the straits, baffled for many days with contrary winds. How bitterly he felt these delays is told in the following letters :—

> " *April* 19th.
>
> " *Victory* AT SEA, TEN LEAGUES OFF TORO.
>
> " MY DEAR BALL,—My good luck seems flown away. I cannot get a fair wind, or even a side wind. Dead foul ! dead foul ! But my mind is fully made up what to do when I leave the straits, supposing there is no certain confirmation of the enemy's destination. I believe this ill-luck will go near to kill me; but as these are times for exertion, I must not be cast down." [2]

> " To W. MARSDEN.
>
> [Same date and place].
>
> " SIR,—The enemy's fleet having so very long ago passed the straits, and formed a junction with some Spanish ships from Cadiz, I think it my duty, which must be satisfactory to their lordships, to know exactly my intentions. I have detached the *Amazon* to Lisbon for information, and I am proceeding off Cape St. Vincent as expeditiously as possible ; and I hope the *Amazon* will join me there, or that I shall obtain some positive information of the destination of the enemy. The circumstance of their having taken the Spanish ships which were for sea, from Cadiz, satisfies my mind that they are not bound for the West Indies (nor probably Brazils), but intend forming a junction with the squadron at Ferrol, and pushing direct for Ireland or Brest, as I believe the French have troops on board ; therefore, if I receive no intelligence to do away with my present belief, I shall proceed from

---

[1] " The Last Naval War," p. 171. This letter not in the Despatches.
[2] Despatches, vol. vi. p. 410.

FLAXMAN'S BUST OF NELSON.

Cape St. Vincent, and take my position fifty leagues west of Scilly, approaching that island slowly, that I may not miss any vessels sent in search of the squadron with orders. My reason for this position is, that it is equally easy to get to either the fleet at Brest, or to go to Ireland should the fleet be wanted for either station. I trust this place will meet their lordships' approbation ; and I have the pleasure to say that I bring with me eleven ships of war, as ably commanded, and in as perfect order and in health, as ever went to sea,

" I am, &c.,
" N. AND B.

" I shall send to both Ireland and the Channel Fleet an extract of this letter, acquainting the Commander-in-chief where to find me." [1]

" To Viscount Melville.

" About *April* 20, 1805.

" I am not made to despair, what man can do shall be done. I have marked out for myself a decided line of conduct, and I shall follow it well up ; although I have now before me a letter from the physician of the fleet, enforcing my return to England before the hot months. Therefore, notwithstanding, I shall pursue the enemy to the East or West Indies, if I know that to have been their destination, yet if the Mediterranean Fleet joins the Channel, I shall request, with that order, permission to go on shore.

" Nelson and Bronte." [2]

" To Sir Evan Nepean, Bart.

" *May 7th.*

" I am still as much in the dark as ever. I am now pushing off Cape St. Vincent, where I hope to be more fortunate ; and I shall join the *Amazon* from Lisbon, from which place I have accounts to April 27, where they knew nothing of the enemy. If I hear nothing, I shall proceed to the West Indies.[3]

" Nelson and Bronte." [3]

" To Mrs. Bolton.

" *Victory*, May 9. [Lagos Bay.]

" My dear Sister,—God only knows where I shall be on July 1st,

---

[1] Despatches, vol. vi. pp. 411–12.

[2] Clarke and McArthur ; Despatches, vol. vi. p. 414.

[3] Ibid. ; Despatches, vol. vi. p. 428.

and, therefore, I send you a bill for one hundred pounds ; and when I get home, I hope to be able to keep Tom at college, without one farthing's expense to Mr. Bolton ; and both you and him may be assured, that I would do more, if in my power.   I should have been a very rich, instead of a poor, man, if Lord Melville had not given the galleons to Sir J. Orde.   God bless you, Mr. Bolton and family, and believe me ever, your affectionate brother,

" Nelson and Bronte." [1]

It was at this critical moment that, probably whilst in Lagos Bay, Nelson received a visit from Admiral Campbell, an English officer in the Portuguese service, who informed him in confidence that the real destination of the French and Spanish squadron was the West Indies. Nelson at once decided to follow them, though he had only eleven ships to their eighteen.[2]

On the 11th of May, after having left the *Royal Sovereign* with Rear-Admiral Knight, as an addition to Sir J. Orde's fleet off Cadiz, Nelson sailed for the West Indies.   To Captain Ball he wrote (May 10th) :—

" My lot is cast, and I am going to the West Indies, where, though I am late, yet chance may have given them a bad passage, and me a good one.   I must hope for the best."

How characteristic of Nelson's feeling for his comrades are the few words to Captain Keats of the *Superb*, notwithstanding the overwhelming anxiety that his squadron should fly in pursuit :—

" I am fearful that you may think that the *Superb* does not go so fast as I could wish.   However that may be (for if we all went ten knots, I should not think it fast enough) yet I would have you be

---

[1] Despatches, vol. vi. p. 429.

[2] Notwithstanding the rigid secrecy observed by Nelson, a complaint was made by the Spaniards' Commander at Algiers to the French ambassador at Portugal, and Campbell's appointment was closed, and though the British Government assured him of their support, the admiral's death involved his widow and family in distress.   Clarke and McArthur, vol. iii. p. 96, and note.

assured that I know and feel that the *Superb* does all which is possible for a ship to accomplish ; and I desire that you will not fret upon the occasion." ¹

On the 4th of June his fleet was at anchor in Carlisle Bay, Barbadoes, and joined there by Rear-Admiral Cochrane, with the *Northumberland* and *Spartiate*, thus bringing his squadron up to twelve sail-of-the-line, whilst Villeneuve's had been increased to twenty-eight. Here, it being reported that Tobago and Trinidad were the enemy's objects, he embarked two thousand troops, and in consequence of a letter from Brigadier-General Brereton, sailed for Trinidad. On the 7th of June Nelson entered the Bay of Paria, found the anchorage deserted. The false news had brought him sixty leagues out of his way. The following is his own account of the chase :—

" I arrived at Barbadoes 4th of June, where I found Lieutenant-General Sir William Myers, who the night before had received information from Brigadier-General Brereton at St. Lucia, that twenty-eight sail of the enemy's fleet had been seen to the windward of St. Lucia, steering to the southward. As there was no reason to doubt this information, the General offered to embark himself with two thousand troops for the relief of either Tobago or Trinidad, which were supposed to be the intended objects of the enemy's attack. On the 6th we were off Tobago, on the 7th at Trinidad, on the 8th I received an account that the enemy had not moved on the 4th from Fort Royal, but were expected to sail that night for the attack of Grenada. On the 9th I was at Grenada, when I received a letter from General Provost to say that the enemy had passed Dominica on the 6th, standing to the northward, to the lee of Antigua, and took that day a convoy of fourteen sail of sugar-loaded ships, which unfortunately left St. John's in the night for England. On the 11th I was at Montserrat, and on the 12th anchored at St. John's Antigua to land the troops, which was done on the morning of the 13th, and at noon I sailed in pursuit of the enemy; and I do not despair of getting up with them before they arrive at Cadiz or Toulon, to which

¹ Despatches, vol. vi., May 19th.

ports I think they are bound, or at least in time to prevent them from having a moment's superiority. I have no reason to blame Dame Fortune. If either General Brereton would not have wrote, or his look-out man had been blind, nothing would have prevented my fighting him on June 6th ; but such information, and from such a quarter close to the enemy, could not be doubted." [1]

The following extracts from Nelson's letters and Private Diary describe his feelings at this period :—

"To the Duke of Clarence.

"*June* 12, 1805.

"Your Royal Highness will easily conceive the misery I am feeling at hitherto having missed the French Fleet ; and entirely owing to false information sent from St. Lucia, which arrived at Barbadoes the evening of July 3rd. This caused me to embark Sir W. Myers and two thousand troops, and to proceed to Tobago and Trinidad. But for that false information, I should have been off Port Royal as they were putting to sea ; and our battle, most probably, would have been fought where the brave Rodney beat De Grasse. I am rather inclined to believe they are pushing for Europe to get out of our way ; and the moment my mind is made up, I shall stand for the Straits' mouth. But I must not move, after having saved these Colonies and two hundred and upwards of sugar-laden ships, until I feel sure they are gone." [2]

From his Private Diary :—

"*July* 17, 1805. Our whole run from Barbadoes day by day was 3,459 miles ; our run from Cape St. Vincent to Barbadoes 3,227 miles ; so that our run back was only 232 miles more than our run out—allowance being made for the difference of latitudes and longitudes of Barbadoes and Barbuda ; average per day, 34 leagues, wanting 9 miles."

"*July* 18, 1805. Cape Spartel in sight, but no French Fleet, nor any information about them ; how sorrowful this makes me, but I cannot help myself." [3]

---

[1] To Lord Robert Fitzgerald, June 15th.   Despatches, vol. vi.
[2] Despatches, vol. vi. p. 455.   [3] Ibid., vol. vi. p. 471.

"To Vice-Admiral Collingwood.

"My dear Collingwood,—I am, as you may suppose, miserable at not having fallen in with the enemy's fleet; and I am almost increased in sorrow at not finding them. The name of General Brereton will not be soon forgot. But for his false intelligence the battle would have been fought where Rodney fought his, June 6th."[1]

From his Private Diary :—

"*June* 21, 1805. Midnight, nearly calm, saw three planks, which I believe came from the French Fleet. Very miserable, which is very foolish."[2]

"To W. Marsden, Esq., Admiralty,

"Near Gibraltar.

"I am, my dear Mr. Marsden, as completely miserable as my greatest enemy could wish ; but I neither blame fortune, nor my own judgment. Oh, General Brereton ! General Brereton ! "

"To Alex. Davison, Esq.

"*July* 24, 1805.

"My dear Davison,—I am as miserable as you can conceive. But for General Brereton's information, Nelson would have been, living or dead, the greatest man in his profession that England ever saw. Now, alas ! I am nothing—perhaps shall incur censure for misfortunes which may happen and have happened. I resisted the opinion of General Brereton's information till it would have been the height of presumption to have carried my disbelief further. I could not in the face of general and admiral go N.W., when it was *apparently* clear that the enemy had gone S. But I am miserable. I now long to hear that they are arrived in some port in the bay ; for until they are arrived somewhere, I can do nothing but fret. Then I shall proceed to England. I can say nothing, or think anything, but the loss my country has sustained by General Brereton's unfortunate, ill-timed, false information. God bless you, and believe me ever, my dear Davison, your most faithful and affectionate friend,

"Nelson and Bronte."[3]

---

[1] Despatches, vol. vi. p. 473.

[2] Clarke and McArthur ; Despatches, vol. vi. p. 464.

[3] Despatches, vol. vi. p. 494.

On the 17th of June, the vessel *Sally*, bound for Antigua, was boarded by Captain Parker of the *Amazon*, and gave the following intelligence : " At 7 p.m. on Sunday evening last, saw about twenty-eight sail of large ships steering, master's account, N.N.E., mate's account, N.N.W. in latitude ; on Saturday noon 27° 28″, longitude, 60° 58″ W." In transmitting this intelligence to the Admiralty, Nelson on the 19th said :—

" I send you a report of a vessel spoke, which with the circumstances attending it, can leave no doubt but that I am hard upon the heels of the enemy's fleet. In addition, Captain Parker reports to me that there was a note in the American's log, that they supposed they were the French Fleet from Martinique. The master was anxious to know if the French had taken Antigua, as he was bound there, and had traded to that island many years. The remark of seeing the fleet in the log of the vessel, with the difference of the course the master and mate supposed the fleet to be steering, satisfies my mind that there could be no intended deceit in the information (which sometimes happens) ; nor did the vessel see our fleet until she was spoke by the *Amazon.* I think we cannot be more than eighty leagues from them at this moment, and by carrying every sail, and using my utmost efforts, I shall hope to close with them before they get either to Cadiz or Toulon." [1]

I agree with Professor Laughton that this report may have been the very slight foundation for the following romantic story, related by Clarke and McArthur, vol. ii. p. 417, which I give on their authority for what it is worth :—

" An American merchant ship, spoken by one of the frigates, had fallen in, a little to the westward of the Azores, with an armed vessel, having the appearance of a privateer dismasted, and which had evident marks of having been set fire to, and run on board by another ship, the impression of whose stem had penetrated the top sides. The crew had forsaken her, and the fire had most probably gone out of its own accord. In the cabin had been found a log-book and a few seamen's

---

[1] To W. Marsden, Despatches, vol. vi.

jackets, which were given to the officer, and taken on board the *Victory*; and with these the admiral immediately endeavoured to explain the mystery, and to discover some further intelligence of the enemy. The log-book, which closed with this remark, "Two large ships in the W.N.W." showed, in his opinion, that the abandoned vessel had been a Liverpool privateer cruising off the Western Islands. In the leaves of this log-book, a small scrap of dirty paper was found, filled with figures, which no one could make anything of but Lord Nelson, who immediately on seeing it remarked, 'They are French characters,' which probably stimulated him to a stricter observation. After an attentive observation, he said, 'I can unravel the whole : this privateer was taken by the two ships that were seen in the W.N.W. The prize master, who had been put on board in a hurry, omitted to take with him his reckoning ; there is none in the log-book ; and this dirty scrap of paper, which none of you could make anything of, contains his work for the number of days since the privateer left Corvo, with an unaccounted-for run, which I take to have been the chase, in his endeavour to find out his situation by back reckonings. The jackets I find to be the manufacture of France, which prove the enemy was in possession of the privateer ; and I conclude, by some mismanagement, she was run aboard of afterwards by one of them and dismasted. Not liking delay (for I am satisfied these two ships were the advanced ones of the French Squadron), and fancying we were close at their heels, they set fire to the vessel and abandoned her in a hurry. If my explanation, gentlemen, be correct, I infer from it that they have gone more to the northward, and more to the northward I will look for them.' Subsequent information proved that he was correct in every part of his interpretation." [1]

It is doubtful at what precise date the following most able paper of instructions was drawn up by Nelson. The general opinion, however, is that it ought to bear a date during the protracted chase to the West Indies. The following copy is from the St. Vincent Papers :—

"The business of an English commander-in-chief being, first, to bring an enemy's fleet to battle, on the most advantageous terms to himself (I mean that of laying his ships close on board the enemy, as

---

[1] "This," says Southey, "more than any event in real history, resembles those whimsical proofs of sagacity which Voltaire in his 'Zadig' has borrowed from the Orientals."

expeditiously as possible) ; and, secondly, to continue there, without separating, until the business is decided; I am sensible beyond this object it is not necessary that I should say a word, being fully assured that the admirals and captains of the fleet I have the honour to command will, knowing my precise object, that of a close and decisive battle, supply any deficiency in my not making signals ; which may, if extended beyond these objects, either be misunderstood, or if waited for, very probably, from various causes, be impossible for the commander-in-chief to make : therefore, it will only be requisite for me to state, in as few words as possible, the various modes in which it may be necessary for me to obtain my object, on which depends not only the glory and honour of our country, but possibly its safety, and with that of all Europe, from French tyranny and oppression.

" If both fleets are willing to fight, but little manœuvring is necessary ; the less the better—a day is soon lost in that business ; therefore, I will only suppose that the enemy's fleet being to leeward, standing close upon a wind on the starboard tack, and that I am ahead of them standing on the larboard tack, of course I should weather them. The weather must be supposed to be moderate ; for if it be a gale of wind the manœuvring of both fleets is but of little avail, and probably no decisive action would take place with the whole fleet. Two modes present themselves ; one to stand on, just out of gunshot, until the van ship of my line would be about the centre ship of the enemy, then make the signal to wear all together, then bear up, engage with all our force the six or five van ships of the enemy, passing certainly, if opportunity offered, through their line. This would prevent their bearing up, and the action from the known bravery of the admirals and captains would certainly be decisive ; the second or third rear ships of the enemy would act as they please, and our ships would give a good account of them, should they persist in mixing with our ships.

" The other mode would be, to stand under an easy but commanding sail, directly for their headmost ship, so as to prevent the enemy from knowing whether I should pass to leeward or windward of them. In that situation I would engage the enemy to leeward, and to cut through their fleet about the sixth ship from the van, passing very close ; they being on a wind, and you going large could cut their line when you please. The van ships of the enemy would by the time our rear came abreast of the van ships be severely cut up, and our van could not expect to escape damage. I would then have our *rear* ship, and every ship in succession, wear, continue the action with either the van ship or second ship, as it might appear most eligible

from her crippled state : and this mode pursued, I see nothing to prevent the capture of five or six ships of the enemy's van. The two or
three ships of the enemy's rear must either bear up or wear ; and in
either case, although they may be in a better plight than our two van
ships (now the rear), yet they would be separated, and at a distance to
leeward, so as to give our ships time to refit ; and by that time I
believe the battle would, from the judgment of the admirals and captains, be over with the rest of them. Signals from these moments are
useless, when every man is disposed to do his duty. The great object
is for us to support each other, and to keep close to the enemy, and to
leeward of him.

" If the enemy are running away, then the only signals necessary
will be to engage the enemy as arriving up with them ; the other
ships to pass on for the second, third, &c., giving, if possible, a close
fire into the enemy on passing, taking care to give our ships engaged
notice of your intention." [1]

When off Cape Spartel Nelson fell in with the
squadron of Collingwood. After writing to him on the
18th of July, how miserable he was at the escape of the
French Fleet, and of the mischief done by Brereton's
letter, Nelson said : " The moment the fleet is watered
and got some refreshments, of which we are in great need,
I shall come out and make you a visit ; not, my dear
friend, to take your command from you (for I may probably add mine to yours), but to consult how we may
best serve our country by detaching a part of this great
force."

Collingwood had already written to Nelson that the
sailing of the French to the West Indies was a feint to
draw off the English Fleet, and then return, liberate the
French squadron which Calder was watching, and then,
taking the Rochefort fleet with them, assemble some thirty
ships off Ushant, and make a dash for Ireland. This he
repeated in his reply to Nelson's letter of the 18th.

[1] Despatches, vol. vi. pp. 443–5.

On the 20th of July, Nelson wrote from Tetuan Bay
to the Admiralty :—

"I anchored yesterday morning without having obtained the
smallest intelligence of the enemy's fleet, except what is contained
in the enclosed paper [the report of boarding the *Sally* before
quoted]. The squadron is in perfect health, except some symptoms of
scurvy, which I hope to eradicate by bullocks and refreshments from
Tetuan, to which I shall proceed to-morrow."

In his Private Diary he made this notable entry :—

"*July* 20th. I went on shore for the first time since June 16,
1803 ; and from having my foot out of the *Victory* two years, wanting
ten days."

Three days after Nelson wrote to Lord Barham, the
First Lord of the Admiralty : "The fleet is complete,
and the first easterly wind I shall pass the straits. I have
yet not a word of information of the enemy's fleet ; it
has almost broke my heart."

To Admiral Cornwallis he wrote on the 27th of
July :—

"The enemy's fleet from the West Indies being certainly gone to
some port in the Bay, I am proceeding northward with eleven sail-of-
the-line. I shall either call off Cape Clear or proceed direct to
Ushant, to form a junction with you, as circumstances may in my
judgment (from intelligence) require. I shall only hope, after all my
long pursuit of my enemy, that I may arrive at the moment they are
meeting you ; for my wretched state of health will force me to get on
shore for a little while."

On the 3rd of August, 1805, he made the following
entry in his Private Diary :—

"I feel every moment of this foul wind, but I trust in Providence
that it is all for the best; although I, poor weak mortal, suffer severely
from the mortification of so apparently a long passage as this will pro-

bably be from the continuation of northerly winds. We are in lat. 39, long. 16, course west. No information ; all night light airs." [1]

On the 15th of August, still baffled in his persistent pursuit of the enemy, Nelson joined the Channel Fleet under Cornwallis, off Ushant, and, " on doing so I received an order from him to proceed immediately with *Victory* and *Superb* to Spithead, where I arrived this morning." [2] On the 19th he struck his flag and went to Merton, where he resided during the few weeks he was on shore. Notwithstanding his failure to intercept the French Fleet, Nelson's popularity was as great as ever :—

" I met Lord Nelson," says Lord Minto, " in August, 1805, in a mob in Piccadilly. I got hold of his arm, so that I was mobbed too. It is really quite affecting to see the wonder and admiration and love and respect of the whole world ; and the genuine expression of all these sentiments at once, from gentle and simple, the moment he is seen. It is beyond anything represented in a play or a poem of fame." [3]

---

[1] Despatches, vol. vii. p. 2.
[2] To William Marsden, Spithead, August 19th.
[3] Quoted in the *Edinburgh Review*, as above, pp. 373–4.

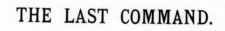

THE LAST COMMAND.

CHAPTER XV.

THE LAST COMMAND.

(1805.)

Nelson at Merton—Blackwood's news—Nelson at the Admiralty—Early sketches of the intended attack—Sir R. Keats and Lord Sidmouth—Leaves Merton—Embarks at Portsmouth, September 14th—Joins the fleet off Cadiz, September 28th—Watching the enemy—The enemy coming out of port—The enemy at sea—The last letters before the battle—The Hamilton codicil.

LORD NELSON remained at Merton until the 2nd of September, 1805, visited by the whole of his family.[1] As I have in another chapter given an account of Nelson's private life, both during his journey from the Mediterranean after the Battle of the Nile, through the continent, and subsequently at Merton, it is needless to repeat it here. As a resident landlord he spared neither pains nor money to render his poorer neighbours comfortable and happy during the brief period of his last residence, which by this time had been

---

[1] In August, 1805, Nelson, writing to Beckford, excused his not accepting his invitation to Fonthill, on the ground that all his family were with him, his stay uncertain, and that he has refused all invitations. Every ship, even the *Victory*, ordered out. According to Harrison, vol. ii. p. 454, Dr. Nelson and his wife and children ; Mr. and Mrs. Bolton, and Thomas Bolton (second Earl Nelson); Mrs. Matcham and her son George (see his account of the life at Merton (Chapter XIX.), and her two daughters and Lady Hamilton.

rendered commodious by his liberal outlay in building. Conscious that his enemies were carefully watched by Cornwallis and Collingwood, and convinced that Napoleon would sooner or later force the combined fleet into action, he was not surprised that intelligence had been brought to the Admiralty that the combined fleet had put into Cadiz, and that his services were urgently required for his last command.

On the 2nd of September, 1805, Captain the Hon. H. Blackwood, of the *Euryalus*, arrived at the Admiralty with the intelligence that the combined fleets had put into Cadiz. At five o'clock in that morning he called on Lord Nelson at Merton for a few minutes, and found him already up and dressed. Immediately on seeing Captain Blackwood, he exclaimed, " I am sure you bring me news of the French and Spanish Fleets, and I think I shall yet have to beat them." According to the statement in *Blackwood's Magazine*, July, 1833, "Lord Nelson followed Blackwood to London, and in talking over the operations that were intended in the Mediterranean, often repeated, ' Depend on it, Blackwood, I shall give M. Villeneuve a drubbing.' " [1]

At the Admiralty Nelson was received by Lord Barham with open arms. "Choose," said the First Lord, "the officers you would like to have under your command." "Choose them yourself," replied Nelson, "the same spirit animates the whole Navy ; you cannot go wrong." Wisely he was given unlimited powers, and his secretary desired to give the names of the ships which he wished to be added to his command.

"I hope," he wrote, on the 6th of September, to Davison, "my absence will not be long, and that I shall soon meet the combined

---

[1] The story in Harrison, vol. ii. p. 457, that he hesitated to go to town, and was overpersuaded by Lady Hamilton, is apocryphal.

fleets with a force sufficient to do the job well ; for half a victory would but half content me.   But I do not believe the Admiralty can give me a force within fifteen or sixteen sail-of-the-line of the enemy ; and, therefore, if every ship took her opponent, we should have to contend with a fresh fifteen or sixteen sail-of-the-line.   But I will do my best, and I hope God Almighty will go with me.   I have much to lose and little to gain : and I go because it is right, and will serve my country faithfully."

Yet amid all his anxiety he did not forget poor Mrs. Maurice :—

" I send you," he wrote to Davison, on the 6th of September, " a memorandum which I am sure you will comply with.   Poor blind Mrs. Nelson I must assist this morning.   A Mr. Brand, an apothecary, called upon me for £133 2s. 6d., as due from my brother Maurice to him.   I shall refer him to you, and if it is a just demand he must have it."

Before Nelson left Merton he had sketched out his plan of attack in the following conversations with Sir R. Keats and Lord Sidmouth :—

" One morning, walking with Lord Nelson in the grounds at Merton, talking on naval matters, he said to me, ' No day can be long enough to arrange a couple of fleets and fight a decisive battle according to the old system.   When we meet them ' (I was to have been with him), ' for meet them we shall, I'll tell you how I shall fight them.   I shall form the fleet into three divisions in three lines. One division shall be composed of twelve or fourteen of the fastest two-decked ships, which I shall keep always to windward, or in a situation of advantage, and I shall put them under an officer who, I am sure, will employ them in the manner I wish, if possible.   I consider it will always be in my power to throw them into battle in any part I may choose ; but if circumstances prevent their being carried against the enemy where I desire, I shall feel certain he will employ them effectually, and perhaps in a more advantageous manner than if he could have followed my orders.'   (He never mentioned, or gave any hint, by which I could understand who it was he intended for this distinguished service.)   He continued, ' With the remaining part of the fleet, formed in two lines, I shall go at them at once, if I can, about one-third of their line from their leading ship.' He then said, 'What do you think of it?' Such a question, I felt, required consideration. I paused. Seeing it, he said, 'But I'll tell you what I think of it. It will surprise and confound the enemy. They won't know what I am about. It will bring forward a pell-mell battle, and that is what I want.' [1]

"On the 24th of August, 1805, Nelson called on Lord Sidmouth in Clifford·Street. 'Surprised me,' wrote Lord Sidmouth, 'without a coat, having just undergone the operation of bleeding. He looked well, and we passed an hour together. Our conversation will be renewed to-morrow, when he has promised to call after church' (letter to his brother). Lord Sidmouth's serious illness and Nelson's engagements prevented their meeting, and on the eve of Nelson's departure with the fleet Lord Sidmouth wrote that he would call on Nelson at Merton if he could not take Richmond Park on his way to town. To this Nelson replied (September 8th), 'On Tuesday forenoon, if superior powers do not prevent me, I will be in Richmond Park, and shall be glad to take you by the hand, and to wish you a most perfect restoration to health.'

"To this note Lord Sidmouth has appended the following words : 'Lord Nelson came on that day, and passed some hours at Richmond Park. This was our last meeting.' He was accustomed in after years to relate that, amongst other things, Nelson explained to him, with his finger, on the little study table, the manner in which, should he be so fortunate as to meet the combined fleets, he proposed to attack them. 'Rodney broke the line in one point ; I will break it in two.' 'There,' said Lord Sidmouth to Miss Halsted, who has reported the anecdote, 'is the table on which he drew the Battle of Trafalgar but five weeks before his death. It is strange that I should have used this valued relic for above thirty years without having once thought of recording upon it a fact so interesting. Now,' pointing to a brass plate inserted in the centre of the table, 'I have perpetuated it by this brief record :

"'On the 10th day of September, 1805, Vice-Admiral Lord Viscount Nelson described to Lord Sidmouth, upon this table, the manner in which he intended to engage the combined fleets of France and Spain, which he expected shortly to meet. He stated he would attack them in two lines, led by himself and Admiral Collingwood, and felt confi-

---

[1] In the hand-writing of E. H. Locker, Esq., who wrote on it, "Copy of Paper communicated to me by Sir R. Keats, and allowed by him to be transcribed by me, October 1, 1829."

dent that he should capture either their van and centre, or their centre or rear. This he successfully effected on the 21st day of October following, in the glorious victory of Trafalgar.'" [1]

On the 7th of September Nelson wrote to Collingwood off Cadiz that he should be with him in a very few days, and on the 13th, as related in his Private Diary, he left Merton :—

"*Friday Night*, 13*th September*. At half-past ten drove from dear, dear Merton, where I left all which I hold dear in this world, to go to serve my King and my country. May the great God whom I adore enable me to fulfil the expectations of my country ; and if it is His good pleasure that I should return, my thanks will never cease being offered up to the throne of His mercy. If it is His good providence to cut short my days upon earth, I bow with the greatest submission, relying that He will protect those dear to me that I may leave behind. His will be done. Amen, Amen, Amen."

The further extracts describe Nelson's voyage until he joined the fleet off Cadiz :—

"*Saturday, September* 14, 1805. At six o'clock arrived at Portsmouth, and having arranged all my business, embarked at the Bathing Machines [2] with Mr. Rose and Mr. Canning at two ; got on board

---

[1] Pellew's " Life of Lord Sidmouth," vol. ii. pp. 380–2.

[2] The spot on Southsea beach where Nelson embarked, and now marked by a memorial stone, has been questioned by an anonymous correspondent of the *Standard*, who asserts on the authority of Admiral Lyons and the widow of Admiral Sir J. Hillyar that it took place at the Sally Port. Nelson could hardly have been mistaken : see letter from "a Late Lieut., R.N.," January 23, 1889.

"LINKS WITH THE PAST.
" TO THE EDITOR OF THE *STANDARD.*

"SIR,—Upon a stone on Southsea beach rests one of H.M.S. *Victory's* anchors. An inscription states that near this spot Nelson embarked when he left England for the last time before the Battle of Trafalgar.

" As naval officers enter their boats, not from Southsea beach, but from a landing place at the sally-port within Portsmouth Harbour, I one

the *Victory* at St. Helen's, who dined with me ; preparing for sea." [1]

"To Rear-Admiral Murray.

"Portsmouth, *September* 14, 1805.

" My dear Admiral,—I am this moment getting in the boat at the Bathing Machines." [2]

Still anxious about the poor blind Mrs. Nelson :—

"To Davison.

"*Victory*, off Portland, *September* 16*th*.

"I am gone and beating down Channel with a foul wind. . . . Poor blind Mrs. Nelson, I have given £150 to pay her debts, and I intend to pay her house rent in future, in addition to the £200 a year, which, I take it, will be about £40 a year.

---

day called the late Admiral Lyon's attention to the inscription, and inquired why Nelson chose so unusual a spot for embarking.

"The Admiral (who was a midshipman on Nelson's flag-ship the *Victory*) replied, ' Nelson never shoved off in his boat from Southsea beach. I have good reason for knowing this, since I was with him on the occasion.'

"He then told me the following incident. Said he : ' My uncle was Dockyard Admiral at the time, and as I wanted a run up to London, he mentioned the matter to Lord Nelson, when the latter was calling at my uncle's house. Lord Nelson at once gave the required leave, and added, addressing me, " I am going up to town myself, and shall be glad to see you to breakfast ; you will find me in apartments at ——, a saddler's, in Piccadilly." On reaching London, I accordingly went to the saddler's, but was informed that Nelson had gone that morning to Lady Hamilton's. So off I went to her house, and found her and Lord Nelson, and Nelson's clerical brother, at breakfast. On my return to Portsmouth, Lord Nelson offered me a passage in his boat to the *Victory*, and we entered the boat at the sally-port.'

"On mentioning this story to the widow of the late Admiral Sir J. Hillyar, she at once replied, ' The latter part is perfectly true, for I witnessed Nelson's embarkation myself.' Lady Hillyar died in 1884, aged, I think, ninety-five years.

"I am, sir, your obedient servant,

" A Late R.N.

"*January* 23rd."

With all due respect to the anonymous writer, I take the liberty of presuming that Nelson knew best where he embarked on his last command.

[1] Despatches, vol. vii. pp. 33–5.   [2] Ibid., p. 36.

In a letter to Lieut.-General Hon. H. E. Fox, Gibraltar, of about September 30, 1805, Lord Nelson requested that the publisher of the *Gibraltar Gazette* should be forbidden to mention the force of the fleet, much less the names and strength of the ships, adding :—

"For I much fear that, if the enemy know of our increased numbers, we shall never see them out of Cadiz. If my arrival is necessary to be mentioned, the ships with me need not ; and it may be inserted that an equal number or some ships of Admiral Colling-wood's are ordered home. I rely upon your goodness to accord with my wishes.

"I am, &c.,
"NELSON AND BRONTE." [1]

"To SIR A. J. BALL, BART., MALTA.

"*September* 30, 1805.

"MY DEAR BALL,—I got fairly into the fleet yesterday, and under all circumstances I find them as perfect as could be expected. The force at present is not so large as might be wished, but I will do my best with it ; they will give me more when they can, and I am not come forth to find difficulties, but to remove them." [2]

Nelson's reception by the Fleet :—

"I joined the fleet late on the evening of the 28th of September, but could not communicate with them until the next morning. I believe my arrival was most welcome, not only to the commander of the fleet, but also to every individual in it ; and when I came to explain to them the '*Nelson touch*,' it was like an electric shock. Some shed tears, all approved—'it was new—it was singular—it was simple ;' and from the admiral downwards it was repeated, 'It must succeed, if they will allow us to get at them ! You are, my lord, surrounded by friends whom you inspire with confidence.' Some may be Judas's ; but the majority are certainly much pleased with my commanding them." [3]

[1] Despatches, vol. vii. p. 35.   [2] Ibid., pp. 34–5.
[3] To Lady Hamilton, *Victory*, October 1, 1805.   From Letters of Lord Nelson to Lady Hamilton, vol. ii. p. 100 ; Despatches, vol. vii. p. 60.

On October 3rd Nelson sent Rear-Admiral Louis with six sail-of-the-line to water at Gibraltar and Tetuan. Vice-Admiral Austen, then Captain of *Canopus*, states :—

"I had been dining with Lord Nelson on board the *Victory*, having accompanied my admiral (Louis) ; and on taking leave in the evening Admiral Louis said, ' You are sending us away, my lord ; the enemy will come out, and we shall have no share in the battle.' To which Lord Nelson replied, ' My dear Louis, I have no other means of keeping my fleet complete in provisions and water but by sending them in detachments to Gibraltar. The enemy will come out, and we shall fight them ; but there will be time for you to get back first. I look upon *Canopus* as my right hand [she was his second astern in the line-of-battle] ; and I send you first to insure your being there to help to beat them." [1]

The following were the final instructions which Nelson issued to his fleet :—

"*Victory*, off Cadiz, *October 9th.*

"Thinking it almost impossible to bring a fleet of forty sail-of-the-line into a line-of-battle, in variable winds, thick weather, and other circumstances which must occur, without such a loss of time that the opportunity would be lost of bringing the enemy to battle in such a manner as to make the business decisive, I have, therefore, made up my mind to keep the fleet in that position of sailing (with the exception of the first and second in command) that the order of sailing is to be the order of battle, placing the fleet in two lines of sixteen ships each, with an advanced squadron of eight of the fastest sailing two-decked ships, which will always make, if wanted, a line of twenty-four sail, on whichever line the commander-in-chief may direct.

"The second in command will, after my intentions are made known to him, have the entire direction of his line to make the attack upon the enemy, and to follow up the blow until they are captured or destroyed.

"If the enemy's fleet should be seen to the windward in line-of-battle, and that the two lines and the advanced squadron can fetch them, they will probably be so extended that their van could not succour their rear. I should, therefore, probably make the second in command signal to lead through about their twelfth ship from their

---

[1] Despatches, vol. vii. p. 63, note.

rear (or wherever he could fetch, if not able to get so far advanced) ; my line would lead through about their centre, and the advanced squadron to cut two or three or four ships a-head of their centre, so as to insure their getting at their Commander-in-chief, on whom every effort must be made to capture.

" The whole impression of the British fleet must be to overpower from two or three ships ahead of their Commander-in-chief, supposed to be in the centre, to the rear of the fleet. I will suppose twenty sail of the enemy's line to be untouched ; it must be sometime before they could perform a manœuvre to bring their force compact to attack any part of the British fleet, or to succour their own ships, which indeed it would be impossible without mixing with the ships engaged. The enemy's fleet is supposed to consist of forty-six sail-of-the-line, British Fleet forty. If either is less, only a proportionate number of enemy's ships are to be cut off ; British to be one-fourth superior to the enemy cut off.

" Something must be left to chance ; nothing is sure in a sea fight beyond all others. Shot will carry away the masts and yards of friends as well as foes, but I look with confidence to a victory before the van of the enemy could succour their rear, and then that the British Fleet would most of them be ready to receive their twenty sail-of-the-line, or to pursue them should they endeavour to make off.

" If the van of the enemy tacks, the captured ships must run to lee-ward of the British Fleet ; if the enemy wears, the British must place themselves between the enemy and the captured and disabled British ships ; and should the enemy close, I have no fears for the result.

" The second in command will in all possible things direct the movements of his line by keeping them as compact as the nature of the circumstances will admit. Captains are to look to their particular line as their rallying point. But in case signals can neither be seen or perfectly understood, no captain can do very wrong if he places his ship alongside of that of an enemy.

" Of the intended attack from windward, the enemy in line of battle to receive an attack.

Enemy's line.

B

E

" The divisions of the British Fleet will be brought nearly within

gun-shot of the enemy's centre. The signal will most probably be
made for the lee line to bear up together, to set all their sails, even
steering sails,[1] in order to get as quickly as possible to the enemy's
line, and to cut through, beginning from the twelfth ship from the
enemy's rear. Some ships may not get through their exact place, but
they will always be at hand to assist their friends, and if they are
thrown round the rear of the enemy, they will effectually complete
the business of twelve sail of the enemy.

"Should the enemy wear together, or bear up and sail large, still
the twelve ships composing, in the first position, the enemy's rear, are
to be the object of attack of the lee line, unless.otherwise directed by
the Commander-in-chief, which is scarcely to be expected, as the
entire management of the lee line, after the intentions of the Commander-in-chief (are) signified, is intended to be left to the judgment
of the Admiral commanding that line.

"The remainder of the enemy's fleet, thirty-four sail, are to be left
to the management of the Commander-in-chief, who will endeavour to
take care that the movements of the second in command are as little
interrupted as is possible.

"NELSON AND BRONTE."[2]

To the copy signed by Lord Nelson, and delivered to
Captain Hope of the *Defence*, was added, "N.B.—When
the *Defence* quits the Fleet for England, you are to
return this memo. to the *Victory*."

On the same day he wrote to Collingwood :—

"I send you my plan of attack, as far as a man dare venture to
guess at the very uncertain position the enemy may be found in. But,
my dear friend, it is to place you perfectly at ease respecting my intentions, and to give full scope to your judgment for carrying them
into effect. We can, my dear Coll., have no little jealousies. We
have only one great object in view, that of annihilating our enemies,
and getting a glorious peace for our country. No man has more confidence in another than I have in you ; and no man will render your
services more justice than your very old friend.

"NELSON AND BRONTE."

---

[1] In upper part of the margin of the paper, and referred to by Nelson
as in text, he wrote "Even steering sails," *vide* instructions for signal,
yellow with blue flag, p. 17, 8th flag with reference to appendix.

[2] Despatches, vol. vii. pp. 90–2 and note.

In his Private Diary he wrote :—

"Fresh breezes easterly. Received an account from Blackwood that the French ships had all bent their topgallant sails. Sent the *Pickle* to him, with orders to keep a good look out. Sent Admiral Collingwood the Nelson touch. At night wind westerly."

Convinced as he wrote to Collingwood that if his fleet was "in sight of Cadiz, the enemy would never move," and relying on the activity of Captain Blackwood and the light squadron under his charge, Nelson kept the bulk of his fleet from fifteen to eighteen leagues west of Cadiz. "I rely on you," he wrote to Blackwood on the 11th of October, "that we can't miss getting hold of them, and I will give them such a shaking as they never yet experienced ; at least I will lay down my life in the attempt. We are a very powerful fleet, and not to be held cheap." Two days after he wrote to Sir A. J. Ball :—

"I am aware that there will be moments when it might be wished we were closer ; but I have considered all possible circumstances, and believe there will often be times, in strong gales of westerly wind, when we may often wish ourselves further off, as we are in danger of being driven into the Mediterranean, when if they choose to go westward, they will have no interception. However, whether I am right or wrong, I act from the best of my judgment."

"The enemy coming out of port." Extract from Nelson's Private Diary :—

"*19th October.* Fine weather, wind easterly. At half-past nine, the *Mars* being one of the look-out ships, repeated the signal, that 'the enemy was coming out of port.' Made signal for a general chase, S.E. Wind at south. Cadiz bearing E.N.E. by compass, distant sixteen leagues. At three *Colossus* made the signal that 'the enemy's fleet was at sea.'"

On the same day Nelson wrote to Lady Hamilton and Horatia :—

" The signal has been made that the enemy's combined fleet are coming out of port. We have very little wind, so that I have no hopes of seeing them before to-morrow. May the God of battles crown my endeavours with success ; at all events, I will take care that my name shall be most dear to you and Horatia, both of whom I love as much as my own life. And as my last writing before the battle will be to you, so I hope in God that I shall live to finish my letter after the battle. May Heaven bless you, prays your

" NELSON AND BRONTE."

" TO MISS HORATIA NELSON THOMPSON.

" MY DEAREST ANGEL,—I was made happy by the pleasure of receiving your letter of 19th of September, and I rejoice to hear you are so very good a girl, and love dear Lady Hamilton, who most dearly loves you. Give her a kiss for me. The combined fleets of the enemy are now reported to be coming out of Cadiz : and, therefore, I answer your letter, my dearest Horatia, to mark to you that you are ever uppermost in my thoughts. I shall be sure of your prayers for my safety, conquest, and speedy return to dear Merton, and our dearest good Lady Hamilton. Be a good girl ; mind what Miss Connor [her governess] says to you. Receive, my dearest Horatia, the affectionate parental blessing of your father,

" NELSON AND BRONTE."

One more entry from his Diary—the last he wrote :—

" *Oct.* 21. At daylight saw the enemy's combined fleets from East to E.S.E. ; bore away; made signal for order of sailing, and to prepare for battle ; the enemy with their heads to the southward, and seven of the enemy wearing in succession. May the great God whom I worship, grant to my country, and for the benefit of Europe in general, a great and glorious victory ; and may no misconduct in any one tarnish it, and may humanity after victory be the predominant feature in the British fleet. For myself individually, I commit my life to Him who made me, and may His blessing light upon my endeavours for serving my country faithfully. To Him I resign myself and the just cause which is entrusted to me. Amen. Amen. Amen."

On the eve of the battle Nelson wrote the well-known codicil to his will, in which, believing what Lady Hamilton had told him, he commended her and the child Horatia to the beneficence of his country. Of the value of her statements of her services I have spoken in a former chapter ; of the fate of the document I will speak in a subsequent one.

"*October* 21st, 1805, then in sight of the combined Fleets of France and Spain, distant about ten miles.

"Whereas the eminent services of Emma Hamilton, widow of the Right Honble. Sir William Hamilton, have been of the very greatest service to our King and country to my knowledge, without her receiving any reward from either our King or country : *First*, that she obtained the King of Spain's letter in 1796, to his brother, the King of Naples, acquainting him of his intention to declare war against England, from which letter the Ministry sent out orders to then Sir John Jervis to strike a stroke, if opportunity offered, against the Arsenals of Spain or her fleets ; that neither of these was done is not the fault of Lady Hamilton, the opportunity might have offered.

"*Secondly*, the British Fleet under my command could never have returned the second time to Egypt, had not Lady Hamilton's influence with the Queen of Naples caused letters to be written to the Governor of Syracuse, that he was to encourage the fleet being supplied with everything, should they put into any port in Sicily ; we put into Syracuse, and received every supply, went to Egypt, and destroyed the French Fleet. Could I have rewarded these services, I would not now call upon my country, but as that has not been in my power, I leave Emma Hamilton, therefore, a legacy to my King and country, that they will give her an ample provision to maintain her rank in life. I also leave to the beneficence of my country my adopted daughter, Horatia Nelson Thompson, and I desire she will use in future the name of Nelson only. These are the only favours I ask of my King and country at this moment, when I am going to fight their battle. May God bless my King and country, and all those who I hold dear. My relations it is needless to mention ; they will, of course, be amply provided for.

"Henry Blackwood, T. M. Hardy, Nelson and Bronte."

TRAFALGAR.

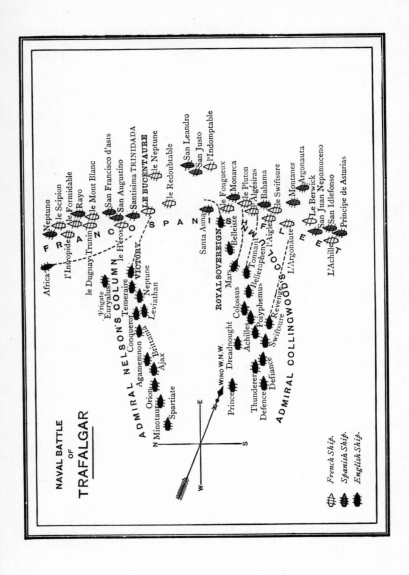

NAVAL BATTLE
OF
TRAFALGAR

French Ship.
Spanish Ship.
English Ship.

CHAPTER XVI.

TRAFALGAR.

(1805.)

 HAT Villeneuve was forced by Napoleon to risk a great battle can no longer be denied ; in his own better judgment he felt that while reliance could be placed on the ships of his own nation, those of the Spanish contingent " were for the most part coming out of port for the first time, commanded by inexperienced captains and ill-manned." Napoleon would not hear of delay. Aware that English and Russian troops were proposed to be landed in Italy, he had ordered General St. Cyr with his forces to take Naples, disperse and annihilate the Neapolitan army, before the expected English and Russians could arrive.

" Some days after signing these instructions (to St. Cyr), on the 17th of September, 1805," writes his French biographer, " Napoleon sent Villeneuve orders to sail with the combined fleet, steering first for

Carthagena, to pick up Admiral Salcedo there; from Carthagena to proceed to Naples, and land the troops he had embarked to join General St. Cyr. 'Our intention,' added the Emperor, 'is that whenever you find the enemy in inferior force, you should *attack him without hesitation, and bring on a decisive action.* . . . You must be aware that the success of these operations will mainly depend on the promptitude of your departure from Cadiz. We feel that you will neglect nothing to effect it without delay; and we require the utmost bravery and activity in this important expedition.' With Villeneuve the Emperor did not fear saying too much, as according to his expression the admiral was 'one who required the spur more than the curb.' Convinced, moreover, while ordering him on this unfortunate expedition, that 'his excessive pusillanimity would prevent his undertaking it,' he had privately despatched Admiral Rosily from Paris. That flag-officer, if he found the combined fleets still at Cadiz, was to take the command, hoist his flag on the *Bucentaure*, and send Vice-Admiral Villeneuve to France 'to account for his conduct.'"[1]

"It was in vain that Admiral Décres, the Minister of Marine, warned the Emperor of the real condition of the Spanish portion of the combined fleets—that a council of war assembled by Villeneuve expressed the same opinion as Décres. 'The English,' said the Emperor, 'will look very small when France shall have two or three admirals willing to die.' 'No one,' adds our author, 'was more resigned to such a sacrifice than Admiral Villeneuve; too happy, if at that price, he could have hoped to save his fleet.' 'But to leave Cadiz,' he wrote to Décres, 'without being able to enter the Straits immediately, and with the certainty of having to fight a superior enemy, would be to lose everything. I cannot believe that it is his Imperial Majesty's wish to expose the greater part of his naval force to such a desperate chance, which does not even promise them the reward of glory.'

"These scruples were, unhappily, to be soon removed. Vice-Admiral Rosily was already at Madrid; an accident which happened to his carriage at Madrid had prevented his setting out on the 14th of October; and during that time Admiral Villeneuve had heard of his arrival in Spain. That news cut Villeneuve to the heart. 'I should be happy,' he wrote to the Minister of Marine, 'to give up the first rank to Admiral Rosily, if, at least, the second were allowed to me; . . . but it would be too painful to me to lose all hope of

---

[1] Jurien de la Gravière, vol. ii. pp. 235–6.

having an opportunity to prove myself worthy of better fortune. If the wind permits me to sail, I will sail to-morrow.' At this moment he was informed that Nelson had despatched six ships to Gibraltar ; he immediately summoned Admiral Gravina on board the *Bucentaure*, and, after consulting with him for some minutes made the signal to his fleet to prepare for sea." [1]

At seven in the morning the combined fleet commenced to move, and by ten in the morning they were all out of Cadiz. Whilst the combined fleet was slowly drawing off shore, Nelson acquainted by his frigates with all their movements, was hastening to the struggle. " At nine that night the signal-guns ordered by Nelson to be fired to indicate the course the enemy were taking were heard at intervals, proving that the British Fleet was only about two miles off." [2]

In his memorandum of the 20th, he wrote to " Captain Blackwood to keep with two frigates in sight of the enemy by night. Two other frigates to be placed between him and the *Defence*, Captain Hope. *Colossus* will take her station between *Defence* and *Mars*. *Mars* to communicate with *Victory*." And added :—

" If the enemy are standing to the southward, or towards the straits, burn two blue lights together every hour, in order to make the greater blaze. If the enemy are standing to the westward, three guns, quick, every hour.

" Nelson and Bronte.

" Signed by Nelson the day before he fell, the last time I saw him,
" George Hope."

Convinced by this report that it was in vain to make any further attempt to conceal his course, Villeneuve about ten at night gave the order to collect his somewhat scattered fleet and form line-of-battle, and the next sunrise saw the two fleets off Cape Trafalgar. How the

---

[1] Jurien de la Gravière, vol. ii. pp. 238-9.
[2] Report of the chief of Gravina's staff to the Prince of Peace, Oct. 22nd. Gazette of Madrid, Nov. 5, 1805.

battle commenced is so well told by Captain Jurien de la
Gravière, that I take the liberty of borrowing his account
of it :—

" Divided at first into two lines, of which Collingwood led the one
in the *Royal Sovereign,* and Nelson the other in the *Victory,* the British
Fleet steadily neared their enemy, who had now, by wearing together,
turned their heads to Cadiz. Eleven sail followed the *Royal Sovereign,*
and fifteen the *Victory.* Of the combined fleet eighteen were French
ships of 80 and 74 guns, and fifteen Spanish ships of which four
were three-deckers. The French and Spanish ships were intermixed,
and though at the commencement of the action the British formed
only two lines, during its course four ships of Collingwood's column
separated themselves from their companions, and made a dash at the
rear-ships of the combined fleet.

" The fleets were now within a few miles of each other, when
Nelson having made all necessary signals, asked Captain Blackwood
of the *Euryalus* whether he did not think one more was wanting.
Reflecting for a few minutes he called the acting signal lieutenant (Mr.
Pasco) to him. ' Make signal to the fleet that England confides that
every man will do his duty.' Pasco suggested ' expects ' as there was
a signal for that word in the vocabulary. Nelson consented, and
added, ' Make it quickly, as I have one more signal to make—Close
Action.' Then at 11.15 flew out the flags of that ever-memorable
signal—

" ' ENGLAND EXPECTS THAT EVERY MAN WILL DO HIS DUTY.' [1]

" ' Now,' said Nelson, ' I can do no more, we must trust to the great
Dispenser of all events, and the justice of our cause. I thank God
for this great opportunity of doing my duty.' When Blackwood
suggested that he should transfer his flag to some other ship in a less
exposed situation ; ' No, Blackwood,' replied Nelson, ' on such
occasions as these it is the Commander-in-chief's duty to set the
example.' "

How Collingwood began the fight :—

" Feigning to yield to the entreaties of others," writes our noble
Frenchman, "Nelson allowed the order to be given to the *Temeraire,*

---

[1] The following were the Nos. in the signal book :

253	269	863	261	471	958	220	374	4.21.19.24
England	expects	that	every	man	will	do	his	duty.

Neptune, and *Leviathan*, to take the lead ; but very soon after, by making more sail on the *Victory*, he rendered the execution of the order impossible. At this moment when this last action evinced the increasing impatience of the Commander-in-chief, the *Royal Sovereign* showed no external symptoms of imitating the example. That ship, whose superior sailing excited Nelson's envy at the moment, seemed to await, under easy sail, for the ships she had left astern ; but notwithstanding this apparent prudence, Collingwood had taken his own measures to ensure himself the honour of striking the first blow. Hardly had the *Belleisle* and the *Mars* approached him, when at a wave of Collingwood's hand (the signal impatiently awaited), her studding sails expanded in the air, and the *Royal Sovereign*, leaving the British columns far astern, appeared singly to throw herself upon the enemy.

"It was noon. The flag of St. George, with the red cross, was flying along the English line, while with reiterated cries of 'Vive l'Empereur,' the French Fleet hoisted the tricolour ; the Spaniards at the same time the banner of Castile, and suspending a large wooden cross beneath it. At this moment Villeneuve gave the signal of battle. A single gun aimed at the *Royal Sovereign* immediately burst from the *Fongueux*, and was quickly followed by a rolling fire to which no English ship replied. The *Royal Sovereign* was then nearly a mile ahead of the *Belleisle*, and about two miles from the *Victory*. Still uninjured by this ill-directed fire, she bore down on the *Santa Anna*, singly, silently, unswervingly, as if protected by some secret spell. The crew lying down at their quarters, presented no object to the few shots which struck her hull, and the stray ball which boomed through her masts had not yet done any injury.

"'Rotheram,' said Collingwood, to his flag-captain, when, after bearing the fire of the combined fleet for ten minutes, he was about to plunge into the ranks of our rear-squadron, 'what would not Nelson give to be here now?' 'See,' said Nelson, at the same instant, 'how that noble fellow, Collingwood, takes his ship into action.'

"The *Fongueux* vainly endeavoured to bar the way ; from the triple tiers of the *Royal Sovereign*, burst a dense storm of shot and smoke. Each gun doubly charged, poured its contents into the stern of the *Santa Anna*. One hundred and fifty cannon balls swept the decks of that ship, and left four hundred men stretched upon them. The *Royal Sovereign* then ranging up to leeward, engaged the Spanish vice-admiral, yard-arm to yard-arm ; but she soon had other enemies to contend with. The *San Leandro*, *San Juste*, and *Indomptable*, closed up to surround her. *Fongueux* opened obliquely upon her, and her sails were soon in shreds. Nevertheless, in the midst of that hail-storm of shot which were seen striking each other in the air, the *Royal Sovereign* did not less furiously cannonade the enemy she had singled out. The Spaniards' fire slackened, and above the clouds of smoke which enveloped the heroic group, Nelson's anxious eye could still discover the lofty flag of Collingwood." [1]

The Log of the *Victory* :—

"*Oct.* 21*st.* A.M., Moderate breezes. At four, wore ship. At six, observed the enemy's fleet bearing E. by S., distant ten or twelve miles. Bore up to the eastward and made all possible sail, out reefs, topsails, set steering sails, and royals, and stay-sails. Cleared for quarters. At eight, light breezes, and cloudy. Body of the enemy's fleet E. by S. nine or ten miles. Enemy's line from N.N.E. to S.S.W., consisting of thirty-three sail-of-the-line, six frigates, and two brigs. Still standing for the enemy's van. The *Royal Sovereign* and her line-of-battle steering for the centre of the enemy's line. At 11.30, enemy opened upon the *Royal Sovereign.* At 11.40, *Royal Sovereign* commenced firing on the enemy. At 11.50, the enemy began firing upon us and the *Temeraire.* At noon, standing for the enemy's tenth ship with all possible [sail] set. Light breezes and hazy weather. Swell from N.N.W.

"Light airs and cloudy, standing towards the enemy's van with all sail set. At four minutes to twelve, opened our fire on the enemy's van, in keeping down their line. At twenty minutes past twelve, in attempting to pass through the enemy's line we fell on board the tenth and eleventh ship, when the action became general. About 1.15 [Lord Nelson] was wounded in the shoulder. At 1.30, the *Redoutable*, having struck her colours, we ceased firing our starboard guns, but continued engaged with the *Santissima Trinidada*, and some of the enemy's ships on the larboard side. Observed the *Temeraire* between the *Redoutable* and another French ship-of-the-line, both of which had struck. The action continued general until three o'clock, and several of the enemy's ships around us had struck. Observed the *Royal Sovereign* with the loss of her main and mizen-masts, and some of the enemy's ships around her, dismasted. At 3.10, observed four sail of the enemy's van tack, and stood along our line to windward. Fired our larboard guns at those which could reach them. At 3.40, made signal for our ships to keep their wind, and engage the enemy's van coming along our weather-line. At 4.15, the Spanish Rear-Admiral to wind-

---

[1] Jurien de la Gravière, vol. ii. pp. 259–60.

ward struck to some of our ships which had tacked after them. Observed one of the enemy's ships blow up, and fourteen sail of the enemy standing towards Cadiz, and three sail of the enemy's ships standing to the southward. Partial firing continued until 4.30, when a victory being reported to [Lord Nelson], he then died of his wound."

Such is the simple record in the log of this portion of the memorable struggle, of which other authorities afford most affecting details. With a failing wind the *Victory* had advanced slowly towards the *Santissima Trinidada*, and the *Bucentaure*. But the enemy's line had closed up. The *Redoutable* had frequently grazed the taffrail of the *Bucentaure*, and the *Neptune* had closed the *Santissima Trinidada* to leeward. A collision appeared inevitable. At this moment, according to our French authority, the following dramatic incident occurred :—

" Villeneuve at this moment seized the eagle belonging to his ship and displayed it to the sailors who surrounded him. 'My friends,' he exclaimed, ' I am going to throw it on board the English ship ; we will follow and recover it, or perish in the attempt.' Our sailors answered these noble words with loud acclamations. Full of hope for the issue of a combat hand-to-hand, Villeneuve, before the smoke had shrouded the *Bucentaure* (which had commenced firing on the *Victory*) from the view of the squadron, addressed this last signal to his ships : ' Every ship not in action is out of her station, and must take any position which shall more quickly bring her under fire.' His duty as an admiral was terminated ; it only remained for him to prove himself the bravest captain in his fleet." [1]

Hardy in the meantime had told Nelson that from the closing-up of the enemy's line, it could not be pierced without a collision. " Choose which you please," said Nelson, and the *Victory* was steered at the *Redoutable*, passing under the stern of the *Bucentaure* at half-pistol shot, pouring a fearful discharge into her stern, and then leaving the *Neptune*, came on the starboard tack and ran

Jurien de a Gravière, vol. ii. p. 263.

on board the *Redoutable*. From the tops of the French
ship, which were filled with marksmen, the decks of the
Victory were swept with musketry. Hardy and Nelson
were together on the quarter-deck, when suddenly the
admiral tottered and fell with his face on the deck. A
musket-ball from the French ship's mizen-top had passed
downwards through his left epaulette and lodged in the
spine; the chaplain ran to him; but a sergeant and two
sailors had already reached him, and lifted him off the
deck covered with the blood that stained it. Hardy, who
had not heard the noise of his fall, turned round, and,
pale and more stricken than Nelson, exclaimed : " I hope
you are not dangerously wounded, my lord?" "They
have done for me at last, Hardy; my backbone is shot
through." The sailors who lifted him up, carried him
in their arms to the cockpit, where he was left amidst a
crowd of wounded. Such is Captain Jurien de la Gravière's account of Nelson's fatal wound.

The following is Dr. Beatty's account of Nelson's
death :—

" The captain ordered the seamen to carry the admiral to the cockpit ; and now two incidents occurred strikingly characteristic of the
great man, and strongly marking that energy and reflection which in
his heroic mind rose even superior to the immediate consideration of
his awful condition. While the men were carrying him down the
ladder from the middle-deck, his lordship observed that the tiller-ropes
were not yet replaced ; and desired one of the midshipmen stationed
there to go upon the quarter-deck and remind Captain Hardy of that
circumstance, and request that new ones should be immediately rove.[1]
Having delivered this order, he took his handkerchief from his pocket
and covered his face with it, that he might be conveyed to the cockpit
at this crisis unnoticed by the crew. . . . The surgeon had examined
these two officers, and found them dead, when his attention was
arrested by several of the wounded calling to him, ' Mr. Beatty, Lord
Nelson is here ; Mr. Beatty, the admiral is wounded.' The surgeon,

---

[1] The possibility of this is doubted. Certainly no such order reached
Captain Hardy. James's " Naval History," vol. iv. p. 30.

on looking round, saw the handkerchief fall from his lordship's face ; when the stars on his coat, which had also been covered by it, appeared.   Mr. Burke, the purser, and the surgeon ran immediately to his lordship's assistance, and took him from the arms of the seamen who had carried him below.   In conveying him to one of the midshipmen's berths, they stumbled, but recovered themselves without falling.   Lord Nelson then inquired who were supporting him, and when the surgeon informed him, his lordship replied : ' Ah, Mr. Beatty ! you can do nothing for me.   I have but a short time to live ; my back is shot through.'   The surgeon said, ' He hoped the wound was not so dangerous as his lordship imagined, and that he might still survive long to enjoy his glorious victory.'   The Rev. Dr. Scott, who had been in another part of the cockpit administering lemonade to the wounded, now came instantly to his lordship, and in his anguish of grief wrung his hands and said : ' Ah, Beatty, how prophetic you were,' alluding to the apprehensions expressed by the surgeon for his lordship's safety previous to the battle.

" His lordship was laid upon a bed, stripped of his clothes and covered with a sheet.   While this was effecting, he said to Dr. Scott, ' Doctor, I told you so ; I am gone ; ' and after a short pause, he added, in low voice, ' I have to leave Lady Hamilton and my adopted daughter Horatia as a legacy to my country ' [Dr. Beatty then describes the examination of the wound, and that, from Lord Nelson's symptoms as described by himself, the case was hopeless, but that this was not told to Lord Nelson until the victory had been certain and communicated to him.]

" Then came an ardent thirst.   He called frequently for drink and to be fanned with paper—' Fan, fan, drink, drink.'   This he continued to do until a very few minutes before he expired.   Mr. Burke told him the enemy were decisively defeated, and that he hoped he would still live to be the bearer of the joyful news.   ' It is nonsense, Mr. Burke, to suppose I can live.   My sufferings are great, but they will all be soon over.'   Dr. Scott entreated him ' not to despair of living,' and said, ' he trusted that Divine Providence would restore him once more to his dear country and friends.'   ' Ah, doctor,' he replied, ' it is all over, it is all over.'

" Many messages were sent to Captain Hardy by the surgeon, requesting his attendance on his lordship, who had become impatient, and often enclaimed : ' Will no one bring Hardy to me ? he must be killed ; he is surely destroyed.'   The captain's *aide-de-camp* now came below (Mr. Bulkeley), and stated that circumstances respecting the fleet required Hardy's presence on deck, but that he would avail himself of the first favourable moment to come. On hearing him say this to the surgeon, Nelson asked who had brought it. 'It is Mr. Bulkeley, my lord,' said Mr. Burke. 'It is his voice,' said Nelson; and then to Bulkeley : 'remember me to your father.' After about an hour and ten minutes Hardy came.

"They shook hands affectionately, and then Nelson said, 'Well, Hardy, how goes the battle ? How goes the day with us ?' 'Very well, my lord ; we have got twelve or fourteen of the enemy's ships in our possession ; but five of their van have tacked, and show an intention of bearing down on the *Victory*. I have, therefore, called two or three of our fresh ships round us, and have no doubt of giving them a good drubbing.' 'I hope,' said Nelson, 'none of *our* ships have struck, Hardy !' 'No, my lord, there is no fear of that.' Nelson then said : 'Hardy, I am a dead man, Hardy ; I am going fast ; it will be all over with me soon. Come near to me. Pray let dear Lady Hamilton have my hair, and all other things belonging to me.' Mr. Burke was about to withdraw at the beginning of this conversation, but Nelson perceiving his intention, desired him to remain. Captain Hardy observed 'that he hoped Mr. Beatty could yet hold out some prospect of life. 'Oh, no, it is impossible. My back is shot through. Beatty will tell you so.' After a parting shake of the hand, Hardy returned to the deck.

"About fifty minutes after Hardy returned. They again shook hands, and while the captain retained Nelson's hand, he congratulated him, even in the arms of death, on his brilliant victory, which, he said, was complete ; though he did not know how many of the enemy were captured, as it was impossible to perceive each ship distinctly. He was certain, however, of fourteen or fifteen having surrendered. 'That is well, but I bargained for twenty ;' and then, emphatically, '*Anchor*, Hardy ! *Anchor*.' To this Hardy replied : 'I suppose, my lord, Admiral Collingwood will now take upon himself the direction of affairs ?' 'Not while I live, I hope, Hardy,' cried the dying chief, and at that moment tried ineffectually to raise himself from his bed. 'No,' added he, 'do *you* anchor, Hardy.' 'Shall we make the signal, sir ?' 'Yes ; for if I live, I'll anchor.' He then told Captain Hardy 'he felt in a few minutes he should be no more,' adding, in low tone, 'Don't throw me overboard.' 'Oh, no, certainly not,' replied Hardy. 'Then you know what to do ;' and he continued : 'Take care of my dear Lady Hamilton ; take care of poor Lady Hamilton. Kiss me, Hardy.' The captain now knelt down, and kissed his cheek, when Nelson said : 'Now, I am satisfied ; thank God, I have done my duty.' Hardy stood for a moment or two in silent contemplation ; he knelt down again, and kissed his lordship's forehead. Nelson said, ' Who is that ? ' ' It is Hardy,' answered the captain. ' God bless you, Hardy.' After this affecting scene, Hardy withdrew, and returned to the quarter-deck."

I will conclude the account of this sad scene in the words of his excellent chaplain, Dr. Scott :—

"After this, the Admiral was perfectly tranquil—looking at me in his accustomed manner when alluding to any prior discourse. ' I have not been a great sinner, doctor,' said he. ' Doctor, I was right—I told you so—George Rose has not yet got my letter. Tell him '—he was here interrupted by pain. After an interval, he said, ' *Mr. Rose will remember.* Don't forget, doctor. Mind what I say.' There were frequent pauses in his conversation. These sentences refer to what he had told Dr. Scott at his first interview.

"When I first saw him he was apprehensive he should not live many minutes, and told me so, adding, in a hurried, agitated manner, though with pauses, ' Remember me to Lady Hamilton—remember me to Horatia—remember me to all my friends. Doctor, remember me to Mr. Rose : tell him I have made a will and left Lady Hamilton and Horatia to my country.' He repeated his remembrances to Lady Hamilton and Horatia, and told me to mind what he said several times.

"The confusion of the scene, the pain endured by the hero, and the necessity of alleviating his sufferings by giving lemonade to quench his thirst, and by rubbing his body, of course precluded the reading of prayers to him in a regular form, but otherwise during the three hours and a half of Nelson's mortal agony they ejaculated short prayers together, and Nelson frequently said, ' Pray for me, doctor.' Every interval, indeed, allowed by the intense pain, and not taken up in the conduct of the action or in the mention of his own private affairs, was thus employed in low and earnest supplications for Divine mercy. The last words which Dr. Scott heard murmured on his lips were, ' God and my country,' and he passed so quietly out of life that Scott, who had been occupied ever since he had been brought below, in all the offices of the most tender nurse, was still rubbing his stomach when the surgeon perceived that all was over." [1]

So died Nelson.

[1] " Life of Rev. Dr. Scott," pp. 187, 189, and 190.

As it has been disputed by some naval writers how and when the sad news reached Collingwood, I insert here his letter to the Duke of Clarence, though written at a later date :—

"TO THE DUKE OF CLARENCE.

"*December* 12, 1805.

" MOST GRACIOUS PRINCE,—The loss which your Highness and myself have sustained in the death of Lord Nelson, can only be truly estimated by those who had the happiness of sharing his friendship. He had all the qualities that adorn the human heart ; and a head, which for quickness of perception and depth of penetration, qualified him for the highest offices of his profession. But why am I making these observations to your Royal Highness, who knew him ? Because I cannot speak of him but to do him honour.

" Your Royal Highness desires to know the particular circumstances of his death. I have seen Captain Hardy but for a few minutes since, and understood from him that at the time the *Victory* continued very closely engaged in rather a crowd of ships, Lord Nelson was commending some ship that appeared to be conducted much to his satisfaction, when a musket ball struck him on the left shoulder. Captain Hardy immediately hastened to support him. He smiled, and said, '*Hardy, I believe they have done for me at last.*' He was carried below ; and when the ship was disengaged from the crowd, he sent an officer to inform me he was wounded. I asked the officer if his wound was dangerous ? He hesitated ; but I saw the fate of my friend in his eye—his look said what his tongue could not give utterance to. About an hour afterwards, when the action was over, Captain Hardy brought me the melancholy news of his death. He inquired frequently how the battle went, and expressed joy when he heard the enemy were striking : in his last moments showing an anxiety for the glory of his country, regardless of what related to his person." [1]

An extract from Captain Blackwood's letter to his wife must close the record of this sad scene :—

" I closed my last sheet in a great hurry to obey my signal on board

---

[1] Clarke and McArthur, vol. iii. p. 161 ; Correspondence of Lord Collingwood, vol. i. p. 234.

the *Victory*, and I really thought that I was sent for to take command of one of the ships vacant. It was only, however, to talk to me—explain what he expected from the frigates in and after the action—to thank me (which he did but too lavishly) for my intelligence, and the look-out we kept, and to tell me that if he lived he would send me home with the despatches. Have I not, therefore, my dearest love, but too much cause to regret such a considerate friend. How completely he has acted up to the letter I send you, which I am sure you will be glad to see and keep, the issue has proved. How glad I am to possess such a letter I cannot express. I stayed with him till the enemy commenced their fire on the *Victory*, when he sent me off. He told me at parting we should meet no more ; he made me witness his will, and away I came with a heart very sad." [1]

Collingwood's Despatch :—

" To William Marsden, Esq., Admiralty.

" *Euryalus*, off Cape Trafalgar,
October 22, 1805.

" Sir,—The ever-to-be-lamented death of Vice-Admiral Viscount Nelson, who in the conflict with the enemy, fell in the hour of victory, leaves to me the duty of informing My Lords Commissioners of the Admiralty, that, on the 19th instant, it was communicated to the Commander-in-chief from the ships watching the motions of the enemy in Cadiz, that the combined fleet had put to sea. As they sailed with light winds westerly, his lordship concluded their destination was the Mediterranean, and immediately made all sail for the straits entrance with the British squadron, consisting of twenty-seven ships, three of them sixty-four's, where his lordship was informed by Captain Blackwood (whose vigilance in watching and giving notice of the enemy's movements has been highly meritorious) that they had not yet passed the straits.

" On Monday, the 21st instant, at daylight, when Cape Trafalgar bore E. and by S. about seven leagues, the enemy was discovered six or seven miles to the eastward, the wind about west, and very light. The Commander-in-chief immediately made the signal for the fleet to bear up in two columns, as they are formed in order of sailing ; a mode of attack his lordship had previously directed, to avoid the inconvenience and delay in forming a line-of-battle in the usual

---

[1] Appendix to Despatches, vol. vii. p. 225.

manner. The enemy's line consisted of thirty-three ships (of which eighteen were French and fifteen Spanish), commanded-in-chief by Admiral Villeneuve; the Spaniards, under the direction of Gravina, wore with their heads to the northward, and formed their line-of-battle with great closeness and correctness; but as the mode of attack was unusual, so the structure of their line was new—it formed a crescent converging to leeward—so that in leading down to their centre I had both their van and rear abaft the beam. Before the fire opened every alternate ship was about a cable's length to windward of her second, ahead and astern, forming a kind of double line, and appeared, when on their beam, to have a very little interval between them; and this without crowding the ships. Admiral Villeneuve was in the *Bucentaure* in the centre, and the *Prince of Austurias* bore Gravina's flag in the rear, but the French and Spanish ships were mixed without any apparent regard to order of national squadrons.

"As the mode of our attack had been previously determined on and communicated to the flag officers and captains, few signals were necessary, and none were made except to direct close order as the lines bore down. The Commander-in-chief led the weather column; and the *Royal Sovereign*, which bore my flag, the lee.

"The action began about twelve o'clock by the leading ships of the columns breaking through the enemy's line, the Commander-in-chief about the tenth ship from the van, the second in command about the twelfth from the rear, leaving the van of the enemy unoccupied; the succeeding ships breaking through in all parts, astern of their leaders, and engaging the enemy at the muzzles of their guns; the conflict was severe. The enemy's ships were fought with a gallantry highly honourable to their officers, but the attack on them was irresistible; and it pleased the Almighty Dispenser of all events to grant his Majesty's arms a complete and glorious victory. About three p.m., many of the enemy's ships having struck their colours, their line gave way; Admiral Gravina, with ten ships, joining their frigates to leeward, stood towards Cadiz. The five headmost ships of their van tacked, and standing to the southward, to windward of the British line, were engaged, and the sternmost of them taken; the others went off, leaving to his Majesty's squadron nineteen ships-of-the-line (of which two are first-rates, the *Santissima Trinadada* and the *Santa Anna*), with three flag officers, viz., Admiral Villeneuve, the Commander-in-chief; Don Ignatio Maria d'Alava, Vice-admiral; and the Spanish Rear-admiral, Bon Baltazar Hidalgo Cisneros.

"After such a victory it may appear unnecessary to enter into encomiums on the particular parts taken by the several commanders;

the conclusion says more on the subject than I have language to express; the spirit which animated all was the same. When all exert themselves zealously in their country's service, all deserve that their high merits should stand recorded; and never was high merit more conspicuous than in the battle I have described.

" The *Achille* (a French seventy-four), after having surrendered, by some mismanagement of the Frenchmen, blew up ; two hundred of her men were saved by the tenders.

" A circumstance occurred during the action, which so strongly marks the invincible spirit of British seamen when engaging the enemies of their country, that I cannot resist the pleasure I have in making it known to their lordships. The *Temeraire* was boarded, by accident or design, by a French ship on one side and a Spaniard on the other ; the contest was vigorous, but in the end the combined ensigns were torn from the poop, and the British hoisted in their places.

" Such a battle could not be fought without sustaining a great loss of men. I have only to lament, in common with the British nation, in the fall of the Commander-in-chief, the loss of a hero whose name will be immortal, and his memory ever dear to his country ; but my heart is rent with the most poignant grief for the death of a friend, to whom by my years of intimacy, and a perfect knowledge of the virtues of his mind, which inspired ideas superior to the common race of man, I was bound by the strongest ties of affection—a grief to which even the glorious occasion in which he fell, does not bring the consolation which perhaps it ought.

" I have also to lament the loss of those excellent officers, Captains Duff of the *Mars*, and Cooke of the *Bellerophon*. I have yet heard of no others.

" I fear that the numbers that have fallen will be found very great when the returns come to me ; but it having blown a gale ever since the action, I have not yet had it in my power to collect any reports from the ships.

" The *Royal Sovereign* having lost her masts, except the tottering foremast, I called the *Euryalus* to me while the action continued, which ship lying within hail made my signals, a service Captain Blackwood performed with great attention. After the action I shifted my flag to her, that I might more easily communicate my orders to, and collect the ships ; and towed the *Royal Sovereign* out to seaward. The whole fleet were now in a very perilous condition ; many dismasted ; all shattered ; in thirteen fathoms of water, off the shoals of Trafalgar ; and when I made the signal to prepare to anchor, few of the ships had an anchor to let go, their cables being shot ; but the same good Providence which aided us through such a day preserved us in the night, by the wind shifting a few points, and drifting the ships off the land, except four of the captured dismasted ships, which are now at anchor off Trafalgar, and I hope will ride safe until those gales are over.

"Having thus detailed the proceedings of the fleet on this occasion, I beg to congratulate their lordships on a victory which, I hope, will add a ray of glory to his Majesty's crown, and be attended with public benefit to our country.

"I am, &c.,

"C. COLLINGWOOD." [1]

In the Appendix will be found in more detail the account of the losses on both sides according to the reports of the Spanish and French commanders.[2] Of the Spanish reports there are three, varying in details, the sum of which may be briefly given :—*British Ships :* The *Victory*, sunk off Gibraltar on the 22nd ; *Britannia* and *Prince of Wales*, and the *Prince*, sunk in the action ; *Tigre*, sunk on the Playa of Santa Maria. *Tonant*, burnt by the English Fleet five or six leagues off Cadiz ; *Spartiate*, sunk after the battle on the coast of Rota.

---

[1] *London Gazette,* November 6, 1805 ; Despatches, vol. vii. pp. 212–15.

[2] The following is the fate of the combined fleet ; British returns :—
Prizes *saved,* four—*Ildefonso, Nepomuceno, Bahama,* and *Swiftsure.*

Prizes *wrecked,* ten—*Monarca* (S.), *Fongeux* (F.), *Indomptable* (F.), *Bucentaur* (F.), *San Francisco a'Asis* (S.), *El Rayo* (S.), *Neptuno* (S.), *Argonaute* (F.), *Berwick* (F.), *Aigle* (F.).

Burnt, three—*Achille* (F.), *Intrepede* (F.), *San Augustin* (S.).

Sunk by orders of British, three — *Santissima Trinadad* (S.), *Redoubtable* (F.), *Argonauta* (S.).

Escaped into Cadiz, nine—*Santa Anna* (S.), *Algesiraz* (S.), *Pluton* (F.), *San Juste* (S.), *San Leandro* (S.), *Neptune* (F.), *Heros* (F.), *Principe de Asturias* (S.), *Montanez* (S.).

Escaped to sea but captured by Sir R. Strachan, November 4th, four (all French)—*Formidable* (80), *Mont Blanc* (74), *Scipion* (74), *Dugancy-Trouin* (74).

British losses : Killed—Officers, 21 ; petty officers, 16 ; seamen, 299 ; marines, 116. Wounded—Officers, 43 ; petty officers, 59 ; seamen, 900 ; marines, 212. Killed, 452 ; wounded, 1,204.

To these were added the following ships which were not in the battle :—*Prince of Wales, Tigre, Queen Donegal, Canopus, Spencer, Zealous*, and *Carnatic*, and five sail-of-the-line are reported as having joined the English Fleet during the action—the *Duke of York*, the *Royal Sovereign*, the *St. Leger*, the *Relampayo*, and the *Aquila*. Of these only the *Aquila* and the *Royal Sovereign* were in the British Navy.[1]

Of their own ships they admit that the *Santa Anna* had surrendered, but afterwards came into Cadiz Bay with the prize crew, that the *San Francisco de Asis* and *Neptuno* were aground near Puerto de Santa Maria, and that of eight sail the " fate is not known " ; of these they subsequently allow that two, the *Rayo* and *St. Ildefonso*, had been captured.

The Spanish reporter has the coolness to say that the report of the English losses is taken from that despatched from Gibraltar by Admiral Collingwood, and sets our losses at ten thousand four hundred and seventy-one killed and wounded.

In the same account five sail-of-the-line are reported at anchor in Cadiz Bay, the *Algesiraz* as having surrendered, but afterwards came into the Bay with the prize crew ; *Aigle* and *Fongeux* stranded ; *Achille* blown up during the battle ; the *Bucentaure*, with Villeneuve, captured. Of the four French ships in the Bay not one ever returned to France.[2]

Twenty-nine British sail-of-the-line are represented to have been in the battle (according to the French account of it), and five more to have joined in the afternoon, making thirty-four in all. Of the twenty-nine enumerated eight, viz., the *Prince of Wales, Queen*

[1] Egerton MS. ; Despatches, vol. vii. pp. 297–9.
[2] Jurien de la Gravière.

Canopus, Donegal, Tigre, Spencer, Zealous, and Le Caine
(probably *Carnatic,* then an old receiving hulk at Plymouth), were not in the action. *Two Queens* are
mentioned, but the second is probably the *Orion,* which
was in the action. Of the five ships which are said to
have joined in the afternoon of the 21st (though none
joined till the 23rd) the *Royal Sovereign* led the lee
division in the action, and was the first ship that opened
her fire. There were no such ships in the British Navy
as the *Duke of York, Le Leger,* or *Relampayo,* and the
Achille was included in those previously mentioned.
Relampayo was probably the *Thunderer,* which was in
the battle ; *L'Achille* is probably meant for the *Eagle,*
which was neither in the battle nor joined the fleet
afterwards. Those present but not mentioned were
Belleisle, Ajax, Africa, and *Agamemnon.*

The following extracts from Spanish letters will conclude this chapter :—

"Dear Friend,—Although I wish very much to be able to give
you a circumstantial account of the calamitous battle, which I
announced to you in my former letter, yet the reports in circulation
here are so vague and uncertain that I have my doubts if the admirals
themselves could do it with any degree of accuracy. Of this, however, there is no doubt, that Nelson and his Englishmen have gained
a complete and decisive victory, and that our fleet has been, all of it,
absolutely destroyed. The number killed and wounded is from ten
to twelve thousand ; Villeneuve taken prisoner, Magon killed, Gravina severely wounded in the arm, Escaño in the leg, and Alava in the
head ; Cisneros and Dumanoir are by some reported to have been
made prisoners, by others to have been killed. Out of the thirty-
three ships which left this port only nineteen have re-entered it, and
that in so miserable and shattered a condition that the hulls of some
are almost unserviceable. The rest of the fleet have either been
taken, burnt, or sunk. In the offing some are seen dismasted, which
the English have manned, and are towing away. Two or three have
run ashore upon the coast, without the possibility of receiving any
assistance, in consequence of the furious tempest which raged imme-

diately after the battle. In the Playa the sea is continually throwing up portions of wreck, together with numbers of dead bodies, all which increases the desolate appearance of that shore. All have exhibited a courage worthy of a better issue ; but the event has demonstrated that valour is not sufficient to insure success, and that victory always inclines towards intrepidity united to skilful discipline. Perhaps in eight or ten days the details of the action may be learnt with some degree of certainty, but the disorder and confusion which reigned throughout the fearful battle have rendered it almost impossible for the commanders themselves to know what occurred on board their own ships." [1]

" In short," writes another Spaniard, "the number of vessels belonging to the combined fleet is now reduced to those riding at anchor in the bay, of which only three have their masts standing ; but if this weather continue they are far from being out of danger. Of these ten ships five are Spanish and five French, which, with the other four French ones that entered the straits of Gibraltar after the action, under the command of Admiral Dumanoir, are all that remain of this once splendid and efficient fleet." [2]

" The dreadful and calamitous loss is owing to the rash and injudicious resolution of Admiral Villeneuve, who hurried into battle without having previously ascertained the numbers, strength, and position of the enemy, and at a time when the tempest which afterwards raged with such fury was hanging over him. History does not record a better contested action, as is proved by the crippled state of our ships and the slaughter on board of them. There are more than one thousand wounded in our hospitals, besides others expected, as well as such as are still on board the ships taken by the enemy.

" It appears that the rash and unfortunate departure of our fleet was in some measure a great mercy for the city of Cadiz, for the English had determined to blockade it in order to force the combined fleet to come to action.

" Scarcely a third part remains of the French troops who were embarked on board the fleet, and it is really heart-breaking to see their soldiers wandering about the streets." [3]

In another report it is stated that the English failed three times to break the line of the combined fleet.

[1] Letter dated Cadiz, Oct. 25th.
[2] October 29th. Egerton MSS. pp. 382–441.
[3] Despatches, vol. vii. pp. 290–1.

PERSONAL I.: NELSON'S PERSONAL
INFLUENCE.

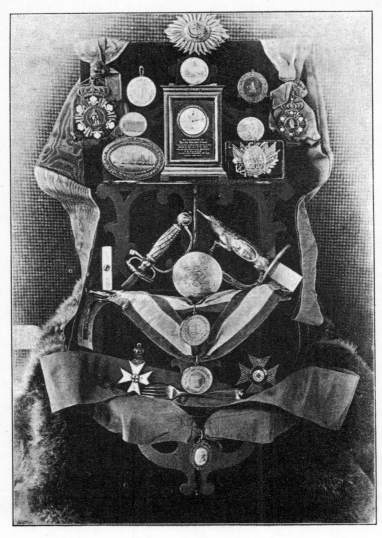

TROPHY OF MEDALS, ORDERS, AND RELICS OF NELSON, PRESERVED AT
VISCOUNT BRIDPORT'S.

CHAPTER XVII.

PERSONAL I.: NELSON'S PERSONAL INFLUENCE.

The sources of his unbounded influence—His rule of kindness and love
—Young Hardy—Captain Ball and Nelson—Kindness to a prisoner
—Anxiety for Troubridge—Captain Layman—Appeal for Captain
Hellyer—Youthful imprudence ; the runaway—Rear-Admiral Camp-
bell—Sir Robert Calder—Captain Westcott's mother—The sailors'
love for Nelson—The old *Agamemnon*—The old sailor of the Nile—
The mutineers of the *Minotaur*—Sailors and soldiers—Discipline—
The Captain of the American schooner—Nelson's opinion on pro-
motions—Advice to young Connor.

HE object of the present chapter is to
show the grounds of that unbounded
personal influence which Nelson exercised over his comrades of all ranks,
and which made him the best served
of all English admirals. The great
Lord Howe thought that the most
marvellous part of the Battle of the Nile was that no
captain failed in doing his duty, and believed that there
was something special in the admiral to produce this result
and make them the "Band of Brothers" of whom Nelson
was so justly proud. Great as had been the exertions of
his predecessors in the glorious roll of English admirals,
no one of them had, ere Nelson came, ruled rather by
kindness and love than by fear. Even Jervis, respected as
he was, and readily obeyed, was rather feared than loved.
Nelson was adored. He realized the duty of his being
known by report to every man and boy in his fleet, and

in his flagship his personal ways, his habits, his gestures, walk, voice, temper, and methods were familiar to everybody. "He lived in public and impressed it in one way or in another, according to his conduct under it. Hence the personal character of the admiral in a fleet may almost have a greater influence on what is called the public character, and what the man is may be as important a national consideration as what the admiral is." [1]

In the previous chapters evidence has been given of the source of this influence—his fatherly method of instructing his young midshipmen, his habit of taking them with him on all occasions into official society, his kindness and offered liberality to the two poor lunatic seamen, his sorrow for the loss of the two brave boys that fell at Boulogne, his assiduous care of and poignant grief at the death of poor young Parker. The record of other instances may be introduced by an anecdote with reference to Hardy related by Lady Minto :—

"It was on February 11, 1797, only three days before the great Battle of St. Vincent. Nelson was on board a frigate in the Mediterranean, just east of the straits of Gibraltar. He was on his way to join the commander-in-chief, whose fleet lay at some distance on the west. The frigate was close to the straits, when she found herself chased from the eastward by two Spanish ships-of-the-line. Suddenly there was a cry of 'Man overboard !' A boat was soon lowered by young Thomas Hardy, known eight years later as the flag-captain of the *Victory*, to whom Nelson gave his farewell instructions as he lay dying of his wound. A very rapid current sets in eastwards through the straits. This current quickly carried the boat far astern of the frigate—further and further from her friends, closer and closer to the pursuing enemy. It was a critical moment. To go after the boat was to lose time, and risk capture from the powerful line-of-battle ships. Nelson, they say, cast an anxious look

---

[1] From the *Edinburgh Review* for 1886, pp. 551-2. A review of Professor Laughton's digest of the Despatches, in which the true character of Nelson is most carefully worked out.

at the receding boat, then exclaimed, 'By heaven I will not lose Hardy! Back the mizen-topsail!' No sooner said than done; the frigate was stopped, the boat's crew was recovered, and the Spaniard, not knowing what to make of the manœuvre, and fearing some trap, shortened sail, and was soon lost to sight." [1]

It may be remembered that during the trip to France in 1783, Nelson met Captain Ball and another officer at St. Omer, wearing the then unusual ornament of epaulettes, borrowed from the French service, and not as yet introduced in that of our navy. The result was that Nelson entertained a poor opinion of these decorated officers—an opinion which evidently, from the following anecdote, he still entertained when Ball, in the *Alexander*, joined Nelson's squadron in the Mediterranean.

"On joining, Captain Ball went on board the *Vanguard* to pay his respects to the rear-admiral, and met with a by no means flattering reception. 'What,' said Nelson, 'are you come to have your bones broken?' Ball quietly replied that he had no wish to have his bones broken, unless his duty to his King and country required such a sacrifice, and then they should not be spared. Soon after, in the storm of May, 1798, the *Vanguard* was taken in tow by the *Alexander*, and Nelson, fearing from the state of the weather that both ships would go down, peremptorily ordered that his ship should be abandoned to its fate. Ball held on, and when the ships arrived at St. Pierre's, Nelson at once went on board Ball's ship, and, cordially embracing him, said, 'A friend in need is a friend indeed.' From this time their close friendship commenced, and he highly esteemed him." [2]

To Captain Ball the very arduous and difficult defence of Malta was entrusted by Nelson after the Battle of the Nile, a position in which, it is evident from the following

[1] Recorded by Lady Minto and quoted in the sermon of the Rev. Montague Butler, Master of Trinity College, Cambridge, at a meeting of the Church of England Young Men's Society, July 5, 1889, at St. Peter's, Mancroft, Norwich.

[2] *Ex relatione* Rev. Francis Laing, who was told it by Ball; Despatches, vol. iii. p. 21, note.

letter, he was the subject of reports that he had forfeited Nelson's esteem—far from it :—

" My dear Ball," wrote Nelson, on hearing of his anxiety, " I love, honour, and respect you ; and no persons ever have, nor could they, were they so disposed, lessen you in my esteem, both as a public officer and a private man : therefore, never let such a thought come into your head, which was never more wanted to be clear from embroils than at this moment."

Then, fortifying his perseverance by informing him that Troubridge is coming with ships and Colonel Graham with troops, he thus proceeds :—

" But, my dear friend, you holding your port so long as you have, is a matter of the greatest credit to you.   If you are forced to quit the island, it cannot lessen your exertion or abilities ; and do not let such an event, should it unfortunately happen, depress your spirits for a moment, and believe me as ever, your obliged and affectionate friend,
" NELSON." [1]

In the following letter to Daniel Williams, Esq., father of Lieutenant C. D. Williams, a prisoner, we have another instance of Nelson's kindness [2] :—

" LEGHORN, *Feb.* 27, 1795.

" DEAR SIR,—I only received your letter of December 29th yesterday, on the return of the fleet from sea.

" I had some time learnt with pleasure that your son was a prisoner and not lost, which I feared was the case from the bad account I heard of the vessel.   I at that time made inquiries if any little money could be got to him, but was told at this place it was impossible ; however, I will make further inquiry, and, if possible, get a remittance to him.   I shall have, I assure you, great pleasure in doing so on your son's account, who is a very good young man, and who at a future time, I shall be glad to serve.   I need no reference to any

---

[1] November 24, 1799.   See in Appendix the account of how Captain Ball gave his worn out crew twenty minutes rest during the heat of the Battle of the Nile, as told by him to the poet Coleridge.

[2] The prisoner was a lieutenant on board the *Agamemnon.*   Mr. Williams was afterwards a police magistrate and knighted.

person for your character. Mr. Prestwood's recommendation of him to me was sufficient for every purpose.

"I can acquit myself of his misfortune. I was at sea ; and the English consul thought fit, which I never should have consented to, to desire your son and others belonging to the *Agamemnon* and other ships, to navigate a vessel with bullocks to Toulon—a vessel by no means proper for the purpose—and left no doubt in my mind of his being lost. However, in case we cannot send him money, his case is not singular ; a great number of English are in the same situation. I will not willingly miss this post, although it may be long in reaching you ; and you shall hear again from me before I leave Leghorn." [1]

"LEGHORN, *Agamemnon, May* 5, 1795.

"DEAR SIR,—The last time I was here, the neutrality of Tuscany being just settled, I could not send your son the £20 which you desired, and which I should, had it been possible, have had the greatest satisfaction in sending : and at this time cartels are expected from Toulon (with) sick prisoners, amongst whom I hope, and have little doubt, is your son. I therefore have not sent the money, but have desired Mr. Sidney, the consul, to advance him £20 immediately on his arrival, to get those things which he must want ; and assure you I shall, with his other friends, be very glad to see him. I think that this account of your son will be acceptable.

"I am, dear sir, &c.,

"HORATIO NELSON."

Nelson's anxiety for Troubridge :—

"TO EARL ST. VINCENT.

"BEGUN *Oct.* 19TH, ENDED (ON THE 24TH).

"MY DEAR LORD,—Had *Leander* got to you, perhaps you would have been overwhelmed with my private letters upon numerous subjects, but of which I have no copies. On the subject of our dear friend Troubridge—I should have been glad if you had received my letter—it was authorizing you to add a paragraph to my public letter, if you thought it more to the advantage of Troubridge, but I thought it better to make no mention of his disaster ; for I consider Captain Troubridge's conduct as fully entitled to praise as any one officer in the squadron, and as highly deserving reward. He commanded a division equally with Sir James Saumerez, by my orders in June, and

---

[1] *European Magazine*, vol. xlix. p. 101.

I should feel distressed if any honour is granted to me that is not granted to the other. This part I write, my dear lord, to make use of to Lord Spencer, should any difference be made. I know the knight has wrote to the First Lord, but the eminent services of our friend deserve the highest reward. I have experienced the ability and activity of his mind and body. It was Troubridge that equipped the squadron so soon at Syracuse — it was Troubridge who saved the *Culloden*, when none that I know of in the service would have attempted it—it was Troubridge whom I left as myself at Naples to watch movements—he is a friend and an officer, a *nonpareil.*" [1]

Again, on hearing of his peerage he did not forget Troubridge :—

"To Lord Spencer.

"Naples, *Nov.* 7, 1798.

"My dear Lord,—On my arrival from Leghorn I received your lordship's letter of October 7th, communicating to me the title his Majesty had been graciously pleased to confer upon me—an honour, your lordship is pleased to say, the highest that has ever been conferred on an officer of my standing who was not a commander-in-chief.

"I receive as I ought what the goodness of our Sovereign, not my deserts, is pleased to bestow ; but great and unexampled as this honour may be to one of my standing, yet I own I feel a higher one in the unbounded confidence of the King, your Lordships, and the whole world, in my exertions. Even at the bitter moment of my return from Syracuse, your lordship is not insensible to the great difficulties I had to encounter in not being a commander-in-chief. The only happy moment I felt was in view of the French : then I knew that all my sufferings would be at an end.

"I observe what your lordship is pleased to say relative to presenting myself, and the captains who served under my orders, with medals, and also that the first lieutenants of the ships *engaged* will also be distinguished by promotions, also the senior marine officer. I hope and believe the word '*engaged*' is not intended to exclude the *Culloden :* the merit of that ship and her gallant captain are too well known to benefit by anything I could say. Her misfortune was great in getting aground, while her more fortunate companions were in the full tide

---

[1] Tucker's "St. Vincent," vol. i. p. 455.

of happiness. No ; I am confident that my good Lord Spencer will never add misery to misfortune. Indeed, no person has a right to know that the *Culloden* was not as warmly engaged as any ship in the squadron. Captain Troubridge on shore is superior to captains afloat. In the midst of his great misfortune he made those signals which prevented certainly the *Alexander* and *Swiftsure* from running on the shoal. I beg your pardon for writing on a subject which I verily believe has never entered your lordship's head ; but my heart is, as it ought to be, warm to my gallant friends.

" Yours, &c.,

" NELSON." [1]

In the following year he again urged his friend's claims :—

" PALERMO, *Jan.* 24, 1799.

" MY DEAR LORD,—I have just received, and with the greatest pain, a postscript of a letter from my gallant friend Troubridge, dated Syracuse, Jan. 14th, viz. : 'I am truly miserable. Do pray, my lord, explain to Lord Spencer, that my accident at Aboukir was not intentional, or through fear of my *head*, for, I assure you, it preys so much on me that it would be a charitable act to shoot me.' Such a postscript and from such a man, it makes my heart (bleed). Indeed, my lord, Captain Troubridge's merit is equal to any officer in that fleet. I would say it as an Admiral to the Board of Admiralty, that Captain Troubridge performed the most important service, and was highly instrumental in making the victory what it was. Could Ball or Hallowell have been in action but for Troubridge ? They will tell you ' *No.*' We know of no distinction of merit, and yet, unfortunately, it has been found out so many hundred leagues distant—not found out from public despatches, but from private information. The stab has been given by the Board in not promoting the first lieutenant. Lord St. Vincent, it is true, by the same conveyance, sent a commission for Captain Hargood. I trust, I believe that your lordship's goodness of heart and regard to justice, will recommend Captain Troubridge to his Majesty as equal in merit to any one on the 1st of August, and I am sure you will add as one of the bravest and very best sea-officers in his service. With every sentiment of respect, believe me, your most obliged,

" NELSON." [2]

---

[1] Despatches, vol. iii. p. 187 ; December 7, 1798.

[2] To Lord Spencer, Spencer Papers, Despatches, vol. vii. add. clxxi.

Again he urged Troubridge's claim in a letter to Lord
St. Vincent of Dec. 6th.

"I received, yesterday, a private letter from Lord Spencer, of Oct.
7, saying that first lieutenants of all ships engaged would be promoted.
I sincerely hope this is not intended to exclude the first of the
Culloden ; for heaven's sake, if it is so, get it altered. Our dear friend
Troubridge has suffered enough, and no one knows from me, but that
the *Culloden* was as much engaged as any ship in the squadron. His
sufferings were in every respect more than any of us. He deserves
every reward that a grateful country can bestow on the most meritorious sea officer of his standing in the service. I have felt his
worth every hour of my command. I have before wrote to you, my
dear lord, on this subject, therefore I place Troubridge in your
hands." [1]

During the tedious operations in the Mediterranean in
the year 1804, the brig *Raven*, commanded by Captain
Layman, was driven on shore during a heavy gale, and
her captain brought to a court martial, which censured
him for "running in with the land."   As the truth was
that had her captain been properly assisted by his officers,
and the ship had not carried away her mainmast and
parted from her anchors, she would have got off safely,
Nelson, with his accustomed love of justice, at once
interested himself in the cause of the censured captain.
Nelson, as he truly said, was not of the school of sailors
who feared running in towards the shore, when duty
called for the risk, and Captain Layman's duty was never
to be from the shore whilst cruising in the Straits.   "If
he did not every day risk his sloop," said Nelson, "he
would be useless."   Hence the following manly letter,

[1] Lord Spencer wrote to Lord St. Vincent Oct. 9, 1798, that the exception was necessary from *Culloden* not being engaged, but that he was so
fully convinced of the merit of Captain Troubridge and his officers on
all occasions, that he begged him to give the first vacancy of commodore
that arose to the first lieutenant of the *Culloden*. (Despatches, vol. iii.
p. 183, note.)

and his subsequent interference on behalf of Captain Layman :—

" To Viscount Melville.

" At Sea, *March* 10, 1804.

" My dear Lord,—I enclose some remarks made by Captain Layman whilst he was in Spain, after the very unfortunate loss of that fine sloop which your lordship was so good as to give him the command of. Your lordship will find the remarks flow from a most intelligent and active mind, and may be useful should any expedition take place against Cadiz ; and, my dear lord, give me leave to recommend Captain Layman to your kind protection ; for notwithstanding the court martial has thought him deserving of censure for his running in with the land, yet, my lord, allow me to say, that Captain Layman's misfortune was, perhaps, conceiving that other people's abilities were equal to his own, which very few people are.

" I own myself one of those who do not fear the shore, for hardly any great things are done in a small ship by a man that does ; therefore, I make great allowances for him. Indeed, his situation was intended never to be from the shore in the Straits, and if he did not every day risk his sloop, he would be useless in that situation. Captain Layman has served with me in three ships, and I am well acquainted with his bravery, zeal, judgment, and activity ; nor do I regret the loss of the *Raven* compared to the value of Captain Layman's services, which are a national loss.

" You must, my dear lord, forgive the warmth which I express for Captain Layman, but he is in adversity, and therefore has the more claim to my attention and regard. If I had been censured every time I have run my ship or fleet under my command into great danger, I should long ago have been *out* of the service, and never *in* the House of Peers. I am, my dear lord, most faithfully, your obedient servant,

" Nelson and Bronte."

Commander Layman arrived at Portsmouth May, 1805, and Nelson still urged his merits. He took him to the Admiralty, and a promise was given that he should be sent out to the Mediterranean, but to use the words of Layman, " the next month terminating his lordship's glorious career, the promise was forgot, and my offer of service rejected." He offered to prevent premature decay in our ships ; to divulge a plan for rendering forest trees fit for immediate use, provided he was entrusted with the measure ; but his applications were disregarded. He published some works, the " Precursor," and others connected with this subject ; but he could not get his suggestions accepted. He is said to have terminated his existence in 1826.[1]

His appeal for Captain Hellyer must find a place here.

" Captain Hellyer is most truly deserving of all your lordship can do for him, and in addition to his public merits has a claim upon us. At twenty-four years of age he maintained his mother and sisters, and a brother, until I made him a lieutenant for his bravery a short time ago. For these reasons he declined the *Ambuscade*, which was offered him ; because, although he might get his rank, yet if he were put upon half pay, his family would be the sufferers. From all these circumstances, so honourable to Captain Hellyer, independent of his services, which every one thought would have obtained him promotion in the late war, I beg to submit that as the *Niger* (Captain Hellyer's ship), is a very fast sailing frigate, well manned, and in excellent condition, she may be fitted with the *Madras's* thirty-two carronades, which are not so heavy as her present 9-pounders, and that your lordship would recommend her being considered as a port ship. . . . I will not venture to say more ; I am sensible of your attention to merit." [2]

The appointment was made.

The following letters show with what kind consideration Nelson dealt with a case of " youthful imprudence " :—

" To W. Marsden.

" *Victory* at Sea, *April* 11, 1805.

" Sir,—I am extremely concerned to acquaint you, for the information of the Lords Commissioners of the Admiralty, that Lieutenant —— (son of that excellent and respectable officer, Captain ——) from an unfortunate desire to travel, and perhaps an imprudent attachment to an Italian female, quitted the *Hydra* when she was last

---

[1] Pettigrew, vol. ii. p. 381, note.

[2] To Earl St. Vincent, Jan. 20, 1804 ; Clarke and McArthur, vol. iii. p. 25.

at Malta, without, I fear, the smallest inclination of ever returning to
his duty in that ship ; . . . and I must beg that you will interest their
lordships in favour of this unfortunate young officer, whose youthful
imprudence I trust their lordships will take into consideration, and on
account of his worthy and respectable father, Captain ——, allow
his name to remain on the list of lieutenants.   Their lordships will
readily conceive the feelings of Captain ——, and, I hope, enter into
my wishes on this occasion." [1]

The following letter refers to the same officer :—

"*Victory, Sept.* 30, 1805.

"DEAR CAPTAIN SOUTHERON,—Captain ——'s son is adrift in Italy,
at Naples or Rome, we think, very probably in prison for debt.   His
father is very anxious to save the lad.   He was lieutenant of the
Hydra, and ran away with an opera dancer from Malta.   Pray try
with Mr. Elliot at Naples, and Mr. Jackson at Rome, to get word
of Mr. ——.   Captain —— will pay the bills he has drawn on
England—supposed to be some two or three hundred pounds—and
if now a few more are necessary to liberate the youth, I will be
answerable.   All we want is to save him from perdition." [2]

The following letter shows how truly Nelson judged
the acts of his comrades :—

"TO REAR-ADMIRAL CAMPBELL.

"*May* 24, 1804.

"I am more obliged to you than I can express, for your not allow
ing a very superior force of the enemy to bring you to action.
Whatever credit would have accrued to your own and your gallant
companions' exertions, no sound advantages could have arisen to our
country ; for, so close to their own harbour, they could always have
returned, and left your ships, probably, to keep the sea.   I again, my
dear admiral, thank you for your conduct.   Some day, very soon, I
have no doubt but an opportunity will offer of giving them fair battle,
and that it may arrive very, very soon, is the most sincere wish of,
my dear Campbell, your most obliged friend,

"NELSON AND BRONTE." [3]

---

[1] Despatches, vol. vi. p. 403.   [2] Ibid., vol. vii. p. 58.
[3] On May 24, when off Cape Septet, reconnoitring with three sail-of-
the-line, Admiral Campbell was gradually threatened with five sail-of-the-
line and three frigates, and after a brief action, made sail, and the
French, finding pursuit useless, returned to port.

If, as many of his biographers state, Nelson was warranted in believing that Sir Robert Calder was his jealous rival since the Battle of St. Vincent, his consideration for him, when he was ordered home from Nelson's fleet before Cadiz for a court martial, was a marked proof of that fraternal affection that prevailed in any fleet commanded by Nelson.

Sir Robert, on the 22nd of July, 1805, had engaged a superior force of the enemy, and after four hours' hard fighting, captured two Spanish ships, an 80 and a 74. The fleets were still near each other, but Calder, deeming it imprudent to renew the action the next day, the enemy escaped, and eventually arrived in Cadiz to swell the fleet for which Nelson so eagerly watched. Spoilt by the decisive victories of Duncan and Nelson, the feeling of the English at home was so bitter, and the attacks on Calder so severe, that the Admiralty offered him a court martial, and instructed Nelson to send him home, with such captains who had been in the action as were willing to come and give evidence.

" My dear lord," Nelson wrote to the First Lord of the Admiralty, on the 30th of September, after communicating his instructions to Sir Robert :—

" Sir Robert thinks that he can clearly prove that it was not in his power to bring the combined squadrons again to battle. It would be only taking up your time were I to enter more at large on all our conversation ; but Sir Robert felt so much, even at the idea of being removed from his own ship (the *Prince of Wales*), which he commanded in the force of the fleet, that I much fear that I shall incur the censure of the Board of Admiralty, without your lordship's influence with the members of it. I may be thought wrong, as an officer, to disobey the orders of the Admiralty, by not insisting on Sir Robert Calder's quitting the *Prince of Wales* for the *Dreadnought*, and with parting with a 90-gun ship before the force arrives which their lordships have judged necessary ; but I trust that I shall be considered to have done right as a man, and to a brother officer in affliction—my

heart could not stand it, and so the thing must rest. I shall submit to
the wisdom of the Board to censure me or not, as to them may seem
best for the service ; I shall bow with all due respect to their decision.
I am, &c.,

"NELSON AND BRONTE." [1]

And so Sir Robert sailed for England in his own three-
decker, instead of in a frigate, almost on the eve of
Trafalgar. "Nelson saw his departure with joy, though
on the eve of the great battle ; he little regretted the
magnificent ship which he gave up, for the melancholy
and desponding mood of the unhappy officer fretted his
sanguine mind and seemed to cast a gloom over the
cheerfulness of the fleet." [2]

On this painful subject Nelson had previously written
the following feeling and chivalrous letter to Captain
Fremantle :—

"*August* 16*th.*

"I could not last night sit down to thank you for your truly kind
letter and for your large packets of newspapers, for I was, in truth,
bewildered by the account of Sir R. Calder's victory, and the joy of
the event; together with hearing that *John Bull* was not content,
which I am sorry for. Who, my dear Fremantle, can command all
the success which our country may wish ? We have fought together,
and therefore well know what it is. I have had the best-disposed fleet
of friends ; but who can say what will be the event of a battle ? And it
most sincerely grieves me that in any of the papers it should be insinu-
ated that Lord Nelson could have done better. I should have fought
the enemy, and so did my friend Calder ; but who can say that he
will be more successful than another ? I only wish to stand upon my
own merits, and not by comparison one way or the other upon the
conduct of a brother officer. You will forgive this dissertation, but I
feel upon this occasion." [3]

Captain Westcott, who fell at the commencement of
the victory in the Battle of the Nile, was a self-made

[1] Despatches, vol. vii. p. 56.
[2] Jurien de la Gravière, vol. ii. p. 224.
[3] Despatches, vol. ii. p. 5.

man, the son of a baker in Honiton. When on one day
he was at a mill, where he had been sent by his father on
business, from the accidental breaking of a rope the whole
machinery was disorganized. Neither the owner of the
mill nor his men being equal to the task of repairing the
damage, young Westcott volunteered to splice the rope—
no easy matter. So well was his task accomplished that the
miller told him that he was fit for the navy, and that if he
liked he would get him a berth. As a cabin-boy he began
his naval career, and solely by his own abilities he rose
step by step till, on the glorious First of June, 1794, he
commanded the *Impregnable*, Rear-Admiral Caldwall's
flagship. At the Nile he commanded the *Majestic*, where
he encountered the *Henreux* and the *Tonant* at the same
time, and fell from a musket-shot—a sad loss to his
parents, who were very poor. When Nelson was visiting
his friends and admirers in Devonshire, in the commencement of 1801, he made a point of seeking out Westcott's
aged mother. "At Honiton," he wrote to Lady Hamilton on the 17th of January in that year, "I visited Captain
Westcott's mother—poor thing. Except from the bounty
of the country and Lloyds, in very poor circumstances.
The brother is a tailor, but had then been chimney sweep;
it was my duty to show them respect." It was on this
occasion that Nelson took from his neck the medal for
the Nile, presented by Alex. Davison to all who were
engaged at the Nile, saying to Mrs. Westcott, "perhaps
you will not think less of it because it has been worn by
Nelson." This medal has been handed down as an heirloom in the Westcott family, and is now in the possession
of Mr. G. B. Westcott, a retired navy paymaster.[1]

Among the numerous instances which are recorded of

---

[1] Captain Simcoe, R.N., of Wolford, Honiton, has a letter from Nelson
to his father, Lieutenant-General Simcoe, speaking of Nelson's coming
to Honiton, probably on this interesting occasion.

the feelings of his sailors for Nelson there will be given only a few instances.   When Nelson went home with the Hamiltons and the Queen of Naples " an expedition," of which, according to Miss Knight, he disapproved, and was against his own convictions, he received the following letter from the crew of his barge :—

" Foudroyant, June 26, 1800.

" MY LORD,—It is with extreme grief that we find that you are about to leave us.   We have been along with you (though not in the same ship) in every engagement your lordship has been in, both by sea and land ; and most humbly beg of your lordship to permit us to go to England as your boat's crew, in any ship or vessel, or in any that may be most pleasing to your lordship.   My lord, pardon the rude style of seamen, who are but little acquainted with writing, and believe us to be, my lord, your ever humble and obedient servants,

" BARGE'S CREW OF THE *Foudroyant.*" [1]

Again, after he received his death wound, writes Mr. Duncan :—

" A thorough seaman himself, nursed in the lap of hardship, he knew how to adapt his behaviour to those he commanded, and never did an officer possess their affections in a higher degree.   To this love and affection he was not only indebted for his early successes, but even for his life, for there was scarcely one of his crew who would not have sacrificed himself to save his commander.   A striking instance how much he was adored by his men occurred during the last fatal conflict off Trafalgar.   A seaman of the *Victory* was under the hands of the surgeon, suffering the amputation of an arm. ' Well,' said he, ' this by some would be considered a misfortune ; but I shall be proud of it, as I shall resemble the more our brave commander-in-chief.' Before the operation was finished tidings were brought below that Lord Nelson was shot ; the man, who had never shrank from the pain he endured, started from his seat, and exclaimed, ' Great God ! I would rather the shot had taken off my head, and spared his life.'

" Another generous instance of the same nature was soon after evinced on board the *Brilliant* frigate.   Being on a cruise, she fell in

[1] Despatches, vol. iv. p. 264, note.

with several vessels, whicl acquainted the crew with the defeat of the combined fleet, and the death of Lord Nelson. A concern, the most general and sincere, pervaded the ship's company. While it was yet the subject of conversation, a boatswain's mate, who was then doing duty as boatswain, was ordered to pipe all hands to quarters ; he did not do it readily, and the lieutenant upon duty went to inquire the cause, with orders to pipe instantly. The honest fellow, after several attempts, began to sob bitterly, and said, ' Hang me, if I can do it ; poor, dear fellow, that I have been in many a hard day with, and to lose him now. I wouldn't have cared if it had been my old father, brother, or sisters, if there were fifty more of them ; but I can't think of parting with Nelson.' And he went below immediately." [1]

In his Private Diary, under date November 7, 1803, Nelson wrote : " I had the comfort of making an old *Agamemnon*, George Innes, gunner into the *Chamelion* brig."

" This ship, called by the sailors ' old eggs and bacon,' was wrecked in Maldonado Bay in the River Plate, under the command of Captain Rose, June 20, 1809. Many of Nelson's old tars were on board. ' I well remember,' writes the old sailor, ' witnessing the distress pictured on their furrowed countenances, as they were compelled to quit the ship so powerfully endeared to them by old associations. The address of Captain Rose, previously to their being distributed amongst the fleet of Admiral de Courcy, drew tears from many an eye that was undismayed by danger, even when death appeared inevitable.' " [2]

Nelson's meeting with the old sailors of the Nile and Santa Cruz :—

" At the reception at Salisbury by the Corporation, on the bestowal of freedom of that city, in the crowd assembled before the Council House, Nelson recognized a sailor who had fought at the Battle of the Nile, called him forward, expressed the gratification he felt at meeting one who had stood with him in the dangers of that celebrated day, and dismissed him with a handsome present. He also perceived another

---

[1] " Life of Lord Nelson," by Archibald Duncan, Esq., London, 1805, p. 518.
[2] " The Old Sailor." Clarke and McArthur, vol. iii. p. 142.

man loudly huzzaing, who had been with him at the time he under-
went the amputation of his arm. He beckoned him to approach, and
also made him a present ; upon which, on withdrawing, the man took
from his bosom a piece of lace, which he had torn from the shirt-
sleeve of the amputated arm, as a token in memory of his gallant
commander."

Nelson's ill-repaid kindness to those sailors who deserted to the Spaniards has already been noticed, to which
the following incident forms a natural pendant :—

"To Capt. Louis, H.M.S. *Minotaur.*

"*Nov.* 7, 1798.

" Sir,—I have this moment received your letter enclosing a petition
from the ship's company of the *Minotaur*. In the common course of
service, I ought not to pay attention either to the petition of your
ship's company, or to your kind interference in their behalf. I am
glad, however, that the prisoners have not presumed to say a syllable
on their conduct, which merits the yard-arm.

" But, sir, I can never forget your noble and effectual support to my
flag on the most glorious First of August; and in remembrance of the
gallant conduct of the *Minotaur's* ship's company, in obedience to your
orders, I do, from these considerations alone, permit you to withdraw
your letter for a court martial on the prisoners.

"I am, &c.,

"Horatio Nelson."

" To the same, but private.

" I have endeavoured to write such a letter as I wish to be placed in
public, and read to your ship's company. Believe me I shall never
forget your support. A friend in need is a friend indeed. Never
was it better applied than to the *Minotaur*. I have written to Troubridge to stop the court martial, according to your request.

"H. N."

One John Jolly, a private of Marines, struck his officer,
and threatened to shoot him when released. Having been
found guilty by court martial and sentenced to death,
Nelson, on July 6th, ordered Troubridge to carry out the

sentence ; but on the 9th sent the following remission of
the penalty :—

"To Capt. Troubridge, commanding British and Portuguese
Troops landed from the Squadron.

"*Foudroyant, July* 9, 1799.

"Sir,—You will, in obedience to my orders, prepare everything
for the execution of the sentence of the court martial held on John
Jolly; but when all the forms, except the last, are gone through, you
will acquaint the prisoner, that although there has been no circumstances to mitigate the severity of the law, yet that I have reason to
hope that the sparing of his life will have as beneficial effect for the
discipline of the service as if he suffered death. You will, therefore,
respite the prisoner from the sentence of death, till his Majesty's
pleasure is known. I hope that this extraordinary mark of lenity will
have its full effect on the minds of those under your command, and be
a beacon to them to avoid the crime of drunkenness, which brings with
it even the punishment of death. And here I pledge myself to them,
that if any similar circumstance happens in future, that I will most
assuredly order the sentence to be immediately carried into execution.
"Nelson."

Whether at sea or on shore Nelson had but one mode
of fighting—to lay his ship or his battery alongside the
enemy. In the San Juan Expedition it may be remembered how he spoke of having boarded the Spanish fort
from his ship ; and when before Bastia and Calvi how, in
disregard of the utmost military rules, he had placed his
batteries at once close to the defences of the enemy. In
the following letters Nelson contrasts the way of sailors
with that of soldiers in such duties.

Nelson to the Duke of Clarence, November 9,
1799 :—

"General Koehler does not approve of such irregular proceedings
[when Nelson attacked and carried Bastia], as naval officers attacking
and defending fortifications. We have but one idea, to get close
alongside. None but a sailor would have placed a battery ónly a
hundred and eighty yards from the Castle of St. Elmo ; a soldier

must have gone according to art and the Z Z way; my brave Sir Thomas Troubridge went straight, for we have had no time to spare."

Again to Lord Spencer, November 6th :—

"The services of Captain Ball will not, I am confident, be forgot by you, but I feel sensible that my pen is far unequal to do justice to the merit of my friends ; for could I have described the wonderful merits of Sir T. Troubridge, and his gallant party in the kingdom of Naples—how he placed his battery, as he would his ship, close along side the enemy—how the French commander said, 'This man fancies he is on board his ship—this is not the mode a general would adopt'; in what a few days this band went to the siege of Capua, where whatever was done, was done by the English and the Portuguese."

His reply to an appeal by a friend of Sir John Warren's in favour of a young officer who had behaved improperly to his captain, shows Nelson's earnest desire ": to prevent rather than to punish " offences :—

"We would all do everything in our power to oblige so gallant and good an officer as our friend Warren ; but what would he do if he were here ? Exactly what I have done, and am still willing to do. The young man must write such a letter of contrition as would be an acknowledgment of his great fault, and with a sincere promise, if his captain will intercede to prevent the impending court martial, never to so misbehave again. On his captain's enclosing me such a letter, with a request to cancel the order for the trial, I might be induced to do it ; but the letters and reprimand will be given in the public order-book of the fleet, and read to all the officers. The young man has pushed himself forward to notice, and he must take the consequence. We must recollect, my dear admiral, it was upon the quarter-deck, in the face of the ship's company, that he treated his captain with contempt, and I am in duty bound to support the authority and consequence of every officer under my command. A poor ignorant seaman is for ever punished for contempt to his superior." [1]

One more instance of Nelson's generosity must be given.

---

[1] Clarke and McArthur, vol. iii. pp. 25–6.

When in command on the American station he captured a schooner belonging to Plymouth (in America) which was evading the orders as to trading, the captain of which he put on shore to go to his home. Some time after, when sailing up the Bay of Boston with his prize, the captain of the schooner fitted out a boat with one or two sheep and vegetables, and on coming alongside threw the articles on to the *Albermarle's* deck, jumped on deck, and begged Nelson to accept them. When Nelson asked the reason, the captain, with some hesitation, said, " that though he could hardly expect it, it was the return of his schooner; it was his all." Nelson at once wrote the following certificate, which it is said still hangs framed and glazed in a gentleman's parlour in Boston :—

"This is to certify, that I took the schooner *Harmony*, Nathaniel Carver, master, belonging to Plymouth : but on account of his good services I have given him up the vessel again.

"Dated on board his Majesty's ship *Albermarle*, August 17, 1782, Boston Bay.

"HORATIO NELSON." [1]

I conclude this portion of the extracts with Nelson's views on promotions :—

"On the subject of promotions, I beg to say a few words, because I feel now exactly as you have felt in a similar situation to mine ; and I rejoice that you, my dear lord, are not only alive, but in office to bear witness to the truth of my words, which I should have quoted even if you had not been in office, *that it was absolutely necessary merit should be rewarded on the moment ; and that the officers of the fleet should look up to the Commander-in-chief for their reward : for that otherwise the good or bad opinion of the Commander-in-chief would be of no consequence.* You always promoted meritorious officers out of the *Victory* and *Ville de Paris*, and many private ships for their merit. The good effect was, that whatever was undertaken succeeded.

---

[1] Duncan's Life, p. 327.

I myself stand in that situation, and Hardy was rewarded by you as Commander-in-chief." [1]

In a letter to Charles Conner, the brother of Horatia's governess, Nelson wrote :—

"DEAR CHARLES,—As Captain Hellyer has been so good as to say he would rate you mid., I sincerely hope that your conduct will ever continue to deserve his kind notice and protection, by a strict and very active attention to your duty. If you deserve well you are sure of my assistance. Mr. Scott (his secretary) will furnish you with money to begin your mess, and I shall allow you £30 a year, if it be necessary, which Captain Hellyer will supply you with. As you from this day stand in the world as a man, I trust that your future conduct in life will prove you both an officer and a gentleman. Recollect, that you must be a seaman to be an officer, and that you cannot be a good officer without being a gentleman. I am always, with most sincere good wishes, your true friend,

"NELSON AND BRONTE." [2]

Do not these instances, out of many that could be cited, prove the words of an able critic that, "at the bottom of his great success under all circumstances, as a commander, we must place Nelson's power of pleasing which was inherent in his nature, and arose in a great measure from that sort of 'enthusiasm for humanity' with which he was filled towards those associated with him"? [3]

---

[1] To Earl St. Vincent, January 11, 1804, in reply to a letter asking Nelson to notice the son of Lord Duncan. Clarke and McArthur, vol. iii. p. 20.

[2] Clarke and McArthur, vol. iii. p. 7. No date or place given.

[3] *Edinburgh Review*, previously quoted.

PERSONAL II.: NELSON AND HIS FAMILY.

CHAPTER XVIII.

PERSONAL II.: NELSON AND HIS FAMILY.

(1779 to 1805.)

Nelson's liberality to his family—His brother Maurice's widow—His sister, Mrs. Bolton—Affection for Burnham—His charity and goodness at Merton—His narrow means—His god-children—the estate of Bronte—The Hon. A. Nelson Hood's account of Bronte—Nelson in Parliament—Anxiety about his proxy—Advice on the Navy—Lawsuit with Lord St. Vincent.

ELSON was a poor man for his position until after the victory of the Nile. As he truly said, foreigners could not understand the really small pecuniary means of the captain of a man-of-war, or the necessity which in such a position he had of incurring expenses which the routine of the Treasury forbad it to repay. Still, however, he found means to send his Christmas gifts to his father for the deserving poor of Burnham, and of helping many a young officer to maintain his position in his ship. It was in vain that he asked for some remuneration for acting as a land officer—practically in the position of a brigadier for his conduct at the siege of Bastia and Calvi. It was also in vain that he applied for a wound pension for the loss of his eye at the latter siege ; it was not, as the Treasury replied, equal to the loss of a limb. After St. Vincent his pay rose as an admiral, and after Teneriffe a wound pension was awarded. Still he had nothing to spare, his necessary expenses as he advanced

in his rank were barely met by his increased pay and pension. He never, however, forgot his aged father; what money there was in his agent's hands was at the service of his father and his family. Though he had earned prize money, the cream of it was skimmed by his commanders-in-chief, and even of what was left to the working captain the payment was long delayed. After the victory of the Nile, however, the liberal gift by the East India Company made him able to give substantial help to his family. Of the ten thousand pounds then voted to him, he immediately instructed Davison to divide two thousand among them, and in his ignorance of business was much surprised to find that it had not been immediately paid to his wife. See the following letters to his wife and his agent, and from his aged father, so truly marking his unselfishness, and its appreciation by his family :—

" To Lady Nelson.

"Naples, *July* 14, 1799.

" I rejoice that you gave Mr. Bolton the money, and I wish it made up to £500. I never regarded money, nor wanted it for my own use; therefore, as the East India Company have made me so magnificent a present, I beg that £2,000 of it may be disposed of in the following manner :—Five hundred pounds to my father; five hundred to be made up to Mr. Bolton, and let it be a God-send without any restriction; five hundred to Maurice, and five hundred to William. And if you think my sister Matcham would be gratified by it, do the same for her. If I were rich I would do more ; but it will very soon be known how poor I am, except my yearly income. I am not surprised at my brother's death [Suckling]. Three are now dead, younger than myself, having grown to man's age." [1]

" To Alex. Davison.

" *September* 26, 1799.

"In my state, of what consequence is all the wealth of this world, I took for granted the East India Company would pay their noble gift

---

[1] Laughton, p. 203.

to Lady Nelson, and whether she lays it out in house or land is, of course, I assure you, a matter of perfect indifference. I have given away £2,000 of it to my family, in expectation it had been paid. Ah, my dear friend, if I have a morsel of bread and cheese in comfort, it is all I ask of kind heaven, until I reach the estate of six feet by two, which I am fast approaching. I had the full tide of honour, but little real comfort. If the war goes on, I shall be knocked off by a ball, or killed by chagrin. My conduct is measured by the Admiralty, by the narrow rule of three, when I think it should have been done by that of common sense. I restored a faithful ally by breach of orders ; Lord Keith lost a fleet by obedience, against his own sense. Yet as one is censured, the other must be approved. Such things are." [1]

Letter from his father :—

> "*December* 15th, 1799.

"MY DEAR HORATIO,—You are too prudent to judge either of things or persons by appearances, and too good to believe that the few letters you receive from me can happen from any cause except the insecure conveyances which offer, or that indolence, which 1 find is in the train of infirmities, which accompany those years when we shall say in the morn, would the even was come, that I may rest; and at night we are weary before the twilight returns. This is too often my case, even in the midst of blessings ; and allow me to say, that yourself, under Providence, are the cause of many of these. Your public merit every mouth proclaims ; your private virtues every day are experienced. A recent generous act has made your family happy by so handsome a present of £500 each, Bolton's more especially ; he has occasion for all. The boy George is got so gay—I hope a happy omen. There is another boy, whom I have desired to be kept at school two years longer, and then brought forward. 1 have hoped he may be got to the East Indies. This was intended for a very long letter, but [I] must curtail it ; the courier is going off directly. Our hopes of seeing you one day are revived, another destroyed ; all I can say, you know best, and in the end will do what is right. If honour is your object, all men say you have enough ; if riches, you are too generous to heap up many ; if the *amor Patriæ*, you have shown it. If your dearest friends are to be gratified, they are, no doubt, very much so, by hearing of your health and prosperity, which pleasure can be

---

[1] Laughton, p. 214.

increased only by seeing you. Memento—your father is seventy-seven years of age. December 16, 1799. God bless you."

" EDM. NELSON." [1]

His brother Maurice, who was in the Navy office, and for whom he had in vain applied for promotion, and who for very many years had treated a Miss Sarah Ford as his wife, died suddenly in May, 1802, leaving her all but penniless. She had been blinded by an accident, and became a cripple, and at once on the news of his brother's death, Nelson came forward with ready help. To Davison on the 22nd and 25th of May he wrote :—

" *St. George*, ROSTOCK BAY, *May* 22, 1802.

"MY DEAR DAVISON,—By a letter from Sir A. Hammond, I first heard of the death of my dear brother Maurice. As the dead cannot be called back, it is no use dwelling on those who are gone. I am sure you will do everything which is right for his blind wife.[2] I hope he has left her well provided for ; if not, I beg you will arrange a proper and ample subsistence, and I will make it up. It is the only true regard I can pay to his memory. He was always good and kind to me ; but enough on this subject." [3]

" BAY OF ROSTOCK, *May* 25, 1802.

"MY DEAR DAVISON,—The morning I sailed from Yarmouth I wrote you a letter, and several others, which were on board a ship left behind, in which I requested you to give Mrs. William Nelson £100 for me, and I do not hear, either from you or any person, that the letter got safe to you. Respecting poor Maurice's wife, if her necessities require it, every farthing which his kindness gave me shall be used, if she wants it ; therefore, I beg you will be everything generous towards her, for she shall ever by me be considered as his honoured wife." [4]

---

[1] Despatches, vol. iv. note p. 183.
[2] Nelson always considered her as his brother's wife.
[3] Despatches, vol. iv. p. 378.   [4] Ibid., vol. iv. p. 391.

In a letter to the same, dated September 6, 1805, he again reverted to the case of the widow.

"I send you on the memorandum which I am sure that you will comply with. Poor blind Mrs. Nelson I must assist this morning. A Mr. Brand, an apothecary, called upon me for £133 2s. 6d., as due from my brother Maurice to him. I shall refer him to you, and if it is a just demand, he must have it. I shall leave the bill in St. James' Square. Ever, my dear Davison,

    "Your most obliged and affectionate friend,
        "NELSON AND BRONTE."

When off Portland in the *Victory*, September 16th, he again wrote Davison as to what he had done about the poor blind widow :—

"Poor blind Mrs. Nelson, I have given £150 to pay her debts, and intend to pay her house rent in future, in addition to the £200 a year, which I take will be about £40 a year."[1]

In the fifth codicil to his will (April 7, 1804) he had provided for her in the case of his death.

"I desire that the sum of £100 sterling money of Great Britain may be annually paid unto the reputed widow of my brother Maurice Nelson by whatever name she may assume, be it S. Nelson, S. Ford, or any other name, and if I have not the means to pay this sum, exclusive of my other legacies, I then trust that my friend, Alexander Davison, will pay it for me regularly every year, and to be paid quarterly, as it is at present."[2]

Gifts to his sister, Mrs. Bolton :—

        "MERTON, *June* 11, 1802.

"MY DEAR SISTER,—Here is £100, which I shall pay you on the 11th of June for three years, towards the education of your children ; by that time other things may turn up, and this is a trifle in case you want any little thing going through London. All I desire is, that

---

[1] Despatches vol. vii. pp. 36, 39.   [2] Ibid., vol. vii. p. ccxxxviii.

you would not say or write a syllable on the subject, for I am sorry I cannot do more, being truly,

"Your most affectionate brother,

"NELSON BRONTE." [1]

"To MRS. BOLTON.

"*Victory, Jan.* 11, 1804.

"With respect to Tom (second Earl Nelson), although I do not know if it be absolutely in my power to say, I will entirely keep him at college, yet you may be sure of my assistance; and when poor blindy [Mrs. Maurice] goes the way of all flesh, and please God some other vacancies which at present draw my pocket very deeply, I shall be more at my ease in pecuniary matters, and, of course, better able to afford permanent assistance. You know, my dear sister, how I have leazed and leazed for that paltry prebendary (Canterbury for W.), and I really believe no minister would give me a place of £50 a year; but if I know what Mr. Bolton looks to, I shall then know how to act. My sincere friendship for him, independent of his relationship, would induce me to do everything in my power to meet his wishes, and that, I trust, he is sure of; but he knows I have, in reality, not an atom of interest. The French having no trade in the Mediterranean, but very little has been done in the prize way; indeed, I am afraid my pursuit lays another way. I never did, or could, turn my thoughts to money-making." [2]

The following shrewd letter on the choice of a profession naturally finds its place here :—

"To HIS BROTHER WILLIAM.

"*Victory*, March 29, 1804.

"With respect to Horace, you know so much better than I how to educate him that I can say nothing; and as to what mode of life he is to follow, that must be a matter for future consideration, as events may turn out. A good education and languages fit him for anything. The Corps Diplomatique, as far as I have seen, is the road to ruin. I never knew or heard of any one who made a fortune in it, and it is very easy to spend one; indeed, without much more prudence than is considered right, a minister cannot exist upon his salary. We must not judge, because perhaps Lord Elgin at a par-

---

[1] Despatches, vol. v. p. 15.   [2] Ibid., vol. v. p. 363.

ticular moment got money at Constantinople, and even a Scotsman,. I dare say, would have been richer with his interest if he had set up as a master tailor. But you may be sure that in any way that I can be useful to Horace, whom I really love, nothing will be wanting on my part, as far as is within the reach of my abilities." [1]

His affection for Burnham :—

"To Dr. Allott, Dean of Raphoe.

"*May* 11, 1804.

"I remember you, dear sir, most perfectly at Burnham, and I shall never forget the many little kindnesses I received from your worthy brother (the Rector of Burnham), with whom I was always a great favourite. Most probably I shall never see dear, dear Burnham again; but I have a satisfaction in thinking that my bones will probably be laid with my fathers in the village that gave me birth. Pardon this digression; but the thought of former days brings all my mother into my heart, which shows itself in my eyes. May heaven, my dear sir, long preserve you in health, for the sake of your family and friends; and amongst the latter allow me to place the name of your very faithful servant,

"Nelson and Bronte." [2]

Again from Mrs. Ullock, daughter of the vicar of his charity and goodness, in the following letter to Sir H. Nicolas :—

"In revered affection for the memory of that dear man, I cannot refrain from informing you of his unlimited charity and goodness during his residence at Merton. His frequently expressed desire was, that none in the place should want or suffer affliction that he could alleviate; and this I know he did with the most liberal hand, always desiring that it should not be known from whence it came. His residence at Merton was a continued course of charity and good-ness, setting such an example of propriety and regularity, that there are few who would not be benefited by following it."

---

[1] Despatches, vol. v. p. 479.

[2] Ibid., vol. vi. p. 18; Clarke and McArthur, vol. ii. p. 363. In the Appendix will be found an account of the present movement to restore Burnham Thorpe Church, in which Her Majesty and the Prince of Wales take so great an interest.

" To the Rev. Mr. Lancaster, Merton.

" *Victory,* Feb. 14, 1804.

" My dear Sir,—Many thanks for your kind letter, and for all the good wishes of my friends at Merton, who I shall some day hope to thank in person.   Nothing shall be wanting on my part to merit the continuance of their esteem by every exertion in my power to bring about an honourable and speedy peace—with respectful compliments and good wishes to all your family, believe me, ever, my dear sir, your much obliged friend,

" Nelson and Bronte." [1]

From the following letters Nelson appears to have by no means shared in the opinions of the Duke of Wellington as to the duty of evading the responsibility of being a godfather.   It was quite contrary to his nature to refuse such requests, especially when they came from one like Mr. Ross, who had so liberally assisted him during his dangerous illness in Jamaica, or from a relative or a comrade, however humble.

On an application from Hercules Ross, Esq., whom he had known in Jamaica in 1779–80, and from whom he received great attention, to be godfather to his son, Nelson wrote :—

" Whatever call public duty has to my services, yet I must not altogether forget the duty of private friendship.   You do not think me capable of forgetting when your house, carriages, and purse were open to me ; and to your kindness, probably, I owe my life, for Green Bay had very often its jaws open to receive me.   But as money was never my object, so I am not much richer than when you knew me, except by my pension.   No !   The *two* Parkers have had the sweets of Jamaica, but I would not change with them.   I pray God we may have peace, when it can be with honour ; but I fear that the scoundrel Buonaparte wants to humble us, as he has done the rest of Europe— to degrade us in our own eyes by making us give up all our conquests, as a proof of our sincerity for making a peace, and then he will condescend to treat with us.   He be ——, and there I leave him." [2]

---

[1] Despatches, vol. vii. add. ccxix.

[2] Pettigrew, vol. ii. p. 233 ; Despatches, vol. iv. p. 488.

" To R. Nelson, Esq., Plymouth Dock, Devon.

"London, *July* 7, 1801.

"Dear Sir,—I received your kind letter from Plymouth, and congratulate you on the birth of a grandson, who I am much flattered with your intention to call after me. I trust that the name of Nelson will remain with credit to our country for many ages, and although I do not despair but that I may have fruit from my own loins, yet the honour of the Nelson family will not, I am confident, be lost in yours. I beg my compliments to Colonel Nelson, and that you will believe me, your most obliged servant,

"Nelson and Bronte." [1]

Archibald Duncan tells the following interesting story of a godchild of very humble parents :—

" As Colonel Tyrwhitt with other gentlemen was looking at the prizes going up Plymouth harbour on Nov. 12, 1805, he observed a fine little boy, of an open countenance, cheering with his playfellows, who frequently called him 'Nelson.' This, being several times repeated, roused the curiosity of the gentlemen to inquire who the boy was. Colonel Tyrwhitt went to the cottage of his father, a quarryman, who lived at Rusty Anchor, under the West Hoe. The boy soon afterwards arrived, and at first appeared rather shy, but after a little conversation his timidity wore off, and he said that Lord Nelson was his godfather, but that he was shot and killed the other day in a great battle. This served to excite the colonel's curiosity, and he entered the hut, where he found the father (who had lost a limb in the *Minotaur* at the Battle of the Nile), and his wife and four children, clean enough, but poorly dressed. He inquired whether it was true that Lord Nelson was the godfather of the little boy, and was answered in the affirmative. The mother then produced the certificate of his baptism at the British Factory Chapel, Leghorn, 1800, attested by the Rev. Mr. Comyns, and signed by Lady Hamilton, Sir W. Hamilton, and Lord Nelson, after whom the child was named Horatio Nelson. His mother was a washerwoman on board the *Minotaur* when the child was born in the bay of Leghorn, and his lordship, when he stood sponsor, promised when the boy grew up, to give him a nautical education and put him to sea. When he sailed for England he desired these poor people to write to him when they should be settled ; but this, through ignorance, they had neglected to do. The *Minotaur* was paid off at Plymouth, and the father, with

---

[1] Despatches, vol. iv. p. 421.

the aid of his small pension, had by his industry contrived to maintain
his family ever since.   Colonel Tyrwhitt immediately resolved to
prosecute his lordship's intentions, and to give the child a nautical
education so as to fit him for the naval service of his country." [1]

Such was Nelson's liberality to his family, friends,
the poor, that his income was very narrow for his
position, especially after the unfortunate separation from
his wife, to whom he allowed £1,800. a year.   In his
statement to Mr. Addington, when applying for a similar
pension on the Irish pension list to that given to St.
Vincent and Duncan, he sent the following balance-sheet.
His house at Merton he had purchased mainly out of
borrowed money, and he had drawn heavily on his income
for its improvements [2] :—

" NELSON'S INCOME.

*Statement to Mr. Addington when asking for same pension as Irish
Parliament gave to St. Vincent and Duncan.*

INCOME AND PROPERTY.

My Exchequer Pension for the Nile £2,000
Navy Pension—loss of one arm and eye 923
Half-pay as Vice-Admiral 465
Interest of £1,000, 3 per cent. 30
	£3,418

OUTGOINGS OF LORD NELSON.

To Lady Nelson £1,800
Interest on money owing 500
Pension to brother's widow 200
To assist educating my nephews 150
Expenditure £2,650
Income 3,418
For Lord Nelson £768

[1] Duncan's " Nelson," pp. 284–5.
[2] From first to last Merton had cost him £20,000.

" Therefore Lord Nelson is free of house rent, but has to pay charities necessary for his stadon in life, taxes, repairs, servants, and to live on £768 per annum.

Property of Lord Nelson.

Merton House, land, plate, and furniture   ...   £20,000
In 3 per cents., £1,000 stock.

Debts.

By mortgage on Merton to assist purchase   ...   £6,000
Fitting out for the Baltic, and again for my command on coast summer of 1801   4,000
_____

£10,000

" Real property of Lord Nelson, £10,000 ; in 3 per cents., £1,000 stock." [1]

It has been a favourite topic with many biographers of Nelson to accuse the Hamiltons of living on the charity of Nelson : it was not so.   The cost of living at Merton was shared by Sir William Hamilton, who had a pension of £1,200 a year as a retired ambassador.

The formal gift of the apparently magnificent estate of Bronte by the King of Sicily was not made until the 13th of August, 1799, though it is said by one of his biographers to have been offered and declined by Nelson on a previous occasion.   According to this authority, on Nelson's refusal the King said, '' Lord Nelson, do you wish that your name should pass with glory to posterity, and that I, Ferdinand de Bourbon, should appear ungrateful." Whether this was so or not, at the above date it was accepted, and so far as can be traced in Nelson's correspondence, was of more trouble than profit to the recipient. It will be noted that in his estimate of his income in 1803, previously given, nothing is credited by Nelson to this property, and the following extracts show that it was

[1] Despatches, vol. v. p. 107.

a constant source of anxiety and expense. The history of this estate, and its present condition, is shown in the admirable memoir so kindly furnished to me by the Hon. Alexander Nelson Hood, the son of the present popular Viscount Bridport, who for many years has been the resident manager at the Castello Maniace.

"PRINCE DE LUZZI TO LORD NELSON.

"PALERMO, *Aug.* 13, 1799.

"His Majesty has resolved and ordained that the ancient and famous town of Bronte, on the skirts of Etna, with its territory and dependencies, shall be constituted a feudal tenure, and shall be raised to the dignity and title of a Duchy, with full and mixed authority— that is, the right of absolute jurisdiction, both civil and criminal ; and that the said Duchy and Title, with its revenues and jurisdiction, shall be conferred on your Excellency, and on the heirs of your body in a right line, according to the laws of this kingdom : and, in default of the same, to any one of your relatives, in whatever degree, whom your Excellency may think proper to appoint, to whom His Majesty will grant a new investiture and testamentary powers according to the laws of this kingdom, enlarging from the present moment the limits of feudal succession." [1]

"TO HIS MAJESTY THE KING OF THE TWO SICILIES.

"PALERMO, *Aug.* 13, 1799.

"SIRE,—The bounty of your Majesty has so overwhelmed me that I am unable to find words to express my gratitude ; but it shall be my study to continue in the same line of conduct which your Majesty has been pleased to approve, and to mark with such very extraordinary proofs of favour, and which has also gained me the approbation of my own most gracious sovereign, your Majesty's faithful ally.

"That the Almighty may pour down His choicest blessings on your sacred person, and on those of the Queen and the whole Royal Family, and preserve your kingdom in peace and happiness, shall ever be the fervent prayer of your Majesty's faithful servant,

"BRONTE NELSON." [2]

---

[1] Nelson did not sign "Bronte" except to foreigners until he received his own sovereign's license, issued Jan. 9, 1801.

[2] Despatches, vol. iii. pp. 438-40.

After the usual grant, "*prædicto Horatio Nelson pro se suisque Heredibus de suo corpore legitime descendentibus,*" the following clause is added :—

"*Et ad Majus Gratiæ Nostræ testimonium, tam existentibus quam deficientibus hæredibus de corpore suo legitime descendentibus, de certâ Nostrâ scientiâ ac de Nostræ Regiæ Potestatis plenitudine, facultatem sibi concedimus et impertimur, ut quem voluerit etiam extra suam agnationem, vel cognationem, tam directam quàm transversalem nominare possit, et valeat, cui a Nobis solemnis paritur Investitura concedetur juxta leges, et capitula hujus Siciliæ Regni, et servata, quoad successionem, ejusdem Juris Francorum forma.*"

In a previous paragraph it was provided :—

"*Ita quod in eodem Ducatu, oppido, et terra sic per Nos, ut antefertur concessis, Hæredes sui vivant jure Francorum nimirum, ut in successione Major Natu Minoribus fratribus, ac Masculus fæminis præferatur.*" [1]

How Nelson dealt with the estate in the interest of his family is shown in the following letters :—

"To the Rev. Edmund Nelson.

"Palermo, *Aug.* 15, 1799.

" My dear Father,—His Sicilian Majesty has created me a Duke by the title of Bronte, to which he has attached a feud of, it is said, about £3,000 a year, to be at my disposal. I shall certainly not omit this opportunity of being useful to my family, always reserving a right to the possessor of leaving one-third of the income for the payment of legacies. It shall first go to you, my dear father, and in succession to my elder brother and children male, William the same, Mrs. Bolton's boys, Mrs. Matcham's, and my nearest relations. For your natural life the estate shall be taxed with £500 a year, but this is not to be drawn into a precedent, that the next heir may expect it. No, my honoured father, receive this small tribute as a mark of gratitude to the best of parents from the most dutiful son.

"Nelson."

"To the Rev. Mr. Nelson, Hillborough.

"Palermo, *Aug.* 21, 1799.

" My dear Brother,—I am truly sorry that the Administration

---

[1] Despatches, Appendix, vol. iii. pp. 524–5.

have neither done that for me or my family which might have been
expected.   Lords St. Vincent and Duncan have £1,000 a year from
Ireland : I have heard no such thing for *Nelson*.   You may be assured
I never have (forgotten) or will forget my family : I think that would
be a crime, and if you will tell me to whom and what I am to ask for,
for the descent of the title and pension goes with it, I will do it.   My
father, Maurice, yourself and children, Mrs. Bolton's and Mrs. Matcham's—this is the way I have fixed the Bronte estate, as I have wrote
our dear father; that letter you will see.   You may be assured that
when a year comes round, and I really know my income, no brother
will be more ready to assist than myself.   How is Aunt Mary ?   Assure
her she shall want for nothing, and if she does, pray write Lady
Nelson, and she will send her anything she desires." [1]

How Nelson resisted the proposed injustice to his
people, is described in the following letter of June 2,
1800, to Sir J. Acton :—

" I am told that I either have been, or am to be, induced to consent
that a superior, or rather all Bronte causes, should be tried at Palermo.
Now, as this is a measure so repugnant to justice, and which must
heap ruin on those whom it is my wish to render happy, I entreat that,
except such causes as the present laws of Sicily oblige to resort to some
superior court, it may never be imagined that I will consent to do an
unjust act.   It is possible, from my not reading Italian, that I may
sign a very improper paper—(which God forbid)—if men in whom I
place confidence lay it before me for my signature.   In his Majesty's
most gracious gift of Bronte has been omitted the word *Fragilé*, a farm
belonging to me.   The reasons for this omission are, I fear, too clear ;
and at a future day I may lose it, and his Majesty may not retain it." [2]

He then asks for the insertion of the farm of *Fragilé*
in the patent, and a billet-royal to annul the present con-
tract of the feuds of St. Andrea and Porticelli.   This was
done.   The following letters show that the Estate brought
more trouble than profit to Nelson :—

" ABRAHAM GIBBS, PALERMO.
" *Victory, Aug.* 11, 1803, OFF TOULON.
" MY DEAR SIR,—I yesterday received your truly friendly letter of

---

[1] Despatches, vol. iii. pp. 456-7.   [2] H., vol. ii. pp. 242-4.

July 5th with much pleasure, and I shall be truly thankful, if you will have the goodness to put my Bronte Estate in a train, that if I cannot receive the value of it, and have done with it, that at least I may receive the full rental regularly ; for I never will lay out another sixpence on it, but am content to pay a certain sum for the attention of some respectable person to receive the rents and transmit them to London. As you are so good as to offer to attend to this serious concern to me, I will enter at large into the subject. I told Grafer [his steward] on first setting out, that I would give up two years' rent for fitting up a house and improving. I paid more attention to another sovereign than my own ; therefore, the King of Naples' gift of Bronte to me, if it is not now settled to my advantage, and to be permanent, has cost me a fortune, and a great deal of favour which I might have enjoyed, and (much) jealousy which I should have avoided. I repine not on these accounts ; I did my duty, to the Sicilifying my own conscience, and I am easy. It will be necessary, before you can take any steps beyond inquiry, to know from Sir J. Acton what has been done and what intended. All that I beg is, that the just thing may be done immediately, and that I may have it permanent. I shall never again write an order about the estate. If the estate cannot be returned, my receiving the whole value, the income net ought to be paid me, which the Hospital received, as delivered to me, 6700 ounces on the average for seven years preceding. Your kind assistance will truly oblige, my dear sir, &c.

" NELSON BRONTE." [1]

Again Nelson writes to his agent, August 12, 1803.

" Mr. Broadbent made a sort of an offer to hire the farm, and when I passed the Faro of Messina I wrote him a letter to explain himself more fully on that subject, but I have not heard since. If that farm was let with its improvements, all the others are so let that a person resident in Sicily sees in a moment what the whole lets for, and, taking an average of seven years, would probably make an offer to give me so much a year for three, five, or seven years, as might be agreed upon." [1]

In a letter to Lady Hamilton, October 18, 1803, he writes :—

" You see what interest [Gibbs] is taking about Bronte. I begin to think, without some assistance like his, that I never should have

---

[1] Despatches, vol. v. p. 160.   [2] Ibid., vol. v. pp. 163-4.

touched a farthing. It will be 1805, before I touch the estate. Neither principal nor interest of seven thousand ounces have been paid ; and it is now eight thousand ounces debt." [1]

Subsequently Nelson writes to his steward :—

"I am so little versed in business, that I hardly know how to answer your letter. Ungrateful as the Brontese have behaved, yet the Prince . . . shall never, upon any consideration, be their master for an hour. In Sicily, I suppose, they have certain forms and customs as we have in England. The gentry may forget that I am master. I consider that we deal on the strictest honour, *our words are our bonds.* You may assure the Brontese that I shall never consent to anything which can oppress them. At this moment I can only think of the French Fleet." [2]

On the death of Lord Nelson, this estate, according to his intention, passed to his brother, the Rev. William Nelson, the first Earl, and on his death to his daughter, the first Viscountess Bridport. In 1845, the trustees of the present Earl Nelson, then a minor, contested this claim, on points of the Sicilian law of inheritance, but after argument, the claim of the Bridport family to the estate was maintained by the then Master of the Rolls, Lord Langdale, in whom the estate is now vested. The arguments in this most interesting case are too recondite to be even analysed in this volume, in which it is sufficient to state the result.

The following paper, contributed by the Hon. Alexander Nelson Hood, furnishes a complete description of the exertions made by his father in the improvement of the estate and its present satisfactory condition.

"The Duchy of Bronte is situated in the province of Catania, in Sicily, about thirty miles from the eastern coast, and the same distance from the northern coast of that island. It is of great extent, though not so large as when granted to Lord Nelson by Ferdinand IV. of Naples. It was then encumbered by vexatious claims on the part of the town-

---

[1] Despatches, vol. v. p. 253.
[2] To his steward some date in 1804 ; Clarke and McArthur, p. 30.

THE CASTELLO MANIACE, BRONTE.

ship of Bronte, to settle which a portion of the property had to be ceded as the price of peace. It contains vineyards, and arable lands which grow magnificent crops of wheat, and lava lands which produce the valuable pistachio nut, the olive, and the almond. Orange groves flourish in the more sheltered parts. Forests of oak and beech stretch away many miles on the sides of the mountains, which rise six thousand feet above sea-level, and from that altitude a magnificent panorama of Etna and its countless parasitic caves is obtained on the one hand, while on the other lies the blue Mediterranean, dotted with the isles of Lipari, which sparkle like jewels on its surface. The country is very beautiful, and a marvel of fertility. The climate is genial, though winter brings frost and snow.

" The 'Castello di Maniace' is the principal residence and seat of administration of the Duchy. It is built on the southern bank of that sometimes impetuous torrent, which, uniting with others, forms the ancient river Symœthus, now called Simeto. Distant some eight miles from the town of Bronte, and up the valley of the same name as the river, the Castello stands on a mass of lava rock which is washed on two sides by the stream above mentioned. To the north rise mountains well wooded, to the south is mighty Etna—a preponderating feature in the landscape—a giant itself, as it was formerly held to be the home of giants. The central crater of the volcano, nearly eleven thousand feet high, is distant sixteen miles, and the Castello stands on the further point of its north-western slope.

" There has been difference of opinion as to the origin of the 'Castello di Maniace.' It is incontestable that the designation of Castello or castle appertained to it in the remote past. The name of Maniace was given to the surrounding country in commemoration of a signal victory gained by the Byzantine general, George Maniaces, over the Saracens, about A.D. 1032, and it is probable that ' the first Swordbearer and Master of the Palace of Michael, Emperor of Constantinople,' as he was styled, constructed a fortified residence near the small town which also sprung up in the neighbourhood and took his name. This town has long since disappeared. There is no doubt, however, that a monastery was founded on this spot by Queen Margaret of Sicily, in 1173, and until 1693 it was inhabited by monks of various orders. Among the abbots were the brother of our own Pierre de Blois, Bishop of London, and Pope Alexander VI., the evil Borgia. The rights and privileges of this foundation, obtained by several Bulls from the popes, which documents are preserved, still appertain to the Duchy; and, in addition to other honours, Lord Nelson enjoyed that of Father Abbot of the Abbadia di Santa

Maria di Maniace, which dignity, with full ecclesiastical jurisdiction over the church and territory, has also descended to his successors.

"The present buildings are large and commodious. The church remains much the same as when it was built. The pointed Norman arches of the interior, and windows of the same period are architecturally interesting, as is also, and artistically, the beautiful door, with its marble and granite pillars, ornate capitals, and deep moulding. Immense granaries, wine cellars, and store-houses, with the monks' kitchen and cells, now turned to modern uses, surround two spacious courtyards.   On the first floor are the living rooms of the Castello, which combine the comfort of an English home, with the tasteful elegancies of a collection of majolica, old embroideries, and Etruscan and Roman pottery. A feature of this part of the building is the long corridor, in which hang prints of the exploits of the great Naval Hero.   The Muniment rooms contain many ancient documents, dating from the year A.D. 900, which are full of monkish lore and legal cunning. Among them is the hero's will, by which the Duchy was conveyed to his brother, Earl Nelson, the father of Charlotte Mary, Duchess of Bronte (Lady Bridport), and grandfather of the present Duke.

"The Castello stands alone, distant some four miles from the nearest village. At the corners are pierced turrets, which serve as a warning to marauding hands ; and in old days they have not been without use in restraining revolutionary bands from arson and pillage. Plantations and oliveyards surround the building, and a vineyard adjoins the old-fashioned gardens which lie beneath the windows. The larger vineyards, wine presses, and cellars are a mile down-stream. There in soil of great depth and fertility grow the vines which produce the wine called the 'Duchy of Bronte ;' which has now found its way to the English market.   All that science and skill can do to perfect the yield of the grape has been done, and pure wines, well matured, take their place on English dinner tables, and will doubtless rival the Marsalas and Madeiras, to the majority of which they are vastly superior.

"Life in this Duchy of Bronte is comparatively easy. Though a kind of feudal state is maintained, and campieri, or mounted guards, in uniforms of red and blue, with silver facings, the Bronte colours, protect the family when in Sicily, and the property on other occasions, there is much kindliness of feeling between employer and employed. Dependents pass a lifetime in the service of the Duchy ; and there died but recently one who had worked for nearly eighty years as dairyman on the property. The jealousy of a foreigner that might be expected on the part of the natives does not exist here. Trust and confidence in English integrity are manifested by tenants and servants alike ; and it is not unfrequently that the former leave their receipts for rent unasked for, as willingly as they accept the consignment of payments in kind without questioning the measure or the measurer. The people do not repose the same confidence in their fellow countrymen. It is difficult to give a correct idea of the character of Sicilians without dwelling too harshly on their shortcomings. The standard of morals must be put on a lower level than that which holds in more northern lands. Where redemption from slavery is but recent, a true conception of liberty is not to be expected. Liberated but yesterday from the thraldom of superstition as gross as can well be imagined, and from an ignorant priesthood, the people have yet to learn the value of veracity and straightforwardness. Cleanliness and morality may also be designated virtues which might be more thoroughly recognized in practice. But the people are hard-working and diligent ; and when their own interests are not too deeply involved, they are kindly disposed and affectionate. It is said that the natural sharpness of the inhabitants precludes even Jews from gaining a living at their expense, indeed, none of the latter race are to be found in the island.

"The economic state of the island is not good. Taxation is a burden well-nigh too grievous to be borne. Commercial failures, partly caused by bad times, partly by fraud and dishonest practices have shaken trade to its foundations. The gradual but steady disappearance of agricultural capital by the enforced division of property not only causes great misery, but swells the statistics of crime. Brigandage appears to be a thing of the past, but marauding parties still roam the country in the winter, and a fray resulting in the death of two persons recently occurred within a short distance of the town of Bronte. That town is composed of small houses in the principal thoroughfares, and of buildings little better than hovels in the poorer parts. The population is about sixteen thousand, of which seventy are priests. The streets are not clean, and though the town boasts a college capable of holding four hundred boys, a palazzo belonging to the Duchy of Bronte, and many churches, it produces a melancholy impression on the visitor, which the bright sun and blue sky do not entirely dispel.

"Since 1868, when the present Duke (General Viscount Bridport) succeeded, much has been done to improve the property. Many miles of road have been constructed, where formerly none existed ; and farm and other buildings have been erected. A vast cellar capable of storing many hundred butts of wine has been built.

Bridges now span torrents, which formerly to cross entailed risk of life to man and beast. Vineyards, and almond and orange groves have been made, and large plantations will soon give the much needed shade from the fierce glare of the summer sun. Steam machinery and saw-mills have been introduced into the forests. The superannuated dependents pass a peaceful old age with suitable pensions ; and the spiritual requirements of the neighbourhood are provided for by the weekly celebration of the mass in the old church built, as has before been said, by Queen Margaret." [1]

The control of the affairs of the Duchy, has for many years been in the hands of the Duke's third surviving son, Hon. Alexander Nelson Hood ; and it may be said, that by associating himself with the people and their aspirations, he has not been unmindful of the words of his great uncle, respecting King Ferdinand's gift which Nelson described as "worthy of a king." "I am determined on one thing," he wrote, "that the inhabitants shall be the happiest in all his Sicilian Majesty's dominions."

On the 22nd of October, 1802, Nelson, for the first time since his election to the peerage, took his seat in the House of Lords. In the strictest sense no party politician,[2] and anxious only for the honour of his King

[1] A most interesting report on Bronte and its wine, is given in the Report of Mr. Consul Stigand to the Foreign Office, on The Sicilian Vintage of 1890, from which some extracts will be found in the Appendix. Mrs. Lynn Linton's account of her visit to Bronte in *Bentley's Magazine* for February, 1884, with the curious legends of the locality, and that of Mr. Hamilton Aide's paper in the *English Illustrated Magazine* of June, 1890, with its clever illustrations, are well worth reading.

[2] About July, 1804, he thus expressed to General Villettes his opinion of "party men." I am of no party man : I hope and believe that any administration would ever act to the best of their judgment for the power and advantage of their country. I am not one of those who think that the State depends upon any *one* or upon one hundred men ; let them go off the stage and others would ably supply their places." And again, "The coalition of parties, the most opposite in principles, ought not to surprise us. Wyndham and Fox may again meet at Holkam, and Pitt join the party—such things are. Politicians are not like other men, and probably all other men would be politicians, if they had the sense."

and country, his name is not found in debate, save when
those interests and the claims of his comrades in every
class in the navy were being discussed.   Hence he gladly
took the opportunity of the vote of thanks to Sir James
Saumarez, on the 30th of October, for his brilliant action
with the combined fleet off Algesiraz in July, to enter into·
the details of the action, lauding the conduct and skill of
the commander, and complimenting Lords Hood and St.
Vincent as the formers of the school in which Sir James
had been educated.   Again, on the 12th of November he
spoke, on the vote of thanks to Lord Keith on the
successful landing in Egypt, giving his opinion on that
hazardous service, with his accustomed frankness.

The preliminaries for the peace of Amiens, by which
with the exception of the islands of Ceylon and Trinidad,
which we had taken from the allies of the French, we
surrendered all our conquests, Nelson defended in his
place in the Lords.   " Minorca he considered of little
value to us, and Malta of no consequence, but an object
of importance to rescue it from the French—estimating
its garrison at seven thousand, and expressing admiration
of the extent and convenience of its harbours.   The Cape
of Good Hope he looked on as a tavern on the road to
India, and therefore often acting as a delay to the voyage.
When the Dutch possessed it," he said, " we could buy a
cabbage there for twopence, now that it belonged to us
we had to pay a shilling."   It could only, in his idea, be
maintained at an enormous expense, and produced little
that made it worth our holding it.   It was, no doubt, in
Nelson's mind, sufficient that we had obtained the empire
of the seas ; he cared little for distant islands, the defence
of which only divided our forces.

In seconding the address in reply to the King's.
speech on November 23, 1802, Lord Nelson said
emphatically :—

"I, my Lords, have in different countries seen much of the miseries of war. I am, therefore, in my inmost soul, a man of peace. Yet I would not for the sake of any peace, however fortunate, consent to sacrifice one jot of England's honour. Our honour is inseparably combined with our genuine interest. Hitherto there has been nothing greater known on the Continent than the faith, the untainted honour, the generous public sympathies, the high diplomatic influence, the commerce, the grandeur, the resistless power, the unconquerable valour of the British nation. Wherever I have served in foreign countries, I have witnessed these to be the sentiments with which Britons are regarded. The advantages of such a reputation are not to be lightly brought into hazard. I, for one, rejoice that his Majesty has signified his intention to pay due regard to the connection between the interests of this country and the preservation of the liberties of Europe. It is satisfactory to know that the preparations to maintain our dignity in peace are not to be neglected. Those supplies which his Majesty shall for such purposes demand, his people will most earnestly grant. The nation is satisfied that the Government seeks in peace or war no interest separate from that of the people at large ; and as the nation was pleased with that sincere spirit of peace with which the late treaty was negotiated, so, now that a restless and unjust ambition in those with whom we desired sincere amity has given a new alarm, the country will rather prompt the Government to assert its honour, than need to be roused to such measures of vigorous defence as the exigency of the times may require." [1]

On November the 12th he spoke on the convention with Russia. He approved it, contending that it put an end to the principle, endeavoured to be enforced by the Armed Neutrality of 1780, and by the late combination of the Northern Powers, that *free ships make free goods*, a proposition he looked upon as monstrous in itself, and contrary to the law of nations, as well as injurious to the maritime rights of this country. The rashness and violence of the Emperor Paul, he considered, had formed the confederacy against us to support and enforce that proposition ; but the moderation and temper of his successor, Alexander, had consented to give it up and

[1] P. 275.

renounce it. He approved of the article restricting the right of search of ships under convoy of a neutral flag-ship of war to our navy, only during hostilities ; and stated what would have been his own conduct if he had met with such a convoy, declaring that he would have endeavoured to discharge his duty with all possible civility to the captain of the neutral frigate ; should have inspected his papers, and if, from the information of any seaman, he was led to entertain a suspicion that the papers were fraudulent or fabricated, and that the convoy did contain what was contraband or illicit, he would in that case have insisted on search, and if he found any contra-band articles on board, he should have detained such ship or ships.

In his speech at the Monmouth dinner, to the toast of his health, August 19, 1802, Nelson offered his advice to the officers of the navy :—

"It was my good fortune to have under my command some of the most experienced officers in the English Navy, whose professional skill was seconded by the undaunted courage of British sailors ; and whatever merit might attach to me, I must declare that I had only to show them the enemy, and victory crowned the standard. The British Navy has received a large portion of public applause ; but however well it deserves it, it should be told, that the same valour and sense of duty would have marked the British Army had it been placed in such situations as would have afforded it equal opportunity of displaying its national courage ; but it has happened that the same good fortune in this instance did not occur, or we should have had equal reason for praising its heroism and public service. When the English Army was sent to Egypt, it was the opinion of many intelligent characters that it would be destroyed. For my own part I never thought so ; for wherever British soldiers have been opposed to those of France, they have uniformly conquered them. In my own person I have received an overflowing measure of the nation's gratitude—far more than I either merited or expected ; because the same success would have crowned the efforts of any other British admiral, who had under his command such distinguished officers and such gallant crews. And here let me impress upon the mind of every officer in the service, that to whatever quarter of the globe he may be destined, whether in the East or West Indies, to Africa or America, the eyes of his country are upon him ; and so long as public men, in public stations, exert themselves in those situations, to fulfil the duty demanded from them by the public, they will always find the British nation ready to heap upon them the utmost extent of its gratitude and applause."[1]

Again in his speech on the Naval Inquiry Bill, Dec. 21, 1802, note his vigorous defence of our merchants :—

" My Lords, in the absence of my noble friend who is at the head of the Admiralty, I think it my duty to say a few words to your lordships in regard to a Bill of which the objects have an express reference to the interests of my profession as a seaman. It undoubtedly originates in the feeling of the Admiralty that they have not the power to remedy certain abuses which they perceive to be most injurious to the public service. Every man knows that there are such abuses ; and I hope there is none among us who would not do all that can be constitutionally effected to correct them. Yet, if I had heard of any objection of weight urged against the measure in the present Bill, I should have hesitated to do ought to promote its progress through the forms of this House. But I can recollect but one thing with which I have been struck as possibly exceptional in its tenour. It authorizes the Commissioners to call for and inspect the books of merchants who may have had any transactions of business with any of the Boards and prize-agents, into whose conduct they are to inquire. But the credit of a British merchant is the support of the commerce of the world ; his books are not lightly, nor for any ordinary purpose, to be taken out of his hands ; the secrets of his business are not to be too curiously pryed into. The books of a single merchant may betray the secrets, not only of his own affairs, but of those with whom he is principally connected in business, and the reciprocal confidence of the whole commercial world may, by the authoritative inquiry of these Commissioners, be shaken. All this, at least, I should have feared as liable to happen, if the persons named in the Bill had not been men whose characters are above all suspicion of indiscretion or malice. I may presume it to be the conviction of the merchants, that in such hands they will be safe ; since they have

---

[1] *Naval Chronicle*, vol. xx. p. 110.

made no opposition to the Bill in its former progress, and since they have offered no appearance against it by counsel, at your lordships' bar ; and truly, my Lords, if the Bill be thus superior to all objections, I can affirm that the necessities of the case, the wrongs of those who are employed in the naval service of their country, most loudly call for the redress that it proposes. From the highest admiral in the service to the lowest cabin-boy that walks the street, there is not a man but may be in distress, with large sums of wages due to him, of which he shall by no diligence of request be able to obtain payment : there is not a man whose entreaties will be answered with aught but insults, at the proper places of his application, if he come not with particular recommendations to a preference. From the highest admiral to the meanest seaman, whatever the sums or prize-money due to him, he may scarcely call any part his own. A man may have £40,000 due to him in prize-money, and yet be dismissed without a shilling, if he ask for it at the proper office, without particular recommendation. Are these things to be tolerated ? Is it not for the interest—is it not for the honour of the country, that they should be as speedily as possible redressed ? I should be as unwilling as any man to give an over-weening preference to the interests of my own profession; but I cannot help thinking, that under all the circumstances of the affair, your lordships will be strongly disposed to advance this Bill into law as speedily as may be consistent with order of your proceedings, and with due prudence of deliberation.' His lordship also on the third reading of the Bill, on the following day, expressed his desire that the necessary inquiries into the flagrant abuses by prize-agents might be made the subject of a separate Act ; observing, at the same time, that there might be instances in which the delay of payment resulted from unavoidable accidents."[1]

A few days before Lord Nelson left England in 1805, he expressed to his solicitor, Mr. Hazlewood, his anxiety about his proxy, which he had entrusted to Lord Moira, who he feared, although a man of too much honour to abuse so sacred a confidence, might have his judgment clouded by partiality, or he might become attached to a party. Next day Nelson told Mr. Hazlewood, who had left him at Mr. Pitt's door :—

---

[1] Clarke and McArthur vol. ii. 458.

"I was so full of the subject we were speaking of yesterday, as to continue it in my interview with Mr. Pitt. I told him I had not been bred in courts, and could not pretend to a nice discrimination between the use and abuse of parties, and, therefore, I must not be expected to range myself under the political banners of any man, in place or out of place : that England's welfare was the object of my pursuit ; and where the tendency of any measure to promote or defeat that object seemed clear, I should vote accordingly, without regard to other circumstances : that in matters where my judgment wavered, or to the full scope of which I might feel unequal, I should be silent; as I could not reconcile to my mind giving a vote without full conviction of its propriety."

Pitt listened patiently, and said, " he wished every officer held the same sentiments." [1]

The course of his lawsuit with Lord St. Vincent, for his share of prize-money, during the brief period that he was left as commander-in-chief in the Mediterranean, was a sore subject with Nelson. To his faithful agent, Davison, he wrote on April 15, 1801 : "I send home the lawyer's opinion. Justice is all I want. My commanders-in-chief run away with all the money I fight for : so let them. I am content with the honour ; of these they cannot get a scrap. But —— me if I suffer any man to swindle me out of my property, whilst he is at ease in England." And again, two days afterwards, he wrote : "*Elephant*, April 17, 1801. I think that we shall fire no more, though the Swedish Fleet was at sea on the 14th. I shall be in England in May, for both my health and affairs absolutely require it." [2]

Again, he wrote to Davison, on the 22nd of the same month :—

"*April* 22, 1801.

"My dear Davison,—I know my health requires it, and my affairs, particularly my lawsuit, require that I should be in England before the 25th of May. I intend to be in court when it is tried, and can and will remind the jury, if I am allowed to open my mouth, that I

---

[1] Despatches, vol. v. p. 371, note.   [2] Ibid., vol. vii., appendix ccvi.

have full as much claim to their consideration as Lord St. Vincent, and my truth brought home to their minds will, I doubt not, have as much weight as Mr. Erskine's eloquence. You may say to Nepean, Troubridge, and even the great earl, that I must be in England for my *health*, and to take care of *my private affairs*. I could say much, but I reserve myself till we can breakfast together at seven o'clock. I get now to breakfast at half-past five. In fact, I cannot rest; for neither body nor mind is happy, but for your ever affectionate friend,

"NELSON AND BRONTE." [1]

Lord St. Vincent having despatched a frigate on a cruize in which she made a prize, afterwards, by Admiralty permission, left the Mediterranean command, and had arrived in England before the capture; but he still retained the pay, title, and table money of Commander-in-chief, and as such made official appointments and promotions, and did not resign his commission till after the prize was taken. When he quitted the Mediterranean, the command devolved upon Lord Keith; and upon Lord Keith's departure to the Channel Fleet, upon Lord Nelson, who was the senior officer in the Mediterranean, when the captor, a frigate belonging to his station, took her prize. Lord Keith, though at the moment of the capture actually serving in the Channel Fleet, memorialized the King in Council to share prize-money with Lord Nelson. Upon which Lord St. Vincent, and the other Mediterranean flag-officers had no alternative but to present separate counter memorials. To all of them the reply was, "This is a subject for the decision of a court of law"; and thus an amicable suit being unavoidable, Lord St. Vincent found himself driven into a proceeding at law, against the very man, of all others in the world, with whom he would have most avoided the mere appearance of a dispute. But his lordship's legal adviser's opinion was, that it was a very doubtful point

[1] Despatches vii. Add. ccvi.

(and so it afterwards proved), and an important one, which ought to be settled for the service ; and the King in Council having pointed out the course, if his lordship did not pursue it, it would have been said that he had abandoned the service from apprehension of the expense of the suit.   Proceedings therefore being thus instituted, Lord St. Vincent commanded his solicitor to afford every possible assistance to Lord Nelson and to his legal advisers, and to pay every farthing of Nelson's expenses, howsoever incurred, if the decision were in Lord St. Vincent's favour.   At the first trial a special verdict was found ; on the argument of it, so refined was the point of law, that the Court of Common Pleas was equally divided.   At the prayer of Lord Nelson's counsel, one of the judges in his favour withdrew his opinion ; and the judgment, which thereby followed, was removed to a higher court, where it was reversed.   In giving the opinion of the court Lord Ellenborough said : " The moment a superior officer left his station the right of the next flag-officer commenced, and consequently Lord St. Vincent having returned to England, the enterprise and conduct of the fleet devolved on Lord Nelson, who thereby becomes entitled to the whole of the admiral's share of prize-money." [1]

How little Nelson was justified in his complaint is shown in the following letter of Lord St. Vincent :—

" To ALEXANDER DAVISON.

" *Ville Paris*, OFF USHANT, *June* 19, 1800.

"SIR,—Surely my excellent friend Lord Nelson could not have been informed of the conduct which I directed Mr. Tucker to observe in all his proceedings with you and Mr. Booth, or he never would have written the letter, a copy of which you enclosed to me. From the commencement of the transaction I doubted my claim, and

---

[1] Tucker, vol. ii. pp. 68–9, note.

was actuated entirely by the judgment of other men, not lawyers, who were by no means unfriendly to Lord Nelson : although what passed between you, Mr. Booth, and Mr. Tucker, must be fresh in your memory. At my desire, the latter has collected all the material points, which are enclosed, and I have only to add, that I would forfeit all I am worth rather than have a dispute with Lord Nelson : at the same time there is something due to the profession we are both in." [1]

------

[1] Tucker, vol. ii. pp. 68–9.

PERSONAL III.: NELSON AT HOME AND ABROAD.

CHAPTER XIX.

PERSONAL III.: NELSON AT HOME AND ABROAD.

(1801 to 1805.)

Nelson's private life at home and abroad—The rupture with his wife—
 Hazlewood's account—Mrs. St. George's account of Nelson and the
 Hamiltons at Dresden—Mr. Matcham's account of Nelson's life at
 Merton—His adopted child Horatia—Lady Hamilton and the ninth
 codicil.

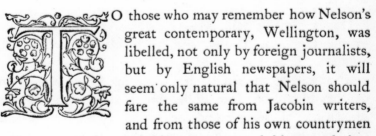

O those who may remember how Nelson's
great contemporary, Wellington, was
libelled, not only by foreign journalists,
but by English newspapers, it will
seem only natural that Nelson should
fare the same from Jacobin writers,
and from those of his own countrymen
who were envious of his successes and his popularity.
Whilst at Naples and Palermo the first of this class
of writers declared that so outraged were the feelings
of Sir W. Hamilton by Nelson's behaviour to his wife,
that he had challenged and fought him—that his immorality was obvious, and that the whole party gambled.
Believing as I do, after the most careful consideration
of all the reliable evidence available that, as his chaplain
Dr. Scott, and his most intimate friends held, there was
no criminality in his friendship—that as Lord St. Vincent
used to call them "they were a pair of sentimental fools"
—I pass by these Jacobin stories. In his continued absence
from England after the day of the Victory of the Nile,
it is not surprising that Lady Nelson began to believe
in them, and that on his return home the exaggerated

attention which he showed to Lady Hamilton, brought about the unfortunate rupture, as related by Mr. Hazlewood.[1] Had there been real ground for the accusation, it is impossible to believe that his sisters and their families would have been his frequent visitors at Merton, and that after his death they would have treated Lady Hamilton with such respect and kindness as we know that they did. As for the charge of being a gambler, Miss Cornelia Knight supplies an anecdote.

"Lord Nelson says that when he was seventeen years of age, he won £300 at a gaming table ; that he was so shocked on reflecting that, had he lost them, he should not have known how to pay them, and that from that time he never played again."[2]

Oh, it may be said, Miss Knight was practically one of the Hamilton family, and her evidence is therefore tainted.   True it was, that on her death-bed her excellent mother had recommended her daughter to the protection of the Hamiltons, no slight proof that with all her knowledge of society and her strict views, she would not have done so had she believed the stories about Lady Hamilton and Nelson.

In a letter from Mr. Hazlewood to Sir H. Nicolas, we have the history of the rupture :—

"KEMP TOWN, BRIGHTON, *April* 13, 1846.

"DEAR SIR,—I was no less surprised than grieved when you told me of a prevailing opinion, that Lord Nelson of his own motion withdrew from the society of his wife, and took up his residence together with Sir William and Lady Hamilton, and that you never received from any member of the family an intimation to the contrary. His father, his brother Dr. Nelson (afterwards Earl Nelson), his sisters,

---

[1] The growing jealousy of Lady Nelson may be traced in Davison's letter to Nelson, December 7, 1798 (Despatches, vol. iii. p. 138) in which he writes that she had just told him that unless Nelson "returned home in a few months, she would come out and join the standard, at Naples—excuse a woman's tender feelings ; they are too acute to be expressed."

[2] "Journals of Miss Cornelia Knight," vol. ii. p. 286.

Mrs. Bolton and Mrs. Matcham, and their husbands, well knew that the separation was unavoidable on Lord Nelson's part; and as I happened to be present when the unhappy rupture took place, I have often talked over with all of them, but more especially with Mr. and Mrs. Matcham, the particulars which I proceed to relate, in justice to the memory of my illustrious friend, and in the hope of removing an erroneous impression from your mind.

"In the winter of 1800–1801, I was breakfasting with Lord and Lady Nelson at their lodgings in Arlington Street, and a cheerful conversation was passing on indifferent subjects, when Lord Nelson spoke of something which had been done or said by 'dear Lady Hamilton,' upon which Lady Nelson rose from her chair, and exclaimed with much vehemence, 'I am sick of hearing of dear Lady Hamilton, and am resolved that you shall give up either her or me.' Lord Nelson, with perfect calmness, said, 'Take care, Fanny, what you say. I love you sincerely; but I cannot forget my obligations to Lady Hamilton, and speak of her otherwise than with affection and admiration.' Without one soothing word or gesture, but muttering something about her mind being made up, Lady Nelson left the room, and shortly after drove from the house. They never lived together afterwards. I believe that Lord Nelson took a formal leave of Lady Nelson before joining the Fleet under Sir Hyde Parker, but to the day of his glorious death, she never made any apology for her abrupt and ungentle conduct above related, or any overture towards a reconciliation.

"I am, dear Sir, your faithful servant,
"W. HAZLEWOOD."[1]

Shortly after this ill-fated interview, Nelson with his brother William—the Canon of Canterbury—travelled to Southampton, from whence he wrote this, his last letter to Lady Nelson :—

"SOUTHAMPTON, *Jan.* 13, 1801.
"MY DEAR FANNY,—We are arrived and heartily tired; and with kindest regards to my father and all the family, believe me, your affectionate   "NELSON."

On quitting his wife, Nelson emphatically said, "I call God to witness, there is nothing in you or your conduct

[1] Despatches, vol. vii. pp. 391–2.

I wish otherwise " ; and with his accustomed liberality he apportioned to her £1,800 a year out of his by no means large income.[1]

In justice to this lady, I insert here a sketch of her character by a personal friend : —

" I will only say on this sad subject, that Lord Nelson always bore testimony to the merits of Lady Nelson, and declared in parting from her, that he had not one single complaint to make—that in temper, person, and mind, she was everything he could wish. They never had a quarrel ; but the syren had sung, and cast her spell about him, and he was too guileless in his nature, and too unsuspecting, to be aware of his danger until it was too late. I am aware of your intention not to touch upon this delicate subject, and only allude to it in order to assure you, from my personal knowledge, in a long and intimate acquaintance, that Lady Nelson's conduct was not only affectionate, wise, and prudent, but admirable throughout her married life, and that she had not a single reproach to make herself. The affections of her lord were alienated, not when they were together, but at a distance, and beyond the reach of her mild and feminine virtues.

" I say not this to cast unnecessary blame on *one* whose memory I delight to honour, but only in justice to that truly good and amiable woman, the residue of whose life was rendered so unhappy by circumstances over which she had no control. If mildness, forbearance, and indulgence to the weaknesses of human nature could have availed her, her fate would have been very different. No reproach ever passed her lips ; and when she parted from her lord, on his hoisting his flag again, it was without the most distant suspicion that he meant it to be final, and that in this life they were never more to meet again. Excuse my troubling you with these observations, as I am desirous that you should know the worth of her who has often been misrepresented, from the wish of many to cast the blame anywhere but on him who was so deservedly dear to the nation. There never was a kinder heart than Lord Nelson's ; but he was in the hands of a very designing person, and few could have resisted the various artifices employed to enslave the mind of the Hero, when combined with

---

[1] Despatches, vol. iv. p. 279.

great beauty, extraordinary talents, and the semblance of an enthusiastic attachment."[1]

It is probable that the Palermitan tales, which had
begun to be disbelieved when Nelson in person visited
Germany on his way home, would have died away, but
for the presence there of a young widow of an Irish
Colonel on a visit in 1800 to Mr. Elliot, our Resident
Minister at Dresden.   This lady left a voluminous journal
of her travels on the Continent, and happening to marry
a relation of Dr. Trench, the late Archbishop of Dublin,
in the year 1846, he, then Dean of Westminster, had them
published, with all her caricatures of Nelson and the
Hamiltons at Dresden, drawn chiefly from the gossip of
the English Minister, who had evidently taken a strong
prejudice against the Hero, and his travelling companions.   "It may be noted," writes the able critic of
Nelson's despatches, to whom I have before referred, "that
Mrs. St. George did not see the inebriate and boorish
behaviour, which she records against Nelson.   The strong
probability is that she was never really told what she has
set down.   Mr. Elliot may have told her something
which, passing through her prejudice, took the form in
which it appeared in her journal."   Happily it met with
the following reply from a great-nephew of the Hero,
who could speak truthfully about Nelson and his friend's
life.

After excusing his interference on the score of the natural
prejudice he must feel as a relative against the extracts from
Mrs. St. George's journal,[2] relative to the Hamiltons and
Nelson, published in the *Times* in 1861, Mr. Matcham
contrasts the real character and habits of Sir William

---

[1] Note in Despatches, vol. ii. p. 353.   Lady Nelson died, *æt.* 68, May
4, 1831.

[2] From a copy in pamphlet form, published by J. Ridgway, Piccadilly,
1861, lent to me by Earl Nelson.

Hamilton, as known to his contemporaries, with the caricature which the journalist had given, on the authority of Mr. Elliot. Except as bearing on the old adage, *Noscitor a sociis*, this portion of the reply does come within the scope of this volume, and the writer himself " refers to them only to show the inaccuracy, or at least, the false colouring of this recital with regard to Lord Nelson.[1]

"I too, Sir," continues Mr. Matcham, " as well as 'the Lady,' had some knowledge of that person, so much honoured and so much maligned; and although I do not defend his one great error (though in that, with some palliation, there were united elements of a generous and noble nature), I venture to say that whoever forms a notion of his manners and deportment in private life from this account of him, will labour under a very great delusion.

"I visited my uncle twice during the short periods in which he was on shore—once in 1802, during his journey to Wales, when he was received at Oxford and other places; and the second time at his house at Merton, in 1805, for three weeks preceding the 15th of September, when he left to embark at Portsmouth to return no more; and I can assert with truth that a more complete contrast between this lady's portrait and my thorough recollection of him could not be forced on my mind. Lord Nelson in private life was remarkable for a demeanour quiet, sedate, and unobtrusive, anxious to give pleasure to every one about him, distinguishing each in turn by some act of kindness, and chiefly those who seemed to require it most.

"During his few intervals of leisure, in a little knot of relations and friends, he delighted in quiet conversation, through which occasionally ran an undercurrent of pleasantry, not unmixed with caustic wit. At his table he was the least heard among the company, and so far from

---

[1] Mrs. St. George, on the authority of Mr. Elliot, gives a graphic description of a drunken bout of the Hamiltons and Nelson, after she herself had left the party, which ended with Sir William, as she describes him, "hopping round the room on his backbone." As to the saying of Nelson when told that the Elector would not receive Lady Hamilton at his court—that "if there was any difficulty on her being received, Lady Hamilton would knock the Elector down," the writer says, "If a passing pleasantry or jocular expression is converted into a serious threat, there is an end to all true delineation of character." That these words were uttered, rest on the veracity of Mr. Elliot. (Diary, Oct. 7).

being the hero of his own tale, I never heard him voluntarily refer to any of the great actions of his life.

"I have known him lauded by the great and wise; but he seemed to me to waive the homage with as little attention as was consistent with civility. Nevertheless, a mind like his was necessarily won by attention from those who could best estimate his value.

"On his return from his last interview with Mr. Pitt, being asked in what manner he had been received, he replied that he had reason to be gratified with his reception, and concluded with animation, 'Mr. Pitt, when I rose to go, left the room with me, and attended me to the carriage'—a spontaneous mark of respect and admiration from the great statesman, of which, indeed, he might be well proud.

"It would have formed an amusement to the circle at Merton, if intemperance were set down to the master of the house, who always so prematurely cut short the *sederunt* of the gentlemen after dinner.

"A man of more temperate habits could not, I am persuaded, have been found. It appears that the person of Lord Nelson (although he was not as described, a little man, but of the middle height and of a frame adapted to activity and exertion) did not find favour with the lady; and I presume not to dispute her taste, but in his plain suit of black, in which he alone recurs to my memory, he always looked what he was—a gentleman. Whatever expletives of an objectionable kind may be ascribed to him, I feel persuaded that such rarely entered into his conversation. He was, it is true, a sailor, and one of a warm and generous disposition; yet I can safely affirm that I never heard a coarse expression issue from his lips, nor do I recollect one word or action of his to which even a disciple of Chesterfield could reasonably object. If such did arise, it would be drawn forth when a friend was attacked, or even an enemy unjustly accused; for his disposition was so truly noble, that it revolted against all wrong and oppression. His heart, indeed, was as tender as it was courageous. Nor do I think, Sir, that it is a necessary concession to truth that you or others should lower your conception of this popular personage, on account of the exaggerated colours in which he is here drawn. Those who best knew the man the most estimated his value, and many who like myself could not appreciate his professional superiority, would yet bear witness to his gentleness, kindness, good-breeding, and courtesy.

"He was not 'a rude and boisterous captain of the sea.' From his early years, by the introduction of his uncle, the Comptroller of the Navy, he was associated with the *élite* of his own profession; and the influences of his own paternal home, and his acquaintance with the first families of his native country, to many of whom he was related, would not allow a man of his intelligence and proper pride to foster coarseness beyond the habits of his age.

" It appears to me that, however flattering or consolatory the recital of the follies or foibles of great men may be to that mediocrity which forms the mass of mankind, the person who undertakes to cater for mere amusement withdraws something from the common stock of his country. The glory of Great Britain depends as much on the heroes she has produced, as on her wealth, her influence, and her possessions ; and the true patriot and honourable man, if he cannot add to their lustre, will at least refrain from any premeditated act which may dim their fame, and diminish that high estimation of them which expedience, nationality, and gratitude, should alike contribute to sustain.

" A NEPHEW OF ADMIRAL LORD NELSON." [1]

The parentage of Nelson's adopted child, Horatia, has been a fertile topic of dispute between many of the biographers of Nelson, so far as her mother was concerned, they all agreeing only in one point, that she was a daughter of Nelson. The child was born sometime in January, 1801, brought to Nelson's house in London by a Mrs. Gibson (who seems to have been the confidential nurse of some at least of Lady Hamilton's illegitimate offspring), and baptized in 1803 in the name of Horatia Nelson Thompson. In the previous October, if the keen eye of the widow St. George can be trusted, Lady Hamilton had no appearance of being about to be a mother. She also at that time " repeated her attitudes, danced the Tarantella, and went through a great deal more of exertion than a woman in her supposed condition would be likely to undertake." Lady Hamilton denied the parentage ; Sir H. Nicolas is certain she was not the mother ; Dr. Pettigrew equally certain that she was, in which Mr. Jeffreson agrees. How about the paternity? Lord Nelson always called her and generally wrote to her as his adopted child.

It is said that was only the society way of desig-

[1] November 6, 1861.

nating illegitimate offspring. But it must be borne in mind that Nelson was never guilty, throughout his adventurous life, of either acting or speaking a lie, and even if he would have descended to a falsehood to strangers, can it be believed that he would have written the following letter to his niece Charlotte, afterwards Lady Bridport, at the time when she was staying with Lady Hamilton at Merton with the child :—

"MY DEAR CHARLOTTE,—I thank you for your kind letters of January 3rd and 4th, and I feel truly sensible of your kind regard for that dear little *orphan*, Horatia. Although *her parents are lost*, she is not without a fortune, and I shall cherish her to the last moment of her life, and curse them that curse her, and heaven bless them who bless her. Dear innocent ! she can have injured no one. I am glad to hear that she is attached to you, and, if she takes after her parents, she will love those who are kind to her. I am ever, dear Charlotte, your affectionate uncle,

"NELSON AND BRONTE." [1]

The statement to his niece Charlotte that Horatia is "an orphan," and that "her parents are both lost," if Nelson is to be believed in so solemn a matter, puts an end to the supposed parentage,[2] whilst the deep interest which he felt in the child suggests the possibility that her mother having been that one of Lady Hamilton's earlier children who died, it is generally understood, soon after Horatia's birth, and from whom there is a most piteous letter to Mrs. Gibson, in the Morrison MSS., begging to be told who her mother was. If, as is probable, this poor woman was in Naples or Sicily with Lady Hamilton, her

[1] Despatches, vol. v. p. 586.
[2] It is true that in his letters to the child Nelson addresses her as "My dear child," and signs himself "Your affectionate father," terms only natural in addressing an adopted child. But it must also be borne in mind that in his last most solemn act, when on the eve of his death—a fate of which it is evident he had the most firm presentiment, she is spoken of as his "adopted child."

betrayer might be wen described as of high rank, and
the theory would fit in with Mr. Hazlewood's statement
in the following letter to Mrs. Ward in 1846.

Writing in November, 1874, to Mr. Paget, Mrs.
Ward (Horatia) says, " This is a copy of a letter I had
from Mr. Hazlewood ; Dr. Scott's account was the
same " [1] :—

" BRIGHTON, Sept. 26, 1846.

"MY DEAR MADAM,—I dare not write so fully as I could wish on
the topics referred to in your kind letter of the 23rd, lest the secret
which I am bound to keep should be rendered too transparent. Thus
much only may be said without incurring much risk. *Your mother
was well acquainted with Lady Hamilton, and saw you often during your
infancy, but soon after her marriage she went to reside a considerable distance from London, which or* (sic) *never visited afterwards.*

"Lamenting that I cannot be more communicative, I remain
always, my dear madam, fathfully yours,

" WM. HAZLEWOOD." [2]

The claims of Lady Hamilton on the gratitude and
liberality of the country, so earnestly put forward by
Nelson in the last codicil to his will have been a subject
of bitter controversy. By her friends Nelson's brother is
accused of having withheld the document itself from Lady
Hamilton until Parliament had secured to him and his
family its liberal provision, and then only to have thrown
it across to her at an interview, with the expression, " Do
what you like with this." By the same writers no terms
are too severe in condemnation of the meanness of the
Ministry in not responding to the last wishes of the Hero,
and leaving Lady Hamilton to die in poverty abroad, and
be buried at the cost of almost strangers.

If the information given by one of the latest con-

---

[1] On the 6th of March, 1881, at Beaufort Villa, Woodridings, Pinner,
Mrs. Horatia Nelson Ward, widow of the late Rev. Philip Ward, vicar
of Tenterden, Kent, in her 81st year. On her grave, in the cemetery,
Pinner, is the inscription, " The adopted daughter of Vice-Admiral Lord
Nelson." [2] J. Paget, *Blackwood*, May, 1888.

tributors to Nelsonian Literature is trustworthy, the earl, as soon as he received the document from Captain Hardy, took it with him to Sir W. Scott (the future Lord Stowell), at Doctors Commons, and was advised by him that, as it spoke freely of the exertions of the Queen of Naples in support of the British Fleet, it should not be published, and that as it did not deal with Lord Nelson's estate it need not be proved by Nelson's executor. The earl, therefore, left the paper with Sir William from the 23rd of December, 1805, to the 15th of February, 1806, and then took it to Lord Grenville and read it to him.[1]

There was really no secret about the codicil; it was well known to Mr. Rose, Lady Hamilton's friend, to Hardy, and Dr. Scott. That the claim was not recognized by the Government was due in all probability to two reasons. None knew better than the Ministry how far the claims were founded in fact, and how far due to the fertile invention of the lady herself—our reasons for throwing grave doubts on both claims have been previously given. Again, they could not be ignorant of the ample provision which Sir William and Lord Nelson had made for the lady. The following is what they had done :—

" Lady Hamilton's Income.

Sir William's legacy of £600...	...	...	...	£40
Charge on his Welsh estates ...	...	...	...	800
Nelson's legacy of £2,000 ...	...	...	...	100
Nelson's annuity on Bronte ...	...	...	...	500
Interest on the £4,000 for Horatia ...	...	...	200
Merton Place and land could be let for £200		...	200

£2,140

" Pictures, plate, and furniture at 23, Piccadilly, worth about £5,000."

_____

[1] "Lady Hamilton and Lord Nelson," vol. ii. pp. 292-3. Mr. Jeffreson has called my attention to a curious fact, that this statement

It must be admitted that with such an income she was no urgent claimant on the country's bounty. By her sheer extravagance everything that could be was anticipated, and after some miserable years in England she was enabled by the aid of a friend to escape to Calais, where she died January 15, 1815.

The story of her state of semi-starvation, as told by a Mrs. Hunter, is denied by Horatia, who lived with her. "On her arrival in Calais," writes Horatia, "she had apartments at Quillac's Hotel; then moved to a house two miles from the town, and in consequence of a dispute with the landlord left after one night and took lodgings in a neighbouring farmhouse, and after some months removed to a house of Mons. Damas in Calais, where she died. Although often certainly under distressing circumstances, she never experienced actual want or received any assistance from any one of the kind which Mrs. Hunter imagined she afforded." She was buried in a coffin, followed by the captains of the vessels in the harbour. The service was performed by a Roman Catholic priest, who attended her in her last illness, as ever since she had been in Calais she had been a professed Roman Catholic.

Again, a few days after, Horatia wrote :—

"She was not in such pecuniary difficulties until a few weeks of her death. I then, knowing the state of her finances, wrote to Earl Nelson (trustee for my money) requesting him to advance me a sum from my dividends for the necessities of the household. Therefore, I can pronounce Mrs. Hunter's tale utterly fabulous." [1]

Of the nature of Nelson's attachment to Lady

follows closely, in the second volume of Pettigrew's life, on the previous one so seriously reflecting on the Earl.

[1] Letters of Mrs. H. Nelson Ward to Mr. John Paget, *Blackwood's Magazine*, May, 1888, written soon after the publication of Mr. Paget's articles, in his volume of Paradoxes and Puzzles, 1874. Mr. Clark Russell has adopted Mrs. Hunter's story, in ignorance of these letters.

Hamilton, Professor Laughton says, with great truth, "Those speak most positively who have least examined it." That her kindness to him during his illnesses in Naples, her extraordinary beauty, and her great though untutored abilities, worked a commanding influence over Nelson's sensitive temper, cannot be doubted. But that they were more than merely "a pair of sentimental fools," as Lord St. Vincent called them, and that as Dr. Scott and Nelson's most intimate friends believed, and there was nothing criminal between them may reasonably be held.

Surely the charge of criminal immorality is utterly inconsistent with the religious feelings which Nelson showed on every occasion of his hazardous life—that firm dependence on his God before the battle, his heartfelt thanks to Him when he had survived the hazard of the fight—the example which he set to his comrades of immediately offering public prayer to the Almighty for the victory :—

"He was," said Dr. Scott, "a thorough clergyman's son. I should think he never went to bed or got up without kneeling down to say his prayers. He was firmly attached to the Established Church in which he had been educated, and he proved the sincerity of this by the regularity and respect with which he always had Divine service performed on board the *Victory* whenever weather permitted. After the service he had generally a few words with the chaplain on the subject of the sermon, either thanking him for its being a good one, or remarking it was not so well adapted as usual to the crew—the admiral always being anxious that the discourse should be sufficiently plain for the men, and his chaplain, with the liability of a scholar, being sometimes tempted into a too learned disquisition. More than once on such occasions has Lord Nelson taken down a volume of sermons in his own cabin, with the page already marked at some discourse which he thought well suited to such a congregation, and requested Dr. Scott to preach it on the following Sunday." [1]

I take the liberty of concluding this chapter of Nelson's

[1] "Life of the Rev. Dr. Scott," pp. 191–2.

private life with the following noble defence by his latest
biographer from the popular charge of an early and lasting
criminal intrigue between Nelson and the lady :—

"Forgetting for the moment that these two men (Sir W. Hamilton
and Lord Nelson) were cordially sympathetic and strongly attached
friends, that Nelson held to old-world sentiments of honour, and that
he was averse to ordinary libertinism, the biographers who insist that
he threw himself precipitately into a vicious *liaison* with Lady
Hamilton, and was infatuated with his love of her from September,
1798, or even from September, 1793, overlook also that he was an
earnestly religious man, thinking of the Deity very much as the
seventeenth-century Puritans thought of the Creator and Ruler of the
Universe.   Though in moments of excitement he used to rattle forth
an idle storm of oaths in sailor-like fashion, Nelson was at every stage
of his career a devout and prayerful man.   The courage which
Buonaparte drew from fate and his star came to Nelson from a
simple and unwavering belief in the omnipresence of the ever-
watchful God Almighty, who, using His creatures for wise and
merciful ends, punished them for their misdeeds, and regarded them
favourably in proportion to their righteousness.   On the eve of a
battle he used to fall on his knees and entreat God to guard him
in coming perils, and give him the victory.   If he came unscathed
out of the fray, he attributed the escape to the beneficence of a
personal God, who, with an omnipotent right hand, had changed the
course of the deadly missiles or kept him out of the way.   When his
ship was shattered, and his fleet driven to confusion by the wide-
sweeping hurricane, he regarded the storm as the rod with which the
Almighty had chastised his indolence.   He had no sooner fought the
glorious fight of Aboukir than he called upon his sea-mates to join him
in returning thanks to God, who had given them the victory.   Was
a man of this sort likely to violate his most solemn notions of right on
the first temptation to error, and to join lightly in a guilty league with
his friend's wife, because she smiled upon him and proclaimed him
her supreme hero ? "[1]

---

[1] "Lady Hamilton and Lord Nelson" (Jeffreson), vol. ii. p. 160.

CONCLUSION.

CHAPTER XX.

CONCLUSION.

(1805 to 1806.)

Nelson's funeral—·Letters and speeches of the Duke of Clarence and others—Effect of Nelson's death on Pitt—Lord Malmesbury's record of the general sorrow—Rewards by the Crown and Parliament—Purchase of the estate of Trafalgar—Memorials and monuments—Nelson's will and codicils—Poetical tributes, Canning and Lord Carlisle—The Queen's visit to the *Victory*—The bust of Nelson in the armoury at Windsor—Lady Castlereagh's letter to her son.

N the 5th of November, 1805, the *Pickle* schooner arrived at Spithead from the fleet, and the news of Trafalgar began to spread about the country. Early on the following morning an extraordinary *Gazette* announced the gain and the irreparable loss. It is no fiction to record so universal was the sorrow for the death of Nelson, that the victory, great as it was, was almost forgotten in the grief for the loss sustained by England of her own hero. "England did mourn," as Collingwood had written, for there was nothing left like him. From Royalty to the poorest subject condolence preceded congratulation, and the victory was deemed too dearly purchased by the death of Nelson. When the King, on the receipt of Collingwood's despatch, realized the truth of the rumour that Nelson had fallen in the hour of victory, he was so deeply affected that some time passed ere he could speak. When the Queen read the despatch to the Princesses, the whole

Royal group burst into tears.   When the despatch was read by all classes the tear stood in many an eye, and all devoured it in silence.   Its effect on Pitt and the English public is thus related by Lord Malmesbury :—

"On the receipt of the news of the memorable battle of Trafalgar (some day in November, 1805)," writes Lord Malmesbury, "I happened to dine with Pitt, and it was naturally the engrossing subject of our conversation.   I shall never forget the eloquent manner in which he described his conflicting feelings when roused in the night to read Collingwood's despatches.   Pitt observed that he had been called up at various hours in his eventful life by the arrival of news of various hues, but that, whether good or bad, he could always lay his head on his pillow and sink into a sound sleep again.   On this occasion, however, the great event announced brought with it so much to weep over, as well as to rejoice at, that he could not calm his thoughts, but at length got up, though it was three in the morning." [1]

Of the effect of the sad news on the public the same diarist furnishes the following graphic and affecting record :—

"The first impression was not joy, for Nelson fell !   The Hero, who was regretted with all the tenderness of gratitude, and all the more selfish feeling that the bulwark of England was gone, and this circumstance would be equivalent to Buonaparte for the loss of his fleet.   He added to genius, valour, and energy, the singular power of electrifying all within his atmosphere, and making them only minor constellations to this most luminous planet.   The confidence he inspired in his followers, and the terror of his name to our enemies, are what make his loss an irreparable one.   Others may be great in many points : nay, admit that another, like himself, might appear again amongst the disciples he has formed, there would yet be wanting all he had done, and all the circumstances of the times in which he did these wondrous deeds.   Every victory was greater than the last. Every additional difficulty seemed only to bring out some new proof of the combination and powers of his mind as well as the invincible force of his arms ; and had he survived this last victory, the next and the

---

[1] Lord Malmesbury's Diary, vol. iv. p. 311.

next would have still surpassed each other. All this is sorrow for ourselves, but still more deeply do I regret that he cannot see the effect his death has produced. Not one individual who felt joy at this victory, so well timed, and so complete, but first had an instinctive feeling of sorrow, not selfish sorrow (for it came before the reflection of the consequences of his loss to us), but the sorrow of affection and gratitude for what he had done for us ; and the first regret was, that he who did the deed should be deprived of the enjoyment which he, above all other men, from his character, would have derived from its effects.

"Could he have lived but long enough to have known, that no victory—not even his victories, could weigh in the hearts of Englishmen against his most precious life, it would have been some consolation. I never saw so little public joy. The illumination seemed dim, and, as it were, half-clouded by the desire of expressing the mixture of contending feelings ; every common person in the streets speaking first of their sorrow for him, and then of the victory. Collingwood's letter (which is admirable) proves that it was his act to make all under him love him, and own his superiority without a ray of jealousy.

"He never was a party man himself, and there never was a party in his fleets. All were governed by one mind, and this made them invincible. He was a true patriot, which is nearly as rare a character as to be the hero he was. He had the aim and spirit of chivalry, and he was the most loyal subject—living and dying for his country, without reference to those who held the helm under that sovereign, to whom, next to her, he considered himself bound. This completes a character which cannot, I fear, appear again in our time." [1]

On the 4th of December the *Victory*, with Nelson's corpse in charge of his faithful chaplain, Dr. Scott, arrived in St. Helen's Road, Nelson's honoured flag flying half-mast high. Immediately every ship lowered their flags and pendants to the same position. From Spithead the *Victory* sailed to the Nore, and there the corpse was transferred to the Admiralty yacht, and conveyed to Greenwich. From the 5th to the 8th of January in the following year the Painted Hall at Greenwich was

---

[1] Lord Malmesbury's Diary, vol. iv. p. 311.

filled from morning to evening with crowds that passed
through it before the coffin of Nelson—the old *L'Orient*
coffin—as he lay in state in that noble chamber.   On the
last day the river presented a singular scene, as the State
barge bore the body up the stream ; the banks were filled
with eager crowds, and the procession was lengthened out
by numerous other barges and boats.   On its arrival at
Whitehall stairs, the coffin was carried with every solemnity
to a room in the Admiralty purposely prepared for its
reception.   On the next day the funeral ceremony filled
the streets [1] with an attentive and serious crowd, as it
passed slowly to St. Paul's.   Nelson's oldest friend, Sir
Peter Parker, was there as chief mourner, every prince of
the Royal family was present, and some of the oldest and
ablest of Britain's admirals bore their part in the solemn
ceremony.   When the Duke of Clarence ascended the
steps of St. Paul's he suddenly stopped, and took hold of

[1] The fact that a waxen figure of Nelson is exhibited in the cupboard
in Westminster Abbey, has given rise to the report that at his funeral
one of those effigies in old days carried in the funerals of Royal and
great personages, was present in the procession to St. Paul's.   The truth
is that finding that the unabated popularity of the hero led sightseers to
flock to the tomb at St. Paul's, and to desert the sights at the Abbey,
induced its vergers to have such a figure made in hopes of reviving the
attraction to that fane.   It is probably little known that for a time the
coffin of Wellington rested on that of Nelson, after the funeral of the
former, for more than a year.   Hence Tennyson's lines in which Nelson
asks—

> " Who is he that cometh like an honoured guest,
>   With banners and with music, with soldiers and with priest ?
>   With a nation weeping, and breaking on my rest ? "

And the answer—

> " Mighty sailor, this is he
>   Was great by land, as thou by sea.
>   Thine Island knew thee well, thou famous man
>   The greatest sailor since the world began !
>   Now to the roll of muffled drums,
>   To thee the greatest soldier comes ;
>   For this is he
>   Was great by land, as thou by sea."

the colours that were borne by the *Victory's* men, and, after a few words with one of the gallant fellows, burst into tears.   When the tattered flags were borne within the altar rails the Prince of Wales requested that they might be carried as near the grave as possible ; and when he looked on these records of the fight he could not forbear from weeping.   At last when the coffin slowly descended into the grave, and Nelson's flag that covered it was about to be withdrawn, with one accord the sailors who held it rent it into pieces, and eagerly treasured up these relics of their beloved chief.[1]

"I wish," wrote the Duke of Clarence to Captain Hargood, " another brave fellow could have witnessed our rejoicing for this victory, but he is gone—I mean my friend Nelson.   You know well my attachment and friendship for him, and you can, therefore, easily conceive what I must have felt, at the moment of the most brilliant victory, to lose my friend covered with glory, and entitled to the first honours of a grateful country.   I did not think it was possible, but for one of my dearest relations, to have felt what I have, and what I do still for poor Nelson."

Again, when offering a sword to Collingwood, the Duke wrote :—

"To Lord Collingwood.

"St. James, *November* 9, 1805.

"Dear Sir,—As a brother admiral, and as a sincere well-wisher to my King and country, permit me to congratulate you on the most important victory gained on the 21st of October under your gallant self and the brave officers, seamen, and royal marines under your command, and formerly under my lamented and valuable friend, Lord Nelson.   The country laments the Hero, and you and I feel the loss of our departed friend.   Five-and-twenty years have I lived on the most intimate terms with Nelson, and must ever, both publicly and privately, regret his loss.   Earl St. Vincent and Lord Nelson both in the hour of victory accepted from me a sword, and I hope you will now confer on me the same pleasure."[2]

---

[1] "Life of Nelson," by the author, S. P. C. K., 1851.
[2] Despatches, vol. vii. p. 240, note ; Correspondence of Lord Collingwood, vol. i. p. 220.

Speech of the Duke of Clarence on the vote of thanks
to Collingwood and his comrades, must find a place here:—

"On the vote of thanks to Lord Collingwood, January 29, 1806,
the Duke of Clarence observed 'That it was unnecessary for him
to trouble their lordships at any length, after the very full, able,
and eloquent speech of Lord Hawkesbury (Secretary of State),
in which he had touched upon the character of his noble and
lamented friend; he had also the happiness of knowing that
illustrious officer through a great part of his professional career,
and could bear ample testimony to every part of the eulogism of the
Secretary of State. He had been in habits of intimacy and friendship with him for twenty-three out of the forty-seven years of his age;
and his character, as arising from his professional conduct in almost
every part of the world, eclipsed that of every other officer he had
known. The heroic actions of his noble friend since the year 1793,
the commencement of the last war, were so recent and so fresh in the
recollection of their lordships as to render it unnecessary for him to
dwell upon them. There were parts of the professional conduct of
his noble friend which he could not avoid alluding to.' His Royal
Highness then particularized a variety of circumstances (the passage of
the Straits of S. Bonifacio among them) indicative of the nautical skill,
the strictness of discipline, and the unshaken perseverance of the
illustrious commander. 'But no part of his recent conduct he
thought more deserving of applause than his vigorous decision immediately to pursue the enemy to the West Indies, where the terror of
Nelson's name was such as to frustrate their designs and paralyze
their exertions. They fled precipitately from that quarter of the
globe; but still they were pursued by the intrepid and enterprising
commander.' He adverted to the circumstance of the unavoidable
want of fresh provisions in the British Fleet under his noble friend's
command, whose provident care and strictness of discipline was such
that scarcely one sick man was found in it. With respect to the
influence of religion, he believed its effect upon the mind of his
noble friend was unequalled in the example of any other officer. He
quoted part of his address to the officers and men under his command
previous to the battle of Trafalgar, which manifested his pious resignation to the will of Providence, and confidence with respect to a
successful issue where the cause was just." [1]

The Crown and Parliament hastened to ensure a noble,

[1] Abstract in Clarke and McArthur, vol. iii. pp. 192-3.

but by no means inadequate reward for her hero's services.
In furtherance of Royal messages on the 18th of February,
1806, the Royal assent was given to a Bill granting Viscountess Nelson an annuity of £2,000 a year for her life,
and on the 12th of May, after the usual Easter holidays,
a perpetual pension of £5,000 was secured to the holder of
the title, and the sum of £120,000 proposed to be voted
for the purchase of an estate to go with the title, and for
gifts to Nelson's sisters.   At first it was proposed that
£99,000 should be set apart for the purchase of the estate,
£10,000 paid to the present holder of the title to make
such reparations and improvements as might be deemed
necessary, and £10,000 given to each of Nelson's surviving sisters.   Eventually an additional sum of £9,000
was found necessary for the purchase of the property; the
£10,000 for outlay on it was abandoned, and the shares
of his two sisters, Mrs. Bolton, and Mrs. Matcham,
increased to £15,000 each.   In the negotiations for an
estate the sum of £70,000 was refused by the trustees of
one in Suffolk, which they were afterwards glad to sell
for half that money, and one near Salisbury, called
Stralynch, originally the property of the ancestors of
the first Viscountess Nelson, was purchased and named
Trafalgar.   By a contemporary grant Nelson's brother,
who had succeeded to the viscounty, was raised to an
earldom.   Nor were the other leaders neglected.
Collingwood was created a baron, and an annuity of
£2,000 secured to him and the two next successors to
the title ; and the grant of £1,000 a year to Sir Richard
Strachan.   The Committee of the Patriotic Fund voted
vases of great value to Nelson's relic, Collingwood, and
Lord Northesk ; and swords to the surviving captains and
commanders of the ships that shared in his glory ; and gifts
of money to the officers and men, and to the widows,
orphans, and parents of those that fell at Trafalgar.   The

general subscription for the widows and orphans exceeded £100,000.

The monuments that were raised to Nelson's memory were so numerous that it must suffice to note only the most important. By Parliament the monument in St. Paul's was raised, the work of Flaxman—a full-length figure of Nelson leaning on an anchor, Britannia directing the attention of a young seamen to him, with the inscriptions NILE, COPENHAGEN, TRAFALGAR.

The tomb in which he lay in the old *L'Orient* coffin was a sarcophagus of black and white marble on a square pedestal resting on a square of coarse masonry, with the inscription, " *Horatio Viscount Nelson.*" The sarcophagus and pedestal in the vault beneath were brought from the Wolsey Tomb House at Windsor, originally prepared for the great Cardinal's body. In the same vault, in 1808, the young Lord Trafalgar, the son of the first earl, was buried, and then the vault closed for ever.

By the City of London a monument was erected in 1810 of three figures—Britannia weeping over a bust of Nelson, the emblematic figure of the City recording his victories, and Neptune leaning on a dolphin. The inscription on this monument was by Richard Brinsley Sheridan.

Norwich, Bristol, Birmingham, Yarmouth, Edinburgh, Glasgow, Dublin—each raised a monument ; nor was he forgotten in Canada and Barbadoes.

On Portsdown Hill his comrades in the victory raised their memorial. The first memorial, however, was raised by the captain (Wilson) and men of the Sea Fencibles in the park of Castle Townsend, Cork—an arch erected in five hours, with the inscription that it was done by himself and twelve hundred of his Sea Fencibles, assisted by eight masons.[1]

---

[1] According to Lord Cockburn, in his interesting volume of Circuit journeys in Scotland, there is, or was in 1840, a very unpretentious

The will of Nelson and its codicils, eight in number, which is preserved at Bronte, is too detailed to need more than an abstract. It is dated May 10, 1803, and commences thus : —

"If I die in England, my body to be buried in the parish church of Burnham Thorpe near the remains of my deceased father and mother, and in as private a manner as may be. Bequests : £100 to the poor of Burnham Thorpe, Sutton, and Norton, in equal third parts, to be distributed by the clergy of the respective parishes to such objects and in such manner as they shall think fit.

"To Emma Hamilton my diamond star and the silver cup marked 'E. H.,' which she gave me.

"To my brother William the gold box presented to me by the City of London, and the gold sword given me by the captains who fought with me at the Nile.

"To my sister, Catherine Matcham, the sword presented to me by the City of London.

"To my sister, Susannah Bolton, the silver cup presented to me by the Turkey Company.

"To Alex. Davison my Turkish gun, scimitar, and canteen.

"To Captain Hardy all my telescopes and sea-glasses, and £100.

"To each of my executors £100."

Then follows a liberal provision for his widow and brother and sisters out of the residue of his personal estate, but to be supplemented if necessary by a charge on Bronte. These provisions became unnecessary from the Parliamentary grants :—

"Bronte is then settled on William Nelson in tail male, with

---

monument to Nelson in a small parish near Loch Etive. "Lest Ben Cruachan, whose summit was glittering all day, as well as the other solemnities of the district, should not be sufficient for the honour of Mackairn, the Heritors, or somebody, have erected a thing in the church-yard about the size of a large broomstick, and not more attractive in form. I asked the driver what it was. 'It's a moniment to a gentleman.' 'What gentleman?' 'Oh, I dinna mind his name. He deed a while ago. Oh, ay. A mind noo. It is to Lord Ne—elson.'" ("Circuit Journeys," p. 78).

remainder over to the male issue of his sisters in succession. The diamond Aigrette the gift of the Sultan, his Collar of the Order of the Bath, his Medals of the Order of St. Ferdinand, and Insignia of other orders, are made heirlooms of the possessor of his real estates in further Sicily, or lands purchased in lieu thereof.

"To Lady Hamilton, her heirs and assigns, Merton and its lands limited to seventy-six acres, to exonerate all charges on it out of my personal estate; [1] the remainder to be sold and the money added to the residue. My plate, linen, pictures, and wares to Lady Hamilton.

"His brother William and William Hazlewood, executors."

About the 6th of September Nelson sent a private letter to Hazlewood—to be burnt when read—charging Bronte with all his legacies, which Hazlewood proved as a third codicil.

By another, the second codicil, he bequeathed the £4,000 he had already settled on Horatia.

By the fourth, fifth, and sixth codicils he charges Bronte with £500 a year in favour of Lady Hamilton, to be paid quarterly, the first payment in advance; £100 a year to the widow of his brother Maurice; confirms his former will and codicils; and gives £2,000 additional to Lady Hamilton; £100 to Scott, his secretary, to buy a ring; his papers and effects to Hardy for his executors; and £200 to Dr. Alexander Scott, his chaplain.

Finally, we have the codicil written a few minutes before the commencement of the action at Trafalgar commending the services of Lady Hamilton and his adopted daughter, Horatia, to the bounty of his country. Of the grounds of these claims I have spoken elsewhere. It is needless, therefore, to repeat the document here.

From the very numerous poetical tributes to Nelson two only are selected—that by Canning in his poem,

---

[1] Varied by codicil i. To trustees for Lady Hamilton and any one she may appoint by will, deed, or writing, and in default after her death to his own right heirs.

contrasting the triumph of Napoleon on the cowardly
surrender of Ulm to the Emperor, with the utter defeat
of his hopes of regaining the Empire of the Sea, by the
victory of Trafalgar. With reference to the word
"Trafalgar," in which Canning had pronounced the scene
of the victory in the usual way, Dr. Scott relates the
following amusing anecdote :—

"Dr. Scott was one day dining at Fife House in company with Mr.
Canning, when the latter very mysteriously let him into the *secret*
(which he so cautiously divulged to the rest of the company before the
evening was over) that a poem by himself was to be published next
day, in which the grand naval triumph would be celebrated. He
repeated some lines for Scott's opinion, who immediately found fault
with the accent being thrown on the middle syllable, instead of on
the last in the word Trafalgar. Mr. Canning defended his pronunciation by the example of Gibraltar. Such a discussion as this Scott
loved to his heart, and gave his oppponent the pronunciation of Gib-
ral-tār with the most delicate precision, informing him that it was
only an English corruption which miscalled that word as it was
generally spoken.[1] So for the future we must talk of Gibraltār and
Trafalgār, a somewhat difficult task after so many years' use of the
other accent."

The poem represents Napoleon as rejoicing over the
defeat of the Austrian Armies, and the capitulation of
Ulm, and then shows how in " an insolence of power,"

" O'er England's seas his new dominion plann'd—
Whilst the red bolt yet flamed in Nelson's hand ;
That had, which erst by Nile's affrighted tide,
Smote with dread fire the godless warrior's pride,
And strewed his flaming wrecks on Egypt's shore—
Exhausted Europe by the distant roar.
Roused from her trance, her shattered force combined,
And half redeemed the freedom of mankind."

The subsequent success of Buonaparte's legions is then

---

[1] " Life of the Rev. Dr. Scott," pp. 220-1. Gibraltar, says Butler, is a
corruption of Gibel Tarik, the Mountain of Tarik, a Moorish general who
first led the Moors into Spain, A.D. 710.

described, which it is said made him "in hope dare profane."

> " With impious grasp the Sceptre of the Main :—
> But England heard the vaunt, and Nelson made it vain.
> Nelson once more (though taught by him, we own
> The thanks, the triumph due to Heaven alone).
> Once more the chosen instrument of good,
> Fixed on the waves, and stablished on the flood,
> His country's rights, but sealed them with his blood.
> O price, his conquering country grieved to pay,
> O dear-bought glories of Trafalgar's day."

> "Lamented Hero ! When to Britain's shore
> Exulting fame those awful tidings bore,
> Joy's bursting sound in whelming grief was drowned,
> And Victory's self unwilling audience found ;
> On every brow the cloud of sadness hung,
> The sounds of triumph died on every tongue !
> Not joy thus doubtful, sadness thus sincere
> Shall grace erewhile, the Tyrant conqueror's bier—
>
> .   .   .   .   .   .
>
> But thee, loved chief !   What genuine griefs bemoan !
> Fleets, cities, camps, the cottage and the throne !
> Round thy thronged hearse those mingling sorrows flow,
> And seek faint solace in the pomp of woe.
> Yet not the vows thy weeping country pays,
> Not that high meed, thy mourning Sovereign's praise ;
> Not that the Great, the Beauteous, and the Brave,
> Bend in mute reverence, o'er thy closing grave ;
> That with such grief as bathes a kindred bier,
> Collective Nations mourn a death so dear ;—
> Not these alone shall soothe thy sainted shade,
> And consecrate the spot where Thou art laid !
> Not these alone.   But bursting from the gloom,
> With radiant glory from thy trophied tomb,
> The sacred splendour of thy deathless name,
> Shall grace and guard thy country's martial fame,
> Far seen shall blaze the unextinguished ray,
> A mighty beacon, lighting glory's way !
> With living lustre this proud land adorn,
> And shine and save, through ages yet unborn !

By that pure fire, before that hallowed tomb,
Heroes and chiefs in valour's opening bloom,
Frequent in solemn pilgrimage shall stand,
And vow to prize, like Thee, their native land;
With pious ardour thy bright course pursue,
And bid thy blended virtues live anew :——
Thy skill to plan, thy enterprise to dare;
Thy might to strike, thy clemency to spare;
That zeal in which no thought of self had part,
But thy loved country fill'd up all thy heart;
That conscious worth, from pride, and meanness free,
And manners mild as guileless infancy;
The scorn of worldly wealth; the thirst of fame
Unquenchable : the blush of generous shame;
And bounty's genial flow, and friendship's holy flame."

Besides erecting a small rostral column in the Court of Castle Howard, on the sides of which are the words " Aboukir, Copenhagen, Trafalgar," Lord Carlisle placed the following lines on an ancient altar from the Temple of Delphi, which was brought from the Mediterranean to England in Nelson's ship :—

" Pass not this ancient Altar with disdain,
  'Twas once in Delphi's sacred Temple reared;
From this the Pythian poured her mystic strain,
  Whilst Greece its fate in anxious silence heard.

What Chief, what Hero, of th' Achaian race,
  Might not to this have bowed with holy awe;
Have clung, in pious reverence, round its base,
  And from the voice inspired, received the law?

A British Chief, as famed in arms as those
  Has borne this relic o'er th' Italian waves;
In war, still friend to science, this bestows,
  And Nelson gives it to the land he saves."

The following is the history of Nelson's ship, the *Victory* :—

" Successive ships bearing the name of *Victory* have been in the Navy since 1670. Nelson's *Victory* was built in 1765, and has carried the flags of Keppel, Sir Peter Parker, Lord Howe, Lord Hood, Sir John Jervis, and Nelson. Paid off, December, 1805. Re-commissioned in 1806 and in service to 1812 ; once proposed to be broken up. Now, after a thorough repair, again lying in Portsmouth Harbour, where she was visited by the Queen, Trafalgar Day, 1844, on her progress with Prince Albert. Noticing that she was decorated with flags, and her mastheads adorned with laurel, the Queen inquired the cause and went on board. On being shown the spot where Nelson received his death wound, Her Majesty read aloud the inscription, ' HERE NELSON FELL,' and plucked a couple of leaves from the laurel with which the inscription was enshrined. Her Majesty then went over the poop-rail, where over the wheel is the memorable inscription in golden letters, and then went to the cabin where he died, where the spot is marked by a funeral urn in paint, surmounted by Nelson's flag, and on the top encircled in a wreath, the words, ' HERE NELSON DIED.' " [1]

Our Sailor King, after his accession to the crown, placed a bust of Nelson at Windsor on an appropriate pedestal :—

" In the armoury stands, on the right hand, the bust of Wellington, facing that of Marlborough ; on the left, and in the centre of the recess at the head of the room, surrounded by a neat iron rail, stands the bust of Nelson on a portion of the foremast of the *Victory*. The nature of the pedestal, the black hoops which bind it together, and the tremendous shot hole with which it is perforated, all combine to give an indescribable interest in the museum of a British monarch : nor will the *nautical* observer overlook the *horse-shoe* nailed on the forepart of the foremast. This is ever done by sailors, either for good luck, or as I have heard some say, ' to drive away the witches.' " [2]

To this chapter a letter from Lady Castlereagh to her son will form an appropriate conclusion :—

" MOUNT STEWART, IRELAND, *Nov.* 15, 1805.

" I thank you a thousand times for your interesting letter. Never was there indeed an event so mournfully and so triumphantly important to England as the battle of Trafalgar. The sentiment of lamenting the individual, more than the rejoicing in the victory, shows the

---

[1] Letter of John Poole, author of " Paul Pry ; " Despatches, vol. vii. p. 343.

[2] Brereton's " Naval History," vol. ii.

humanity and affection of the people of England; but their good sense on reflection will dwell only on the conquest, because no death at a future moment could have been more glorious, and might have been less so. The public would never have sent him on another expedition ; his health was not equal to another effort, and he might have yielded to the more natural but less imposing efforts of more worldly honours ! Whereas he now begins his immortal career, having nothing to achieve on earth, and bequeathing to the English Fleet a legacy which they alone are able to improve. Had I been his wife or his mother, I would rather have wept him dead than seen him languish on a less splendid day. In such a death there is no sting, and in such a grave everlasting victory." [1]

---

[1] Clarke and McArthur, vol. iii. p. 180, note. There is an interesting account in the sixth essay of the third volume of " The Friend," by the poet Coleridge, of the effect of the news of Nelson's death on the Neapolitans. " The tidings," he writes, had arrived on the day that he returned from Calabria. " I never can forget the sorrow and consternation that lay on every countenance. Numbers stopped and shook hands with me, because they had seen tears on my cheek, and considered that I was an Englishman, and several as they held my hand burst into tears."

APPENDICES.

APPENDICES.

I.

THE BIRTH-PLACE OF NELSON. RESTORATION OF BURNHAM THORPE CHURCH.

Y the kindness of the Rev. Lister-Knight, the ·rector of Burnham Thorpe, at the vicarage of which Nelson was born, I am enabled to give a brief account of its church, the restoration of which is being attempted by a committee of which H.R.H. the Prince ·of Wales is the chairman, and to which her Majesty has gladly contributed.

"This building," says Sir Arthur Bloomfield, in his report, "apart from the interest which it must always inspire in connection with the great name of Nelson, is itself a good specimen of the churches of a country unusually rich in mediæval ecclesiastical architecture.

"The columns and arches on each side of the nave, dating from the thirteenth century, are good in character, and very finely proportioned, the rest of the church, including the clerestory, is of the different date of Perpendicular, and the exterior of the east end a beautiful and effective composition. The chancel arch is poor and mean, its poverty no doubt being hid in past days by a rich rood-loft.

"Its present condition is sad. Some time in the last century the upper part of the tower fell down, injuring the roof and partially ruining the south aisle, since taken down, its arches built up, and a slated roof put up, quite unworthy of the church, and the upper part of the tower built up, quite regardless of anything like a restoration of the former one. At the same time the western arch was built up and a gallery erected. The old font much injured by the fall of the tower, the stone and base destroyed, lay for many years in the rector's garden, but has now been restored to the church. In the north aisle the ancient roof remains, but much out of repair. The side windows in this aisle are of a very graceful design. In the chancel is the grave of Nelson's father, who was for forty-seven years the rector of the parish. Except some fragments of the lower part of the screen, which formerly divided the eastern bay of the north aisle, no doubt as a chantry chapel, there are no remnants of ancient woodwork. The recess for the reredos and altar in this chapel still remain at the east end, and a small priest's door in the north aisle."

Thanks to the interest which the Queen with the Prince of Wales and the Duke of Edinburgh are taking in this movement for the restoration of the church, and the very liberal responsibility which the rector has taken towards its cost, we may trust that it may be made a fitting monument of the great man whose father was so long its rector.

II.

NELSON AND ALEXANDER DAVISON. ACCOUNT OF DAVISON'S MEMORIAL TO NELSON, FORMED OUT OF THE GUINEAS FOUND IN HIS PURSE AT TRAFALGAR.

If Clarke and McArthur are correct (vol. i. p. 77), Nelson became acquainted with his future friend and naval agent, during his command in the *Albermarle* on the American station, when, as they relate, he prevented Nelson from ruining his early career with his attachment to a young Canadian lady. "The *Albermarle* was ready for sea at Quebec, when A. Davison met the frigate's captain as he sprung from his boat to the beach. Davison eagerly asked him the occasion of his return. 'Walk up to your house,' replied Nelson, 'and you shall be acquainted with the cause. I find it utterly impossible to leave this place without again looking on her who has so much added to its charms, and laying myself and my fortunes at her feet.' 'Your utter ruin,' cried Davison, 'situated as you are at present, must irretrievably follow.' 'Then let it follow,' exclaimed Nelson, 'I am resolved to do it.' Davison, however, talked him over, and watched on the beach until the *Albermarle* was blowing out to sea." Mr. C. Russell has adopted this anecdote, but it seems to me too like "a stage Nelson," as he says with respect to similar stories, to be worthy of insertion in the text.

It is sad to think of the close of the hitherto most successful career of this firm and kind friend of Nelson. Navy agent, banker, commissariat contractor, he had acquired a large fortune, was the political friend of successive cabinets, many differences in which were more than once arranged at his mansion in St. James' Square. Tempted to try to acquire a seat in Parliament, he was convicted of outrageous bribery, and imprisoned for a long period ; but on his release—such was the lenient view then entertained of election bribery—he was appointed to important posts by the Government,[1] and continued his previously successful career. In 1808, however, at the time of the investigation of the commissariat frauds, he was tried and convicted, and sentenced to twenty-one months' imprisonment. Of his subsequent career I have no knowledge. After the battle of the Nile he had struck medals for all ranks, of his presentation of one of which he gives the following interesting account to Nelson :—

"St. James' Square, *April* 6, 1799.

"I waited upon the King early last Sunday morning, at the Queen's House, and presented him with a gold and silver medal. He received them most graciously, and with much joy and pleasure, and paid me compliments upon the occasion. I was *alone* with the king for a full hour, when much of the conversation was about you. It is impossible to express how warmly he spoke of you, and asked a thousand questions about you. I promised his Majesty a copper gilt and a bronze medal, as soon as I received them, which I shall also have the honour of presenting."

"St. James' Square, *May* 7, 1799.

"I have been again at the Queen's House, and have given the King a copy of your last letter to me, giving an account of your health, which he read twice over with great attention, and with apparent emotion of concern. I said a great deal (but not too much) regarding my idea of your situation. His Majesty speaks of you with the tenderness of a father. He was much pleased with the portrait I presented to him of you, and said he thought it much like."[2]

Medal. Hope with the emblem standing on a rugged rock, olive branch in right hand, medallion profile of Nelson on the left. Hope

---

[1] Commissary-General of the Forces and Treasurer of the Ordnance, and in the latter position—though without salary—had full employment, as a banker, of the millions of money that passed through his hand. ("State Trials in the Nineteenth Century," vol. i. p. 223–5.)

[2] Autographs in Nelson Papers ; Despatches, vol. iii. pp. 321–2, note.

crowned with oak and laurel. Motto round medallion, "Europe's Hope and Britain's Glory." Legend, "Rear-Admiral Lord Nelson of the Nile." Reverse, the Bay of Aboukir with British Fleet advancing on French Fleet at anchor. Legend, "Almighty God has blessed his Majesty's arms," and on the exergue, "Victory of the Nile."

One of these medals is in the possession of G. Blagden Westcott, the grand-nephew of Captain Westcott, who was killed at the Nile, to whose aged mother it was given by Nelson when he visited her at Honiton, and through whom it has come as an heirloom.

"Lord Nelson, not long before his death, on his way through Devonshire, slept a night at Honiton, the native place of Captain Westcott, who was killed at the battle of the Nile. Finding that the captain's mother and sister still resided there, Lord Nelson invited them to breakfast with him at the inn. In the course of conversation he inquired of Mrs. Westcott if she had received the gold medal, which her son would have been entitled to had he survived. On her replying that she had not, he immediately took off his own medal, which he was wearing suspended from a blue ribbon, and presented it to her, saying, 'You will not value it less because Nelson has worn it.' The medal is now, we believe in the possession of the great-nephew of the captain."[1]

This was one of the medals struck by Alexander Davison, inscribed on the rim, "A tribute of regard from Alexander Davison, Esq., St. James's" (Letter from G. B. Westcott, July 14, 1890).

After Nelson's death at Trafalgar, Davison formed the guineas found in the hero's purse into the following curious memorial, of which, through the kindness of its present possessor, I am enabled to give an engraving. The memorial was exhibited at the opening of the New Town Hall, Portsmouth, by the Prince of Wales :—

"A curious memento of Lord Nelson was offered for sale lately, and purchased by Mr. James Griffin, bookseller, The Hard, Portsmouth. When the admiral received his fatal shot at Trafalgar, eighty-four guineas, mostly of the spade-ace pattern, were found in his purse, and these, with other effects of the Hero, were sent to Mr. Alexander Davison, Nelson's intimate friend and naval agent. Davison had the guineas soldered together and formed into a pyramidal roof, with the obverse and reverse faced alternately uppermost, the whole being supported at the angles on the shoulders of four full-length weeping female figures, in dull metal gilt, a polished

THE DAVISON MEMORIAL.

ball intervening between the supports and corners of the roof. In the centre of the canopy thus formed is a metal gilt miniature sarcophagus, which stands on a plinth, formed of four steps, and is surmounted by a viscount's coronet resting upon a cushion. The handles of the sarcophagus are composed of the stern and prow of an admiral's barge. The trophy, which is capped by a trident, bears on its front the following inscription : ' *These Guineas were in Lord Viscount Nelson's purse at the time he received the fatal wound off Trafalgar, Oct.* 21, 1805.' The back and sides are inscribed thus : ' *Battle of St. Vincent,* 14*th Feb.,* 1797 '; ' *Battle of the Nile, Aug.* 1, 1798 '; ' *Battle of Copenhagen,* 2*nd April,* 1801.' The trophy became the property of the late William Joy, of Cheam, in whose possession it remained forty years and by whose executors it was put up to auction. It is satisfactory to know that the relic is now within sight of the old *Victory,* Nelson's flagship, and at the centre of the naval service." (Newspaper cutting sent to me July 14, 1890, by G. B. Westcott, Captain Westcott's grand-nephew.)

III.

FEES ON THE GRANT OF A KNIGHTHOOD OF THE BATH.

Copy of Bill sent to Nelson.

	£	s.	d.
Secretary of State's office	6	7	6
Lord Chamberlain's office	26	14	0
To the Seven Officers of the Order—			

	£	s.	d.
Dean	£22	6	8
Genealogist	22	0	0
Bath King of Arms	22	0	0
Register	22	0	0
Secretary	22	0	0
Gentleman Usher	22	0	0
Messenger	18	13	4
	£151	0	0
Bath King at Arms—Book of Statutes...	6	13	4
Secretary, for Notice of Election ...	6	13	4
Seal of the Order to the Book	0	10	6
	164	17	2

¹ *Gentleman's Magazine* (cut out of the *Exeter and Plymouth Gazette Daily Telegram,* December 4, 1866, by G. B. Westcott, R.N., the grand-nephew). See also *Notes and Queries,* Third Series, vol. viii. p. 263.

	£	s.	d.
To the Garter and Officers of Arms for Patent of Supporters	40	12	6
To the King of Arms and other officers of Arms for the Patent of Confirmation and Exemplification of Arms	43	12	6
To Fees of Honour to King's Household...	128	6	0
Warrant for dispensation for wearing the Star	7	13	6
Two suits of Ribbons	0	16	9
Soliciting the same...	10	10	0

	£	s.	d.
	£428	7	5

Fees to King's Household.

	£	s.	d.
Earl Marshal of England	3	13	4
Garter and Heralds at Arms	8	10	0
Lyon and Heralds of Scotland	8	10	0
Gentlemen Ushers, Privy Chamber	5	0	0
Do. do. Daily Waiters	5	0	0
Do. do. Assistant	1	5	0
Do. do. Quarter Waiters	4	0	0
Grooms of the Privy Chamber	5	0	0
Exons of the Yoemen of the Guard	5	0	0
Knight Harbinger	3	6	8
Gentlemen and Yoemen Harbingers	5	6	8
Office of Robes	4	0	0
Removing Wardrobe	2	5	4
Pages of the Bed Chamber	7	0	0
Sergeants at Arms	5	0	0
Sergeants' Porter	1	0	0
Sergeant and office of Trumpets	3	0	0
Barber	1	0	0
Servers of the Chamber	2	0	0
Household Drums	0	13	4
Pages of the Presence	0	10	0
Surveyor of the Ways	0	10	0
Yeoman of the Month	1	16	0
Gentlemen of the Buttery and Cellar	1	12	0
Surveyor of the Dresser	0	10	0
Yoemen Ushers	1	0	0
Master Cook	1	5	0

					£	s.	d.
Keepers of the Council Chamber ...	...	...	...	...	1	0	0
Footmen and Coachmen ...	...	...	...	...	2	10	0
Porters at Gate ...	...	...	...	...	1	0	0
Closet Keeper ...	...	...	...	...	0	10	0
Registrar of the College at Arms ...	...	...	...	...	1	8	2
Principal Usher of Scotland	...	...	...	...	3	6	8

$$^1 £98 \quad 0 \quad 0$$

IV.

BRITISH FLEET AT THE BATTLE OF THE NILE.

SHIP'S NAME.	CAPTAIN.	GUNS	CREW.	KILLED.	WOUN-DED.	TOT.
Culloden ...	T. Troubridge ...	74	590			
Theseus ...	R. W. Miller ...	74	590	5	30	35
Alexander	A. J. Ball ...	74	590	14	58	72
Vanguard	{ Sir H. Nelson } { Edward Berry }	74	595	30	75	105
Minotaur	T. Louis	74	640	23	64	87
²*Leander* ...	T. B. Thomson ...	50	343		14	14
Swiftsure	B. Hallowell ...	74	590	7	22	29
Audacious	Davidge Gould ...	74	590	1	35	36
Defence ...	John Peyton ...	74	590	4	11	15
Zealous ...	Sam Hood ...	74	590	1	7	8
Orion ...	Sir J. Saumarez ...	74	590	13	29	42
Goliath ...	Thos. Foley ...	74	590	21	41	62
Majestic ...	G. B. Westcott ...	74	590	55	143	193
Bellerophon	H. D. E. Danby...	74	590	49	148	197

Killed, 218.   Wounded, 677.   Total, 895.

---

[1] Despatches, vol. ii. p. 467.   Appendix.

[2] Captured by *Le Généreux*, August 16th, off Candia, with Captain Berry on board going home with despatches ; he and his crew plundered and ill-treated by the captors.

FRENCH LINE OF BATTLE.

SHIP'S NAME.	COMMANDER.	GUNS.	MEN.	
Le Guerrier...		74	600	Taken ; burnt, Aug. 16th.
Le Conquerant		74	700	Taken.
Le Spartiate		74	700	Taken.
L' Aquilon ...		74	700	Taken.
Le Souverain Peuple ...		74	700	Taken.
Le Franklin...	{ Blanquet, Contre Admiral ... }	80	800	Taken.
L'Orient ...	{ Brueys, Commander in chief ... }	120	1,040	Burnt.
Le Tonnant ...		80	800	Taken.
L'Henreux ...		74	700	Taken ; burnt, Aug. 16th.
Le Timoleon...		74	700	Burnt.
Le Mercure...		74	700	Taken ; burnt, Aug. 16th.
[1]*Le Guillaume Tell* ...	{ Villeneuve, Contre Admiral ... }	80	800	Escaped.
[2]*Le Généreux*		74	700	Escaped.
FRIGATES.				
La Diana ...		48	300	Escaped.
La Justice ...		44	300	Escaped.
L' Artemise		36	250	Burnt.
La Serieuse...		36	250	Sunk by *Orion.*

V.

CAPTAIN BALL AT THE BATTLE OF THE NILE.

In the third and fourth essays in the third volume of " The Friend," the poet Coleridge, who was an intimate friend of Captain Ball of the *Alexander*, in Nelson's fleet at the Battle of the Nile, gives

---

[1] Taken by Lord Nelson, February 10, 1800.
[2] Taken by Sir E. Berry, March 30, 1800.

the following anecdotes of him, in a biography of his friend, contained in those essays :

"In the plan of the Battle of the Nile, it was Lord Nelson's design, that Captains Troubridge and Ball should have led up the attack. The former was stranded; and the latter, by accident of the wind, could not bring up his ship into the line of battle till some time after the engagement had become general. With his characteristic forecast and activity of (what may not improperly be called) practical imagination, he had made arrangements to meet every contingency. All the shrouds and sails of the ship not absolutely necessary for its immediate management were thoroughly wetted and so rolled up that they were as hard and as little inflammable as so many solid cylinders of wood ; every sailor had his appropriate place and formation, and a certain number were appointed as firemen, whose sole duty it was to be on the watch if any part of the vessel should take fire, and to these men exclusively the charge of extinguishing it was committed. It was already dark when he brought his ship into action, and laid her alongside the French *L'Orient.* One particular only I shall add to the known account of the memorable engagement between these ships, and this I received from Sir Alexander Ball himself. He had previously made a combustible preparation, but which, from the nature of the engagement to be expected, he had proposed to reserve for the last contingency. But just at the time, when from several symptoms, he had every reason to believe that the enemy would soon strike to him, one of his lieutenants, without his knowledge, threw in the combustible matter, and this it was that occasioned the tremendous explosion of that vessel. Yet the incident which followed, and which has not, I believe, been publicly made known, is scarcely less impressive, though its sublimity is of a different character. At the renewal of the battle, Captain Ball, though his ship was on fire in three different parts, laid her alongside a French eighty-four, and a second longer obstinate contest begun. The firing on the part of the French ship having at length for some time slackened, and then altogether ceased, and yet no sign given of surrender, the first-lieutenant came to Captain Ball and informed him that the hearts of his men were as good as ever, but that they were so completely exhausted, that they were scarcely capable of lifting an arm. He asked, therefore, whether as the enemy had now ceased firing, the men might be permitted to lie down by their guns for a short time. After some reflection, Sir Alexander acceded to the proposal, taking, of course, proper precautions to rouse them again at the moment he thought requisite. Accordingly, with the exception of himself, his officers, and the appointed watch, his ship's crew lay down, each in the place in which he was stationed, and slept for twenty minutes. They were then roused, and started up, as Sir Alexander Ball expressed it, more like men out of an ambush than from sleep, so instantaneously did they all obey the summons! They recommenced their fire, and in a few minutes the enemy surrendered; and it was soon afterwards discovered that during that interval, and almost immediately after the French ship had first ceased firing, the crew sank down by their guns, there slept, almost by the side, as it were, of their sleeping enemy." [1]

Captain Miller of the *Theseus*, in his letter to his wife, speaks of "his anxiety on seeing the *Alexander* on fire in several places, and of his own men being so extremely jaded that, as soon as they had hove his sheet-anchor up, they dropped under the capstan bars, and were asleep in a moment in every sort of posture, having been then working at their fullest exertion or fighting for twelve hours." [2]

VI.

COPY OF THE LETTER FROM NELSON'S FATHER TO THE REV. BRYAN ALLOTT, WHITEHAVEN, CUMBERLAND, AFTER THE BATTLE OF THE NILE.

"MY GOOD SIR,—Your letter gave me much pleasure, as well as from your kind remembrance of our friendly intercourse and good neighbourhood in years past, as from your polite congratulation upon the success of my great and good son over the avowed enemies of this and all civilized nations. He went into the world without friends or fortune, but with a heart replete with every moral and religious virtue. These have been his compass to steer by, and it has pleased God to be his shield in the day of battle, and give success to his wishes to be useful to his country, now sensible of his services. If he should meet with ingratitude, his scars will cry out and plead his cause. At the siege of Bastia, the loss of an eye; at Teneriffe, an arm; on the memorable 14th of February he received a severe blow upon the body, which he feels; and now a wound on his head. After all this you may suppose the bloom of his countenance is faded, but the spirit beareth up still as vigorous as ever. The 19th of last month he completed his fortieth year, cheerful, generous, and good, fearing no ill because he has done none, an honour to my grey hairs which, with every other mark of age, creeps very fast upon me. During the

---

[1] "The Friend," vol. iii. pp. 237-9, Pickering's edition, 1850.
[2] See his letter in Laughton, pp. 158-9.

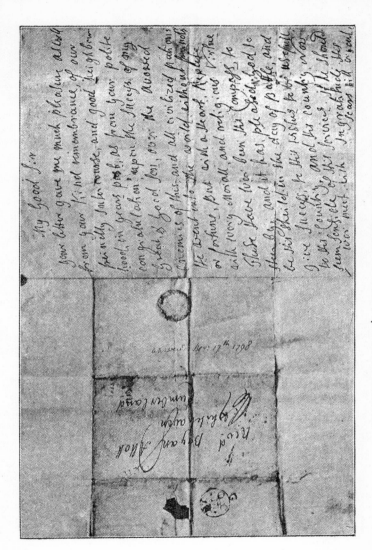

LETTER FROM NELSON'S FATHER TO THE REV. BRYAN ALLOTT.

LETTER FROM NELSON'S FATHER TO THE REV. BRYAN ALLOTT.

whole war I have been with Lady Nelson, a good woman, and attentive to an infirm old man. We are now fixed in a purchased house within a small distance of Ipswich, in Suffolk, in the winter. I still continue at S. P., at Bladus Springs. You have seen my youngest son is rector of Bm. Sutton, and that he resides at Thorpe.

"I am truly glad to hear you say you are fixed for life, which indicates something good and pleasant, such as after passing through a tempestuous sea may bring you to a peaceful port—pray God it may be so! Miss Allott is, I am certain, a good woman, a cheerful companion, and your staff in age.

"I shall always be glad to know that you are both happy, and am, my dear sir, to herself and yourself, a very sincere friend and servant,

"EDM. NELSON.

"Ipswich, Oct. 16, 1798."

The house mentioned in the foregoing page is Roundwood.

VII.

SIR WILLIAM BEECHEY'S PORTRAIT OF NELSON'S FATHER.

Extract from letter to Lord Nelson from his wife, March 4, 1800 : —"I think you will be surprised when I tell you our good father is sitting for his portrait. Sir W. Beechey is the fortunate man. You must know it is a profound secret. . I went to Sir W. to ask his price, look at his pictures, and then inquire whether he would go to an invalid. The answer, ' No,' puzzled me ; however I said, ' Sometimes general rules were broken through.' Sir William, finding I was rather anxious about this picture, said that really he never went to any person excepting the King and Royal Family. The Duke and Duchess of York had that instant left the house. I knew that. ' But, madam, may I ask who is the gentleman ?' ' Yes, sir ; my Lord Nelson's father.' ' My God, I would go to York to do it ! Yes, madam, directly.' He was as good as his word, and has been here twice. I think the likeness will be an exceeding good one. I don't know whether the picture is for you or me—the picture is for you, so I hear this morning."[1]

---

[1] Nelson Papers (Auto.) ; Despatches, vol. iv. p. 514, note. This portrait is in the possession of Earl Nelson at Trafalgar.

VIII.

WELLINGTON AND NELSON'S INTERVIEW.

" The news of Sir Robert Calder's action had just been received, and this naturally formed a principal topic of their discourse. Sir A. Wellesley said to Lord Nelson, ' *This measure of success wont do now-a-days, for your Lordship has taught the public to expect something more brilliant.*' Shortly after this Lord Nelson left the waiting-room, evidently to find out who his new friend was, and, returning in a minute, renewed the conversation on a fresh footing. Nelson had at that time some project of occupying Sardinia, and he wished Sir Arthur to take charge of the troops on the occasion. But he replied that he would rather not—that he had just returned from India—in short, he did not enter into that view." [1]

IX.

SPANISH AND FRENCH ACCOUNTS OF THE FLEETS AT TRAFALGAR.

Spanish Account.

Victory, entirely dismasted in act of cutting the line ; taken in tow by frigate ; foundered off Gibraltar.

Prince of Wales 98, sunk in action. (*Not in the battle.*)

Britannia 98, sunk in action.

Dreadnought 98, hull riddled with balls.

Temeraire 98, without any masts.

Neptune 98, and *Prince* 98, both sunk, and masts of the first and rudder off ; found on the Playa de Conil.

Queen 98, in Gibraltar ; much damaged. (*Not in the battle.*)

Donegal 80, dismasted on the coast of Barbary. (*Not in the battle.*)

Canopus 80, dismasted ; alongside of pontoons in Gibraltar. (*Not in the battle.*)

Tigre 80, dismasted ; sank on the Playa of Santa Maria. (*Not in the battle.*)

Tonant 80, burnt by fleet five or six leagues off Cadiz.

Spencer 74, towed by frigate into Gibraltar. (*Not in the battle.*)

---

[1] Review of Barrow's "Howe," *Edinburgh Review*, July, 1838, p. 322. Wellington may have so spoken, but if he did it is strange that he never mentioned it to Mr. Croker, to whom he related the incident at Strathfieldsaye, March 25, 1834. See author's " Life of Wellington," p. 8.

Le Spartiate 74, sunk after action.

Defence 74, without mainmast in Gibraltar.

Swiftsure 74, without mainmast at Gibraltar.

Orion 74, dismasted; coast of Africa.

Leviathan, under sail; lost topmast.

Zealous 74, hull damaged; in Gibraltar. (*Not in the battle.*)

Conqueror 74, under sail.

Revenge 74, and *Achille* 74, in Gibraltar; second without topsail-yard.

Minotaur 74, and *Colossus* 74, ran ashore on coast of Conil and Santa Maria.

Mars 74, and *Bellerophon* 74, under sail.

Polypheme 74, under sail, without mizenmast.

Esparciata 74, sunk after battle on coast of Rota.

Carnatic 74, with jury masts; under sail. (*Not in the battle.*)

Ships that joined the Fleet at 5 p.m.

The Duke of York 90, under sail. (*No such ship in the navy.*)

Royal Sovereign 100, lost with £400,000 on way to Malta.

Le Leger 80, *Relanpayo* 74, *Aquila* 74. (*No such ships in the navy.*)

Admiral Beckerton was wounded at the beginning of the action, and died three hours after it was ended. A one-hundred-gun ship, three frigates, and one sloop have sailed from Gibraltar to the westward, to protect the vessels which have grounded or were dismasted. This account is taken from the despatch from Gibraltar of Admiral Collingwood, and from those given by those ships who have come into port. It is to be expected that the English would not exaggerate their losses, but they are much greater than they chose to represent. But it is sufficiently evident that their fleet is destroyed, and some accounts from Cadiz state their loss to be seven or eight thousand men —a loss which England can with difficulty repair.

FRENCH LIST OF BRITISH SHIPS IN ACTION.

Victory, Le Prince de Galles,* Le Britannia, Le Neptune et Le Prince, Le Driognaute, Le Temeraire, Le Queen,* Le Canopus, Le Donegal,* Le Tigre,* Le Tonant, Le Spencer,* Le Spartiate, Le Defens, Le Swiftsure, La Reine, Le Leviathan, Le Zele,* Le Conquerant, La Revanche et L'Achille, Le Colossus et Le Minotore, Le Mars, Bellerophon et Le Polyphemus, Le Carne (query *Carnatic*), *Hardron, L'Effronte* (query *Defiance*).

Joined at 5 *p.m.*

Le Duc de York,† *Le Royal Souverain, Le Legar,*† *Le Relampayo,*†
L'Achille † (query *Eagle**).

The ships marked * were not in the action. No such ships as
those † in the British navy.

A further Spanish Account of the Losses of the British Fleet at Trafalgar, in detail.

First Division.—Admiral Nelson.

Victory—killed : 2 captains, 1 rear-admiral, 11 officers ; wounded, 7
officers. Seamen—killed 500, drowned 96, wounded 209.

Britannia, dismasted and sunk by *Santissima Trinadada*—killed : 7
officers, wounded 11. Sailors — killed 359, drowned 200,
wounded, 132.

Prince 98, sunk in action by Spanish ship *Argonaute* and the
French *L'Aigle* — killed : 5 officers, wounded 2. Seamen —
killed 125, drowned 121, wounded 321.

Total in First Division—killed and wounded : Admirals 2, captains
9 ; officers killed 53, wounded 48. Seamen—killed 2,020, drowned
637, wounded 1,573.

Second Division.—Admiral Collingwood. Total—killed : captains
5, officers 26, seamen 607, drowned 285. Wounded : officers 27,
seamen 740.

Third Division. — Vice-Admiral *Calder. Killed : captains 5,
officers 26 ; wounded : officers 12. Seamen killed 1,044, wounded
278.

Fourth Division. — Rear-Admiral ——. Killed : captains 5,
officers 29, seamen 1,705, drowned 242. Wounded : seamen and
soldiers 452.

Fifth Division (arrived in afternoon). — Rear-Admiral Louis.
Killed : captains 3, officers 6, seamen 158. Wounded : seamen 176,
officers 9.

Sixth Division.—Joined the fleet on the morning of the 22nd, and
after manning part of it, directed its course to Malta, having vessels
under convoy. Killed : captains 2, officers 12, seamen 900 ; these
all in the *Royal Sovereign*, wrecked off Cadiz.

Grand total. — Killed : admirals 2, captains 26, seamen 4,394,
drowned 2,064. Wounded : officers 109, seamen 3,244 ; total,
10,471.

Among the not engaged must be reckoned the *Aboukir*, which did not leave Gibraltar until after the battle, 13 frigates, 5 brigs, and 2 sloops also formed part of the fleet.

Result : sank 7, shipwrecked 3, burnt 1, condemned 8, repairable 11, not engaged 5—35.[1]

X.

WHO KILLED NELSON ?

That in the confusion of such a battle as that of Trafalgar it is not surprising that it should not have been known who fired the fatal shot from which Nelson died. Some time after the battle, however, a French conscript, of the name of Guillemard, put forth his claim to have been the party, and this was his story, as told by himself :—

"He was on board Admiral Villeneuve's ship, the *Redoubtable*, which directly faced the *Victory*. All the topmen of the *Redoubtable* had been killed, and two sailors and four soldiers—of whom Guillemard was one—were ordered to occupy the posts of those who had fallen in the tops. While they were going aloft the ball and grape showered around them striking the masts and yards and cutting the rigging to pieces."

Omitting his imaginative description of the close conflict which he says was carried on between the English and French marksmen from the tops of their respective ships (a very unlikely act on the part of the English, as Nelson was always against having marksmen in the tops for fear of setting fire to the sails), we continue his narrative :

"It was at this juncture," said Guillemard, "that he perceived the officer covered with orders on the poop of the English vessel. Guillemard observed that the officer had only one arm, and having often heard Nelson's personal appearance described he concluded that this must be the English admiral. At the moment when his attention was directed towards the officer several of the English sailors lay dead upon the poop, the heat of the conflict not allowing even time to throw them overboard. Nelson cast a pitying glance on the brave men under him, who with their life-blood were procuring glory for Old England. The French soldier on the tops of the *Redoubtable* took aim and fired ; then through the cloud of smoke Guillemard saw a

---

[1] Egerton MSS., British Museum, No. 31.

group of persons gathering anxiously round the officer who had fallen. But the death of Nelson did not stop the fighting, indeed, after the hero had breathed his last it waxed hotter and more furious. Twenty thousand prisoners were taken, and by this victory, which cost Nelson his life, Napoleon's projects against England were blown to the winds."

If there is any truth in this story, it is curious that Guillemard was not decorated by Napoleon, or, as far as is known, ever obtained any promotion or distinction in the French service. His countrymen evidently did not believe in it.

It is a tradition in the service that after Nelson was shot, the man who fired the fatal shot was marked out by a midshipman of the *Victory* as he put his head over the barricade of the top, fired at by him, and seen to fall back dead.

XI.

REPORT OF CONSUL WILLIAM STIGAND TO THE MARQUIS OF SALISBURY ON THE SICILIAN VINTAGE OF 1889.

(PALERMO, *Dec.* 14, 1889.)

After briefly relating the early history of the estate of Bronte and its descent to the present possessor, and describing the Castello de Maniace and its Nelsonian treasures, Mr. Stigand gives the following account of the past condition of the property :—

" When the estate was erected into a duchy and handed over to Nelson, it was in a bare and wretched plight. It was forty miles distant from any carriageable road, and no proprietor had lived on it for two hundred years. After the flight of the last monastic proprietors, from 1693 to 1799, the property was in the hands of caretakers. Reforms and improvements were commenced on the estate soon after Nelson received it, but little was done on a grand scale until the succession of the present duke in 1868. No members of the family had then visited the place for forty years. Roads were immediately commenced, and Mr. Hood had the satisfaction of being the first to drive to Maniace in 1873, and the mileage of roads on the property has now increased to twelve miles. Farmhouses have been repaired and built, several bridges over torrents at times impassable erected, and the Castello itself restored and enlarged, not only to make a suitable dwelling-house, according to English notions, but also to allow for storage of grain and wine, and for stabling, while the ravages of the Simeto had to be restrained with solid bastions and embankments. Indeed, when the castle was delivered over to Nelson it was quite a ruin, threatening entire disappearance, without a scrap of furniture on the premises. One of the chief events in the history of the improvements which are going on was the introduction of a ten-horse power traction engine from England, from the firm of Messrs. Clayton and Shuttleworth, of Lincoln, whose journey up to Maniace, through Lingualossa, Randazzo, and other places, under the conduct of Mr. Nelson Hood, as chief engine-driver, excited a commotion in the country, the memory of which still survives as something out of the common. Mr. Hood not only acted on this occasion as chief mechanician, but has turned his versatile talents to account on the estate as engineer, architect, cabinet maker, decorator, and master cooper. Roads have been laid out, wine magazines or 'cantine' erected, casks and vats of colossal size fabricated with his designs and under his direction" (p. 10).

Of the careful selection and preparation of the vine, the Consul gives the following account :—

"Experiments were made in nurseries for many years of vines suited to the soil, and from the beginning of the vineyard Mr. Hood, as director-in chief, has been aided by a French gentleman, M. Fabre, with an assistant, M. Ricard. Vines were procured from Madeira, from Bourdeaux, from Ronsillon ; the Palomino vine and the Hermitage vine were also tried, as also some samples of the Pedro Ximenes of Spain, transplanted from the estates of the Duke of Wellington at Grenada. The vine which has been selected as suited best to the soil and climate is the 'Grenache Noir' of Ronsillon. The youngest vines utilised are now seven or eight years old, the oldest has fifteen years' growth. Each vine stands in a square of ground somewhat larger than a square metre, and great care is taken to keep the soil free from weeds by frequent horse-hoeing. The vines are pruned three times over every year, and in summer the exuberant shoots are removed by hand in order that the vigour of the vine may be concentrated on the fruit. Great attention is paid to select the moment of proper maturity for gathering the grape, and only the best bunches are selected for wines for export, the inferior grapes being left for the inferior wines which are consumed in the country. The time of vintage is, as in other places, quite a festal period ; from one hundred and twenty to one hundred and fifty men, women, and children come from all sides to assist in the vintage, and they live wholly on the premises until all is concluded, taking their meals in a somewhat primitive fashion in open-air, out of long wooden troughs, and ignoring, in Oriental fashion, knives and forks (and he might have added spoons), and a fair proportion of the grapes are left hanging on the vines for gleaners after the harvest, in patriarchal fashion " (p. 11).

The Consul's description of the gathering of the grapes reads like a picture of Arcadia : " The boys, prolonging their route to the pressing-house, with the heavy baskets of grapes, by executing a sort of rude 'fantasia,' marching in a circle round the central fountain of the interior quadrangle, and chanting songs in chorus which may be a distant echo of the ' Evoe Bacchi ' of classic times, after which tribute to Liber and the Graces, they deliver in their burdens one after another at the windows of the pressing-house."

I wish I had space to give the Consul's description of the grape pressing, with its sieves, with meshes large enough to allow the grapes to go through, but to retain the stalk, the care taken that the pressers, who go round like mill horses, should be shod not with hobnailed boots, but light moccasins of gutta percha, and the feet carefully washed every morning and evening, of the juice running in continuous streams through the caoutchouc pipes to the reservoirs, and how the juice of the first fermentation is carried across the quadrangle in skins of goats or pigs, such as Don Quixote slashed in his nocturnal adventure. Space, however, must be economized. Suffice to add, that the great tun in which the wine is eventually stored—" La Madre "—can contain the wine for one hundred and eighty thousand bottles, and that in two comparatively smaller ones sixty thousand more bottles can be stored.[1]

---

[1] Report, p. 12, 13.

INDEX.

UNWIN BROTHERS, THE GRESHAM PRESS, CHILWORTH AND LONDON.